The Struggle
and the Triumph

Also by Lech Walesa
A Way of Hope

The Struggle and the Triumph

An Autobiography

Lech Walesa

with the collaboration of Arkadiusz Rybicki

translated by Franklin Philip
in collaboration with Helen Mahut

Arcade Publishing
New York

First English-language Edition

Originally published in France under the title *Les chemins de la démocratie*

Library of Congress Cataloging-in-Publication Data

Wałęsa, Lech, 1943–
    [Chemins de la démocratie. English]
    The struggle and the triumph : an autobiography / by Lech Walesa with the collaboration of Arkadiusz Rybicki ; translated by Franklin Philip in collaboration with Helen Mahut.
        p.   cm.
    Translation of: Les chemins de la démocratie.
    ISBN 1-55970-149-8
    1. Wałęsa, Lech, 1943–   . 2. Presidents—Poland—Biography. 3. NSZZ "Solidarność" (Labor organization)—History. 4. Poland—Politics and government—1980–1989. 5. Poland—Politics and government—1989–
I. Rybicki, Arkadiusz. II. Title.
    DK4452.W34A3 1992
    943.805′6′092–dc20   92-3096
    [B]   91-35875

Published in the United States by Arcade Publishing, Inc., New York
Distributed by Little, Brown and Company

Design and typography by David Frederickson

10 9 8 7 6 5 4 3 2 1

Printed in the United States of America

Contents

Introduction   3

Part I: At Home

1   The Apartment in Zaspa   15
2   The House on Polanki Street   29
3   Danka   32
4   The Children   41
5   Daily Life   56

Part II: Public Life

6   Hatred   73
7   The Law and the Telephone   88
8   Difficult Days   108
9   The Turning Point   112
10   The Referendum   121
11   Auschwitz   128
12   The First Avalanche   137
13   Between the Sickle and Hope   147
14   The Second Avalanche   151
15   The Prime Minister's Revenge   159
16   The Debate   166
17   The Round Table   172
18   Among Ourselves   182

19	The Light from the Vatican	187
20	Turning West	194
21	The Thirty-Five-Percent Democracy	200
22	The Presidents	207
23	The Government of Solidarity	216
24	The Domino Theory	223
25	A Shower of Dollars	230
26	Healing Old Wounds	237
27	Stirring Things Up	244
28	Death of a Dissident	248
29	The Final Days of the PZPR	252
30	The Gloves Come Off	259
31	The Second Solidarity Congress	264
32	Speeding Things Up	269
33	Three Cities	273
34	Electing a President	278
35	Between Rounds	285

Part III: Keeping Faith

36	The Virgin on My Lapel	289
37	Beginnings	297
	Epilogue	305

	A Note on Polish Pronunciation	308
	Names and Acronyms	310
	Chronology	312
	Index	319

The Struggle
and the Triumph

Introduction

"After forty years, communism is healthy. The balance sheet of the fortieth anniversary is decidedly positive." So declared Jerzy Urban, spokesman for the Polish government, during an interview with ABC News in the summer of 1984.

"Decidedly positive"? While Western European countries were speeding toward unification, and competing with each other to take the lead in economic development, technological progress, and environmental protection, in Poland the Communist Party claimed to be solving our problems by creating worthless institutions like the Patriotic Movement for National Salvation, known by its Polish acronym PRON.

Since the mid 1980s, what had become clear was that economic reform would get nowhere without political reform. I reiterated almost daily that the only way Poland could end the economic crisis that gripped it was to revamp the entire political system from top to bottom. But the Polish United Workers' Party — the name given the Communist Party in Poland, known by its Polish initials, PZPR — was incapable of bringing about change on this scale. Could Solidarity do it? Since at that point it was no longer legal, Solidarity was simply trying to survive from one day to the next, to survive not only the moments of high drama, when there was tension and risk, but also — almost worse — to survive the routine daily grind. Progress was slow. Its thousands of members knew that democracy was a just cause, but proving it to the rest of Poland was like trying to move a derailed train.

Even though the Brezhnev Doctrine was dead and the Soviet Union no longer a threat, few things had changed in the People's Republic of Poland. The measures taken by General Jaruzelski were headed in the right

3

direction, but as I said in numerous interviews, it would take two or three centuries for them to bear fruit.

Supporters of Solidarity, particularly younger ones, were growing increasingly impatient with our policy of nonviolence. Some began to insist that we had to prepare for war. Had nonviolent struggle against the Communists ever succeeded? they asked. Comparisons between Solidarity and the Indian independence movement, they argued, were wrong. Gandhi was from another era, and anyway, he had been dealing with the British, with men of principle. He would have failed here because Communists pay no attention either to principle or to public opinion. I told them I agreed — Gandhi would indeed have had a tough time in Poland. But hadn't the Nobel Peace Prize I'd accepted on behalf of Solidarity meant I was committed to nonviolent methods? That argument didn't wash with some of the younger radicals, who would then accuse me of hypocrisy. Sure, I could say that, since I was pretty well off (house, car, some money), but they had nothing and saw no future for themselves. "Mr. Walesa, why don't you join in the demonstrations anymore? As soon as the ZOMO [riot police] show up, you hop into your car and take off." I was in a different position now, I answered, and constrained by my status as an international figure. "Young people can scamper off when the police arrive. But can you imagine Lech Walesa, the Nobel laureate, letting himself get chased down the street?"

In Father Jankowski's vicarage at Saint Brygid's Church in Gdansk I talked and talked about the need for discussion and organization, and about how pluralism was the basis of democracy. After countless hours of discussion, what became clear to me was that many Poles preferred slogans about struggle to the rigors of self-organization. Empty rhetoric let them go on doing nothing. Years of the Moscow brand of socialism had created deep-rooted passivity: even if people didn't support the ideas imposed on them by the state, they wouldn't necessarily be up to doing anything about them. Some Poles couldn't let go of their misery, especially those who had survived Hitler's concentration camps or Stalin's gulags.

I was tired of just getting by. It was time for action, to prove that things could be done. I threw myself into the cause. But while I was feeling impatient and restless, another part of me felt that life was passing me by. My children were growing up fast, and yet I had almost no time to play with them or talk with them about their problems. Every single day I had to convince myself to keep up the struggle for just a little longer, whatever the cost, luring myself into thinking that soon everything would be different, and that someday, somehow, I'd be able to make up for lost time.

Had I been a poet or philosopher instead of an electrician, I might have fought totalitarianism differently — perhaps by taking refuge in an inner world, or articulating my anger in an essay or poem about the imprisoned soul. But I'm a pragmatist, a realist. I look for practical solutions to specific problems. So many magnificently intelligent and intellectual people came to my house or to Father Jankowski's vicarage, and from their mouths flowed words both compelling and profound. I stuck to plain language. It didn't much matter whether what I said squared with elegant theories or not.

When I was released from internment at the end of 1982, I found myself hailed as a national hero. Awarded the Nobel Prize, I was elevated into the pantheon of those to whom monuments might be raised. But I had no desire to be a hero or to have anything to do with statues or sainthood. I knew that I was a political animal trying to untie Poland's Gordian knot — not some wax figure in a museum. The coming years would call more for a doer more than a martyr. Polish history has been drenched in the blood of heroism. We have poured our heart into just causes and then seen others come along and use our martyrdom for their own benefit. This time would be different. This time we were in a marathon, not a war, and in a marathon the only important thing is the finish line. What counts most are those last few meters. And now we were playing to win. Poland has come close in the past, such as during that brief burst of prosperity and peace between the two world wars. But history had overwhelmed us. Our country was attacked and dismembered, wiped off the map. Poles survived World War II heroically, among the few people in Europe not accused of being Nazi collaborators. In return we earned only plots in graveyards. If we were on the winning side, supposedly, what did the victory win us? Yalta. Once again we were drawn and quartered by stronger powers.

From 1945 onward, Poland was governed not so much by criminals as by vulgar and dull-witted apparatchiks who, during the war, had stood firm somewhere in the rear echelons, and when it was over forced their way to the front by assassinating the competition along the way. I had to lecture the radical younger members of Solidarity about Poland's bloody past, since I knew what they wanted to do would contribute another chapter. Violence wasn't the way. After the war, I told them, we had seen tens of thousands of educated Poles revolt against the new occupiers and wage a guerrilla war from underground. Where are they now? They went from the underground to the burial ground. History may not have given that generation any choice, but Poles today had other options.

For all the grumbling it caused among the young, Solidarity's strategy of nonviolent struggle had brought quick results. The state of martial law had proven only that the same power that could break up a labor union with tanks couldn't handle even the smallest social problem. After Solidarity had been outlawed, radicals and hardliners wanted us to change our tactics. "Your union is many millions strong," they would say. "How could you let yourself be beaten so easily?" We were like a boxer who dodges a punch not from weakness or fear, but from cunning, I replied. The best fighters save their strength until it matters and then, when it does, they make their move. Had we fought the Communists with guns, Europe would have witnessed yet one more example of Polish heroism — but at what a cost! Our land would have been strewn with corpses — hundreds of thousands, possibly as many as a million of them. Who would have been left to build a monument to their memory?

Solidarity's strategy of evasion hadn't contributed more gore to Polish mythology, but eventually it put us in the position to land a knockout punch. We toppled a system that had tried for fifty years to fool everyone with false promises.

Over the years, people have often asked me what my philosophy was, what was the theory behind my actions. I know that what I did wasn't always clear to everyone — sometimes not even to my closest friends and advisors. All I can say about my own inconsistencies is that the changes that swept over Europe didn't follow logic, or at least they didn't follow the kind of logic political scientists understand. I owe my own success to the fact that I was good at landing on my feet. Experience teaches that political events often unfold in ways inconsistent with reason. You need to react instinctively, flexibly, to every occasion.

I sometimes feel buried by the myths of who I am *supposed* to be. According to one myth, I was like a helpless child without my advisors: they had all the ideas and I just voiced them. How could someone with my background have any grasp of the political problems facing Poland? The reason I was constantly surrounded by intellectuals, academics, distinguished journalists, and lawyers — people who spoke several languages and frequented (or even constituted) the best society — was that I myself was not an intellectual. In Poland, you see, being an intellectual has value in and of itself. The content of what a professor, a doctor, or a famous actor says when they talk about national problems is unimportant; what is important is that they have the right diploma, present the appropriate bearing, possess "a knowledge of things," and use big words. It didn't seem to matter that elegant rhetoric is very often empty rhetoric. What counts is correctness of speech.

Some of my supporters so badly wanted me to fit their conception of a leader that they would even go so far as to ask me whether I had started taking courses at the Catholic University of Lublin, was actively studying foreign languages, or was reading piles of books at night. They needed me to fit their image of the charismatic leader — rather than a strategist, political animal, or practical man who sets concrete objectives. In other words, they didn't want a fox; they wanted a lion.

Nevertheless, events that even the political scientists hadn't foreseen intervened (political visionaries sometimes have rather limited imaginations): after all those years of Cold War, Europe, in the latter half of the 1980s, was thawing. Who could have predicted Gorbachev and perestroika? Or the demise of the Soviet Union, an imperial power founded on a totalitarian ideology, which until then had seemed unreformable? Rather than a modern country, it was an avatar of tsarism improved upon by a system of omnipresent indoctrination. Students of politics thought Soviet policy was based entirely on the fear that if any one column were to give out, the whole edifice would come tumbling down. Therefore the Soviets would never allow any one column to give out. And that's why programs for Poland's emancipation set forth by opposition intellectuals were based either on the dream of a new "people's springtime" (in other words, a populist revolt within the USSR itself) or on the notion that Poland should remain a loyal vassal to the Soviets and hope for better conditions as a reward.

Behind the latter idea ran the argument that only the various Communist Parties could govern in the countries of the Soviet bloc, for they were the empire's sole guarantors of its vassals' fidelity. All that Poles might hope for was a status like Finland's — geopolitically dependent on the USSR, but free to decide on internal matters. The problem with that theory was that Poland, unlike Finland, was both too large and too strategically positioned for "Finlandization" to be possible.

Not long after my release from internment on November 12, 1982, Leonid Brezhnev died, and a brief period of hope followed. Alas, too brief: a host of doddering old men were in line to succeed him, and for all of them it was imperative that the Soviet empire remain unchanged. Just before martial law was declared in Poland, I was at the height of my popularity. I knew that my choice was either to let myself be enshrined or to get back into the game. I decided to get off my pedestal. During a press conference in my apartment on November 14, I compared my situation to that of a tightrope walker in trouble. Should I go back, or try to reach the other side? No one knew. Whatever I did, the official powers declared me a "private citizen" — albeit one the government would keep under close surveillance. Government spokesman Jerzy Urban, a talented satirical journalist, was assigned the task of undermining my authority. Articles lampooning me as a "mustachioed monkey" or calling me the "cowboy from Gdansk" appeared in the press. Day after day, my children were forced to listen to their government heap insults on their father.

But together Solidarity and I did reach the other side. Commitment to the ideals of liberty proved stronger than all the diktats. This book tells the story of how it happened.

The story must begin by saying that Solidarity's survival was due largely to the Church, which not only provided moral support, but also literally opened its doors so that we could hold both public and secret meetings. I must have given a thousand talks in churches and chapels, particularly in Gdansk. The intelligentsia found refuge in these sanctuaries. Many Solidarity militants criticized the bishops for not taking unequivocal political positions. The highest-ranking archbishop in Poland, whose position traditionally brings with it the full authority of a national leader, did not want to become a political activist. He stressed that the Church's first task was to preach the gospel.

Now, in hindsight, one can see that the Church did a great deal. It brought help to those interned and imprisoned and to their families, as well as to people who had gone into hiding for fear of punishment; it expressed the principles that should govern social life; and it demanded that Solidarity be accorded legal status. Without the Church there would have been no Solidarity.

In fact, without the Church there would be no Poland! Over the centuries, we have been pushed to the east and pushed to the west, and each time, humiliated and massacred, we have lost our homeland. But the Church has remained an immovable and unshakable force that has always protected and nourished the seeds of nationhood. After World War II we recovered our homeland, but in a form imposed by Russia. Once again the Church preserved the bridge to our past and what was best in it. Its Latin has remained incorruptible in an age of ideology and total uniformity. Polish history has visionaries and martyrs aplenty; what we need is the stability of timeless values to sustain our belief in just and lasting solutions.

Some people, surprised at how much I fraternized with priests, have criticized me for it. From a Western viewpoint my behavior may indeed have been perceived as too "churchly." I tried to explain to journalists (in interviews held in church sanctuaries, as a matter of fact) that the authorities don't go after you with nightsticks on ecclesiastical premises the way they do in the street. We couldn't meet in places of business or in factories. State ordinances stipulated that every worker had to leave his post within fifteen minutes after the bell sounded the end of the workday. Nor could we meet in private homes. Unauthorized gatherings of more than three people were prohibited, and the Militia (the urban police) had the right to come in and "disperse the assembly."

How could we not respect the priests? The Church endured under totalitarian regimes because a supernatural ideal had sustained its existence. But it also endured by not getting too involved in policy-making. More than once, I had to persuade overzealous colleagues that Solidarity, though indeed important and marvelous, was but a transitory historical movement. "Priests should not become deeply involved in our affairs," I told them. "The Church must stand above that. We ought to be respectful of their distance, because we don't know what the future has in store for us."

Two men in particular helped Poland survive communism: Cardinal Stefan Wyszynski (1903–1981) and Pope John Paul II. Wyszynski was the prelate of what we proclaimed "the Church Militant," for while the Church had been broken in the USSR and in the other Eastern European countries (by having their bishops imprisoned or "neutralized"), Cardinal Wyszynski still retained the stature of Poland's principal moral authority. His three-year imprisonment was a time of triumph for the Church: the number of those choosing an ecclesiastical vocation rose; practically all Poles had their infants baptized. I met with this great man on many occasions before he died, seeking his advice on the important questions. His stature among his countrymen always helped calm things down. When he spoke, we all listened. Even after his death the Church was relieved of the duty of having to display "national values." It took a few years before our friends in the West realized that in Poland, Catholicism was not synonymous with clericalism.

Before anyone dreamed of perestroika, there was John Paul II, who first visited his native Poland as pope in 1979. At the time, opposition to the government was very weak and consisted of tiny groups with grandiose designs. My participation in one such group cost me my job — and I had five children to feed. Eventually I was permitted employment elsewhere, and that was the moment when the Holy Father arrived in Poland. I wanted desperately to see him, but state-security agents had alerted my new employers, and I was refused time off. All I could do was listen to what other people reported about the millions who gathered to see him and the feelings of strength and purpose those huge celebrations inspired.

A new world was forming. When the shop foreman humiliated you on the job, when a soldier handcuffed you for no good reason and hauled you off to the police station, when a lieutenant in civilian clothes made you strip naked to make sure you weren't concealing suspects' addresses in the cleft of your buttocks, it all seemed to matter less. Poles were already sensing that something in the Communist system was giving way. Antireligious propaganda was still running full tilt, but its ineffectiveness was increasingly evident. During their memorable strike in 1980, the first thing the Gdansk workers did was to affix a cross, an image of the Virgin Mary, and a portrait of John Paul II to the gates of the shipyards. They became symbols of victory.

My foreman may have prevented me from attending the pontifical mass of 1979, but two years later I went to the Vatican as the leader of the delegation from Solidarity — by then a union with ten million members. In their name I said to the Holy Father, "We were raised in the spirit of the faith, and we also know that for a man to be a man, he must believe in the power of reason." After martial law was declared on December 13, 1981, we gathered around our radios every Wednesday to listen to the pope, and every Wednesday we were confirmed in our belief that our resistance to communism had moral justification. Less than a week after the military coup, on December 19, 1981, Archbishop Luigi Poggi handed General Jaruzelski a letter from John Paul II in which the pope appealed to the dictator of Poland not to let blood be shed. (Despite the huge military and police mobilization, we should remember that, undoubtedly thanks to that letter, there was no large-scale bloody repression.) The pope later met with Jaruzelski, which upset a number of people, but it is undeniable that their talks produced only positive results. When in 1987 John Paul II visited Poland for the third time, it was clear that communism was collapsing. The events for which Poles had been waiting for decades were finally occurring. In Poland, our eyes had been always been fixed on the political *nomenklatura,* the ruling Communist elite, so we didn't fully grasp the moral dimensions of our activities within the context of Europe in the 1980s as a whole. But the pope had been among the first to appreciate the momentous nature of what was happening. That is why he spoke of the meaning of the Ten Commandments, morality in politics, and human rights, as well as denouncing violence and pollution. He expressed solidarity with the oppressed and kept up the morale of those struggling wearily against totalitarianism. Under his pontificate, Europe recovered its identity, becoming a continent of free countries.

"There is no freedom without Solidarity" was the slogan repeated over and over again by the shipyard workers when they went back on strike first in May and again in August 1988. No one yet knew they were the vanguard of the political upheaval that was to rock Eastern Europe in the fall of the following year. The workers who took part in these memorable strikes hadn't experienced firsthand the events of 1980–81, the period when Solidarity was legal, because they were only ten to twelve years old at the time. They had been brought up under martial law — under a system that humiliated them and denied them any chance for advancement. Yet, raised though they had been in a repressive state, they had not yielded to the temptations of terrorism. The nonviolent struggle that emanated from Solidarity's philosophy had seemed to them a more attractive alternative — even better, a more effective one.

The example of Solidarity quickly spread to all the other countries of Central and Eastern Europe. Before our very eyes, stock ideological formulas inherited from the Cold War — "the Eastern Bloc," "the community of socialist countries," "the Soviet sphere of influence," and the like — were disintegrating.

Meanwhile, it looked as if I was fated to be a figurehead. I could become president, prime minister, or head of the Solidarity group in parliament; or I could rest upon my laurels, travel all over the world, and give lectures (I had invitations for years to come). But I felt the urge to act as a devil's advocate. In soccer you don't change a winning team; that doesn't hold true in politics. Poland's future would be endangered if the old Communist monopoly were simply replaced by a Solidarity monopoly. The time for political parties, economic associations, and a free press had come.

My position was that while Poland had dropped several points on the scale of political stability, stability depended most of all upon economics. Western nations, which are to some extent morally responsible for what happened at that fateful Yalta Conference, should acknowledge this by forgiving loans, so that the debtor nations do not spend their entire national income making interest payments. If the West doesn't do this, the enormity of the economic chaos inherited from communism, together with the impatience of the banks, may indeed lead to real political instability. Not so long ago, the lending countries devoted enormous portions of their national budgets to manufacturing weapons intended to counter the ambitions of the Soviet Union. Yet now that the order established at Yalta has collapsed, and with it the threat of communism, the developed countries still insist that fledgling democracies assume the financial obligations contracted by their Communist predecessors. Is that fair play?

The fundamental question facing Europe today is this: Can the leaders of the economically powerful nations work out a new and ethical policy toward the smaller and politically weaker nations? A wait-and-see policy seems cynical. Europe's job and fate is unification, and responsibility must be shared by all of its nations. Today Poland is engaged in the most challenging experiment in its history. The West should understand that, though in global terms Poland is but a small-scale experiment in democracy, it's an experiment that *must* succeed.

Part I
At Home

1

The Apartment in Zaspa

For anyone swept up in public affairs and actively pursuing a political career, family obligations can at times get short shrift. Then comes the question: Family life or public life? The dilemma has more than once pushed an exasperated spouse into making an ultimatum: "Choose either one or the other — politics or your family." While this is fodder for divorce lawyers, it can also be a potent weapon against dissidents, one routinely used by Polish policemen attempting to persuade them to cease their "illegal" activities — as I discovered before 1980. "You have children, don't you Mr. Walesa?" the police would often say to me. "Do you want them to grow up without a father?" Or "We know how tough things must be for you — you've got lots of kids, a small apartment, low wages. That's why you're taking these risks and letting yourself be exploited by radical militants. Borusewicz, Kuroń, Michnik — these guys are professionals paid by the CIA. If we put them in jail, there'll always be someone to post bail for them. Besides, they're the elite, and we can always control the elite. You we'll just have to crush. But maybe we can come to an understanding; we certainly have the means. You'd be able to buy a big house, and we could get you a high-paying job. Let bygones be bygones. What do you say? What? No? Come, now — think of your future. In a few years, your children will be asking you why you didn't get them a better start in life. They'll accuse you of spoiling your life and theirs."

My big chance, and I blew it.

Family life was always the most important part of my life. Nothing could ever compete with it. No one, in my view, should be totally absorbed by politics. But on the other hand, being committed to one's family must not be an excuse for inaction. I'm fortunate, because I've been able both

15

to be politically active and to have a family. In my case, I know that my family life has made me a better politician and leader. No one whose family life isn't in order will ever get anywhere — publicly or privately.

My family is the foundation of my life. Having so many children has helped guide me and give me strength. It's no coincidence that the family was among the first institutions undermined by the Communists. Children were dumped into day-care centers, nursery schools, or after-hours centers. Families disintegrated, traditions disappeared, and because of financial hard times, the large family became a thing of the past. One or two children became the norm. Couples with more than two kids were regarded as "unprogressive." You can see why the Communists pushed for small families, because it's hard to brainwash parents of a large family with doctrinal absurdities; they are too grounded in the everyday. Children protected lots of Polish families from Communist indoctrination, and as it has in the past, the family became the last refuge for the old principles of the Ten Commandments.

My children were born at a time when I was becoming politically active, and I am convinced that this fact made my activities more credible. Anyone with five kids (six by the time of the 1980 shipyard strike) has to be seen as more than a starry-eyed theorist. Doesn't he have a better grasp of the burdens of family responsibilities? In August 1980, during the strike, young fathers often told me, "I can't keep going. I've got young kids at home, my wife is threatening divorce, I'm in debt to the shipyards, and I live in a rented room." "If you have to go, then go," I would tell them. "You'll be more useful there than here." There's no point in asking too much from anyone in a situation like that.

Besides having a magnificent family, I now also enjoy the refuge of a real house, a place where I can hide from prying eyes and cut myself off from public life. When I walk in my garden, I often think back to the nomadic years, or to the apartment at Zaspa, where it felt as if our life was lived on a stage with no curtain.

Our beginnings in Gdansk were humble. We went from one garret to the next. We started married life in a rented room — it was something of a public walkway — on Marchlewski Street, where we stayed only four months. From there we moved into the attic of a private little house in Suchanino, where again we had only a single room and a dark kitchen — but at least we had it all to ourselves. After a year we moved again, now with baby Bogdan, this time to a workers' hotel on Klonowicz Street (in what was called a "family unit"). Living there was unbearable, because of the fighting and drunken rowdiness all around us.

Finally we were given a two-room apartment in Stoga, and we could breathe a little. Our family was growing every two years, however, and we were soon cramped again. When it was time for the kids to go to bed, we would unfold the beds and mattresses, and they took up the whole of the two rooms. Most of our life took place in the larger one, where there was a couch, a little bed, a table, and a sewing machine that sometimes served as a stand for a primitive machine to print fliers. The smaller room was used as a bedroom for the children.

Compared to these holes-in-the-wall, the Zaspa apartment seemed palatial. We got it in September 1980, a few days after the memorable August strike. The regional housing board suddenly responded to our request for larger housing, a request that had been sitting on their desks for years. Quite obviously the authorities didn't want the world to learn how a Polish worker — now a labor leader — with a good number of children actually lived. In a single night, the Party vacated a second-story, 1,300-square-foot office in a block of apartment buildings on Pilotow Street, and it became our nest for the next eight years. We didn't have enough furniture to fill it, but we were still overjoyed! Even the ultramodern bugging devices installed in it didn't dampen our enthusiasm (in this area, at least, Polish technology is up to standard).

In the beginning, we used to leave the front door open. Crowds of journalists and visitors came and went freely. Family matters and Solidarity matters became inextricably mixed. Finally, it was too much to take. One day I said, "Enough!" and began demanding some peace and quiet. It didn't last long. After my internment, our apartment once more became Solidarity headquarters. I still remember my first "free" press conference there in November 1982. We had to do it in two shifts, because the largest room was barely 200 square feet.

In short order we set up my office in the middle of the apartment; there was no other solution. Rules prohibited any new construction in the apartment, so we couldn't separate the living and working spaces. My visitors must have thought it pretty cozy and homey. There I would be, giving an interview, and suddenly in would run little Brygidka in tears, or from behind the curtain would appear a grinning Magda, who would curtsy and then run off.

It all became increasingly unbearable for the adults. The year 1987 reinforced that feeling. General Jaruzelski's government was grinding to a halt, and I was talking to dozens of political figures and giving countless interviews in an attempt to convince the government that some kind of compromise with its opposition — Solidarity and all the other opposition groups — was the only recourse. My wife's patience was sorely tested.

Our day began when the alarm clock went off at 5:15 A.M., when I had to get up and go to work. I rarely felt I had had any sleep. I would say a brief prayer: "God, grant me a peaceful, uneventful day and grant me a little time to spend with Danka and with the children. Give me strength and a sense of purpose. I am a union leader, a politician, an activist, a husband, a father, a Nobel laureate, a citizen of Gdansk, a worker at the shipyards, and I don't know what else. Help me also to remain myself." While I washed, shaved, and dressed, Danka made my lunch and breakfast, which I would take with me. I didn't have time to eat and didn't want to be late (I was late only once and remember it to this day). The kids were still asleep, of course; even little Brygidka didn't get up until around six o'clock. It was always in the morning, when everyone was still in bed, that I would realize that even this apartment had become too small.

There were always three cars waiting for me in front of the house: my special group. I was afforded at least as much protection as the Party's first secretary. Sometimes the Security Service agents would be snoozing, so I'd knock on the car windows. The trip to the shipyards wasn't long, maybe three and a half miles. The tram was usually jam-packed.

Today, when people talk about the "gray masses," I always think of the people who take this tram. Worn coats and drab jackets — the colors all looked the same at dawn in that crowded tram. All those tired faces. When jostling with people, trying to ignore the grumbling and avoid the sour-smelling breath, I often reminded myself how easy it was to forget that every human is a child of God.

So I preferred taking the car. That way, at least, I didn't have to answer the endless barrage of questions: "Mr. Walesa, how are we going to sur-vive? When will all this change? When do we attack the Communists?" In the car I felt safe from assaults by discouraged workers or tricks by the political police. "You know where to go for New Year's Eve?" a worker once asked me. "What do you mean?" I replied. "The best place is the Party's regional headquarters. I have my heart set on it. Do you have any extra tickets?" Everyone around me howled with laughter. But three days later, the TV news began with an interview with Militia man "Kowalski," who stated that Mr. Walesa had come to him to get two tickets for the New

Year's Eve ball at the Party's regional headquarters. Stand in line like everyone else, Comrade Walesa!

Or take the tram. For part of the trip, the tram ran along a wall of concrete pillars the color of which constantly changed. Painters hired by the government couldn't manage to cover over the graffiti scrawled there each night by members of the Solidarity underground (mostly high school students). Until martial law was declared, the walls carried messages and demands large enough for all to see. "TELEVISION TELLS LIES," read one slogan. But there were also specific messages, such as "WATCH IT! THE CAR WITH LICENSE PLATE # XXXX BELONGS TO THE SECURITY SERVICE." Some graffiti demanded freedom for Leszek Moczulski of the Confederation for an Independent Poland (KPN), who had prematurely and unpardonably proclaimed Poland's independence; we had not managed to get him out of prison even when our union ranks had swelled to ten million. In 1987, people scrawled, "SOLIDARITY LIVES!" on the walls.

The graffiti could be read clearly even through the coats of paint slapped over them. The painters simply didn't do their job, and sometimes cheated by saying they had run out of paint — and later they would sell the paint on the black market.

The view from the tram was grim. Despite its pretty Gothic churches, Gdansk offers landscapes of dilapidated houses, grimy factories, and potholed streets. Nonetheless, I have thanked Providence more than once for making me a part of this city filled with so many interesting and unusual people. I was used to the eloquence of its gray walls. I understood the smells and sights. I felt like a citizen of the world in Gdansk, and I never once thought of emigrating, particularly at a time when Poland's problems needed to be resolved. We can better understand the wider world if we understand our own, our roots. Solidarity was born in Gdansk; it was as a citizen of Gdansk that I received the Nobel Peace Prize. My eight children will become sixteen people when they are married. When they have children they will form half a parish. Those parishes are what make Poland. I identified with Poland through the prism of my family, the parish, the Gdansk Shipyards. Europe and the rest of the world came later.

If I took the tram to work, I always had to empty my pockets on the docks of the shipyards because by the time I got there all sorts of messages were crammed into them — requests for secret meetings or for medicine, warnings, sometimes even threats.

I returned to work after prison just before May 1, 1983, in order to repair the electric forklifts; their connectors, sometimes even their wheels, had been torn off. Once martial law was declared, the workers stopped caring about the equipment and let it fall apart. In the early days, during breaks, I would go to the canteen. People would sit next to me in order to get into discussions; we were always surrounded by agents with tape recorders and cameras. But those seen with me would later be summoned to the management offices for a "conversation" with the Militia, so I thought it better to hold my conferences outside the shipyards. Religious services were always useful for this, and I was invited to them by workers, students and professors, and intellectuals.

What, you might ask, was a Nobel Prize winner doing at the shipyards? The fact that I went on working there seemed to surprise everyone. Yes, I no doubt could have found a better job practically anywhere. I could have been employed as a sexton at Father Jankowski's church and earned more. But I wanted and needed continuity, even if it meant working in this technological dinosaur of a factory, and repairing equipment much of which dated from before World War II. Every now and then I did get a chance to sweat over something truly modern, an import from the West or the East, and that would give me the opportunity to compare their technology to ours. One particular afternoon when I was scheduled to meet the British ambassador, I could compliment him on the high quality of English transformers, because that very morning, as it happened, I had been involved in taking one apart. My knowledge of a British product impressed him.

Another time, as I was making the usual repairs on a certain model of truck that was constantly breaking down, I made it my business, once and for all, to do preventive work on the model. This was reported immediately by someone who said, "After Walesa meddles with it, the equipment feels different." From that moment on, watchful eyes followed my every move. An investigative committee was formed to determine the reasons for my preventive repairs and to decide whether they conformed with company policy — or whether they constituted sabotage. The technical committee's functional analysis determined after due deliberation that I had made a significant improvement, and I was given a medal as well as a reward. My detractors and the Party did not appreciate that at all. But what could they do? Eliminating an improvement once it has been instituted is a serious misdemeanor.

Often, instead of beginning my day at the shipyards, I was forced to appear at the regional Party office or the Office of Internal Affairs, or even at the

Prokuratura.* I was summoned there as a rebellious citizen who needed a lesson in proper conduct. And so they would routinely grill me about my meetings, asking me what information I was passing to the West. During these interrogations, officials were constantly coming and going, or picking up the phone to get instructions from someone higher up. Responsibility needed to be spread out over several levels, or at least several floors. "Mr. Walesa, if you continue your illegal activities, you risk spending six months in prison," they told me. "That's too short!" I would retort. "A year is what I want! Going to prison is the only thing I haven't really experienced in my career, and I want to do it right!"

Upon leaving I was usually handed the inevitable summons to appear the next day or the following week. After pocketing it, off I would go to Saint Brygid's parish house in a convoy of four cars: two carrying Security Service agents, a third with uniformed Militia men, and in the last, me, Lech Walesa — "private citizen." Besides being an electrician, my second profession was as a public speaker. Journalists usually waited for us all in the square in front of the parish house, and I was always faced with a silly dilemma: to eat lunch first or to talk first. Often, though, a phone call settled the matter — Danka calling to announce that she had fried my favorite fish. "Gentleman," I would then tell them, "you're just going to have to wait. I am going home to have lunch with my wife."

The questions I got from journalists were, for the most part, fairly predictable, almost always about Solidarity's status, our plans, perestroika, Gorbachev. Solidarity, I replied, was a reform movement and the need for its existence was obvious; Poland had become the beggar of Europe; we were beginning to come up with definite and positive programs; it had been Poland's tragedy that Brezhnev died three years too late, etc. Too many people, too many questions — most of the time the same ones again and again. I often fantasized about writing out all my responses, numbering them, and then giving them out to whoever was interested — prepackaged information.

After an hour, the heat of the television lights would make me sweat. Large though Father Jankowski's parish house is, the lack of ventilation or air-conditioning made the atmosphere increasingly oppressive, and with each passing minute it became more difficult to keep one's concentration. I have always enjoyed the press — their probing interviews and aggressive questions, their tirelessness. But since I was usually pressed for time, I would get furious if, when I arrived, the television crew was still

* The state prosecutor's office.

unrolling cables or trying to track down my interpreter. Also, some journalists lacked tact and imagination. They no doubt assumed that since I
could spend eight hours working on some electric forklift, waiting for
them would be no problem. After all, who was I but a local electrician?
They had come from abroad. I would look at my watch and say, "Gentlemen, three minutes out of the ten I agreed to have already gone by. You
have seven left." My meetings with journalists weren't always in the form
of ordinary press conferences; some were interviews planned well ahead
of time and sometimes with great secrecy. For those I needed to be well-
prepared, and rather than arrive straight from the shipyards, I would go
home to change out of my usual turtleneck and into a suit.

One such interview was for the French literary television program
Apostrophes, hosted by Bernard Pivot, on which the first part of my autobiography, *A Way of Hope,* was under discussion. Various aspects of my
life were to be topics, as well as questions about the book:

> *Bernard Pivot:* Isn't your book an elegant way of saying, "This is what I've
> done, this is my assessment, and now it's up to others to carry the torch"?
> *Lech Walesa:* Oh, by no means. Nothing could persuade me to give up my
> struggle — not money, and not glory. You can serve a cause in a number of
> ways, and my book is one, but I didn't write it with the intention of saying
> farewell. My life goes on, and I hope I will still have many more pages to
> write.
> *BP:* Still, as you write in your book, "Hasn't the time come to quit while I'm
> ahead and can bow out gracefully?"
> *LW:* Yes and no. I said that while thinking at one point about my small private
> life and my large public life. Let me put it in context. I was talking about
> the end of a certain stage during which I was very conscious of the mistakes
> I'd made — an important stage in my life, but not the last one; it merely
> marks the beginning of an even better one.
> *BP:* Since your publisher is French, it was a French publisher, Fayard, that
> obtained the world rights to your memoirs. Does the choice of France have
> any particular significance?
> *LW:* The choice wasn't due to chance. I got many proposals during the course
> of the interviews and meetings I had with union leaders and activists in
> France. I sensed that we understood each other very well, and that our two
> nations had much in common. I thought that the project, which would help
> me gain a wider audience, would be undertaken in an atmosphere of un-
> derstanding that would also assure its effectiveness. We have many

friends in France and we know that they will take good care of us, because they are interested in Polish matters, in Solidarity, and in promoting understanding. All that prompted me to entrust them with my thoughts and my aspirations.

I had delayed writing my memoirs for quite a long time. Memoir-writing, in my view, was an occupation for retired people, and I certainly hadn't retired. I was also hard at work organizing Solidarity and barely had a moment to spare. But I let myself be persuaded. The idea of possibly earning some real money was also attractive; my wages at the shipyards barely supported a family of our size. I decided to go ahead with the project, and held taping sessions where I talked about my life. I found it difficult to recount intimate details into a tape recorder. The time I had set aside always seemed to coincide with some extraordinary political event and I was too distracted to concentrate. How could I talk about my first romance when Deputy Prime Minister Rakowski was on his way to the shipyards to debate me in front of the television cameras? I often had to postpone the session. There were times when I feared that I wouldn't be able to meet my deadlines. Eventually, however, the memoirs were finished.

People all over the world know about the electrician from Gdansk. For many I may actually be the only Pole whose first and last name they not only know but can pronounce. Not long ago, for example, I got a letter from a missionary living in Chad. Strangely enough, the letter was addressed to me but contained information about the migratory patterns of certain birds for one of Poland's ornithological stations. It seems that a man and his son had come to the missionary with a pigeon the boy had shot; the pigeon had a band around one leg inscribed with some numbers and the words "GDANSK, POLAND." The missionary realized that these were the markings of an ornithological station that was studying migratory patterns, and that it would want to know where the bird was found. He didn't know anyone in Poland, let alone Gdansk, but he had heard of Lech Walesa. I sent him a copy of my book with my thanks.

When a Polish worker's job includes diplomacy, he'd better have a friend who is a priest. I could always count on using Father Jankowski's apartment when I needed a safe refuge, but I was always slightly nervous in my role as head of state. I remember confiding this to Zbigniew Brzezinski, formerly national security advisor to President Carter, when he came to Poland for a visit.

Lech Walesa: Greetings, Professor Brzezinski. After all the good things I've heard about you, I am delighted finally to meet you. To many Poles you are an example of how it is possible to be successful in politics without abandoning personal conviction. To them you represent a realist who hasn't lost sight of the important things. Please, let's sit down. This is my second job for the day — and it's even more exhausting than a morning at the shipyards.

Zbigniew Brzezinski: It can't be as bad as all that. You seem to handle both pretty well.

LW: It may not look hard, but this second job really wears me out. Especially this high-level diplomatic stuff.

ZB: But that's exactly what you're so good at.

LW: Meeting with important figures still wears me out. I approach a meeting as if it were a prizefight. I'm a worker, and not very good at clever conversation. Diplomats are supposed to make speeches and know how to play with language. Even their intonations count. I'm out of my depth. I tend to go on too long. But with you, professor, it's a different matter. We're two Poles who feel the same about national questions.

ZB: Actually, I consider myself an American — an American of Polish origin. That doesn't mean I try to play down my Polishness, or try to hide it — such as by changing the spelling of my name, which I haven't done. It is my duty to do everything I can to improve Polish-American relations.

LW: The work you do helps a great deal. But to begin: The period of Edward Gierek and Jimmy Carter, when you were working for the American government, was a critical one for Poland. The 1970s ended with Poland opening up to the developed countries.

ZB: I agree, but I still worry about whether the Polish authorities will take advantage of opportunities that offer themselves in the international arena. If they don't, the younger generation might conclude that only violent solutions work.

LW: Professor, what do you think of the changes in Moscow? It seems to me that there really is something brewing there. Gorbachev will make some changes, and his successor will take them even further. They are attempting to rebuild the whole edifice — but we have to be careful that the bricks of this reform don't come crashing down on us. As a worker at the shipyards, I loosen and tighten thousands of nuts. If I screw them on too tight I can ruin them, and if I unscrew them too quickly I can break them. One thing is certain: communism is on its deathbed. The question that remains is how to undo the system it leaves behind.

ZB: Here is what I think: Gorbachev will not be thrown out as Khrushchev was, but he also probably won't be successful. He won't be able to implement reform that would radically change the Soviet system. That system is too rooted in tradition and too centralized to be transformed into a truly pluralistic model of management. The result of his attempts at reform will most likely be several years of political and ideological ferment, but they won't end with any radical changes. Nevertheless, they will force Russia to seek international accords, and that is where I see a chance for Poland.

Professor Brzezinski's analysis and predictions proved to be right on the mark.

Going home at the end of the day was routine enough, although there were some exceptions. Once, for instance, on my way home from work, a man who gave his name as Szczepanski* came over to my car and said he'd been hired by some organization to assassinate me, but had decided otherwise. As for the police who always followed me, I sometimes managed a subterfuge to evade them. Upon arriving home, instead of getting out of my minivan, I would instead lie flat on the floor. In the van with me was a stand-in — someone dressed like me who could imitate my walk. He would get out and walk into my house. I would wait in the cold for a few minutes, long enough for the police to settle comfortably into their normal vigil, then slip out of my van and into a waiting Fiat, which, with me crouched on the floor, would whisk me away to a secret meeting with underground Solidarity leaders. For three days after one such maneuver, I was able to walk around — wearing a hat and sunglasses — feeling free, free from police surveillance and free from crowds. When I returned home I smacked the roof of the police car as I passed it on my street. This visibly upset them. "You know, gentlemen, this could mean you won't get a bonus this year," I chided them.

But usually the return home, where my wife and eight children were waiting for me, was uneventful. I trusted in God and knew that there was no point in being afraid for my life — there was nothing I could do about this fake Szczepanski or some other madman. I wondered, in fact, whether I was taking full advantage of the opportunities the Almighty had given to me.

Afternoons, the house was always in a commotion. In our part of the house, the children played and did their homework, while the living room was always crowded with Solidarity aides and assistants: Zosia Gust, sec-

---

* The real Szczepanski was a Free Union militant; see chapter 3.

retary; Teresa Zabza, interpreter; Bogdan Olszewski, computer expert; Jurek Trzcinski and Wojtek Jamrozik, my bodyguards; and Aram Rybicki, the man who tried to keep everything under control. Add to them various other people with some problem or other, and you have quite a crew. On rare occasions, I managed a half-hour nap before the visits, but most of the time I was immediately caught in a whirlwind the minute I walked through the door.

I doubt I could list all the "visionaries" who came to my home to talk over their often harebrained projects. But I was less dismissive of them than they might have expected. Who knows? They might just be able to change the world. Anyway, all they really wanted me to do was just listen, and I always tried to do that.

Apart from the visitors, there was the correspondence. Zosia opened and classified the letters. I recall once noticing a thick one in the pile. A bomb? There was always that possibility. But my other "secretaries" had already examined and photographed the package in the Office of Special Investigations at the post office. There was no need to panic.

What the gray envelope contained was a pipe sent by an American collector who wondered if I would send him one of mine in exchange. All my pipes had long since gone to various collectors, and I had completely stopped smoking. This after a long and private struggle, for I had once been a chain-smoker.

At first, I smoked ordinary "worker's" cigarettes, but when I became president of Solidarity, I took up Salems, because they were supposed to be less harmful than the others — and besides, I received whole cartons of them as gifts. That brought me nothing but trouble. In 1980, a television commentator, with the camera focusing on my cigarette, made a point of declaring, "Look, everybody — Walesa, the so-called 'worker,' doesn't smoke 'worker's' cigarettes." I received letters begging me to quit. It wasn't proper for a Catholic, some would write, nor for the father of a family, the head of Solidarity, to smoke. Doctors, too, were after me. I did sincerely want to give it up, and after several tries, one day I'd really had enough. "My lips will never touch tobacco again, " I announced. And they haven't since.

My assistants and advisors often met me away from the house, in order to be able to talk openly. The seashore always seemed a good place, since my apartment was bugged from top to bottom, and we didn't rule out the possibility that even those who came to talk might be Security Service agents. Things were different on the beach. It was easy to spot the guys in business suits carrying suitcases with microphones sticking out of them. We also knew from reading spy novels that the sound of the waves muffles listening devices, especially when there's wind. We would walk with Jacek Merkel, Aleksander Hall, Grzegorz Grzelak, Aram Rybicki, Piotr Nowina-Konopka, or Leszek Kaczynski, and the guys in suits would hopelessly run around us trying to catch what we were saying.

There were plenty of occasions when at the end of the day someone would drop in. "I've lost my money and can't get home." Walesa helped everyone, was the word. What could I do? Whether or not he was telling the truth, I usually tried to spare something. I would finally collapse into bed, exhausted — but the doorbell would always ring. Some drunk who'd lost track of time absolutely insisted on showing his personal support for me and wouldn't leave until he'd shaken Walesa's hand. All this was of no interest whatsoever to the government men parked day and night in front of my building. They had more important things to do than stand guard over my domestic tranquillity. But as the drunk would leave my place, they would ask him without fail for his papers. They had to make sure he followed the rules, like all my visitors. These agents must have had a lookout post — in the day-care center across the street, most likely — because even when several people came down the stairs from my apartment together, they always seemed to know precisely which one to ask for papers.

Even our excursions outside of town offered no escape. I love to go fishing or mushroom-picking. On Sundays, I'd take Danka and the kids, and often some friends as well, and we'd all go to the woods of Kaszuby. Behind us our eternal shadow followed, the Militia van, and behind them, the predictable car with Security Service agents. Once, as we were driving through some swampy area, and my minivan just barely made it through, theirs got literally bogged down. In a panic, they must have sent a message to their superiors — "Walesa has given us the slip and has certainly gone to meet with the underground." Minutes later, a helicopter was hovering over us.

Usually I'd pull over in a clearing, and while Danka and the youngest girls set up a picnic, the rest of us went off in search of mushrooms. After I'd parked, the Militia van and the other car would block my minivan by parking ahead and in back of it. Men in suits — carrying mushroom baskets, of course — followed my every step, as always, doing their job of overhearing what I was saying, and trying not to lose sight of me. I would ignore them and stubbornly hunt for mushrooms. When I returned to the car, the Militia van would sound its siren to summon the agents roaming around in the forest; only when they got back would they unblock my car.

Time to go — back home to where live broadcasts were conveniently sent directly from the bugs in the walls to the Militia van. We knew this was the case, because some underground Solidarity members had overheard Militia men discussing the details of my domestic life in the Zaspa apartment.

2

The House on Polanki Street

L ife in the Zaspa apartment eventually became so cramped and unbearable that it was imperative for us to buy a house, where we would
have more space and I could get away from the world, someplace where
I could feel like a truly private citizen, a husband, and a father. In 1980
local authorities in Gdansk had offered us a small house in the suburb of
Sopot, but I had refused, wanting to live under the same conditions as
everyone else and remain in an apartment with no more than a hundred
square feet per person. Later, I still hesitated. I imagined someone on TV
telling the world, "Walesa has gotten rich and lives like a *prominent*" —
a member of the privileged and influential nomenklatura.

Feeling torn about it all, I kept putting off buying while still talking a
great deal about it. Meanwhile, life on center-stage was definitely taking
too great a toll on all of us. I was looking for a house close to the center of
the city, if possible, not too big but large enough for my family, and most
importantly in a location unknown to the Militia — so they wouldn't have
time to install bugs. We therefore had to look in complete secrecy. That
turned out to be no simple matter. As soon as the owners learned who the
buyer was, they immediately responded, "Mr. Walesa? No thanks. I've
decided not to sell." They were afraid, not unreasonably, that selling me
their house secretly would subject them to scrutiny, even persecution, by
the Security Service. They would have to explain how they had gotten the
house, justify where the money had come from to build or buy it, and
prove that everything was legal.

Father Jankowski is the one who in the end found a house for immediate
sale — a dilapidated hundred-year-old place on Polanki Street in Gdansk-
Oliwa, nicely located and with a large garden. The owner was an elderly

widow who was about to emigrate to Germany. We had to make our minds
up fast and move in a flash.

And we did. We took the house furnished, just as the owner left it, so that
we would be in the place before the government team of "movers" and
"plumbers" could come in and install their listening devices. We packed
our things in burlap bags that had once contained sugar, provided by the
wife of my late friend and aide Janusz Paczek, who had worked in a
nearby grocery. We quickly crammed all our things into these sacks, marking the contents on the outside, and drove them to Polanki Street with the
intention of storing them in the garage. Naturally, all the contents of the
bags got mixed up and sugar-coated.

   We had bought the house fully furnished for two reasons. First of all, in
those days you couldn't buy any furniture anywhere, and secondly, nothing from our old apartment suited the new place. This turned out to be a
terrible idea. Having to live amid unfamiliar furniture and other people's
objects as well as utensils was eerie for all of us. We were constantly coming across the former owner's personal effects. In one of the bedrooms,
previously rented to a student from Iraq, there was even a portrait of
Saddam Hussein on the wall. For Danka it was especially uncomfortable.
It was like living with strangers, she complained, or, worse, as if we were
intruding on someone else's life. A kind of aura of death hovering about
the abandoned belongings unnerved us, and we finally decided to pile
everything up, sort carefully through it, discard most, and keep only what
we really needed. And our house — bought furnished — became unfur-
nished overnight.

   The condition of the walls — and the roof, plumbing, and floors —
was terrible. Everything needed repairs. We moved in just after the May
1988 strike. I thought it was a good idea to hire people from the shipyards,
knowing that they would no doubt welcome a little money. I also felt that
they would be trustworthy. I would supervise everything — "it is the
master's eye that fattens up the horse," says the old adage — but in practice this wasn't always feasible, and unfortunately, because of my busy
schedule, things proceeded without my having a chance to monitor them.
My coworkers from the shipyards turned out to be model socialist workers: eight-hour days (including an hour for lunch in a nearby restaurant, at
my expense, of course), after which it was quitting time.

   But we managed, and life in the new house resumed its normal rhythm:
the kids went off to school, Danka prepared the meals and tried to bring

some order to things, and my staff showed up each day to work, since, as before, where I lived was also Solidarity headquarters. The telephone never stopped ringing.

When demonstrations broke out in August, my team of workers, dropping their brushes and hammers, promptly returned to the shipyards to join in. I seized this chance to change personnel, and I hired private workers who had, I knew, a different attitude about what they did. What was important to them was the quality of their work, not the number of hours they put in. Without glancing at their watches, they worked from dawn to dusk, and the renovations finally moved ahead. These private workers, without question, applied themselves more strenuously than their predecessors. They also talked less. The shipyard workers had spent too long in a state enterprise with a distinct absence of work ethic or motivation.

I was doing a lot of juggling in August 1988. Before noon, one could always find me at the shipyards talking to workers and management, and meeting with our advisors. At noon, I rushed home to see how the construction and renovation were progressing. In the afternoon and evening, I returned to the shipyards. But as tensions grew and the calls to Kiszczak and the strike in the mines began, I was less and less able to devote time to our house's renovation.

Because any structural home alteration in Poland was forbidden, we were obliged to keep the existing floor plan with its dozen rooms, which were all very small. And the lack of a large living room became painfully obvious when we held our housewarming celebration in September. Teams of journalists had arrived as well as all our friends, and it quickly became clear that the bishop wouldn't have the space he needed to conduct the service. But no matter, we coped. Despite it all, we knew we had finally moved into the castle of our dreams, one with a fence, a gate, and a large garden (an acre and a half). We loved our new garden, even though it was overgrown and we had to replant it from scratch.

3
Danka

T he family is the main pillar of life, and the wife or mother holds that pillar up. Danka* is both the mainstay of our clan and a woman forced by events to do extraordinary things. We all have reserves and talents, but few of us get the chance to show their true depth. Not so for Danka. Life has demanded a great deal from her, from the very beginning of our marriage. She has consistently met and risen above all of its challenges — whether in our garret under the rooftops, expecting our first child in December 1970, listening to gunshots and not knowing if I was in prison or even alive; or after December 13, 1981, when she spoke out in the name of the thousands of wives and mothers whose husbands and sons had been taken from them; or in Oslo, where in her new role as my ambassador she accepted the Nobel Peace Prize in my place.

Danka combines enormous energy and vitality with restraint and refinement. She continually displays courage, as well as a keen intelligence. She is quicker to judge than I am, perhaps, and that is probably the main difference between our ways of looking at the world. We have had wonderful and rich times together, along with some difficult ones, but we are extremely close and understand each other. We share the same feelings about what really matters in life. We've also touched upon the notion of death (though Danka doesn't care for the subject), and often wonder what it would be like if one of us were left alone. Because of the way my political life has evolved, I have often had to prepare her for the worst. One can anticipate, or prepare, but does life ever go according to plan?

In the early 1970s I tried shielding her from my political activities — partly because she was so caught up with our growing family and our do-

---

* Miroslawa Walesa is known as Danuta, of which Danka is the familiar diminutive.

mestic life, and perhaps also because discussing my plans openly doesn't come easy to me. But I learned early on from experience that she was a lot calmer if I warned her, for instance, "Today they might lock me up for forty-eight hours." The unexpected tends to trigger overreaction in her.

I remember one particular time at the beginning of 1980 as we were getting ready to attend the funeral of the Free Union militant Szczepanski, who had died under mysterious circumstances. We had made a wreath, and a group of us were to meet in my apartment — which, of course, as always, was under surveillance. Just as soon as we had gathered, the secret police burst in and dragged us all down to their car. Danka came rushing out of the building after us and, taking off her shoe, began hammering with it on the car, crying that the Militia had no right to arrest us. Their arresting us was proof that the police had been involved in Szczepanski's murder, she screamed. Danka is impulsive, and when she overreacts, I know, it's always out of her love for me.

She has never tried to steer me away from activism with the argument "You have a family, so don't stick your neck out." She always understood that what I did emanated from my political vision and was also for our children's future. I am fully aware that it has been extremely hard for her. One summer the Security Service arrested me while I was taking little Magdalena for a walk in her stroller. At the time Danka was pregnant with Ania and due to deliver on August 3. She categorically refused to allow the agents — after I had been brought to the police station — to take advantage of my absence and search our apartment without a warrant. When they returned two hours later with me, all they found were broadsheets with prayers and church hymns printed on them. Upon learning that the police were taking me to jail, Danka declared she was going to dress the children and send them along with me, because, she insisted, she was unable to look after them alone in her condition. But while she went into the other room, the agents blocked the door after her and dragged me by force down to the car. I can still hear my poor wife running down the stairs after us, weeping, shouting, swearing. Alas, there were to be many such separations. But that one left the strongest impression on me. I felt so helpless leaving her alone just days before our baby was due.

Until 1980, we lived extremely modestly, but we never lost hope. Like me, Danka is a believer, and so far as I know she has never been through a serious depression: her faith in God permeates her daily life and sustains her and the children. If she has had moments of doubt, she has been able to dispel them, convinced that we would pull through and that things would get better. My job was to help keep that store of precious optimism from drying up. Her optimism was also the source of my own strength and energy.

In spite of a difficult life and more than a few obstacles along the way, we have managed to build the family of our dreams. Together we fed and bathed the children, washed their clothes, took them for walks. There was little time left for entertainment, or for getting together with friends, but that was fine with us. For most of our early life we never had enough money, particularly after I'd been fired. "This is how much we need to get through the month," Danka would suggest. "You need to think of ways of getting it." And, somehow, one way or another, I would scrape together the money we needed.

A young man once appeared at our door and told Danka he'd just been fired and had two young children to support. The situation was desperate; could the Walesas help? My wife, a graduate of the school of hard knocks, always managed to infuse courage into those in distress by telling them about our own past, using us as examples of what can be done to survive. But to a woman wearing furs and jewelry, crying because she didn't have the money for expensive medicine or even enough to eat, Danka said bluntly, looking her straight in the eye, "You'll just have to sell your furs or a ring."

After August 1980, when the massive strike led to the legalization of Solidarity, political events were accelerating at such a pace that our apartment in Zaspa had seemingly become permanently populated with press and colleagues. It had become an open house. We no longer had a family life. From morning till night journalists camped out with us, drinking our coffee or tea, parking themselves in our kitchen making sandwiches. Along with the journalists, there were also workers fixing our apartment. And among all of them ran the kids. The word "chaos" is too mild. Danka, in the middle of it, would sometimes get so upset she would even make a scene. Could I blame her? Trying to find ways of maintaining calm in the household, I suggested putting up a sign on the door saying TYPHUS.

From the moment I was released from internment, my obsession was to devote every free moment to my family. I made the children recite their lessons and looked over their homework, I repaired things around the house, I changed lightbulbs. Saturdays and Sundays were strictly family days — so long as there wasn't some important meeting. I tried to keep so many people from coming to our house, unless they had come a great distance or needed to address an urgent problem.

Meetings and interviews were now being held outside the home. My office, located right in the new apartment — occupying two small storage rooms — was, of course, still a problem, and walling off our private life from public affairs remained a constant challenge. We statesmen of Solidarity were having a meeting once, pondering Poland's future, when Danka burst into the room, looked right at me, and said, "Gentlemen, perhaps one of you could go to the store and stand in line. A shipment of meat has just come in."

Danka would be in one part of my office — otherwise known as the kitchen — drying some mushrooms. One day, overhearing us still discussing the same point, and unable to contain herself any longer, she yelled at me, "You live in your private world, and the children are getting bad grades! Nothing surprising about that, since no one ever goes to the parent-teacher meetings!"

About those important meetings between teachers and parents, more often than not, I didn't want my presence to create unnecessary drama in the school. I was always trailed by two plainclothes secret policeman at the time, and when I attended those meetings they would stand right behind me, edge their way into the back of the classroom, and sit conspicuously in the last row. Not an ideal occasion for serious conversation about my children's progress.

So now I got up from our discussion to chasten the guilty party into studying. (The guilty party was usually Slawek.) When I spanked him, he screamed, "You may have won the Nobel Peace Prize, but you act just like a Communist!" Of course, I was too distracted to return to my prior discussion.

I always felt guilty about punishing Slawek, and was constantly trying to think of ways of making it up to him. But Danka reminded me of my responsibilities — even if it meant, in the case of Slawek, having to play the heavy.

The hardest time for Danka was during the period of martial law. In the beginning she seemed unaware of all the dangers it presented. I was always busy or off somewhere (someone calculated that in November 1981 I spent only five days in Gdansk). When three days after my internment Danka came to visit me at Chylice, not far from Warsaw, it was obvious to me that she was giving in to despair. I comforted her as best I could. We had to act with dignity, I said. We were making history. When she left, I believe she was feeling stronger and even proud.

She came all the time to visit me at Otwock, and later at Arlamowo — either alone or with the children. Danka knew that she was my only link to the outside world. She brought me tapes of various events, such as the May 1 demonstrations in Gdansk, or smuggled in documents. We had long talks, and from these precious conversations I learned that Danka, whom I'd never tried to convert into becoming a "comrade in the struggle," understood issues and problems more profoundly than I could ever have suspected. We discussed things we had never discussed before. Her opinions, her stories, her responses were important to me. She had an intuitive grasp of even the most difficult questions. Danka was generally well treated by those who ferried her to and from my place of isolation, but toward the end of 1982 this changed dramatically. One day, returning from one of her visits at Arlamowo in the Security Service car with three-year-old Ania and four-year-old Magdalena, she and the children were dropped off, not at the residence of the bishop of Przemysl, as usual, but at the Militia headquarters. All three were hustled into the building and searched for a full two hours. Insults were thrown at Danka; but I was pleased to hear that she returned the insults well. Danka speaks her mind, and she let the Security Service flunkies know in no uncertain terms what she thought of their methods.

I actually stopped delivering statements during my internment, since Danka spoke so eloquently and well for me. From where I was, I heard her on the radio giving interview after interview and answering questions about a wide variety of issues. She was one of the thousands of wives and mothers taking care of their families when their husbands or sons were in prison, and she spoke for them all. She also met with representatives of the Polish Church, the Apostolic See, and foreign embassies. To the journalists who came to see her she would not only talk about me and how I was holding up, but discuss with great competence a number of current events as well. My wife had matured politically, and she played her new role with growing skill. I was terribly proud of her.

When Maria Wiktoria was born, her baptism in the Zaspa church turned into a spontaneous demonstration of public support for Solidarity and an expression of sympathy for our family. These displays of goodwill strengthened Danka's morale and touched her deeply. But I couldn't help noticing that our painful separation was becoming increasingly hard for her to bear, try though she did not to show it. All I could think about was how little I could do to help her and yet how much I needed her. I knew she would never let me down. Danka was my ray of hope.

My dear wife is one of those people who, once having started something, have to bring it to its completion. I was totally confident that traveling on my behalf she would conduct herself impeccably in Oslo. Since I couldn't travel, she had decided to go, accompanied by our eldest son, Bogdan, to accept the Nobel Peace Prize in my name. Her greatest joy, she said, came from the fact that the prize would clean off the mud spattered on us by the official Polish propaganda machine. It was our passport to a place in history, and of critical importance for the future of Solidarity. The strain of this new and weighty responsibility made her understandably edgy before their departure. She was aware of representing not only me, but all Polish women as well, and it was daunting. Her mission was to show the world that being a mother of a large family doesn't necessarily turn you into a simpleminded domestic hen. Somewhat intimidated by the task, she also fretted about what to wear, how to act.

But it all worked out in the end. When I heard her voice on the radio at the home of Father Jankowski, I was speechless with emotion and couldn't stop the tears. When she returned home, I was moved all over again by her account of her trip; it was so different from the official accounts provided by the Communist media — the only sources I could hear or read. Meeting the king of Norway had made the biggest impression on her, and she remembered with embarrassment that he had approached her so quickly she hadn't had time to follow etiquette and curtsy. The whole interview went by in a blur.

The Nobel ceremony itself, with all of its elegance, Danka found enormously impressive and gratifying. It lifted her spirits and helped her get through the press conference without a hitch. Late in the evening on the first day of her stay in Oslo, she and our son went window-shopping, and together they marveled at the magical, brightly colored Christmas displays. But she soon had to give up taking these walks because they automatically attracted a crowd of journalists. Walking on the streets of Oslo gave her a new sense of freedom and the feeling that life was easier there.

Letters, telegrams, congratulations, and news clippings, arriving from around the world, gave us enormous pleasure. Journalists were insisting on interviews; but all we craved now was a return to a normal life. Shortly after Danka's return from Norway, two elegantly dressed representatives from Japan's largest newspaper arrived at our apartment. They were received by my secretary, Aram Rybicki, who, upon learning that they wanted to interview Mrs. Walesa, asked them to wait a moment. Danka, meanwhile, was out in the courtyard beating some rugs. When she appeared, looking like a housekeeper with a rug slung over her shoulder, the visitors ignored her, not realizing who she was. When she reappeared, this time dressed more appropriately for the occasion, they recognized their mistake and became so flustered they had great trouble conducting the interview. But Danka, typically, remained cool and collected.

Danka is equally comfortable with housewives or prime ministers. It's one of her special talents. Her natural self-confidence and poise always astound me. Whether she is with Mr. and Mrs. Bush, Mr. Mitterrand, or Mrs. Thatcher, Danka addresses them with equal ease, as people like herself. She feels that they, like us, celebrate the same human joys and are at the mercy of the same mortal dramas as we. Title or rank means nothing to her.

The one exception is John Paul II, who has always made a deep impression on Danka. "The Holy Father radiates such goodness and such serenity that it creates a feeling of security," she said to me. Our first trip abroad together, Danka's and mine, was to Italy — for that unforgettable meeting with the pope in the Vatican in January 1981. Together we expressed to the Holy Father our belief in and yet our concern for the Polish family. Eight years later, once again we knelt before John Paul II in Rome. We thanked him for what he had done to help the Polish people find freedom and for his prayers on our behalf. We thanked him for the simple fact that his prayers had worked.

These two visits to Italy were our only trips abroad together. I visited John Paul II in my role as a union activist, of course, but also as a Catholic Pole, husband, and father, with my wife, the mother of my children. Most of my other trips were purely business trips; I had to leave the family back home. Trips together posed difficulties — how could we leave all those children without parental supervision for any length of time, really?

Danka's trips without me were to Oslo and, in 1989, to Philadelphia. She enjoyed both immensely. My wife is curious about people and the world. I have made an effort to shield her from too much publicity, and we both felt strongly about our right to a private life. So for some time now I have forbidden anyone to use flashbulbs or television lights or cameras in my house; we're under enough scrutiny as it is. Danka makes fun of me, saying that I would happily hide under the stove. Well, it's true that I would much prefer to have no politics in my house.

But now, because she's involved in various organizations (especially those that save lives) and interested in women's issues, Danka does give interviews. The organization to which she devotes the most time is the foundation called Sprawni Inaczej [Alternative Living], which helps handicapped children. Danka is a cofounder, and a great deal of her energy is aimed at raising funds and keeping the charity going. Despite her new interests and obligations, Danka's chief realm remains our home, and it has long been left entirely to her able management. Eight children don't allow her to sleep late or even take a little rest, especially during the school year. Keeping track of which child is going to what school at what time, who is washed, combed, and dressed, or whether he or she has eaten his or her breakfast and has sandwiches for lunch — all of this needs her endless vigilance. Then there is the business of daily marketing for each meal. Danka is on the go every minute. Her domestic standards are very high. Various young people with good intentions and goodwill have applied for the job of helping Danka, but because her standards are so high, no one has made the grade. Once we were sure we had found just the right person: a whiz at housework and shopping, and a good cook who also knew how to look after the children. Danka became very much attached to her. But it turned out that she had been planted there by the Security Service. Even today, as wife of the president of Poland, Danka still has difficulty finding proper household help.

An excellent gardener, Danka also sows, plants, and even turns over the flowerbed. Her flowers and vegetables are an endless source of pride to her, and to me.

With all these occupations, there isn't much time left for socializing, although she enjoys spending time with friends — joking, chatting, asking or giving advice. Spring always inspires her to travel somewhere, even if it's just a few miles from home. She laughs and calls herself a Gypsy. Even moving the household has never been a negative experience for her.

I enjoy talking to attractive women, but my wife and family are the absolute center of my life. Danka knows this. She occasionally looks amused when other women seem attracted to me. For my part, the sight of someone showing too much interest in Danka annoys me. Jealousy, no doubt. But isn't jealousy a part of love?

When someone asks Danka whether she's happy, she always replies affirmatively. Being happy is an integral part of her nature, and it is that positive nature which built our family. Hate and disrespect pain her, whatever form they take and whether in her public or in her private life. Danka is my reference point and my guiding light. She always surprises me with her refinement and the sweet grace of her reactions. Thanks to Danka, I feel that the world can be beautiful. With a simple gesture, a look, or a word, she can change my mind and my mood in an instant.

When Danka and I got married and we started our family, she consciously made the decision to dedicate herself entirely to her responsibilities and enjoy the wonders of motherhood. Danka regrets that today Polish women need to work outside the home, and deplores the fact that this necessity is too often at the expense of the family. The precious time that women spend with their children, she insists, is all-important. Both of us know that our children are the fulfillment of our marriage.

4
The Children

Danka and I had always planned to have a big family. Following in the ancient tradition of workers and peasants, we wanted as many children as God would give us, as many as we could feed. Wasn't I afraid to raise so many little ones when life in Poland was so hard? Since the possibility that I could be assassinated or imprisoned was there every day, hadn't it crossed my mind that my children might have to grow up without a father? I had no easy answer to these questions. Aren't the most important things in life often irrational? If you calculate things in terms of numbers, fewer children definitely mean fewer expenses and fewer cares. But in my life I have seen so many efforts come to naught, and so many ambitions end in disaster, that I find it hard to advise with any certainty how you should calculate anything. I am a man of faith, and by its very nature faith eludes reason, statistics, calculations. To the question of why I have so many children I answer, with a certain fatalism, "Because Providence has allowed it."

Life has always proved complicated for us, and in keeping with that, the births of nearly all our children coincided with some dramatic event. In fact, looking at it subjectively, events in Polish history over the past twenty years form a kind of calendar of my fatherhood. Bogdan, the eldest, came into the world in December 1970 (there are those who enjoy repeating the myth, even to this day, that his parents were killed during the protests and the Walesas adopted him); Slawek was born when we were moving from Stoga into our own apartment; Przemek, when I was fired from the shipyards; Jarek, when I was beginning my Free Union activities; Magda, during the period when the SB had me under particularly close surveillance; Ania, during the strike of August 1980; and Maria Wiktoria, when I was interned. Only Brygidka's birth was not marked by any political turning point.

Each of my children has earned his or her special place in the family. Bogdan is very calm and sensitive, and perhaps overly shy. At the moment he is studying economics at the University of Gdansk, although he hasn't yet focused on his future. His school years went by smoothly. Slawek and Przemek, on the other hand, are what people classify perhaps as real conmen. Always up to some mischief, Slawek can worm his way into just about anything, anywhere. He's ambitious, stubborn, and self-righteous. Danka remarks laughingly that Slawek is a reflection of me. On the other hand, thanks to his computer know-how, he has helped me get a better handle on the illogical system we live in.

From 1980 to 1988, all ten of us lived in a modern but fairly cramped apartment. After I was awarded the Nobel Prize, six hundred letters — usually addressed simply "Lech Walesa, Gdansk" — came every day. Not knowing what else to do with them, we piled them in a heap in the largest room, which served simultaneously as my office, a lecture room, and Solidarity headquarters. I couldn't throw the letters away, because the agents who had me under surveillance day and night parked their car right next to the trash. They would have immediately pulled the letters out and shown them to the press: "Hey, Walesa fans, this is what your hero thinks of your letters!"

Not only could we not throw them out, but keeping up with answering them had become impossible. The mountain of paper accumulated until I learned that the only solution was to store return addresses and responses in a computer; diskettes take up a lot less room than files. A marvelous idea. Underground Solidarity, aided by its foreign bureau in Brussels (which government spokesman Jerzy Urban called "an office of the CIA"), was able to purchase the computer equipment. Because it was contraband (computers were included in the European Economic Community embargo following the Soviet invasion of Afghanistan), it had to be smuggled out of Western Europe. People on our side of the border made things difficult as well. The Security Service, the intelligence communities, and the Communist Party could freely import whatever equipment they needed, but not a private citizen. The government was afraid we'd find and begin using more modern means of encoding and transmitting information. So, like tape recorders and VCRs, computers now had to be registered individually. The government proved it was ready to enforce regulations by confiscating equipment brought in from the West by members of Solidarity (who were accused of collaborating with the CIA). But on the whole the blockade proved ineffective; more computers and VCRs were imported, one way or another, into Poland than into all of the other countries in Eastern Europe combined.

Next to my "office" was a room of just over a hundred square feet, a little storeroom where I stacked the computer and all the other equipment. Right beside it was an oven Danka used to dry mushrooms and make preserves. Stubbornly defending her territory, the domestic half of the apartment, she insisted that the oven stay exactly where it was.

I was uneasy about keeping my archives in a computer. Paranoid? Perhaps. The various secret services were watching every move Solidarity made — and before long the computer would be crammed with data of great interest to them. Sooner or later the men in gray would show up and either confiscate the computer or implant a special bugging device that could transmit impulses generated by the keyboard. We tried unsuccessfully to devise ways of protecting the data. And paper continued to fill shelf upon shelf.

Thanks to my sons, we solved the problem. As soon as the secretaries left at six every evening, the boys booted up the computer and studied the systems. I couldn't stop them. They became computer whizzes in almost no time. They helped me become proficient as well, and the more functions and commands I learned, the more seriously I took an interest in this world-conquering machine, and the more I became convinced it provided the evidence that the Communist era would have to come to an end: information systems bend to no psychological pressure, after all; they know no fear, and they are incapable of lying.

Beginning in the mid-1980s, my watchword was pluralism: the multiplication of approaches and solutions, from computers to unions to political parties. "Let's put the data we have about our system into the computer and see how it tries to organize it," I suggested, and later joked, "I'm surprised the machine didn't go up in smoke, given that the socialist formulas we were feeding it were so illogical." These remarks, picked up by journalists, were touted as an example of Walesa's "wit and wisdom." The old formulas were thrown out. Europe was in search of a new logic.

Slawek has always had a passion for cars, and he is impatient and impulsive. Przemek is stubborn and high-strung. Bogdan claims that Przemek acts this way to deflect criticism while he marches to his own drummer. In Krwia, at Father Lewinski's summer camp for the children of Solidarity members, Przemek always found himself in some kind of trouble with the counselors. There wasn't a single tree he didn't climb up or a single window he didn't climb through.

The youngest of my boys is Jarek. Danka claims he is the one who most resembles me, except that he's better-natured. Very independent, he's the only one who doesn't need to be gotten up or urged to get dressed. He has a strong sense of duty and finishes everything he has to do on time. When he takes on a project, he does it methodically from A to Z. He's been involved in gymnastics for five years now. Every day after school, off he goes to practice. He has already taken part in the Polish championships, and a life in sports seems to attract him more and more.

My children's studies, I'm afraid, haven't gone as well as I might have hoped. When they were smaller, I was able to sit with them and help with their homework. But that was of course when I had more time and more peace of mind. Danka spends a great deal of time with the girls. Meanwhile, the boys need tutors. For them schoolwork seems secondary. They've skipped class more than once, and I've had to tighten the reins by making them bring their teacher's signature, in order to verify that they really attended.

When asked by the press which educational methods and models I believe in, I reply that I don't particularly care for theory, nor do I believe in textbook definitions. Textbooks can answer specific questions. But you can't learn about real life from books. There are no universal standards. Each person is different, and every circumstance is different. I don't put much faith in the educational methods currently used. Children obviously need to be taught to tell the truth, to be honest and conscientious. But this, I am convinced, should be accomplished more by example than by schoolwork. I hope that my children understand my dreams and see that I am guided by moral principles, that if my life has involved struggle, this struggle has had a profound and definite meaning. Values can be taught to children only by example, just as they learn to pray by kneeling with others and saying the words out loud along with them.

Naturally, like all the children in the world, my children can be disobedient. With eight kids, one of them inevitably is going to be up to some mischief. The more serious the mischief, the more vigorous my reaction. At times I would even pick up a belt and use it. Now that the boys are grown, I have had to find other ways of disciplining them. I confiscated Slawek's key to the car, for example, forbidding him to drive alone. But I find it hard to stand by my resolution. All Slawek has to do is come and beg and I'll give in. Buying presents for my children has never been my method of rewarding them. I do buy presents for my daughters when I go on a trip: a doll, a teddy bear, a game, nothing more extravagant than that.

The younger girls are still little and their characters are just beginning to develop. The eldest, Magda, is already a young woman; Ania demands more of our attention — she is very ambitious, always wanting to be first in her class and receive praise. And then there is Brygidka — Bibon, as we call her — a little bit our mascot, who demands the most time. I love all my children equally, but I must pay more attention to the younger ones. I think that's less unfair than it sounds — at one time, each of them was the youngest.

Five years ago, our youngest was Maria Wiktoria (her nickname is Mynia). Lilka Mrowczynska, an acquaintance of ours who devotes her energies to charity work, happened to see two little girls in the street. She noticed that one of them looked especially pale and underweight. She went up to that little girl and asked, "Where are you from, child?"

"Nearby," the child answered.

"And where does your daddy work?"

"At the shipyards."

"And your mommy?"

"She doesn't work. She takes care of us."

"How many are you?"

"Eight."

Mrs. Mrowczynska promised herself she'd have to look in on such a large family, especially since it was obviously such a poor one. "Could your mommy come see me?"

"No, Mommy won't come. She doesn't have time."

"Then give me your name and address, and I'll come see her."

The little girl replied, "Walesa."

Mrs. Mrowczynska burst out laughing. Mynia is indeed quite frail-looking, and I can see that she might even at times pass for a charity case.

I am particularly pleased that none of my children were ever raised like the spoiled progeny of celebrities or public figures. If their last name perhaps sets them apart from their contemporaries, I haven't noticed that this affects how others treat them — by either indulging them or harassing them. Bogdan and Slawek have already been arrested by the Militia. Bogdan was wearing an earring at the time, and that bothered the Polish Militia men. When they challenged him about it, my son stood his ground and refused to take it off; a few insults were exchanged. Do my children take advantage of their name in any way? Bogdan accuses Slawek of parading around boasting that he is a Walesa, but all kids tend to brag at that age.

That's my family. The kids fight among themselves and they also tease each other, but they would also walk through fire for each other. If Bogdan doesn't see Brygidka for two days, he misses her so terribly he comes home. The oldest and the youngest roll around on the floor like puppies. The children, as in other families, can be jealous of one another, the girls especially. If we pay attention to one for a little too long the others will start sulking. We do our best to treat each child in our family as an "only child," giving them as much love and warmth as we can. None of them is particularly useful around the house. The older ones go off with their buddies after school, Jarek returns from his gymnastics exhausted, and the girls are still too little. Nevertheless, during those rare moments when everyone is home, Danka divides up the chores and they all end up doing their share.

I've always taken our children's religious education very seriously. A daily prayer and Sunday mass are basic to our lives. In the evening we all kneel together for prayer. When the children were very young, the whole family went to church together. Now, the boys go to their mass, and the girls attend with Danka. As for me, one day I'll be at Saint Brygid's, another day I might travel somewhere else to attend mass. The children, like children everywhere, will always look for ways out — pleading that they have a headache or that they have an important homework assignment. "Forget your homework," we say. "Mass is more important." Catechism classes are also obligatory, no excuses accepted. These rules are not a matter for round-table discussion, and I am not flexible.

Still, the atmosphere in our house is very different from the one I remember from my own childhood. My mother invoked divine authority every time one of her children was naughty, saying that God, who suffered for mankind's sins, was angry with us. I would rather have been spanked than made to feel guilty about mankind's sins, so I decided that with my own children I would never invoke the Lord's name over trifles.

Questions come up, however, that force us to talk about our faith. One day Bogdan asked how God could have permitted Auschwitz and Katyn Forest,* the concentration camps and the gulags. Answering him that God

---

* Thousands of Polish army officers were massacred in Katyn Forest in early 1940 by the Soviet secret police. Only in 1990 did the USSR admit responsibility; see chapter 31.

endowed man with free will didn't satisfy him, but I am no theologian and it was the best I could do.

My boys sang in the choir, even when they were young. I admit that I would love for one of them to become a priest, just as I would love for one of my daughters to become a nun, though of course I know those callings are a matter of divine, not human, will. I myself have sometimes contemplated becoming a priest.

It is a Walesa family trait to be driven — toward either good or evil. My brother was an alcoholic and nothing could stop him from rushing headlong toward self-destruction. I became a union militant, never pausing to think what it might cost. Perhaps those same genes might have made a good priest out of me. Who can say?

I am painfully aware of never having enough time to give my children. I am away from home too much, and when I am home I'm usually preoccupied and want to shut myself up in my room or take refuge in the garden. When things aren't going well, I like talking with my two eldest sons. They are adults, and even though they are not particularly interested in politics, I always find our talks together helpful.

They were encouraged from the start to worry more about their studies than about politics. Before he graduated from high school, Bogdan dabbled a little in politics — he handed out some fliers — but he didn't really take to it. My children have known or guessed enough about my political activities to be concerned, even at times frightened, particularly during the period when much of what I did was illegal. The kids, by necessity, grew up fast and caught on quickly. The whispering and undertones around them were signs to them that their father was in danger. They didn't tell me, but I saw it in their eyes. Sometimes when they misbehaved I couldn't understand why. One day I realized that if they were misbehaving, they might be doing so to distract me from the danger I was in. During the period after the abduction and murder of Father Jerzy Popieluszko, they were especially afraid and couldn't help but worry that it could happen to me, or that they themselves might be kidnapped.

My life has often been in danger. As I traveled to Italy in 1981, for example, I was informed that an attempt on my life was imminent. There was a contract out on me, and an assassination would be attempted by the Red Brigades, acting on orders from abroad. At the time, few understood the degree to which terrorists benefit from substantial, well-organized support from other countries. No one knew much about East German leader Erich Honecker's weapon-smuggling operations, or knew that Nikolai Ceausescu of Romania — "the genius of the Carpathians" — was really the greatest criminal and psychopath Europe had produced since Stalin. I was therefore surrounded day and night by bodyguards when I was in Italy. So much so, in fact, that I wanted to give them the slip and go walking around Rome at night. Someone urged me to do just that, claiming he could show me how to elude the security agents and go off on my own. I resisted the temptation. I've wondered whether my refusal was why I escaped the bullet that cut down John Paul II five months later.

In 1984, rumors about an attempt on my life were the subject of an investigation conducted by the Polish minister of the interior. As a result of that investigation, two people who had attended the First Congress of Solidarity in Gdansk were arrested in Italy after it was established that they had been in contact with the Red Brigades. Colonel Trafalski, who conducted the investigation at the Polish end, never got to see it through, though. He was killed in October 1984 while driving to Tarnow, where he had gone to hunt down those who had been in contact with Father Popieluszko's murderers. His car collided head-on with a large truck. The truckdriver was never able to explain how the accident happened.

As such events were almost daily occurrences, it was virtually impossible to isolate the children from them. I remember clashes between the police and some young people from our own housing development on May 1, 1983. The Militia arrived to disperse the demonstrators with tear-gas bombs; people leaned out their windows and pelted the Militia with flowerpots, jam jars, whatever was handy. Events such as these fed right into the children's natural aggressiveness. Kids in the neighborhoods formed gangs with names like the Pilots and the Start, which fought among themselves through the next two years. Slawek and Przemek, to my regret, were active in one of these gangs. They were at the right age for revolt, and my nonviolent methods irritated them.

Given everything they've been through, I often wonder what my children will be like when they're grown. For years they endured all kinds of abuse and accusations being made against their father by the official propaganda machine. Week after week they watched how the government spokesman spat on me with total immunity by repeating lies and distortions; I was called a bourgeois laborer who couldn't muster the support of a hundred workers, an ignorant fool with too many children, a religious zealot led around by the nose by priests, a CIA agent awarded the Nobel

Prize for all the work he had done for the Americans (the proof being that seven American universities had given me honorary doctorates!), a tax evader who received cash payments he wouldn't share with the government, an advocate of destroying the Polish economy both because he extorted medical excuses to justify absenteeism and most of all because he approved of the American sanctions that followed martial law. These descriptions of me caused more amusement than alarm in our house. I used to joke that Jerzy Urban didn't realize he was running a kind of one-man publicity show for me by bringing my name up on such a regular basis. There were times, however, when I noticed a troubled look cross Bogdan's face. He was the one who would best understand what was happening, and that look indicated to me that he had been forced to defend me to his friends. I made a point of taking him into my confidence, hoping he would understand what was going on and be able to explain it to others.

I would have liked to explain my life to my children — but could it be done? I would have liked to tell them about my first joys, my failures, my loves. But would they really understand what it was like to grow up using kerosene lamps for light? When electricity finally did make it to our village when I was a young boy, the whole idea of volts, amperes, and ohms fascinated me. It was magic for me — not being able to see an electric current and yet knowing it was strong enough to knock a grown man down and run machines that were stronger than a horse. I was so curious to find out how it all worked that I began picking up various pieces of electrical appliances, taking them apart, and putting them back together. This was the start of my career as an electrician.

How could I explain this early passion to a generation that spends all of its time in front of computer terminals? My children know from my stories that when I was young there were times when we didn't have enough bread for our dinner, but I am not certain that this made any impression on them. I had to walk everywhere because I never had enough money for a bus ticket. Their response was that I should have gotten a monthly pass. Our church was over four miles away, and I used to take my shoes off so I wouldn't wear them out, then put them back on just before entering the church. How can my sons understand what this means, when they throw their shoes away as soon as they get scuffed and dirty? The world I grew up in no longer exists; that reality is gone.

We all learn from our mistakes. I have warned each one of my children not to touch the iron because it was hot, yet each one had to touch it before believing me. Even little Brygidka. Prohibitions don't work, nor does

theory. Life is richer than both, and it doesn't always permit either foresight or remedy. I remember how my mother and my stepfather would
rehearse, down to the last detail, what they would do when they were summoned to some bureaucratic office; but I also remember that none of the
preparations ever did any good. All the bureaucrat would have to do was
spill his coffee when they arrived and their careful planning would come
to nothing.

My children learned that nothing can be foreseen with any accuracy. During the summer of 1987, we received an invitation from a Franco-Polish
family for two of our boys to spend their vacation in France. I was delighted. At their age I had never had the opportunity to set foot outside
Popowo, the village of my birth; there was neither time nor money for
traveling. I had promised myself that for my kids it would be different. We
decided that Slawek and Przemek should go to France, since Bogdan was
already planning to go to West Germany. So they packed their things and
I arranged for my favorite taxi driver, Andrzej Rzeczycki, nicknamed
"the Zlotowka" ["the Dollar"], to drive them to Okecie Airport in Warsaw.
Everything had to be done extremely discreetly in order to avoid running
into journalists. Waiting for Slawek and Przemek at Orly Airport in Paris
were not only the host family, but also my friends Bozena and Maciek
Grzywaczewski. Bozena was the first secretary I ever had, and probably
the best. She and Maciek had moved to Paris to get medical treatment for
thier leukemia-stricken child. I knew that with Bozena there, my boys
would be met and taken care of.

At thirteen and fifteen, Slawek and Przemek were old enough to look
after themselves on the airplane, and because we didn't want to attract any
attention, Andrzej, the taxi driver, hadn't requested that a Polish flight at-
tendant accompany them through customs at Orly, as sometimes is done
with smaller children. Our friends and the host family stood by, waiting to
welcome them. But the boys didn't show up. When the last of the passengers had already gone through customs, the welcomers started to get impatient and upset. An announcement was broadcast in Polish and in
French, asking the children of Lech Walesa to please come to the information desk. It was repeated several times, but to no avail! They concluded that Walesa must have changed his mind about sending his kids
and hadn't bothered to warn them. They called me up.

Now it was my turn to get upset. I knew that my old friend the Zlotowka
had personally taken the kids through customs at Okecie and then watched

from the airport terrace while the plane took off. There was no doubt that they had boarded the airplane. They had to have arrived in Paris. I asked Maciek if it was possible that the boys had gotten out of the airport without being spotted. That was impossible, he replied. He had been informed in rather a haughty tone that at Orly even a mouse couldn't slip by without their knowing it. Armed patrols were everywhere, constantly on the alert for terrorists (there had been a number of bombings in France about that time).

Tension mounted. Danka panicked. I tried playing the role of the man in charge. This was 1987, after all, and the government was still mounting a propaganda campaign against me. There was no way for me to just call the Militia and request their help. I went over their head to the minister of the interior, whose secretary informed me that the affair might indeed be very serious and that it was now a matter for the Security Service. Having discovered that soon after the plane took off for Paris, a plane bound for Ankara had also taken off, they feared that the Organization of Gray Wolves or some other terrorist group trying to liberate Ali Agca (the man who had tried to assassinate John Paul II) might be involved. They might have kidnapped my children with the idea of forcing an exchange. In France, the affair had also fallen within the jurisdiction of their minister of the interior.

An appeal was sent to French television: "Anyone who has seen or knows anything about Slawek and Przemek Walesa is requested to come to . . ." The announcement was sitting on the anchorman's desk, to be read within minutes on the air. Then suddenly Maciek telephoned: "We found them!" he crowed. "Everything's okay!"

After the plane had landed, the boys, having waited for a minute without spotting their hosts, wandered around in the duty-free area. Never having traveled, they hadn't realized that anyone waiting for them wouldn't be allowed into this area, nor that they would first have to go through passport control before reaching the public concourse. From time to time they wandered back to the original spot. Not finding their hosts didn't bother them in the slightest at first, for they had found themselves in a paradise: ads, computer games, shops full of attractions and music. There was even a real motorcycle on display, right within the reach of anyone. Slawek and Przemek imagined themselves riding it, got swept up in their daydreams, and lost track of the time.

After a while they went back again to the arrival spot, but by then everyone had left. Now they started getting worried. They were also hungry, so they sat down on a bench to eat the food they had in their bags. Then Slawek decided to go to the post office to make an international call. He discovered that the police were everywhere, and they had just arrested a suspect — everyone was a suspect in that climate. The policeman on duty said to the boys, "It's all right. Just wait here and someone will come and help you." Of course, he spoke French and the boys didn't. Back they went to their bench. Still nobody. So they returned to the duty-free stores. And then back again to the police checkpoint.

By now they were starved. A different policeman (part of a new shift, probably) told them the same thing as the one before: "Sit and wait." So they sat down again.

It was nearly dawn when Maciek found them. Even though he'd been told to leave things to the police, he wanted to check for himself. Through the customs glass he finally spotted Slawek and Przemek dozing peacefully on their bench.

But not all my kids' trips abroad have turned into such a nightmare. I have, for several years now, tried sending them away (at least the boys, since they're older), abroad if possible, for two months of vacation. It gives Danka some breathing space. Bogdan has gone to Germany to work. He was employed in Bremen at a home for the elderly, first as a food-server and then as an orderly whose job it was to help people walk or to push their wheelchairs. A year later he worked as a dishwasher. The people there knew he was Lech Walesa's son, but treated him like anyone else. And rightly so. Some elderly ladies wanted to give him German lessons, but his boss wouldn't agree to it. Nevertheless, Bogdan did make some progress in German by virtue of being obliged to speak it. Observing the elderly who, despite their age and various ailments, try to remain active and keep their spirits up inspired him greatly. Seeing ninety-year-olds working happily in the garden, writing, and watching television gives a young man a new perspective about age.

Slawek has traveled across the United States and is good at making contacts wherever he goes. I thought it best to make sure before he left that he was to give absolutely no interviews. He didn't listen to me, of course, and over the past year a few articles have appeared about him, saying that he likes girls and beer. I don't object to his having the tastes of a young man, but I wish he wouldn't broadcast it.

As for Jarek, all he wanted to do was spend his summers in sports camp. But in July 1989, he accompanied Danka to the United States. She was to accept the Medal of Freedom on my behalf. They both attended the awards ceremony in Philadelphia, and that changed his mind. On July 4, he was given the thrill of striking the Liberty Bell three times. Seeing and experiencing so many new interesting things developed his taste for travel. Magda has also begun going abroad, to France. As for the other girls, they visit relatives, and especially my sister Iza in Sochaczew. Although they also have participated in church-organized retreats, they are still too young to go far from home.

My sons' reactions to their trips abroad always interested me. Did they feel comfortable there? Had they acquired a taste for an easier, more interesting, and more colorful life? Their first contact with a world so different from the one they knew was a great shock. What fascinated them most, of course, weren't democratic freedoms, but daily life. I recall how excitedly Jarek recounted his experiences in the United States: the shops had plenty of meat and anything else you could want — and they were open twenty-four hours a day! Movie theaters showed several different films at the same time, and they had seats you could adjust, and a refreshment stand with all kinds of goodies! All this made a great impression on the boys. Witnessing this miracle of plenty convinced them that what their father was struggling for wasn't something abstract. There definitely was more to life than deprivation, after all.

For Poland's young people, life is indisputably hard. The sense of powerlessness, of being manipulated, of lacking choices   all these contribute to an overwhelming feeling of frustration. I remember that in 1983, during his second trip to Poland, John Paul II addressed the young people at Czestochowa. He talked of Poland's rich heritage and promise, hoping to discourage them from the temptation of fleeing to an easier life. The temptation has too often been too great. In 1983 alone, 3,339 people actively involved in Solidarity requested permission to emigrate; of that number, 1,170 left Poland (300 of them had been interned, as I had). The authorities concluded that there was no longer a place for them in their homeland. In fact, the government had wanted to ship off Tadeusz Mazowiecki, Bronislaw Geremek, Adam Michnik, and Jacek Kuron — the brains of the democratic opposition — but these men were too stubborn to accept the invitation.

Nearly every week, though, people came to see me seeking a kind of moral absolution before leaving. I neither blamed them nor mourned them. Most often it was Danka who had to listen to their bitter confessions, since I was off at work. So many compatriots didn't know we had seven children (as we did then) or that we were watched around the clock — they assumed that our life was easier than it was. Wiping their tears with handkerchiefs, they said that while life might be tough in Gdansk, it was even tougher where they were from, in Silesia. Terror reigned there.

Behind the desire to emigrate was also the sense that life in Poland had been a failure. Those who advised others to leave suddenly decided they themselves couldn't stand things any longer and began packing. People had their fill not only of martial law, communism, and General Jaruzelski, but of Polish architecture, public transportation, trees, everything. Even the fruits and vegetables had lost their taste. The very air suffocated them and their own homes felt like prisons. It was like an illness that was beginning to permeate the land.

I hope that my sons won't catch that illness. That's why I wanted to expose them early to those things young people might covet. The world is changing and the borders that divide people are disappearing. Right before our eyes the new united Europe is becoming one home shared by Spaniards, French, Germans, Poles, and Russians. Today when I look abroad I can expect a hand extended in friendship rather than a bullet. All the problems threatening humanity today threaten everyone, regardless of nationality — the dangers to our environment are universal.

Patriotism has also changed. I can remember with what reverence my mother and stepfather used to talk about Polish history — its kings, territories, rebellions, and heroes. To them, a Pole's most sacred duty was to defend his homeland against invaders. That was patriotism. But patriotism is also a sentimental attachment to particular times and places — schoolyard days, first dates, cemeteries where grandparents lie in peace. Many who had left Poland for the New World seem to return to spend their old age in Poland. They look for that kerosene lamp they read by as children, for that path in the forest now choked off by undergrowth. Returning to one's roots is a human need, a beautiful need. I believe that it ennobles us. You may have been married five times, but you can't change your original family. The land on which your hands first became calloused cannot be erased from memory.

My children often question how anyone could become attached to a concrete apartment building like the one we lived in — that ecological nightmare — claiming that this is what Poland represents to them. People have only one childhood, I tell them, and, like a dog refusing to abandon a burned-out farmhouse, they cannot let it go.

What will my children become as adults? All parents wonder what life has in store for their children. Had I listened to my own parents, traveled, and gone further with my studies, I might have become — let's say — the manager of a factory: my mother's dream. Perhaps one fine day a company car would have pulled up in Popowo and my mother would have invited Father Placiczewski over to her cottage, boasting, "You see that car? My Lech's. He's really made it to the top." Of course it would have been impossible to ask the priest over, because as a factory manager I would have had to belong to the PZPR, and any family contacts with the clergy would have been frowned upon. Instead my mother would have had to limit her invitation and only ask over some of her friends. "Look at Lech," she'd have said, feigning modesty. "He runs a factory. He's made it up the ladder, and now he drives a company car and lives in a beautiful apartment." Flushed with my success, I would have gone on a vacation and returned home to find . . . that my factory was on strike! I probably would have yelled at the workers, "You can't go on strike!" And they would have promptly put me in a wheelbarrow and carted me right out of the factory. And there would have ended my career as a manager, as well as my mother's dream.

If I hadn't rebelled against the system, I would never have become a part of Solidarity nor won the Nobel Peace Prize. So how am I to know what's best for my children?

5
Daily Life

I have lived through an important and unique period of Polish history, and feel privileged to have witnessed — and perhaps partaken in — the final days of a system that had seemed indestructible. Today, life in Poland is slowly returning to normal. My own life and that of my family are following this pattern of normalization. Our previous daily tension and anxiety have disappeared. And I am pleased to finally be able to separate my private from my public life. This said, every step I take seems to trigger description and commentary. I am still constantly being observed, and people still cling to me and wear me down. If I stumble, say, or fall off a ladder and sprain my wrist, the news is broadcast throughout Poland. What's more, someone somewhere will reveal to the public that actually I didn't fall off a ladder, but was injured in a car accident. I've never been sure what good this uninterrupted flow of information serves, but I do know that being a public figure has its pitfalls.

People who envy me may not understand the price I have to pay. I appear on television talking with VIPs from abroad, but what most don't know is that I suffer from stomach cramps because most of the time I don't have time to eat lunch before the meeting. The glamorous parts of my public life — the house, a car, traveling — are all they see. When absolutely everything you do is public, when everybody wants something and you can't please them all, when someone criticizes you to your face and you feel nauseated, that's the other real side of my life. Take the example of President Bush's visit in June 1989. The meeting and the luncheon we gave at my house were a great pleasure and honor. But before his arrival, his Secret Service agents arrived and turned everything inside out more than a hundred times. Working day and night, they dug up the entire garden, peeked into every corner, and photographed everything. This nonstop intrusion lasted two weeks. There were daily barrages of questions: "What's that lock? No, no, that one. What's under this bush? And under this stone?" Twenty or thirty people swept through my place examining everything, including my socks. They even took the birds out of their cage to make sure no one had slipped in a bomb. It was exhausting; I no longer knew whether I lived in a house or a den of terrorists.

"You showed a lot of nerve, inviting the president of the United State to your house," many told me. I'd met George Bush before he became president, and I knew how much he supported our struggle. Moreover, the United States is a great power that is not content merely to talk about democracy, freedom, and human rights. In the past few years, it has been the country that has best understood the aspirations of the Polish people. I had not invited its president out of swollen self-interest: I hoped for a normal meeting between two people who wish each other well. Furthermore, Americans, I know, place considerable value on the home and family, and opening my house to him, I felt, was symbolically important. It was no coincidence that the American media gave the most coverage to that part of President Bush's visit to Poland.

Over the years, a great number of people have passed through my house, and even more through my office. Talking with prime ministers and their opponents, leaders of parties and organizations, professors, generals, doctors, magicians, visionaries, hordes of journalists — and, most of all, ordinary citizens — has been my main duty. I take cover from no one. My door has always been open to anyone. Anyone coming to Gdansk to knock on my door has always been received by Lech Walesa. It was from these conversations with my visitors that I learned about the world, about politics, and about human nature. I began as an ordinary worker, but was able to fill in the gaps quickly, thanks to the many and varied conversations at my house. I learned a great deal as I went along.

I am indebted to all those who came to see me, for they have enriched me and enlarged my experience of the world. All my visitors — whether celebrity, worker, diplomat, peasant, living legend, or even the occasional child — have helped expand my thinking. Each has given me something.

I must mention in particular Lech Badkowski, a man I admired enormously. This writer, journalist, and social activist from the region of Pomerania showed up at the shipyards one day in 1980, shortly after the strike was declared, at the head of a group of writers from Gdansk who were bringing us declarations of support. He was immediately coopted into a leadership role on the strike committee and chosen to be strike spokesman. He became active on behalf of Solidarity during our negotiations with the government.

Badkowski was a man of great culture and a hardy soul whose opinion I valued profoundly. He watched my actions attentively, judging them in his fashion, sometimes severely. A good organizer himself, able to categorize everything with great skill, he considered me too much of a political improviser and admonished me at times for neglecting Solidarity's organizational needs. When the Gdansk union weekly *Samorzadnosc* [*Self-Governance*] was started, I proposed without any hesitation that Badkowski be named editor-in-chief — he had already been editing the union column in the *Dziennik Balticki* [*Baltic Daily*] since September 1980. Only two issues of *Samorzadnosc* ever appeared; the third was dated December 13, 1981,* and few copies of it ever reached the readers. Even during Badkowski's terminal illness, we remained in close touch. Shortly before he died, worn down by cancer, he miraculously managed to prepare an outline of my acceptance speech for the Nobel Prize.

I don't particularly enjoy official functions, be they receptions, small luncheons, or formal dinners. If there is business to be done, I would prefer to do it in an office and be done with it. But of course, protocol demands that you organize a luncheon for a visiting dignitary, or dine out, or welcome him to your home.

Our family celebrations, however, like Danka's and my saint's days, follow a different rule of order. We don't normally send out invitations; we know that friends will drop by and that the family will show up. Some people will call up to ask to present their wishes in person; others simply appear without warning. Over the years we've gotten used to this. Danka always makes sure there's plenty of food, and I see to the bar — though usually I let my guests help themselves.

Since the birth of Solidarity, my birthday has become something of a group affair. I say "group affair" because at Zaspa sometimes as many as fifty strangers would turn up at our door. Many would have traveled a good distance just to shake my hand, wish me well, and assure me of their support; then they would leave, waving goodbye with the V-for-victory sign that has helped the Polish people stand firm for the last few years. Piles of postcards and telegrams would keep arriving all day long, and the

* The date martial law was imposed.

phone never stopped ringing. I make a point of not leaving the house on my birthday so that no one will be disappointed.

The receptions at the Walesa home became a kind of barometer for the political climate and the social mood. On New Year's Eve in 1982, I invited those associates who were closest to me — those who hadn't been arrested and weren't in hiding, that is — and we drank champagne and talked about the hard times (more accurately, we whispered, always aware that the apartment was bugged). Every minute someone knocked at the door to present their greetings and good wishes. Flashbulbs lit up the room, and it was getting quite hot. By midnight, the doorbell was ringing incessantly.

When I looked out the window, what I saw struck me dumb: there in front of the building was a line of people stretching for more than a hundred yards, mostly men dressed in their best white shirts — even though it was only about 40 degrees out — holding bottles of champagne. This kind of gathering represented one of those "illegal assemblies" prohibited by martial law. But each one would stand for a few seconds in my doorway, noisily pop a champagne cork, fill my glass, and drink to my health. I listened to a long string of New Year's wishes: wishes for things to go well for me, badly for the military regime.

The residents of Zaspa came out of their warm homes on that cold New Year's Eve. Spotting the usual car from the SB, someone threw a snowball at it. A second snowball followed, a third, then a whole bombardment, and the secret agents sped off into the night under a barrage. It was a memorable evening.

Of all the many receptions at my place, the noisiest was my birthday party in 1986, because it came right after Solidarity stalwarts Adam Michnik and Bogdan Lis were freed. We were all so overjoyed to be together again and make plans for the future that even the knowledge of the hidden microphones or the agents positioned in front of the building didn't bother us. We made merry — the alcohol flowed, and the jokes rolled off the tongue. Adam begged me on his knees for the umpteenth time to forgive him for the days when he had opposed me. I had long since forgiven him, but again he was assuring me of his loyalty. But prodigal sons sometimes stray more than once . . .

Then there was the celebration of my saint's day on June 3, 1988. It was right after the end of the May strike. Many people saw that strike as the signal of change they had been waiting for, and they came to see me. Even Anna Walentynowicz came, and this particularly pleased me. I took it as a sign that she was ending the campaign she'd waged for years against me, or at least that she was calling a truce. We badly needed to be united.

The celebrations a year later took place in a different setting — and oh, how different were the political conditions! It was the Saturday before the general elections, a time of great concern and great expectations — of joy and suspicion. Would we be cheated? Had we been sold out to the Communists? The thirty-five percent of the seats we needed to win hadn't seemed like much, but now suddenly it seemed like a great deal. Crowds of journalists showed up at my house in Oliwa, and after setting up the television equipment, they couldn't sit still and wait. So they strolled around, asking questions, formulating hypotheses, playing word games, and whittling away at the stock of my little bar. The day's great attraction was a motorcade through Gdansk organized by Solidarity (Szymon Pawlicki in particular) to solicit votes. Younger enthusiasts and hotheads drove through the city, waving flags and handing out leaflets. Driving down Polanki Street, they formed an impressive spectacle — an endless procession of cars, motorcycles of every make and model, even bicycles, all decorated with Solidarity banners and electoral slogans, each trying to outdo the other in honking. My guests crowded around the front of our house to watch the extraordinary parade, and the celebratory mood spread everywhere. Finally, after four long years, we were able to shout out how we felt.

The Walesa house was packed. Anna Kowalczykowa, my extraordinary secretary from the early days of Solidarity, who still stays in close touch, asked the person sitting next to her his name. She must not have heard his reply, because she went on to ask him what he did. He replied that he was a singer. She retorted impatiently, "Well, that's fine, but what else do you do?" It turns out that this man is one of the most popular Polish singers in recent years, and also one of my personal favorites, Piotr Szczepanik.

Times have changed, and so has the way my saint's day is celebrated. My private life — now more genuinely private — interests the media and the people less. Some of those colleagues who once stood in the first row to offer me their best wishes are now annoyed with me. Others have more important things to do than trek over to Oliwa. But the old guard still comes. In June 1990, fifty guests arrived at the house — some just stopping by, others, closer to the family, settling in for the evening. People began dancing. The party moved out to the garden, where there was more room to breathe. I like being in the garden. I feel, as an old reflex, that I can talk more freely there.

On my wife's saint's day in 1990, three weeks after mine, I had to attend an emergency meeting of Solidarity's Civic Committee in Warsaw. At that meeting I warned my colleagues that if we didn't break up into smaller political groups we would fall into the pattern of a new *nomenklatura*; one regime would in effect be replacing another, and nothing would have changed in Poland. Furious with me, Michnik, Geremek, and Wujec accused me of having turned into an autocrat. These differences in opinion caused me pain, but I knew they were the lifeblood of a new democracy.

The meeting lasted until pretty late, and at six that evening I was still in Warsaw. Meanwhile, in Gdansk, guests were arriving at our house for the party, and I'd promised Danka I'd be back in time. When I finally climbed into the government car, I was preoccupied, still mulling over that meeting. In the front seat sat my bodyguards, ex-colleagues of those who had had me under surveillance not so long ago. After the fall of the Communists, we had discovered most of them to be perfectly nice young people. They drove me home at about a hundred miles an hour, nearly twice the speed limit, and got me there in two and a half hours. Danka's glance when I arrived carried a light reproach.

Then I heard the newscaster on the radio describing the committee meeting I had just come from, and after greeting the guests I felt impelled to go out into the garden and to the little arbor, where we kept another radio. I'm not sure I can describe quite how I felt as I listened out there by myself — as if I'd reached the end of a road on which I had traveled, and suffered, with so many others for so long. I couldn't indulge in that feeling for long. Danka came out to find me. "Weren't you sitting in that room just four hours ago?" she asked. "What good does it do to keep going over it? Come on and join the dance." I did, and I enjoyed the party.

I'm happiest when I'm at home with my immediate family. We also stay in close touch with our more extended family, Danka's and mine. My brother Staszek, who lives in Bydgoszcz, visits Gdansk whenever he can. But I'm closest to my sister Iza. She enjoys giving Danka a hand with things. Sometimes Danka's sister Krystyna appears with her brothers. For a while her brother Marek seemed to be around almost full-time (although he had a rented room elsewhere), and he proved to be very handy around the house, repairing things and overseeing projects when I was away. We can count on him. And now that the boys have driver's licenses, they drive Danka to see her sister in Sokolaw Podlaski.

• • •

I am with people all day long, so when I come home I just want peace. Do
I have any really close friends? I have had good friends in school and at
work. During the time we were organizing free unions at the end of the
1970s, I felt very close to a number of people. We helped each other out
and talked about almost everything. But we were also overworked and
overextended because of job and family, and there was practically no time
left for intimacy.

When Solidarity was founded I could discuss practically everything
with my advisors and supporters. They promised me friendship and loyalty. But I wondered whether this meant something outside of work. I
came to understand that I was surrounded by devoted and goodhearted
people, but that their support was limited to defined areas — and for them,
work and home remained separate realms. At work I had complete faith
in my secretary. For health problems, I put myself in the capable hands of
Professor Penson. And for my spiritual needs, I went to my confessor, Father Cybul. I do have friends for various occasions and settings. However,
none transcends them all. In life's crises, one is alone no matter who is
around.

Not only is my doctor, Professor Joanna Muszkowska-Penson, a bril-
liant physician, but because she's a woman, she displays goodness, which
in my view is part of the feminine gift. Professor Penson is ready at the
drop of a hat to rush to the bedside of someone needing her help. Since
1982 she has worked for the diocesan charitable committee at Saint
Brygid's in Gdansk, and under her leadership it has provided medical care
to all the internees and prisoners as well as their families. She has gradually became a friend of the family. She calls herself "a little old lady," but
her energy and enthusiasm more than match any teenager's. She was
among the first to join the striking workers at the shipyards in May and
August of 1988. She took charge of their health problems when it meant
a few nights of sleeping on the floor for her. For this support and assistance, she paid dearly. She endured the usual harassment we all got, and
on top of it she was denied permission to see her only daughter, who lives
in England. She was also refused permission to travel to France and accept
an invitation by an association of former inmates at the Nazi concentration
camp of Ravensbrück.

The good doctor doesn't believe I can be trusted. She won't let me eat
sweets because of my weight and the risk of diabetes. She won't let me
get upset, because that raises my blood pressure and isn't good for my

ulcers. My ulcers deserve their own story. At first, I tried to treat them myself, and when Danka saw that I wasn't succeeding, she forced me to go to a mind-healer. I went, in pain but indignant. This is the twentieth century, I said to myself, and this guy is a witch doctor. Unbeliever though I was, my ulcers immediately got better. I called my doctors and said, "I refuse to believe it, but the pain is gone." And for two years, I had no pain. When it started up again, my stubborn and enterprising wife took me back to this "healer" who, in this age of computers, once again worked some kind of hocus-pocus, and once again the ulcers stopped hurting. Was this coincidence? If it worked a third time I told myself I'd start believing in it. When the well-known Ukrainian therapist Anatoly Kashpirovsky came to Poland for a visit, I had a chance to speak with him. He explained that what psychotherapy does is soothe the soul, and through it, the body.

I owe a great deal in both my personal and political life to Father Henryk Jankowski. I first met him during the 1980 strike. He arrived at the shipyards on the evening of August 16, at the request of workers who had earlier sought him out, since the shipyards fell within the parish of Saint Brygid's. It was a desperate time. We expected at any moment that the government would send in the tanks. I begged Father Jankowski to take care of my family should the need arise, and gave him my address, and because of that I think he felt he was doing his part to help the cause. He did more than many. His Sunday masses at the shipyards — with the permission of the authorities — helped sustain us. In the period that Solidarity was legal, particularly in the beginning, Father Jankowski was very active; in fact, he seemed to be everywhere. This greatly irritated union leaders not just in Gdansk but nationwide, but because he was a priest, they toned down their attacks on him.

Father Jankowski's greatest service to the cause, though, came when Solidarity was running illegal operations and existed under martial law. When it came to bringing aid and relief to those who had been interned and imprisoned and persecuted — and all of their families — Father Jankowski was tireless. His house was the center of activities of the diocese's service organization for Solidarity, an organization that for many years was directed with total devotion by Dr. Stefan Gomowski, a scientist at Gdansk's technical college.

When I was released from internment, Father Jankowski was waiting for me at my home. I had wanted to go to the window to speak to the crowd that had assembled outside and was calling for me. The good father held me by the arm and said, "Lech, it would be a better idea if you taped your statement, and then I could have it played out the window over a loud-speaker. Martial law makes it clear that anybody who directly participates in a public demonstration in this country can be hauled off to jail. So if the Communists were looking for an excuse to jail you again, you'd be giving them one by speaking to the crowd, and they'd drag you right back." I thought about what he said for a moment, and realized he was right. Some-one brought me a tape recorder. Father Jankowski went to the window to tell the crowd I was going to speak, but as soon as I heard the applause and chanting, I couldn't hold back any longer. These people had been waiting for three days. I pushed the microphone away and began speaking directly to them.

For a good number of long years, my second home and Solidarity's headquarters were located in the parish house of Father Jankowski. All kinds of meeting and press conferences took place there, and it looked almost as if Saint Brygid's did nothing except Solidarity business. Jankowski himself was among the most active in proposing and organiz-ing events, such as anniversary marches, demonstrations, symposia, and talks. When the May 1988 strike started, he made all his resources avail-able to Solidarity — a large house, a car that ran, two telephones, and some financial reserves. The help he offered in organizing an information center was absolutely indispensable. Thanks to him, Poles and the whole world, however bewildered by the information provided by the govern-ment, could find out what was really happening at the shipyards, which were encircled by police and cut off from the rest of Gdansk.

For several years we were so inseparable that I felt like Father Jankowski's Siamese twin. This had its good side: no one is a better orga-nizer than a priest. Today, Father Jankowski can devote himself entirely to his pastoral duties, as I can devote myself to my own pursuits. I will never forget what he did for Solidarity and for me. If the stormclouds gather again, it is a tremendous comfort to me to know that I can turn to Father Jankowski, my trustworthy friend and advisor.

After martial law was lifted, Poles were free to return to the jobs they had before, or find new ones that matched their abilities and qualifications. Of course, there will be other kinds of mistakes, confusions, miscues, and quarrels; but they are a part of what we're fighting for — they represent pluralism, freedom of speech, competition. I returned to my work at the union, where I had won my political spurs.

Every day at 9:30 two official bodyguards from the Bureau of Protection came to take me in their Lancia to union headquarters, where I managed various kinds of union business and met with people. I must confess to not liking office work very much. It's not for me. I might even be accused of working fitfully. I did make an effort to see that the Solidarity office was run smoothly. Sometimes I went to the office before eight in the morning just to find out if everyone got there on time. I prowled around looking at the projects people were working on. My staff didn't like this. They asked me to keep out of their way.

At two o'clock, I always went home for lunch. I could never conceal my love for Danka's cooking (though there was a time when Father Jankowski's soups competed with it), and I eat whatever she puts on the table. In an ideal world, I would eat a roast duck with apples every day, and pastry with hazelnuts — but I can no longer indulge like that. As for alcohol, I am of the opinion that the old system needs to be shaken up a little from time to time. So now and again I take a little "cure" and allow myself to drink a little more than usual. These "cures" involve accepting a cocktail invitation and reassuring my hosts not to worry if they see me indulge just a bit.

I tried to give my family as much of my time as I could. At home I liked to listen quietly to the radio or catch up with the newspapers. Sometimes I'd even pick up a book. What I've always liked best is take a reflective walk in the garden and sit in the arbor. In that little sanctuary I have known moments of real peace.

Sometimes one of the kids would join me with one of our dogs. For quite a long time I was afraid of dogs, but I overcame that fear. When I was eight years old, some other boys and I were walking along the road when suddenly a large dog attacked me and bit me in the calf. Today, not only do we have dogs, but they are wolfhounds: Kuba we inherited from the former owner of the house; Baki is a recent acquisition. Kuba is always trying to run away. At first I couldn't figure out how he could get out. I walked the length of the surrounding wall and didn't find any gaps, and I knew it was too high for him to jump. I discovered that he had dug under the wire fencing. As for Baki, he lost part of his tail when it was run over by a car. I rushed him to the veterinarian, but the crushed part had to be amputated.

I am sometimes asked how I like to spend my leisure time. It depends on what I'm trying to relax from. When I need to get away from my family, I walk in the forest; when I need to get my mind off work, I go fishing.

During the years I was under the most stress, I learned how to monitor my body and find ways of recovering strength. During the early days of Solidarity, when its headquarters were on Grunwald Street, I used to shut myself up in my office and take a half-hour nap as soon as I started feeling very tired. Afterward I was ready to dive back into the thousand matters demanding my attention. During my trips across Poland in 1981, especially when my job was to "put out" a strike that had flared up, I would take a catnap in the car or at the hotel. I've always gone to sleep quickly and I set an internal alarm clock. If I tell myself I can sleep for only three hours, I will wake up exactly three hours later feeling rested.

It was like that as well during the 1988 shipyard strike. The strike committee was in constant session, day and night. Decisions needed to be made and changed from hour to hour, and the atmosphere was tense, especially after the ZOMO attacked the ironworks at Nowa Huta. When there seemed to be a lull I'd roll myself up in a sleeping bag and fall asleep. The ZOMO regularly woke us up by pretending they were launching an attack. One night, very late, they massed at the gates of the shipyards, turned on their floodlights, and began making a racket. We all got up to see what was going on, and as soon as they saw that we were all wide awake, they got back into their cars and drove off. I'd had enough by that point and announced that no one was to wake me up under any circumstances. "If the ZOMO break into my room," I said, "I'll get up all by myself."

Music relaxes me. My ear is a little flat, musically speaking — in fact, you might even say it couldn't be flatter if an elephant stepped on it — but when I am very tired, I enjoy listening to something soothing. When I feel rested, I like listening to something with a beat. But no matter what the hour of day or night, no matter what my mood, I can always listen to patriotic songs. I played "The Anthem of the First Pilsudski Brigade" so many times that I wore out the cassette.

I know very little else about music and don't attempt to keep up with popular songs. In April 1984, I was told that Elton John wanted to come to Gdansk and see me. All I knew about him was that he was a celebrity. A concert was organized at the Olivia Hall, and a crowd of young people gathered at the very place where, three years earlier, I had first been elected president of the union. Elton John came to my apartment in Zaspa before the concert, undeterred by the Security Service agents stationed at the bottom of the stairwell. He seemed very nice and affable, with his big smile and his big glasses, and appeared very much at ease. He asked how I was surviving from day to day and what my prospects for the future were. Then he gave me his hat as a gift, and I gave him one of my pipes. I learned that he not only made records and gave concerts, but was also a supporter and sponsor of the Watford soccer team. Now, that impressed me! He invited me to the concert, and we left together.

I hadn't expected so many people. Martial law was still in effect, and the government was wary of any kind of assembly. Elton John led me down to the front row, right next to the stage, where I sat down among the teenagers in the best seat in the house (I would have much preferred crouching down way at the back). When the music started it was as if 120-millimeter cannons had begun shelling, because I was seated right next to a tower of gigantic loudspeakers. I soon stopped hearing anything at all and wanted nothing more than to escape, but I was surrounded by a delirious crowd of young people swept away in oblivious bliss. I gather it was a great concert. From time to time, Elton John would smile at me and wave, and I would signal back that everything was peachy. Internally, I was really swearing that never again would I let myself be dragged to a rock concert. When, at long last, it was over, I felt like a deflated inner tube.

The Security Service had expected Elton John to invite me onstage and were concerned that I would put on a show of my own. Secret agents were waiting in the wings to prevent this. They were under strict orders not to allow me access to the stage. There they ran straight into the stage personnel, who felt strongly that security in the hall was their own bailiwick and didn't like being pushed around. A sharp quarrel soon turned into a brawl.

I bought my first car — a Warszawa — from a junkyard located not far from a repair center for construction machinery. I worked hard trying to make it work. When I finally succeeded I drove the whole family to visit Danka's family, and all that work seemed worth it. Later, as my life became busier, tinkering with the engine became less and less fun. Now when something breaks down, I ask the ex-cabbie Andrzej Rzeczycki to fix it. I have always liked being behind the wheel — even though these days I get driven more than I drive — and I used to love to travel. When, in 1981, my friend Mietek Wachowski and I traveled all over Poland, we had a lot of fun. We were reckless speed-demons and were lucky we didn't get ourselves killed.

But now I've become a homebody, and I find even plane trips tiring. Trips abroad are no longer my style. The routine is always the same: a

frenetic schedule, constant surveillance, no spontaneity. All I seem to do
is jump from meeting to meeting and from limo to limo. Then I always
long for a daily mass. Sometimes finding a Catholic church is a little difficult, but there is nearly always a Polish community, and where there is
a Polish community you will find a priest and a mass. In the United States,
one was even arranged in my hotel room. Those masses afford the only
private moments on my trips abroad, which are otherwise entirely official
occasions. There is one exception. I spent a whole day as the private guest
of the Polish millionaire Piszek when I was visiting the United States.

The only place that I still enjoy traveling to is the little village of
Wesiora, in Kaszuby (or more precisely, Zdunowice), where for several
years now I have spent my summers. "Summers" may be a bit of an ex-
aggeration, since I go only as often as my schedule permits. Danka and
the girls precede me right at the end of the school year. I enjoy getting
away from the frenzy, the noise, the hot pavement, and the apartment com-
plexes such as the one we lived in at Zaspa, and settling by the water's
edge with a fishing rod.

In 1985, I was talking to a friend who owned a pretty little dacha not
far from Gdansk. I had enjoyed visiting the area, and remembered how
peaceful and sparsely populated it was. My friend told me about other
cottages for sale and I was immediately interested in buying. I obviously
needed to visit the cottage, but not wanting the SB to follow me, I decided
to give them the slip. My friend and his wife joined me at Saint Brygid's.
I left the church with Jurek Trzcinski, dove into the back seat of his car,
and lay down without the SB agents noticing. I visited the cottage without
any of the agencies following me or getting involved — at least for a time.
Eventually, of course, they caught on. And when agents discovered the
name of the man who had sold me the cottage, they searched his property
and harassed him, threatening to deny him a passport or make him pay
extra taxes — "supplements" — on the basis of external signs of wealth.

The dacha suited us perfectly — and we soon had it hooked up with
electricity and plumbing. It was situated near the forest and a pond, and
had a pleasant terrace in the back. After planting trees all around, we
seeded the lawn, and put in a sandbox and seesaw for the girls. In 1989,
we put wire fencing around the whole property on wooden posts. I also
built a dock for the pond, which the SB men immediately turned into an
observation post. My secretary Krzysztof Pusz's father used to fish there
and was upset when he discovered the extent of the surveillance. He complained about it to one of the agents, but to no avail.

Each time I went to my cottage for weekends, the predictable two cars followed me; half of the agents stayed in the car, and the other half pretended they were hiking and fishing, depending on what I was doing. The journalists wouldn't leave us alone, either, but in time their numbers dropped off, and in the end only a few curious pilgrims remained. To this day tour buses continue to stop or at least slow down before our little house, giving their passengers a chance to gaze at Walesa's vacation spot. Vacationers will loiter around upon learning that I am in the neighborhood. None of this is especially annoying, but who likes to be observed night and day?

I escape being persecuted by the telephone by not having had one installed in the country. My secretary Krzysztof always stays in the neighborhood. If the need arises, he can go back and forth between Gdansk and Wesiora.

An afternoon in July 1990. The weather is perfect for lazing about in a small boat with a fishing rod in hand. Danka will fry the fish as soon as we catch them and serve them hot and crusty. I watch the bobber, lost in thought. I have given the last twenty years to the struggle — with all the running, all the pressure it entailed — and for the last ten years my life has been completely public. But I now know it has been successful. We won our nonviolent war, and I was even gratified with the laurels of victory. I never became rich, having always given most of my earnings to Solidarity, but I have enough to live a decent life.

Hasn't the time come for me to stop? Won't others pick up where I left off? Then I'll finally be able to lead a normal life!

There are those who never stop battling for political leverage. I consider them to be political degenerates. What is the point of struggling mindlessly for position and privilege? This is definitely not for me. I crave the ordinary life. I'd rather go fishing, and I don't care for meetings, quarrels, and misunderstandings. I dream of running away. But if I did, the first thing people would scream is "Walesa made a bundle and then he left. He dishonored himself and his country." Or, if I stayed, they would denounce me as bursting with excessive ambition: "Walesa has gotten more than his share!" Life is its own leveler and will resolve this dilemma, I know. I trust in God. I believe that Providence watches over me and will help me to choose what is best — for Poland.

Part II
Public Life

6
Hatred

On November 3, 1984, surrounded by several hundred thousand people at the grave of Father Jerzy Popieluszko, I concluded my eulogy to the fallen priest with these words: "Rest in peace. Solidarity lives because you gave your life for it." I knew that the world had had its fill of Polish martyrdom, its fill of heroic "victories" in which the heroes themselves had perished. I was aware that when the foreign press raised the issue of Poland as the story of a people brutalized and assassinated, it was met with numbed indifference. Yet only five years were to pass before we were to see just how vital Solidarity was.

I had met Father Popieluszko only twice. Once he came to visit me in my home; only once were we able to talk at some length. Yet he had a significant impact upon my life.

We first met on August 13, 1984, at the Church of Saint Brygid in Gdansk, the parish of Father Henryk Jankowski. Preparations were underway for ceremonies to mark the fourth anniversary of the August 1980 strike out of which Solidarity was born. Such ceremonies strengthened our resolve in the struggle against oppression and bolstered our resistance to the state of martial law. They also enabled us to organize public gatherings, which were otherwise banned by the then new regime of General Jaruzelski.

When we announced those anniversary ceremonies at Saint Brygid's, the machinery of the Security Service immediately went on a war footing. The alert sounded at the ZOMO barracks on the edge of Gdansk, and informers spilled out into the alleyways and stairwells of the apartment houses near the church. Father Popieluszko, chaplain of the Warsaw Steelworks, was to arrive on August 13, 1984. During the summer of 1980, Cardinal

Wyszynski had sent the young priest to celebrate mass for the strikers. His knees were quaking, it was said, as he passed through the gate, beyond which milled several thousand workers. This was the first time the priest had held mass in a factory, the first time during a strike. This was also a first for the workers — and the priest seemed so young and so shy!

They soon became friends for life, because the workers sensed how profoundly Father Popieluszko understood them. They would later go to him whenever they had problems, and he to them. He went on outings with the steelworkers in hired buses (where he often had to beg them not to drink). During martial law, he organized assistance for the interned and the imprisoned. Popieluszko was the kind of person who took bread from his mouth to give to others. And every month he celebrated his famous "masses for the homeland," which were attended by half of Warsaw.

At our first meeting, in the sacristy, my initial impression of Popieluszko was of a young priest — rather average, quite young, sensitive, delicate. I had known priests like him and they didn't much appeal to me. This first impression proved, of course, superficial. The next day, in the packed church, facing the congregation and the delegation from Solidarity and the political police, Father Popieluszko showed his true mettle. He turned out to be an excellent preacher: "Our servitude comes from our knuckling under to the reign of the lie. We do not unmask that lie, and by doing nothing about it, by our silence, we encourage it. We are living the lie." I recognized these words. They were from Cardinal Wyszynski's prison notes, notes in which he provides the most succinct diagnosis of totalitarianism I know: a system supported by the Big Lie, whose purpose is not simply to demoralize and liquidate opposition, but also to convince that opposition that the treatment accorded it is just and moral.

"During the demonstrations," Father Popieluszko went on, "you shout unanimously, 'No freedom without Solidarity!' But each and every day at work, when individual acts of courage are called for, where is your voice?" What he said was disagreeable, but it was also true and needed saying. How many had indeed muffled their convictions in the name of illusory rewards? How many shipyard workers had turned away from me when I stood at the foot of the monument, when I was a marked man? "Do not fear those who kill the body, for they can do nothing more!" His words rang out from the height of the pulpit of Saint Brygid's. With new warmth and respect I bade Father Popieluszko farewell, momentarily wondering whether this had been only good theater or something more.

I was soon to have my answer.

...

Symbols take on great significance in a nation robbed of its freedom. And so it was for us. On August 31, 1984, demonstrations to mark the fourth anniversary of the Gdansk accords were held throughout Poland. Close to fifteen hundred people were arrested; criminal proceedings were instituted and fines imposed: a classic "finale" in the repertory of martial law. In Wroclaw, Solidarity leaders were sentenced to two months in jail for trying to place flowers beneath the plaque commemorating the movement. In Gdansk, an armed cordon of ZOMO would let only me approach the monument. So I stood alone facing the shipyards, a copy of my little speech still in my pocket. In it I had written that Solidarity applauded the amnesty granted the political prisoners, despite its having been issued on July 22 — the anniversary of the Communist takeover. I called for new evidence of the government's sincerity. The precondition of any progress in Poland was recognition of the principle and the practice of pluralism.

The government, however, had another agenda. Two months later it set up the pro-government National Alliance of Trade Unions (OPZZ) as "the only legitimate unions" and denied Solidarity any legal role in public life.

Our ceremonies were concluded at the Dominican basilica of Saint Nicholas, a historic monument. I was seated next to Adam Michnik and Janusz Onyszkiewicz, both of whom had recently been released from prison and were now questioning me about the "entente and struggle" proclamation made by General Jaruzelski's cronies. Deputy Prime Minister Mieczyslaw Rakowski, chief ideologist of Jaruzelski's team, had come to the shipyards for the sole purpose of discrediting me in the eyes of public opinion. Our confrontation in the shipyards' main hall was to have been televised live, but my pronouncements were of course edited out by a government censor. Rakowski's mission was to demonstrate that I was insignificant. Some years earlier he had written a "psychological profile" of me, which had been put to wide use during my internment. Now he had written and circulated a new and improved version.

Rakowski declared that I was a man with "a weak mental apparatus" on whose shoulders had fallen too heavy a burden: the leadership of a large organization. For a man as ill-equipped as Walesa, he said, this had to be a crushing load. It was made heavier still by the megalomania that foreign journalists and politicians aroused in him when they cynically manipulated him for their own ends. So long as I was kept in check, I was all right; but all the attention and honorary doctorates bestowed on me had swelled my head, and my head didn't hold a great deal to begin with. How obvious it was that everything I said had been written out for me in one form or another by Bronislaw Geremek and Tadeusz Mazowiecki. And, of course, there was the Church, which everybody knew was leading me around by the nose.

Armed with this assessment of my personality, Rakowski came to the shipyards to teach Solidarity and the workers a thing or two, and to blame them for all the evils that had befallen Poland since 1980. He was jeered. I proposed to him that in commemoration of the anniversary of the signing of the Gdansk accords the two of us jointly place flowers at the foot of the monument. He declined. His refusal was edited out — censorship that spokesman Jerzy Urban justified by arguing that showing this kind of a ceremony would only encourage illegal demonstrations. Television should not promote criminal activity.

In the realm of deceit, Urban had reached new heights. But despite their best efforts, Rakowski and Urban failed to discredit me. What they did not realize was that the more the Communist media heaped abuse on anyone, the higher his popularity rose. The Poles' general reaction to all the slander was, "Walesa must be a pretty good guy." Rakowski was upset. No matter how much television and the press vaunted his so-called victory, all that the viewers remembered was the arrogance that a government representative had shown the workers.

Father Popieluszko didn't need to look very far to find themes for his sermons. He took them from life — his own life. He was not "spreading false information," which the penal code forbade; he was merely describing what the government had put him through. He came to embody the ordinary man, and his sermons, which attracted tens of thousands of people from around Poland, were all the more dramatic because of it:

> In September 1984 a notice was posted on the doors of the offices at the Warsaw district court: CLOSED DUE TO LACK OF PERSONNEL. The court had pronounced judgment against a longstanding employee who had been dismissed for disciplinary reasons despite excellent references from her supervisors. She had been denounced by a drill lieutenant, who said she had been among those accompanying Father Jerzy Popieluszko to the Mostowki Palace — the Militia headquarters — and she had greeted him with flowers at his return. The second reason for her dismissal was this, and I quote: "She came to the aid of the suspect Jerzy Popieluszko on the premises of the Prokuratura." Her "aid" consisted of steering me through the court's maze of corridors. That's it. The

Prokuratura was the very place where I later was to read six volumes of depositions outlining my own "criminal activity."

Father Jerzy soon came back to Gdansk. At the time, he was busy crisscrossing the country delivering sermons on Maximilian Kolbe, the Polish Franciscan who, to save a fellow prisoner named Gajowniczek, had starved to death in Auschwitz. He had recently been canonized by John Paul II. At Saint Brygid's, Father Popieluszko explained that in places like death camps, solidarity among the sufferers is rare. The survival instinct overcomes the impulse to share and commiserate; humanity is lost in the scramble for a hunk of bread or a gulp of water. The weakest succumb in a struggle that those of us who have not been there could only barely imagine, for we can understand horror only if we ourselves have experienced it.

After the mass, Father Jerzy hurried over to my place in Zaspa. Several workers accompanied him, along with a musical group from the hill country who wore traditional costumes and gave our gathering a festive feeling. I got out a bottle of wine and offered them all a glass. They'd brought their instruments along and played with gusto. Everyone had a good time, though Popieluszko did talk about the difficulties he'd been having — the constant surveillance, the insulting graffiti sprayed on the parish house, the gaudy paint smeared on the car another priest had lent him, the planting of explosives and subversive leaflets in his rooms while he was undergoing harsh interrogations at the police station. But he also praised the solidarity he had found among the steelworkers who, despite living in other parts of town, made a point of crossing the city to Saint Stanislaw's Church in Warsaw to hear their chaplain.

In my "office," which was barely large enough to hold all the guests, someone took a snapshot of the two of us beneath a portrait of John Paul II. I would never have imagined that a few weeks later this photograph would be reproduced by the thousands and sold in all the churches, next to the missals and crucifixes.

Father Popieluszko returned to Warsaw, leaving me with the recollection of a man of childlike trust and of enthusiasm for his activities and future projects, a man without political ambitions, one of the few such I have ever known. Most of my visitors seemed to want something from me, a petition signed, some kind of commitment on my part.

On the road from Gdansk to Warsaw that evening came the first attempt on Father Popieluszko's life. At the point where the road is most winding someone heaved large rocks at his windshield; they barely missed. Had they hit, he would have lost control of the car and had a serious, if not fatal, accident.

On October 19, 1984, I issued a statement in support of a government announcement affirming the government's decision to sound out public opinion as to whether Poland should join the International Monetary Fund. It was my hope that this move heralded a new style of policy on the part of the government. My statement was one of my countless "conciliatory" gestures that regularly brought criticism from colleagues.

That same day, Father Popieluszko went to Bydgoszcz to celebrate mass and to meet with Jan Rulewski, regional director of Solidarity, and the priests of the parish in the sacristy of the Church of the Martyred Polish Brothers.

At 9:20 P.M., Popieluszko left the church in his Volkswagen Golf, driven by his chauffeur, Waldemar Chrostowski. They were followed by a Fiat from the Security Service carrying Captain Grzegorz Piotrowski, head of Department IV of the Ministry of the Interior, and Lieutenants Leszek Pekala and Waldemar Chmielewski, from the same department.

At ten o'clock that night, not far from the town of Gorsk, the Fiat forced Popieluszko's car to pull over. A uniformed Militia man got out of the Fiat. The hundred minutes that followed were to have an impact on Poland comparable only to the declaration of martial law. The course of events was reconstructed at the trial:

> *Lieutenant Waldemar Chmielewski:* I approached the car and told Father Popieluszko to get out. When Piotrowski, my boss, joined us, I turned and saw that he was carrying a nightstick in his hand. Father Popieluszko asked what was going on. I remember that Piotrowski grabbed the handle of the door and opened it. The priest undid his safety belt, got out, and headed toward our car with Piotrowski, who called to me, "Waldek! Come here. He doesn't want to get in." I approached them from the right rear of our car. I saw Piotrowski holding the priest by the cassock, at shoulder height. Going up to the priest, I said to him, "Why don't you want to get in?" The priest answered, "Because this gentleman is trying to take me somewhere." I saw that Father Popieluszko had been roughed up by Piotrowski and then that he had sort of fallen forward on the car trunk. I also saw Piotrowski hit the priest on the head and upper body with his nightstick. He definitely hit him more than once.

They then gagged the priest and tied him head and foot with a rope. As the trial progressed it was clear from the depositions that not everything had gone according to plan, which was that there was to have been an "accident."

The earlier attempt to kill Father Popieluszko on October 13 after he was leaving Gdansk was also supposed to look like an accident. That first attempt on the outskirts of Olsztyn had been designed to look as though the car had simply gone off the road. Had the passengers survived, Piotrowski would have incinerated them alive after dousing their car with gasoline.

> *Captain Grzegorz Piotrowski:* I led him to our car and wanted him to get in, but he put up a struggle. I had been holding him gently by the arm, but then he began saying in a very loud voice that he wasn't going to get in the car. He demanded to know what was going on, what we thought we were doing. He was making a racket. . . . I don't know how many times I hit him. I'm sure it was at least twice, maybe three times. . . . Waldek got some rope out of the car, though I don't remember asking for it. I remember that I tied Popieluszko's hands. I have the image in my mind that I put something in his mouth, but that may have happened or never happened. He wasn't moving anymore, just lying there, inert.

Meanwhile, Waldemar Chrostowski, Popieluszko's driver, had been handcuffed and hustled into the front passenger seat of the Fiat

> *Waldemar Chrostowski:* While all this was going on the driver [of the Fiat] held a pistol to my head and told me, "Don't move, don't turn around." I thought that it was simply a holdup. People were getting into the rear car. I had already felt something being heaved into the trunk and heard it being slammed shut. I know this because the car sagged from the weight. . . . Then the one sitting in the back seat snapped at the man at the wheel, "Turn onto the forest road!" I realized that our lives were in danger, the priest's and mine, and that these could be my last minutes. First I thought of grabbing the wheel and causing an accident, but I gave it up. Then I decided to jump from the car. I wanted to do it in front of witnesses, it didn't matter who, to leave some evidence, even if it was just a bloodstain.

Without attracting attention, Chrostowski managed to grab the door handle, open the door, and jump out onto the road. He had been doing some parachuting and was experienced in making rough landings. Bleeding, he ran a long way down the road toward the nearest telephone. He couldn't manage to flag down a passing car. Who would stop in the dead of night to pick up a strange-looking character in torn clothes and handcuffs?

The car carrying Father Popieluszko didn't stop, but continued on toward Torun. It was ten-thirty when the kidnappers' car began having engine trouble. They drove on toward a brightly lit parking lot near the Kosmos Hotel.

> *Piotrowski:* I felt a jolt. I said it was a wheel. I knew that if it was the wheel, we were done for. We felt a second jolt. Then Leszek said that the car had thrown a rod. We stopped. There was another bump. Our car was breaking down and we had Popieluszko in the trunk, which was damaged and couldn't be locked. We all jumped out of the car. Suddenly I saw Popieluszko running across the little square. I charged after him and caught up with him. I hit him on the head with my nightstick, several times. He collapsed and lay motionless.
>
> *Chmielewski:* At one point I saw Piotrowski and Pekala carrying the priest and laying him down on the grass next to the car. I called for someone to help me with the license plates. . . . Then I saw Piotrowski and Pekala tie the priest up and put him back in the trunk of the car.
>
> *Lieutenant Leszek Pekala:* At the parking lot, after changing the license plates, we all knew that things were going badly — especially Piotrowski, because he was the one who would have to account for it. Personally, I was sorry that we didn't give the whole attempt up. An accident is one thing; torture and throwing the body in the water is quite another.

While giving their depositions in court, the defendants did their best to make their answers vague, using phrases such as "I think," "maybe," "probably," "somewhat." But the eloquent facts spoke for themselves.

> *Pekala:* Piotrowski had convinced us that the plan had been approved at the highest levels, even if it involved murder. For two weeks I had been given indications that it was in the country's best interests, both domestically and internationally. [Piotrowski] told me that the kidnapping was a part of our plan and told me not to ask him who was behind all this.

After leaving the hotel, the kidnappers drove to a gas station to buy some oil for their limping car. Father Popieluszko again regained consciousness and struggled to get out of the trunk. So they started the car again and, a few hundred yards farther ahead, turned into the forest. Pekala was ordered to drive very slowly so that Piotrowski and Chmielewski, who were walking behind the car, could keep up with it. Both were assigned to keep pushing down on the lid of the damaged trunk; from time to time they had to sit on it.

> *Pekala:* We went into the underbrush because the priest kept trying to force open the trunk. We stopped in the bushes and I opened the trunk. The first one to approach it was Piotrowski. I think Piotrowski clubbed Father Popieluszko with the nightstick while he was still in the trunk. I heard metal being hit.
>
> *Chmielewski:* Since I was standing next to the car, I picked up the bag of stones we had brought with us. I just kept telling myself that this couldn't really be happening.
>
> *Pekala:* Father Popieluszko was unconscious when we attached the stones. The rope ran the length of his spine, from his hands to his feet. His legs were folded behind him. If he tried to move them, the slipknot would tighten around his throat. . . . I asked Piotrowski if we were just going to leave him there. He said, "No. Tie the bag of stones to his legs. There's no other way." I told him that Chrostowski would recognize me, that the handcuffs were numbered, and they must have fingerprints on them. Piotrowski replied by saying, "Look, don't sweat it. The justice system is behind us. You won't have to face Chrostowski, and if worst comes to worst you can always change your name, your job, where you live." I thought that if Popieluszko was still alive we should let him go. But Piotrowski said, "No! He goes into the river!" Waldek and I both tried to talk Piotrowski into letting Popieluszko go, because we were afraid of what would happen to us. Piotrowski replied that it was important "to the people who had given [him] the orders that Popieluszko disappear once and for all."
>
> *Piotrowski:* We drove to the dam. I looked down and said, "This is it. This is where we get rid of him."

Just before midnight on October 19, 1984, not far from Wloclawek, they dumped Father Jerzy into the Zalew Wislany River. They hadn't even bothered to check to see whether he was still alive. Then they got back into the car, opened a bottle of vodka, and began wondering aloud how all this was going to affect their lives.

Meanwhile, Chrostowski had managed to reach a telephone. He called the ecclesiastical authorities first and the Militia second, so that there couldn't be any sort of cover-up. Roadblocks were set up and all vehicles searched. Toward morning, in a suburb of Warsaw, a road patrol stopped a car carrying three employees of the Security Service returning from a "mission." They had a special "W" pass authorizing them to travel freely, a pass they had obtained from their superior — along with Militia uniforms, white-braided caps, handcuffs, gasoline vouchers, and authorization to travel beyond the regional borders. Doing that, of course, meant ignoring the regulations of the Ministry of the Interior. But no one at the ministry was surprised.

On Saturday, October 20, a television bulletin announced Father Popieluszko's disappearance. The Criminal Bureau of the General Command of the MO (the civil police), trying to maintain its independence from the Security Service, launched an all-out investigation. Tension mounted throughout the country. In every Catholic church there were prayers for the safety of Father Jerzy, although as each day passed the conviction grew that the worst had happened. The urban parish of the Church of Saint Stanislaw went on twenty-four-hour alert. Its priest had received threats, and it was feared that someone might try to abduct him as a political provocation.

Many priests with ties to Solidarity felt threatened. Workers organized themselves into guard units and issued passes to anyone wishing to enter the rectories.

I went to Warsaw to consult with Tadeusz Mazowiecki, Bronislaw Geremek, and other colleagues, to try and figure out who could be behind Popieluszko's disappearance. At the Church of Saint Stanislaw, where I went to pray and share in the anguish of those assembled there, I witnessed at first hand the immense respect Father Jerzy commanded. I returned to Gdansk.

That Monday, as usual, I went to work — followed, of course, by my government escort, who were becoming more suspicious of my movements than ever. I knew that the minister of the interior, General Czeslaw Kiszczak, had ordered that I be kept under even closer surveillance during this difficult time. Nonetheless, I managed to give my escort the slip and attend a secret meeting with underground Solidarity leaders. Knowing all the ins and outs and secret passages of the shipyards, I found it easy to get away. My escort, who had been waiting for me at the gates, sounded the alarm minutes after I failed to show up, but by then I was already far away from Gdansk.

That day we again issued a declaration urging the government to clarify its attitude toward this abduction, which, since it involved one of the most devoted and conspicuous worker-priests, was rocking Polish society. We all knew that this was not an isolated event. After martial law had been declared, there had been a surge in the number of abductions and beatings by "persons unknown." The priest's abduction was yet another sign that torture and extortion were becoming an established means of political struggle.

I returned from my meeting better informed about the escalating tension in the country. Solidarity mobilized all of its forces and created civic committees to guard against violent outbreaks; the Militia and the Security Service closed ranks. "Who are they supposed to be protecting?" I asked from the pulpit at Saint Brygid's. This was a first for me. I'd been in the church countless times and spoken there often, but I'd always felt that the pulpit should be reserved for the clergy. On that particular day, however, at Father Jankowski's urging, I mounted the steps to the pulpit. We both knew that this was an extraordinary occasion, a response to an extraordinarily dark deed.

"Those who dreamed up this provocation," I said,

> want us to take to the streets, to demonstrate violently, and to do battle with the ZOMO. They want to turn us into pawns, a pretext for a new regime that would seize power by establishing "order" in Poland   and with the excuse that the old regime had not only condoned kidnapping, but also proved unable to control the repercussions. Keep this in mind and don't let yourselves be manipulated. Let us show our strength, here, through our prayers and on our knees! We must find a Christian solution, a morally right one that will not involve bloodshed.

Generals Jaruzelski and Kiszczak also sensed the danger. The grisly deed had been directed essentially against them, against their policy of "entente and struggle," which called for maintaining good relations with the Church and good public relations abroad. General Kiszczak, minister of the interior, declared that Poland would not tolerate the disappearance. Whoever was responsible would be arrested and punished to the full extent of the law.

An intensive investigation was ordered and searches were undertaken throughout the country. At Department IV of the Ministry of the Interior, a special operations group was formed under the direction of General Platek. His men handled the Church in Poland, security during pilgrimages, surveillance of priests and their contacts abroad; they were the ones who decided who to wiretap, who was issued a passport, and so forth. The department was now in constant contact with Archbishop Dabrowski, secretary of the episcopate. General Platek even placed his deputy, Colonel Pietruszka, in the operations group.

No one yet knew that the decision to abduct and assassinate Father Jerzy had come from these same thugs, so at first we were surprised that the investigation was ignoring significant and glaring clues: Chrostowski indeed did have a good memory, and Piotrowski had so badly miscalculated in believing that those higher up would protect him that he had not even bothered to get rid of the evidence.

People all over Poland gave their undivided attention to the trial, which opened under heavy security on January 2, 1985, at the court of Torun. In order to save themselves, the authorities had decided to try the assassins publicly and to proceed with a spectacular purge of the state-security apparatus. The trial provided stunning revelations about the workings of certain departments in one of the most important ministries in Poland — who it employed and who it promoted, as well as what their concept of law and ethics was.

Captain Piotrowski outlined the reasons for his having spied on Father Popieluszko:

> One of our first objectives was to bring to light, and to thwart, his subversive activities, which were inspired by the Western intelligence communities. We also needed to monitor his contacts with Western embassies, and his alliance with the secret services of the NATO member states. The second objective was to bring to light and liquidate the information-gathering network that Popieluszko had once called "the forge for the cadres of a new social upheaval." The third objective consisted of opposing the integration of the underground Solidarity organizations, which Father Popieluszko was attempting to foster, as his numerous travels — especially to areas such as Silesia, Gdansk, and Stalowa Wola — attested. The fourth objective was to expose his criminal activity, his nonconformity with the law.

In the course of deliberations within the Ministry of the Interior, nothing was ever said openly, nothing was ever recorded. A general might casually remark that when renegade priests like Popieluszko broke the law, they should be punished outside the law; and a colonel might casually mention that it wouldn't be a bad idea to "give one of these priests a scare, since they don't give a damn about surveillance and searches"; and then a captain would carry it out. In these situations people would use terms like "annoyance," "freak accident," "heart attack," "damaged during transport," "spontaneous fire in the vehicle," and the like. The directors would be annoyed by having to explain things to civil servants: "Show more initiative, gentlemen! The brass expects initiative and results. These priests are getting away with too much. Don't play by the rules. You want to be promoted? Then do something!"

Captain Piotrowski and his subordinates yearned for promotion. Pekala told the court, "I thought that this would change my life, that it could decide the fate of my career." They began preparing an action against a priest — a priest as yet undetermined. There were several candidates: Malkowski of Warsaw, Jankowski of Gdansk, and Popieluszko. The conspirators chose the third, for "his name carried the greatest qualitative weight." The top brass raised no objection to the choice of who was to be "harassed."

Ambitious Captain Piotrowski took it upon himself to act concretely. Borrowing handcuffs and uniform, stealing license plates and gasoline vouchers, falsifying documents to obtain the special "W" pass, buying rope, gloves, and a ration of duty vodka: these were routine preparations for operations in that world of intrigue and espionage. They might walk the same streets with the other citizens of Warsaw, have homes and families; but as civil servants, they inhabited a different world — one of poisoned daggers and paranoia. The trial did not expose those at the top who had assured the assassins immunity. The judicial apparatus is made up of the "right" sort of people, and if things took a turn for the worse, these men could always slip out of the country under assumed names.

The trial exposed to a stunned public the moral degeneracy and contempt for the rule of law prevailing among civil servants in the Security Service. A detailed analysis of the crime, the motives of each of the defendants, the customs and morals peculiar to Department IV, and generally the mentality of its agents — whose job, theoretically, is to protect the citizens — cast a damning light on the socialist system. We all knew about it, of course; but it is another thing to see and hear, up close and firsthand, the spectacle of organized hatred.

Fully aware of the trial's potential political fallout, the government did its best to sway the public. The press published a series of articles on the

various crimes imputed to priests — everything from their supposed collaboration with the Nazis during World War II (there had been no such
cases in Poland), to their supposed wealth, the claim that they didn't pay
their taxes, and so forth. One priest from the United States had a criminal
record, it was said; another had a mistress; still another had murdered a
friend. All these outrageous lies were spiced with allusions to the Spanish
Inquisition, as if the association weren't already obvious. To buttress their
allegations, the press quoted — or misquoted — from Western tabloids.

This propaganda campaign was launched well before the trial began.
Its purpose was not only to undo the impression that the police were mur-
dering innocent people, but also to prove that radical priests were stirring
up problems that could shatter the peace and the security of all citizens.
Some priests preached hatred, others committed murder — not a very
subtle approach. That is why on December 12, 1984, in my Letter to the
Workers of Poland, I called on all Poles to unite under the Church's banner. "At the funeral of this great man, Solidarity will live because he has
given his life for it," I said. "The proof of this is in our demand for a verdict
that lets no one go unpunished — instigators or perpetrators — for the
murder of a priest. Unity is fundamental for the future of our country.
Without it, we can do nothing; with it, we are capable of anything."

On the day that Piotrowski was arrested, Captain Adam Hodysz of the
Gdansk Security Service was sent to the same penitentiary on suspicion
of having collaborated with Solidarity's underground. On October 25, he
was transferred to Cell 5, on the highest floor of the third wing at the
Rakowiecka Street Prison in Warsaw. At the time of his arrest, Hodysz
knew that Father Popieluszko had vanished and that the search for him
was continuing. In Cell 5, he found himself in the presence of a tall man
who introduced himself tersely as Piotrowski, and who said he was in jail
for petty smuggling. The two cellmates were isolated from the other prisoners and placed under constant surveillance. During their two months in
prison together, they were never allowed to meet other inmates in the corridors, in the showers, or on the exercise ground. They weren't even allowed to see the face of the person who served them food: they would
leave their mess kits in the corridor, the door would then close, someone
would pour soup in the kits and disappear, and the door would reopen. At
night the lights were not turned off, though a dimmer bulb was inserted
sometime in the course of the evening. The hatch in the door remained
open day and night, and outside it a man from the Tiger Brigade stood

guard. The prisoners did receive the Party's daily newspaper *Trybuna Ludu,* though anything having to do with the Popieluszko affair had been censored out. Reading between the lines, so to speak, they both guessed that the murdered priest's body had been found. The day of the funeral, lying on their bunks, they heard the bells tolling all over Warsaw.

They spent nine weeks in that tiny cell, talking, playing chess, exercising. During the day, each of them underwent an "intensive interrogation" that lasted up to twelve hours. On Saturdays and Sundays, when the interrogations were shorter, they had more time to themselves. They talked a little about their children. Piotrowski had two, Hodysz one. Piotrowski, who had spent the summer in Bulgaria, was still tanned. He exercised by lifting a pail of water with his outstretched arm. He was in excellent shape, physically and mentally.

Not once in two months did he give the slightest hint that he had had anything to do with the vilest political murder in a decade. But outside Cell 5, all Poland knew it. Like those who had given him his orders, he was sentenced to twenty-five years in prison.

The murder of Popieluszko conformed perfectly to the logic of the system. But the Communist government's reaction to the murder exceeded this logic — and therein lay Father Jerzy's great victory. For all the talk about "entente," everyone now knew that a part of the machinery remained dedicated to a life-and-death struggle to "clarify" the Polish situation. Hard-line comrades believed that things tended to get muddled by compromises with either the Church or any opposition group. On the other hand, the more reasonable part of the government machinery understood, just in time, that if it did not firmly oppose violence, it would soon fall victim to violence itself.

Official recognition of Solidarity and negotiations with the government were still years away, but Father Popieluszko's death helped compromise to take the place of struggle, and put Poland on the right road.

7

The Law and the Telephone

I didn't fully realize how large the telephone looms in the life of a political activist until I read through the court proceedings from my case. On October 14 and 15, 1987, according to the record, I committed two crimes:

Communiqué. Studying voter participation in the election, Solidarity's public-opinion panel made a provisional assessment of the election returns based on a full day's observation of the urban polling places in northern Poland. Voter turnout was 52 percent in Gdansk, 57 percent in Sopot, 65 percent in Gdynia, 70 percent in Elblag, 60 percent in Slupsk, 75 percent in Olsztyn, and 62 percent in Szczecin; in Tczew, Starogard-Gdanski, and Pruszcz-Gdanski, the turnout ranged between 70 and 80 percent.

Lech Walesa

Statement. The elections that were viewed by the authorities as a plebiscite on public support for their so-called policy of normalization took place yesterday. These elections were held under conditions of heightened pressure on, and even intimidation of, Polish citizens, through a blatant propaganda campaign that squandered a great deal of money that would have been better spent on the economic problems facing this country. . . . In many large urban centers, the elections were boycotted by between 35 and 50 percent of the voters, including workers, intellectuals, and young people. . . . The legacy of August cannot be written off. The elections are over; the problems remain. . . .

Lech Walesa

No doubt about it. The prosecutor knew from the start and without further pointless formalities that I was one tough customer.

CRIMINAL RESEARCH DIVISION

OF THE CHIEF COMMANDANT OF THE MILITIA

UJAZDOWSKI ALLEY 7, WARSAW

REPORT # 7KE 4161/85, DATED OCTOBER 22, 1985

VERIFICATION OF STUDIES MADE WITH A TAPE RECORDER

In the sound-recording laboratory of the Criminal Activities Service of the Chief Commandant of the Militia in Warsaw — in conformity with the decision of the Gdansk regional Prokuratura's October 17 decision concerning Affair Number DS 14/5 — examination was made of the following items:

State's Evidence: Eighteen telephone conversations recorded onto two cassette tapes, brand Supertron C-60, designated numbers 13 and 14.

Comparison Exhibits: Statement made by Lech Walesa on the occasion of his hearing at the regional Prokuratura on February 16, 1985, preserved on magnetic tape wound on a reel with a diameter of 7.5 centimeters.

Goal of Research:

1. To determine whether Lech Walesa took part in the telephone conversations serving as evidence;
2. To verify the authenticity of the magnetic recordings serving as exhibits;
3. To reconstitute and transcribe the content of the telephone conversations used as exhibits. . . .

Until that moment, I had had no idea that simple wiretapping could be so impressively scientific!

On the basis of comparative analysis, it has been established that the vocal utterances of one of the men on the tapes serving as evidence, and those in Lech Walesa's depositions, display similar sets of features and individual parameters, such as:

- in the set and the mode of lexical items and phraseology;
- in the expressive and impressive nature of the discourse, marked by dynamism and spontaneity;
- in the type and kind of utterances;
- in the mode and form of the utterances;
- in the speed and rhythm of the discourse;
- in the syntactic-stylistic-schematic structures (including the syntactical function of the intonation, rhythm, and accentuation);

- in the articulatory phonetic properties;
- in the simplification and reduction of consonants;
- in the phonetic manifestations of lexicalization within and between words;
- in the numerous instances of dialect and linguistic colloquialisms;
- in the numerous errors of syntax and style;
- in the voice pitch, intensity, and distribution;
- in the coloration connected with the form and amplitude of the oral resonance;
- in the duration of consonant pronunciation, and the delayed release of stop consonants;
- in the intensity and development of the dynamic range.

The set of measurable linguistic features and language parameters described in this list are reliable, making it possible to assert that in the telephone conversations serving as evidence one of the interlocutors was none other than Lech Walesa.

There followed several pages of scientific analysis of my voice, incontestably demonstrating that I was I and only I. Next began the stenographic transcript of the conversations. I had no idea I was so talkative.

THIRD CONVERSATION

Woman: Hello?

Lech Walesa: Yes.

Woman: Good morning! AP [Associated Press] says hello.

LW: Good morning.

Woman: What's happening there, Mr. Walesa?

LW: What and where?

Woman: Ah, it seems there was a demonstration.

LW: Yes, but I suggest going to other sources, because here we're getting ready for something else.

Woman: No? Oh. I understand. But in any case you can confirm that . . .

LW: Yes . . .

Woman: . . . that this took place?

LW: Yes! A fairly large demonstration, barricades, police searches . . .

Woman: Do you know anything about the people apprehended, arrested?

LW: There were quite a few of them. The roundup was pretty sizable.

Woman: What does that mean? How many people could there have been?

LW: That's hard to say. I'm not going to play any guessing games. But up to eleven o'clock, we had sources . . .

Woman: Oh, I see.

LW: . . . we have figures. Something like 3 percent turned out.

Woman: Oh, good!

LW: That's the tragedy. If it doesn't reach 10 percent, I may have to break my resolution and vote myself.

FOURTH CONVERSATION

Lech Walesa: Hello?

Man: Hello!

LW: Yes, I'm on the line.

Man: I'm calling from the Reuters Agency in Warsaw.

LW: Hello, Reuters.

Man: I'd like to ask you how you're spending your day today.

LW: Well, with my family. I do have a short statement to make.

Man: Aha.

LW: Are you recording this?

Man: One second while I turn on the machine . . . There we are. Please excuse me for taking so long.

LW: That's okay.

Statement: "The public-opinion panels of Solidarity monitored the voter turnout during the so-called elections today. Based on standard statistical methods, these panels can give a percentage estimate of the voters up to 12 noon. In certain towns and cities of northern Poland the percentages were as follows: In Gdansk, 16.6 percent, in Sopot, 17.3 percent; in Gdynia, 17.5 percent; in Elblag, 20 percent; in Slupsk, 21 percent; in Olsztyn, 21 percent; and in Szczecin, 17 percent. On the basis of the data collected, we anticipate that in Gdansk today more than 50 percent of the registered voters will boycott the so-called elections.

"Gdansk, October 13, 1985, 2:30 P.M., Lech Walesa."

SEVENTH CONVERSATION

Lech Walesa: Hello?

Man: Good evening, ANSA [Italian News Agency] calling from Warsaw.

LW: Hello, ANSA.

Man: We have a question: is there anything new in connection with Gdansk?

LW: Well, no, nothing for now.

Man: Nothing for now? Because at the press conference that just took place, Mr. Urban said that up to four o'clock this afternoon more than 50 percent of the eligible voters in Gdansk had voted.

LW: Is that so? Well, well, well! No, no, he's only joking.

Man: Aha. He said that . . . the rate is about two-thirds for the whole of the country.

LW: That's just Urban's little joke . . .

> *Wiretap transcript signed by*
> Chief Expert of the Criminal Research Division,
> Senior Commandant of the MO,
> and Commissioned Lieutenant-Colonel ——— ; *and*
> Chief Expert of the Criminal Research Division,
> Chief Commandant of the MO, and
> Commissioned Lieutenant-Colonel, Engineer ———

But the colonels' work was far from over. I did a lot of talking on the phone. The wiretap service of the Security Service in Gdansk kept sending more tapes to Warsaw, making me an increasingly expensive citizen.

Following analysis of the performance of techno-electro-acoustical parameters and of the set of linguistic-phonetic features, it has been established that twenty-one telephone conversations were recorded on the cassette offered as an exhibit.

IDENTIFICATION EXAMINATION OF PERSONS

These examinations were carried out in conformity with the standard methods of identification measurement of an individual person's vocal patterns, and on the basis of the analysis of continuous discourse. The analyses done in accordance with this method have shown that one of the men taking part in the conversations was Lech Walesa, whose utterances were recorded on magnetic tape and sent for study as material for comparison. . . .

RECONSTITUTION AND TRANSCRIPTION OF THE CONTENT OF CONVERSATIONS

The telephone conversations on exhibit were reproduced and transcribed under laboratory conditions, preserving all linguistic errors and slips of the tongue. Conversations of women or children involving private matters were not transcribed.

ELEVENTH CONVERSATION

Man: Hello?

Woman: May I speak with Danuta?

Man: Certainly.

Woman: Thank you . . . Hello, Danuta?
Danuta Walesa: Yes, it's me.
Woman: Do you know what's in that can?
DW: What?
Woman: Meat hash.
DW: Meat hash?
Woman: Yes.
DW: Oh. Well, very good.
Woman: Does it look OK?
DW: Oh, pretty good.
Woman: Is it red or white meat?
DW: Red.
Woman: Then it's beef.
DW: I see.
Woman: Well, enjoy it.
DW: Thank you.
Woman: Bon appetit!
DW: Thanks . . .
Woman: 'Bye.
DW: 'Bye.

This time the expert colonels of the Criminal Research Division of the Senior Commandant of the MO proved much too suspicious. While in theory you can hide subversive material in a tin can, I'm pretty sure that my wife was thinking of cooking the contents rather than disseminating them.

TWENTY-FIRST CONVERSATION

Woman: Hello?
Man: Good evening. This is the AP calling.
W: Good evening.
M: May I speak with Mr. Walesa?
W: Hold on, please.
Lech Walesa: Hello?
Man: Good evening, Mr. Walesa. Greetings from the AP.
LW: Greetings to the AP.
Man: We'd like to know if there's anything new.
LW: Oh, nothing special. I'm still on sick leave so that I can keep quiet. I was checked over by the health board.

Man: Oh, really?

LW: So I've been excused from work for the next twelve days.

Man: Is that right? When did this board meet? Today?

LW: Yesterday.

Man: The board met yesterday, and you're out for the next twelve days? Is it the ulcers?

LW: There are some ulcers in the duodenum.

Man: Do they bother you all the time?

LW: Yes. I'll need medication that we can't get just now. If I can't get it tomorrow, I'll be asking the agency if it can do something.

Man: Good. In that case, I'll tell my boss.

LW: Ah.

Man: That's good, Mr. Walesa. Anything else aside from that? Were there any summonses?

LW: Well, no. I'm sick. I can walk around, but only in the house. That's where things are at the moment.

Man: Uh-huh.

LW: A sort of semiconfinement.

Foreign correspondents weren't the only ones keeping track of my movements. The Polish Press Agency also collected every statement I made about the upcoming elections:

Comrade Leszek Pietrasinski, Deputy Director
Department of Criminal Behavior
General Prokuratura

Comrade Pietrasinski:

In response to your letter of 29 February, we are sending you a set of photocopies of data gathered from press agencies (along with the translations, as necessary) concerning the statements of citizen Lech Walesa.

Vice-President of the Polish Press Agency

STATEMENTS OF LECH WALESA TO THE WESTERN AGENCIES

10/7/85 (in connection with the complaint lodged by Romaszewski over "the torture practiced by the personnel of the Leczycy Prison" with regard to certain union activists). In his conversation with the Reuters correspondent, Walesa stated that the government had stepped up the number of arrests in connection with the date of the upcoming elections. Walesa declared that these arrests were proof that although Solidarity was gagged during the state of martial law, it continues to be a powerful force. He added, "If we were weak, we would have been left to our own devices." (Reuters)

10/9/85. Lech Walesa, criticizing the absence of independent candidates, said the elections "will neither add to nor erode anyone's credibility." (Reuters)

10/11/85. Lech Walesa stated, "Once again I want to repeat that the official results of the election will not reflect the real opinions of the nation. That is why I don't intend to vote." (UPI)

10/12/85. In a telephone conversation with the agency's representative, Walesa stated, "Arrests have been made throughout the country. Their purpose is to disrupt vote-projection and information-gathering. But we had foreseen this, and everything was organized so that there was no possibility this would paralyze our efforts." (AP)

Walesa added that on Sunday he intended to go to mass and to spend the election day at home, as he has the flu. He also said, "I am closely watched by the police, and Gdansk is like an armed camp." (AP)

Concerning the stepping up of arrests in Gdansk, the UPI wrote that Walesa told its representative, "I have obtained thirty-five names from the families of the persons arrested." Walesa maintains that he is "certain" that many others have not contacted him, since they expect that their relatives will return in the next forty-eight hours. Walesa added, "Before World War II, they used to arrest the Communists just before elections. Now the Communists are doing the same thing to us."

10/13/85. Walesa told the agency by phone that in Gdansk, site of the birth of Solidarity, some one thousand people had headed for the city's center after mass before being dispersed by the police. (AP)

In order to get a fuller view of my character, the prosecutor also decided to seek information from my superiors at the shipyards:

ASSESSMENT OF EMPLOYEE

Citizen Lech Walesa, son of Boleslaw, born on September 29, 1943, in Popowo; basic professional training; began working at the Lenin Shipyards in Gdansk on July 12, 1961. He currently holds the post of electro-fitter at the enterprise. . . . *Professional qualification:* Certificate of mastery in his field. *Area of tasks and duties assigned to him and assessment of performance level:* Makes routine repairs, maintains the electric trucks and forklifts, as well as maintaining and repairing the transformers. He works independently, demonstrating a wide knowledge of problems, determining the causes of breakdowns and how to repair them. He submitted a plan for simplifying the control system for the electric trucks. Among other things, he also improved the method of operating imported forklifts by means of remote control. . . .

My superiors clearly didn't have too low an opinion of me. In contrast, the head of the local MO, an "acquaintance," gave a less flattering testimonial:

INVESTIGATION INTO HIS ASSOCIATIONS

Lech Walesa, son of Boleslaw and Felicja, née Kaminski . . . lives with his wife, Miroslawa, and seven children. He has a six-room apartment. He owns a car, a Volkswagen microbus. He has been found guilty of four infractions by local courts and fined once for a moving violation. . . . Has been arrested many times for taking part in illegal demonstrations. . . . Despite the legal prohibitions, he took part, along with several other people, in illegal meetings in Gdansk, attempting to organize (on February 28, 1985) a nationwide protest strike to stir up public unrest in connection with the state's policy on price reform and the relations between the state and the Church.

Her opinions confirmed by the police and Militia reports, the prosecutor decided to indict me on November 6, 1985.

PROTOCOL OF THE DEFENDANT'S HEARING

Asked whether he wished to present clarifications, the defendant replied that he would refuse to do so and that he would present his deposition in writing. He stated that he would not read the statement aloud, for it was in written form. At this time, the prosecutor read the contents of the statement:

GDANSK, NOVEMBER 5, 1985. STATEMENT BY DEFENDANT
TO THE GDANSK REGIONAL PROSECUTOR.

The scandalous proceedings of the trial of W. Frasyniuk, B. Lis, and A. Michnik, as well as the repressive acts of the authorities, which have continued to intensify in recent weeks, have conclusively persuaded me that it is only appropriate for me, as concerns the court, the Prokuratura, and the Militia, to refuse to make any deposition and to remain silent. . . . I declare that despite the new criminal proceedings instituted against me, I shall continue to act just as I have up to now. Nothing can tarnish the achievements of August or prevent me from keeping the vow I made to the congress of Solidarity — until the inevitable victory.

signed, Lech Walesa

The defendant acknowledged that this was his own signature.

Question from the prosecutor: What basis did the defendant have for the information he disseminated for publication, to wit, that on October 13, 1985, . . . more than 50 percent of the registered voters in Gdansk boycotted the elections?

When asked if he understood the question, the defendant pointed to the statement he had made to the prosecutor. . . . The defendant and his lawyer insisted that they be presented with a justification for the decision to bring these accusations against him. . . .

A recess was granted for the defendant to take counsel with his lawyer.

After this recess, the defendant's lawyer appeared, but the defendant did not. The defense declared that his client had felt ill during the recess and returned home. The lawyer presented a certificate of temporary inability to work, number 523406, issued by the Industrial Health Service of Gdansk to Lech Walesa . . . Illness statistical number 532, with the patient directed to seek treatment. Stamped with the signature of the physician. This certificate was returned to the lawyer . . . and the hearing ended.

The defendant returned home alone.

11:30 A.M.

That hearing was a farce in which I had no intention of playing a part. I had a medical excuse and was feeling distinctly under the weather. So I returned home, followed as always by a crowd of secret-police agents.

SECOND TAPE, NINTH CONVERSATION

Man: Hello! This is the UPI. Is that Mr. Walesa?

Lech Walesa: Hello, UPI. Is your tape machine on? "Communiqué for November 6. At ten o'clock this morning, I appeared at the Prokuratura, leaving the following statement with the regional prosecutors: The scandalous proceedings of the trial of Wladyslaw Frasyniuk, Bogdan Lis, and Adam Michnik, together with the repressive acts of the authorities, which have continued to intensify in recent weeks, have conclusively persuaded me that it is only appropriate for me, as concerns the court, the Prokuratura, and the Militia, to refuse to make a deposition and to remain silent. . . .

"Because of this interrogation, I was unable to attend the funeral of Marcin Antonowicz today, but I sent a letter that will, I hope, be read at the graveside. This is what it said:

" 'We are witness to yet another great tragedy. A young man has died. I would like to convey to the relatives of Marcin, whose memory is sacred to us, our heartfelt condolences and sense of profound sadness . . . at this utterly senseless death, which occurred when he was in the hands of those whose basic duty it is to ensure the safety of all citizens. His death confirms yet again that the machinery of the Polish Ministry of the Interior acts in contempt of the law and with a sense of total impunity. . . . The ministry is not subject to social control, and we may at any moment find ourselves in Marcin's place, our death written off as a tragic accident.'"

Have you got that? Hello?

Man: Hello?

LW: Well, that's all . . .

Man: I still have a question. How long did the proceedings at the Prokuratura last?

LW: All together, it was about an hour. That includes an interruption because I wasn't feeling well. I left my lawyer there alone. So the business has two parts.

Man: I see.

LW: I think you should get the rest from Jacek Taylor, because he was there until the end, not me.

Man: Will he be with the group today?

LW: Probably.

Man: I have another question: were you accused of a particular crime?

LW: Yes, I was.

Man: Do you remember the number?

LW: They were in a big hurry. I think they wanted to get this thing over with today. And in connection with that —

[*Teresa Zabza, Lech Walesa's secretary, interrupts:* Mr. Walesa, the Militia is here for you.]

LW: And in connection with that, I had to act in that way and no other. Hold on a moment. It seems some representatives of "the people's power" are arriving here, so I must go see . . .

[*Zabza to Walesa:* Come quick! Look at how they're pushing and shoving. Look!]

STENOGRAPHIC TRANSCRIPT OF CASSETTE TAPE RECORDED NOVEMBER 6, 1985, IN THE APARTMENT OF THE DEFENDANT LECH WALESA

Captain Marek Rogowski: Where's Walesa?

Danuta Walesa: They're crawling all over the apartment . . . These gentlemen think they own the place. The Militia is here for you! Hey, just a second — look out, come on! Why are you pushing like that? My husband's coming.

MR: You're not the one I came for, ma'am.

DW: Look, now just wait a minute!

LW: Is this "the people's power"?

MR: Please, Mr. Walesa.

DW: Be quiet! Stop! Why are you forcing your way in like that? Wait for my husband to come out. You're acting like an animal.

MR: Go ahead, lady. Keep right on talking.

DW: What an insulting thing to do, sticking a tape recorder under my nose! Right here in my own house!

LW: I demand to know why this guy is taping in my home. He hasn't introduced himself yet.

MR: Because those are the orders.

DW: What orders? Orders to come barging into someone's house with a tape machine?

MR: I have an order from the regional Prokuratura to put you immediately at its disposal —

DW: Why don't you just step all over him? What do you think you're doing, shoving a sick person around like that?

LW: I'm on sick leave.

MR: Keep your hands to yourself and stop pushing me!

DW: Well, excuse me! Whose apartment is this anyway?

MR: I know about the sick leave, but there's an order from the prosecutor.

DW: Would you look at this guy, running around like a beaten dog . . . ! The police are so scared their knees are knocking.

LW: I'm on sick leave. I'm not supposed to leave the house, and you're not permitted to haul off a sick person by force.

MR: Yes, we are.

LW: Oh, come on! How can you have that right? OK, then — I'll show you just so you don't have any doubt. . . .

DW: Four goons have to come to take my husband away from me? You lousy bastard!

MR: Don't get upset, ma'am.

DW: Oh! Right! Sir, do you think all you have to do is give the word and I'll calm down? Sure! That guy over there looks about as "official" as Colonel Pietruszka.* Come on! Get out your pistol and shoot!

LW: You don't have the right to do this. You're violating the law. You can't break the law. I'm on sick leave.

MR: Tell it to the regional Prokuratura. [*To an agent:*] Please call the doctor.

---

* The person behind the assassination of Father Jerzy Popieluszko.

DW: Now, just wait a minute! Urban said that he should stay at home because he's sick. I don't know what the Militia is there for. So the SB [Security Forces] can run the country? They act like they think they're gods. Pigs! Cannibals! All you want to do is scare people with a tape recorder!

MR: You were at the Prokuratura.

LW: But now I don't feel up to it. The doctor told me to stay home.

DW: It's also in writing that he can only walk around the house, and not wherever they want him to go . . . Look at that guy! He just keeps right on taping! I'd like to throw this ashtray at your head so you can go straight to hell! Shit! Why do you keep taping?

MR: Because those were my orders.

DW: Orders? Animals! All you want to do is spit on people! You're all imbeciles!

MR: I warn you that you are insulting a civil servant trying to carry out his duty.

DW: I couldn't care less! A civil servant is someone in uniform, not some low-life in a tacky suit! I am a citizen just as much as you are. How would you like it if I walked into your house with a tape recorder and just started taping?

LW: Come on, honey, please don't get upset. It'll just makes things worse.

MR: Mr. Walesa, again, I should warn you that your wife is harassing civil servants trying to do their job.

LW: Oh, is that so? My wife is doing what she has a right to do in her own home. You are the ones harassing me, a sick man.

DW: And look at him, running all around the apartment like a cat with a frying pan tied to its tail.

LW: This is just plain assault . . . in my own home. . . .

DW: A mugging! . . . And that one over there chasing me all around the house with his tape recorder! . . .

LW: Sweetheart, don't get upset. You're not supposed to get upset. It won't help.

DW: What these thugs are waiting for is for someone to get upset who ought not to. That's what it is. You kill someone in the street and then say that it was an accident. Business as usual. You don't scare me, because I've had it with you! [*The doctor comes in.*] A doctor? This is the first I've heard about a doctor.

MR: I'll ask for the doctor to examine Lech Walesa.

LW: You should honor the medical excuse, which says that I must stay home. Here's my doctor's certificate.

DW: Honey, just let the doctor speak. She can say what she likes, okay? Please.

LW: Doctor, please, I have a medical excuse, which says that besides going to get the prescribed treatment, I must stay home. This copy of the excuse was given to the Prokuratura, and that's why I don't want to go out. . . . All you have to do is confirm that this is so, ma'am. If you have any doubts, I suggest you check with the Prokuratura.

Doctor: Yes, but I'd like to look you over —

LW: I don't *want* to be looked over. . . . Are you challenging a document issued by the board?

Doctor: That's not the problem. That wasn't why I came here.

LW: So tell these representatives of "the people's power" that I have a legal medical excuse and that I'm supposed to stay quietly at home. . . .

DW [*to Teresa Zabza*]: Here, take the phone and tell everyone that —

[*She reaches for it, but is pushed away.*]

MR: Leave that phone alone!

DW: I beg your pardon! What a thug! I've seen your kind before.

LW: Sweetie, cool down.

DW: No thug can just come into my home and lay down the law!

LW: That's it exactly. What gives you the right to boss us around?

MR: I am doing what I was ordered to do.

LW: But what were you ordered to do? You have no jurisdiction here.

MR: Mr. Walesa, can we speed this up? The doctor here would like to check you over. Will you allow it?

LW: No sir, I will not. I have an official medical excuse issued by the board, and the board knows —

MR: OK, fine, Mr. Walesa; you've already told me that. But I'm asking you again: Will you let the doctor examine you?

LW: I don't want to be examined again because I don't feel well.

MR: I'm going to have to ask you to get dressed. You're coming with us.

LW: No, I am not, sir. You will take me only by force, and this doctor will have violated the rules of the medical board.

[*The doctor explains that she has only come to examine Walesa's state of health.*]

LW: If you would, ma'am, please explain to these gentlemen that they are violating doctor's orders. They are upsetting me, and I am not supposed to get upset because what I have demands that I stay calm. . . .

[*Lech Walesa finally permits the examination, which takes place, and the medical conclusions are barely audible.*]

DW: If it were me, I wouldn't have gotten undressed. They'd have had to force me. . . . What a sleazy business! The Militia is supposed to protect common citizens, not invade our homes! . . . Such clean-cut-looking men, but what bastards they are! What pigs!

LW: Why are you getting so worked up? You know you're not supposed to strain yourself.

DW: Some moron just barges in here and sticks a tape machine under my nose! He must think it's the first time I've ever seen one. And in my own house I have the right to say whatever I please! Let God's will be done. I'm going to kick this tape recorder out of your hands. Just take a look at yourself, you animal!

MR: Mr. Walesa, the order was . . . and it's not a secret. . . . Given that there is a permit for sick leave and that you have agreed. . . . We shall simply report to the prosecutor. . . .

LW: If I hadn't put things that way, what would you have done?

MR: I would have carted you off.

LW: Where is your sense of honor and the law? Is that how you want to govern? We have to fight you, really fight you; you're probably going to force us to that point! I can't stand it any longer! You're going to cry over your own fate.

MR: Fine, Mr. Walesa. That's all. Goodbye.

DW: I thought you were better than that . . .

MR: Goodbye.

DW: You don't deserve to be called men!

A citizen of the People's Republic of Poland — one living in Cracow, on Century of the Golden Age Street — sent the following letter to the General Prosecutor:

Thursday's press published the Polish Press Agency's communiqué describing how "the leader of the Polish working world," Mr. Lech Walesa, has once again sneered at the institution called on to uphold the law in Poland. I know I'm not a writer, but I do know that this guy is the pawn of larger outside forces, and scoffed not only at the prosecutor of the Gdansk Prokuratura, but at me and at every other citizen of the People's Republic of Poland. . . . Every ordinary citizen, when summoned by the prosecutor, cooperates . . . and conducts himself in a serious manner. He doesn't disappear, play hide-and-seek, and then pull a valid L-4 sick-leave permit out of his hat. I think it's high time to put an end to Mr. Lech Walesa's plotting, cut him down to size, which he fully deserves, and above all to show him that, despite the Nobel Prize he won by fighting against socialism in Poland, he is neither a lesser nor greater citizen of the People's Republic of Poland than any other Pole.

I was fortunate to have others act in my defense, and in particular to have three remarkable lawyers: Anna Skowronska, Jacek Taylor, and Jan Olszewski. They filed a series of protests against the Prokuratura's prejudicial actions, showing that a whole consignment of petitions had been especially organized to prosecute me and that reckless letters from irresponsible people had been used as evidence. "Our client," they stated, "is not guilty of any infraction. Indeed, it is hard to see in his words and action any desire to slander anyone; we see a desire for the truth."

At the Prokuratura, however, they saw things differently. I was summoned to a new hearing, and it seemed likely that proceedings against me would be instituted. Obviously, I had no intention of subjecting myself to them.

THIRTY-FIRST CONVERSATION

Man: Hello. This is the UPI. Can I . . . ?

LW: Yes. Is your tape machine on?

Man: Yes!

LW: . . . I have received yet another summons to appear at the Gdansk Prokuratura at nine in the morning on December 5, 1985. Despite the state of my health, I shall go and present my views on some important ques tions. . . .

As I mentioned, the people's government spared no expense in the wiretapping of my phone conversations. On December 4, 1985, the director of the Criminal Research Division submitted the bill for expert evaluation of my phone calls, which had taken a qualified specialist 170 hours of work — in other words, three solid weeks of eight-hour days. For a whole month, a lieutenant-colonel pored over my phone conversations; his puttering cost the people 120 zlotys an hour, twice as much as I was making at the shipyards.

Expenses were also incurred for translating my statements to the foreign press, for the writing of innumerable memoranda, and for the dozens of hours that prosecutors, investigators, and secret agents had devoted to my case. To this must also be added the vehicles used in surveillance, the cumbersome and costly wiretapping equipment, and the patrol car that sat in front of my house day in and day out. All this to "reprivatize" a lowly member of the proletariat! For a while I was the center of an immense amount of public attention.

BILL OF INDICTMENT AGAINST LECH WALESA

FOR AN ACT PUNISHABLE UNDER PARAGRAPH ONE OF ARTICLE 178

OF THE CRIMINAL CODE

Basis for Accusation: In October 1985, in Gdansk, in order to spread false information about the success of the boycott of the elections for the Sejm* of the People's Republic of Poland proposed by an illegal antisocialist group, he passed on false information to representatives of the Reuters, United Press International, and Associated Press agencies, as well as Agence France-Presse, and distributed illegal publications throughout the country containing false information about voter turnout in the regions of Gdansk, Elblag, Slupsk, Szczecin, Olsztyn, and Wroclaw. This false information was later published in the foreign press and also broadcast on the radio. These broadcasts were also transmitted in Polish and printed in publications outlawed in Poland, thereby casting doubt on the legitimacy of the authentic tabulations made by the electoral commissions in these regions, and so denigrating the members of these commissions in the public's eyes that they risked losing the trust indispensable to carrying out their assigned public duties — an infraction defined in paragraph one of article 178 of the criminal code. . . .

Furthermore: The elections of October 12, 1985, for the Sejm of the People's Republic of Poland were preceded by propaganda campaigns carried on throughout the country by illegal and antipatriotic organizations calling for a boycott of these elections. These organizations disseminated illegal publications, pamphlets, and slogans across the nation urging Polish citizens to abstain from voting, and the propaganda was widely circulated in foreign anti-Polish publications and broadcast by certain Western radio stations in Polish. The call for a boycott of the election proved ineffective, . . . but from his apartment in Gdansk on October 13 and 14, 1985, Lech Walesa issued statements to foreign correspondents challenging the legitimacy of the figures involving voter turnout established by the electoral commissions. The content of these conversations . . . was recorded and put at the disposal of the investigators. . . .

During this same period, government spokesman Jerzy Urban informed foreign journalists at a press conference in Warsaw of the provisional estimates for voter turnout, based on data provided by the electoral commissions. These figures were markedly higher than those disseminated by Walesa.

---

* The Sejm is the lower house of the Polish Parliament; the upper house is the Senat.

During a telephone conversation, designated Number 7, with the representative of the Italian agency ANSA, Lech Walesa called these provisional official estimates "Mr. Urban's little joke."

On October 15, 1985, at various locations in Gdynia and Gdansk, notably the areas around train stations, pamphlets were found bearing caricatures of prominent state or social figures, as well as containing a statement signed by Lech Walesa. That statement, dated October 15, 1985, characterized the elections as taking place under conditions of increased pressures on the citizens, and declared that 35 to 50 percent of the voters from the larger urban centers had boycotted them. . . .

The alleged falsification of voter-turnout percentages during the elections to the Sejm dated October 13, 1985, elicited a strong reaction from the members of the electoral commissions . . . who expressed their indignation over the slanderous reports by the Western media, which — relying on Lech Walesa's statement — cast doubt on their integrity and accused them of misrepresenting the election results. . . .

When confronted with charges brought against him, Lech Walesa pleaded not guilty, refused to provide clarification, and presented a declaration unconnected with the issues involved in the proceedings.

February 11, 1986, was the date chosen for the matter to go before the regional court of Gdansk. It didn't seem to matter that the final paragraph of the indictment declared that Lech Walesa, "wishing to make credible the information that he had communicated, published figures that appeared to approximate the actual results"; it didn't seem to matter that I had published these results before the official numbers on voter turnout were released; it didn't seem to matter, finally, that the president of the regional court had been one Mr. Zieniuk — who was also the president of one of the "offended" electoral commissions. The government had simply decided to test the strength of the Lech Walesa myth.

PROTOCOL OF THE MAIN SESSION

FEBRUARY 11, 1986

COURT OF THE REGION OF GDANSK

Case: Lech Walesa, defendant, accused according to article 178, first paragraph of the Penal Code.

Presiding: Janusz Lenarcik, president of the regional court.

Jurors: Jan Nowicki, Jerzy Kruszynski.

Court Clerks: Mariola Kus, Malgorzata Wozna.

Vice-Prosecutor: Rajmund Blaszkowski.

Defendant: Lech Walesa, accompanied by his lawyers. . . .

(At this session . . . the parties were forewarned that all the proceedings would be videotaped. . . .)

One of the defendant's lawyers, Anna Skowronska, requested that a member of the Swedish parliament be authorized to enter the courtroom; that individual had submitted a letter to the president of the Gdansk regional court with the request but received no reply. Furthermore, Skowronska requested that the defendant's religious advisor, Father Henryk Jankowski, rector of Saint Brygid's Church of Gdansk, be admitted into the courtroom, and also that a correspondent from ABC News be permitted to act as an observer for the duration of the trial.

Another of the defendant's lawyers, Jacek Taylor, declared that on February 6, 1986, he had passed along a request from Bishop Tadeusz Goclowski to the president of the Gdansk regional tribunal asking that two representatives of the bishopric be allowed in the courtroom, but averred that he had never received any reply. . . .

After consultation, the court allowed Father Henryk Jankowski, as well as the two representatives mentioned in Bishop Tadeusz Goclowski's request, to attend the sessions. Entry was, however, denied to the representatives of the foreign press.

Several hours dragged by.

At the Request of the President: Do the parties see any possibility of settling their differences out of court?

Prosecutor's Declaration: Were the defendant Lech Walesa to submit a statement satisfying the members of the electoral commissions, the charge brought against him would be dropped.

Defendant Lech Walesa's Declaration: It was not my intention to slander anyone; I didn't want to humiliate anyone.

The court recessed to deliberate upon the declarations; then there was another brief exchange:

At the prosecutor's query as to whether the defendant wished to issue a statement giving satisfaction to the offended parties, the defendant declared that he stood by his earlier statement — that it was never his intention to offend or slander anyone.

After another short recess by the court, the prosecutor stated:

> Taking into account the interests of the offended parties as well as the statement provided by Lech Walesa, and citing article 50, paragraph 3, of the criminal procedures code, the Gdansk regional prosecutor withdraws the charge against the defendant.

And that was how I broke free of the clutches of "the people's justice." No one asked for the opinions of the "offended" members of the electoral commissions — probably because they didn't have any. After a time, however, the commissioners did submit statements to the court, each one worded exactly the same, in which they said that they no longer felt offended or slandered, and that they were withdrawing their accusation.

So in the end the government decided not to condemn me, in part because it feared the protests that would have erupted, abroad as well as in Poland. They also somehow understood that I had in my possession a number of documents detailing electoral fraud. I had plenty of proof that in one village, for example, a mayor had distributed ballots to the farmworkers at home, just so they wouldn't have to tire themselves out going to the polling place.

8
Difficult Days

The year 1986 promised to be a turning point for Poland. While the government was still baring its teeth, those teeth were already showing numerous signs of decay. Underground leaders Bogdan Borusewicz and Zbigniew Bujak were arrested, but they were released shortly afterward, along with the remaining political prisoners, following two successive declarations of amnesty that were connected with Poland's joining the International Monetary Fund and the World Bank.

Then in late June, the bishops gathered in Gniezno for the 214th Plenary Conference of the Episcopate of Poland. Among other actions, the bishops issued a statement expressing the expectations and hopes of many social and professional groups in Poland that the government would create and legalize opportunities for political activity by parties independent of the existing system.

Three months later, after brief visits to the most important industrial areas, I formed the Solidarity Provisional Coordinating Board, consisting of Bogdan Borusewicz from Gdansk, Zbigniew Bujak from Warsaw, Wladyslaw Frasyniuk from Wroclaw, Tadeusz Jedynak from Katowice, Bogdan Lis from Gdansk, Janusz Palubinski from Poznan, and Jozef Pinior from Wroclaw. The government reacted nervously and summoned me to a hearing. It was clear that they had finally realized that taking any severe measures against a Nobel Peace Prize laureate was no longer in the cards. Thus once again did the peculiarly Polish version of *Zamordyzm z ludzka twarza* [roughly, "Brass knuckles with a human face"*] hide everything but the human face.

---

* A takeoff on the slogan "Socialism with a human face" — playing on the similarity between *zamordyzm* and *socialyzm*.

Government spokesman Jerzy Urban couldn't pass up the opportunity to take one more swipe at me:

> Had Lech Walesa . . . undertaken to respect the law instead of create organizations designed to oppose it, had he sincerely and openly admitted that the union he led had made some mistakes, had he made unambiguous his willingness for entente, . . . had he not concealed slogans calling for his brand of pluralism and for plotting against our regime, were he not so obviously in cahoots with Western forces hostile to Poland, then the following statement might be applied to this man in whom we once had confidence: "It doesn't matter where he stood before. What matters is where he stands now."

On October 10, together with a group of eight intellectuals (notably Tadeusz Mazowiecki and Bronislaw Geremek), I called on the United States to lift its economic sanctions against Poland. This was, as I recall, one day before the second Gorbachev-Reagan summit in Reykjavik. On October 12, however, I met with the Solidarity Provisional Coordinating Board, expecting that while it would continue to act concretely, its membership would still remain secret. A month later the Security Service began an all-out effort to unmask those members, hoping to demonstrate its own effectiveness, but instead pitifully demonstrating just the opposite. The "members" the police "unmasked" either were completely unconnected with the board and living openly, or had long been living abroad.

On November 19, 1986, an important event filled our hearts with hope: Solidarity was admitted to the International Confederation of Free Trade Unions (ICFTU) and to the World Confederation of Labor(WCL). For only the second time in history, a union was admitted to both organizations, which have very different platforms and outlooks. The first to achieve this was the Basque Union during General Franco's dictatorship. It had taken two full years to gain admission. What clinched it, so far as I know, was the support of the British Trades Union Congress (TUC) and the personal efforts of its secretary-general, Norman Willis; efforts made by Solidarity's Coordinating Bureau, headquartered in Brussels and directed by Jerzy Milewski, had also been crucial. Solidarity's new affiliation with the ICFTU and the WCL immediately boosted our movement's prestige in the eyes of its members, sympathizers, and enemies, and effectively wiped out the absurdly false rumors that Solidarity's organizational structure had collapsed. These rumors had threatened to scare off potential donors; not many people want to support a nonexistent organization.

Solidarity's Coordinating Bureau in Brussels had been created on July 1, 1982, and its most tangible contribution to the cause had been providing funds for Poland's "delegalized" organizations. By the mid-1980s, the bureau was taking in some $500,000 a year, $300,000 of which came from the American AFL-CIO, $100,000 from the ICFTU, and the rest from groups of affiliated unions in Europe, Canada, Australia, and Japan, together with smaller sums from organizations of Polish émigrés and pro-Solidarity groups.

Depending on instructions from the Solidarity Provisional Board, the Brussels bureau sent cash or equipment to Poland. Unfortunately, some of the shipments failed to reach their destination. The worst loss occurred on November 28, 1986, on the dock of the Swinoujscie ferry, when Polish officials impounded a forty-ton truck and its contents, worth $200,000 in all, coming from the bureau. The truck held twenty-three offset presses, forty-nine copiers, sixteen fax machines, a set of IBM-PC computers, four Tandy computers, nine disk drives, and twelve small NL-10 printing calculators, as well as other smaller equipment and books. A Swedish customs agent from Ystad had sent a Telex to the Polish authorities alerting them to the shipment.

On December 10, undeterred by these problems, which came and went like adolescent blemishes, I quite openly organized Solidarity's Legal Defense Committee, whose presidency fell to Zbigniew Romaszewski. Shortly after, Solidarity's legal team was formed under the same leadership. In addition, I asked Wladek Frasyniuk to organize a group to analyze social issues, and Tadeusz Jedynak to do the same with economic issues. Trying to conceal his displeasure, the government spokesman then delivered the following statement to the press:

> The government shares the opinion that union activities must be unified, so that a given firm will have only one union organization within it. . . . Questions involving the structure of the union movement in general are unrelated to the illegal political group operating under the name Solidarity. . . . It is naïve to think . . . that Poles will go down that road again, and it will happen neither in the near nor the distant future.

The year 1987 began rather auspiciously. On January 12, General Jaruzelski traveled to see the pope. I don't know in any precise terms what they talked about, but beyond outlining plans for John Paul II's upcoming visit to his native country, the need for a social entente in Poland was discussed quietly. I am proud to give the pope credit for coming up with the idea for the Round Table negotiations that eventually took place between the government and the democratic opposition.

In March, though, I had to swallow a bitter pill, and it left a bad taste in my mouth for months. A group of former associates, a small band of disaffected visionaries, decided to create a schism in Solidarity; under the guise of "loyal commitment to the statutes," they created a headache called the National Work Group. It was led by militants from Lodz, Szczecin, Gdansk, and Warsaw, who had for some time maintained that Solidarity under Walesa wasn't functioning under true democratic principles. What alarmed me most was the narrowmindedness of these people. They couldn't seem to understand that from time to time Solidarity's activities would have to exceed those of an ordinary labor union. Their noisy self-righteousness, I thought, would lead Poland into economic stagnation. Luckily, they gained no serious influence. They subsequently decided to form a separate union.

In April, after several months of talks, Solidarity's experts decided to go public with the union's views on the reconstruction of the Polish economy — the same views that, with minor corrections, were later set forth at the Round Table negotiations. It was a joy to watch new buds of political life forming with each passing week. My own popularity even made something of a comeback, judging from the number of interviews I was asked to give and by the visits from foreign dignitaries and labor leaders. In May, for example, I had the great pleasure of receiving the French director-general of the International Bureau of Labor (part of the International Labor Organization), François Blanchard.

On May 31, 1987, the day before the arrival of John Paul II on his third trip to Poland, I invited a group of sixty-two eminent writers, scholars, journalists, cultural figures, and economists to Warsaw, and together we formulated a declaration articulating the Poles' right to independence, democracy, freedom, and truth, and their right to shape their own economic destiny. We were all anxious for and inspired by the moment when the Holy Father's feet would again walk on Polish soil. The pope's 1979 visit had had the force of a miracle. Millions of unorganized and unaffiliated Poles had suddenly seen themselves as a community under the leadership of the Church — an experience that a year afterward had led to the creation of Solidarity. What would this trip bring?

9
The Turning Point

The most important event of 1987 for Solidarity, and for all of Poland, was the pope's third visit. While some people might want to interpret the history of Solidarity differently — and emphasize its autonomy from any external influence — the pope's visit was undeniably a turning point in the national mood. For the first time, John Paul II, so beloved by the Poles, was permitted to travel to the forbidden city of Gdansk — and, better yet, to the new community of Zaspa, former site of an airfield, where I was then living. His itinerary was the subject of lengthy negotiations, for in Poland at the time everything was still considered symbolically charged, as well as potentially subversive. Every participant, every building, every ceremony might suddenly assume political dimensions that could endanger the "normalization process," meaning the old order.

The Communist government was acting as though it was less and less sure that its policies were guided by any coherent principles. Only two years later did we become fully aware of the doubts that assailed it. But at the time local and regional authorities behaved arrogantly, overcompensating for their fears that the era of their power was ending. Stanislaw Bejger, first secretary of the Polish United Workers' Party, told the bishop of Gdansk, "The pope's visit to the Monument for the Shipyard Dead will not be possible; however, we do agree to his visiting the Monument to the Defenders of Westerplatte."*

A war of monuments had been going on for some time. Whoever could erect the most, endow them with the greatest significance, and make them the most visible, would prevail. So at night and on the sly, a monument to

---

* The Polish naval base at Westerplatte was heavily bombarded by German forces before being taken in the first days of World War II.

the victims of Katyn Forest was erected by one faction; by day, the government built one to the noble agents of the Security Service who had fallen during the postwar struggle to consolidate the new order. The people put up plaques commemorating the heroic leadership of the Home Army; the authorities put up similar plaques to the memory of various fallen Communists.

In the end, the pope paid his respects to both monuments — to the shipyard dead as well as to the defenders of Westerplatte. As for comrade Bejger, his name is all but forgotten now.

Perestroika had not yet reached Poland by the spring of 1987 (and in the Soviet Union its future was still uncertain), but its effects were already beginning to be felt, and one of those effects was to offer us new alternatives. Deep-seated prejudices against the Russians kept the public from taking any real interest in news from our giant eastern neighbor. Mikhail Gorbachev was regarded as simply a new and more skillful deceiver. I admit to thinking the same myself, initially. Then I realized that he had embarked on a perilous journey, mounted on a horse that might at any moment run away with him; once on, he had no choice but to ride it out. His enemies were waiting for him to fall.

We had often spoken of him with Adam Michnik, who started monitoring the Soviet press carefully and cultivating his own contacts (dissidents from the Soviet Union were still afraid to come see me directly). This was during a period when I was meeting almost daily with journalists, militants, and politicians at the rectory of Saint Brygid's, spurred by a powerful need to be active. To the point of sounding like a broken record, I told my listeners that Solidarity was a reform movement. I said this to Edward Koch, then mayor of New York, and repeated it later to Jane Fonda. I went on, saying it to many visitors, an Irish bishop, and to an Italian reporter with anarchistic leanings who followed him. That I gave so many interviews — that I "talked too much" — displeased some of my colleagues. Cardinal Jozef Glemp, for one, met with me less and less. He frowned on the workers' pilgrimages to the shrine of Jasna Gora at Czestochowa, I was told, because they usually turned into political demonstrations in support of Solidarity. Jasna Gora, Poland's most important shrine, gave the people who gathered there a feeling of safety, and that feeling of safety inspired them to fill the grounds outside the fortified monastery walls with thousands of banners proclaiming anticommunist slogans. As the head of the Church in Poland, Cardinal Glemp was responsible for preparing the

Holy Father's visit; he made it known that the government's policy of normalization was more to his liking than was our ineffectual political activity. A number of his ecclesiastical advisors and some militants from the opposition shared his leanings. Others came right out and said that Walesa was finished, that he had played out his role.

Everything that I or Solidarity had done up to that point, however, was merely the backdrop for the spectacle to follow. Cardinal Glemp had occasion to be convinced of this on his trip to the United States, where he traveled to raise funds for an agricultural foundation whose function was to help encourage the spirit of private enterprise in Poland. The countries in the European Economic Community and the United States were disposed to offer this foundation substantial financing. But one question came up again and again: What does Lech Walesa think of the foundation? Public opinion abroad was of great help in strengthening my position at home.

Preparing for John Paul II's arrival was a major effort. When he came to Gdansk, the pope would recognize our achievements, I told the editor of the Catholic paper *W Drodze* [*On the Way*], and his visit would affect our destiny — whatever that destiny was. I went on to say, "We inhabit a country that has over the centuries has been overrun and overcome by its neighbors. If this ever happens again, at least it can be said that during the Holy Father's visit in 1987, he underscored a simple fact: Without a free Poland, a free Europe is not possible." We were aware that the pope would not solve our problems, but he would tell the world about the will of the majority of the Polish people, and about what millions of Poles prayed for. He would be the instigator of changes outside Poland whose effects would eventually reach us and push Poland in the right direction — toward an era of faith, honesty, and social reform.

In my own neighborhood I could witness the effects that the mere expectation of his visit was having. From a clump of gray apartment blocks — they looked something like huge dormitories — my residential development was transformed into a living organism, a community of people with distinct personalities and angles of vision. Unexpected qualities began to appear in Falowce, home to several thousand people who had patronizingly been nicknamed "the Kolkhozians" [collective farmers] or "the Ants," an allusion to their sheer numbers and to Pharaoh's "swarming ants" in the Bible. Each floor, each balcony, became a shrine loudly proclaiming its residents' attachment to the Faith. I knew that the people weren't as religious as their very gaudy decorations seemed to indicate, but the important thing was that, if only for a moment, for a single day, they wished to be religious. Their souls were stirred.

In the middle of the leftover airstrip at the heart of the suburbs a huge altar was constructed, an ancient ship onto whose bridge the Pilot of the Church was to ascend. Marian Kolodziej, the set designer of the Gdansk Theater (prisoner number 432 at Auschwitz), had drawn the design for this ship; it rose over 130 feet high into the air and had a great billowing sail visible from everywhere in the community. Hundreds of people donated their labor to the construction of this altar, whose beauty almost redeemed the ugliness of the socialist planned community that surrounded it. For days, the pounding of innumerable hammers was heard late into the evening. Residents strolled around as if it were a fair, commenting on the progress of the work, imagining what it would look like when finished, hoping that it would be left standing when everything was over.

A week before the pope's arrival, the central administrative authorities abruptly ordered work on the altar to halt. The masts formed three crosses that echoed the symbolism of the Gdansk shipyard monument; that upset them. It took great powers of persuasion to convince them that *these* three crosses were not *those* three crosses! And so, just three days before the pope's arrival, the ban was lifted, and the altar was completed in the nick of time. In Poland, struggle against the cross has always proven futile.

I remained as calm as I could while getting ready for my audience with the pope. After putting on my white shirt and suit, I inspected the children. All Zaspa had been decked out for the celebration with flowers, and at our home, too, it felt like Christmas Eve. I had a gift ready for the Holy Father: a copy of the first part of my autobiography, bound in white leather, which the French publisher had given to me. It was the most elegant book I had ever seen, and not even in my wildest dreams had I imagined that someday I would be author of so many printed pages. I fretted over the dedication, for the standard phrases seemed so hackneyed. Whenever I find myself in a situation in which people expect eloquence of me, the best I can manage are simple, perhaps simplistic, words. "To the beloved Holy Father, who has shown us the true way of hope, a gift from Lech Walesa and his family." I took the dedication from the book's title, *The Way of Hope*.

My whole family and I went to the bishop's residence, where we were to meet John Paul II. My children wandered around for several hours. They had been told not to go near the windows "for security reasons" and must have been terribly bored.

My mind drifted back to the pope's previous visit, four years earlier. When I saw that negotiations with the regime over that earlier visit were turning out to be difficult, I had met with Cardinal Glemp on March 19, 1983, to recommend that nothing and no one should stand in the way of the Holy Father's visit. If necessary, I would give up any public activity for a period of time in order to avoid turning the question of my audience with the pope into a moral issue. All this was said with a heavy heart, since I was counting a great deal both on having this audience and on the publicity it would bring to Solidarity. The cardinal listened as if he had expected all I was proposing and might accept my terms. Nevertheless, the next time we met, on April 17 in Gdansk, he stated that the Holy Father was determined to meet with me.

And so it was that on June 16, 1983, John Paul II arrived in Warsaw and was greeted by Henryk Jablonski, then president of the State Council — something like the country's president — with these words: "His Holiness's visit testifies to the gradual normalization of life of our country." The government wanted to prove to the world that the state of martial law, which was still in effect, had become accepted as normal and had stabilized a European nation of some thirty-seven million inhabitants.

The pope's opening statement conveyed his rebuttal: "In the name of Christ, I ask that those who are suffering be particularly close to me. I was ill and you came to see me, I was in prison and you came to visit me. I cannot visit all the sick, all the imprisoned, all the suffering, but I beg them to be close to me in spirit."

General Jaruzelski's nervousness grew obvious during these welcoming words. It was becoming clear that the head of the Church would not participate in any propaganda show in the name of "normalization."

As for me, I had another cause for concern. Negotiations about my audience with the pope were still going on. I stayed in my apartment at Zaspa, still not knowing until the last minute whether or not I would be able to meet with him, watching television and listening to the radio — waiting. Under surveillance by dozens of agents of the Security Service, I couldn't move a step. Sometimes my phone worked and sometimes the line was dead.

A few days later at Czestochowa, John Paul II gave us more reason to hope:

I am a son of this nation and that is why I feel profoundly all its noble aspirations, its desire to live in truth, liberty, justice, and social solidarity, its desire to live its own life. Indeed, after a thousand years of history, this nation has its own life, culture, social traditions, spiritual identity. Virgin of Jasna Gora, I want to place under your protection all that has been produced in these difficult years since August 1980, all those truths, principles, values, and attitudes.

The million people gathered there at the spiritual heart of Poland understood his words perfectly. Before the pope's visit, the opposition had feared that he might condone the accursed state of martial law by shaking hands with the general in sunglasses, diplomatically backing away from confrontation, putting the Church's interests ahead of Solidarity's struggle, shying away from explicit criticism. Everyone heaved a sigh of relief as soon as they heard him speak. The Holy Father's words went straight to the hearts of the Poles, immediately overcoming the mendacious propaganda of the police state and the concerns of its censors. A million people raised their arms and extended the V of victory into the air, and by so doing served notice on the government and the world . . .

When I heard some commotion in the hallway, I snapped out of this reverie about the past. It was 1987 and the Lord's Anointed had finally arrived, looking tired. We all knelt and kissed his ring. He apologized for his lateness; he had been greeted with such enthusiasm along the way, he said, that it had thrown his schedule off. I cleared my throat and presented each of my children, which took quite some time. The pope commented graciously on each one: "Drygidka? The youngest? Her name makes her a true daughter of Gdansk. Victoria? It all began with her, and she is the one they show to the world." He made the V-for-victory sign, the most eloquent of all symbols, with his fingers. In fact, little Maria Wiktoria had been a resistance heroine almost from the moment of her birth in 1982. At the time, I was still interned in a small government hunting lodge at Arlamowo, not far from the Soviet border. Meanwhile, my daughter was being christened without me in Gdansk, in the presence of several dozen friends and supporters, as well as an envoy of the Apostolic See. "She began early," I joked.

We went into another room, where John Paul II and I began talking politics, even though it was already nearly midnight. How could I have supposed, when I was locked up in Arlamowo, that a few years later I would be talking with the pope, sitting on the same couch with him in the episcopal palace? The decrees of Providence are mysterious. The pope was here in Poland. He inspired in us feelings for a freedom that we had never even known, not only because he was an exceptional man, but because we all felt that behind him stood God.

I presented him with my gift. John Paul II began leafing mechanically through the pages, and I could see that he was very tired. I also knew that he had already seen the book, for the French publisher had sent him one of the first copies. Yet in spite of his exhaustion he went on talking animatedly. "I wouldn't have come to Poland if the government hadn't allowed me to visit Gdansk," he told me. Then he asked me how the Polish people were managing to survive a crisis that put their future in such doubt. How did people cope while living in the grip of a government in which they played no part?

By way of answer, I repeated what I had said so many times before: that the energies of the nation needed to be liberated and that it could happen only by burying the hatchet; we needed to reform the system, but without violence. I said all this with absolute conviction. Our methods recalled those of Gandhi, the pope observed. I wasn't certain that we deserved such a flattering comparison. "If the world grasps what you are trying to do, if it sees in your movement hope and a way to resolve conflicts," the Holy Father went on, "it is precisely because you have renounced violence and let yourselves be guided by the teachings of the Church."

Neither emigration nor the doubts in the minds of some Solidarity militants could dull the desire for freedom. Poland as a nation had reached the point of no return, I told John Paul II. Our nation was experiencing a time of accelerated change and a spiritual reawakening, and these involved a return to traditional values — family, homeland, and Church.

During the fall of 1980, in a record time of three months, a 140-foot monument had been erected near the gates of the Gdansk Shipyards to honor its dead: three anchors were affixed to three giant crosses. The monument was unveiled on the tenth anniversary of the December 1970 demonstrations, when the Militia had killed forty-eight workers protesting price hikes. During the ceremony, which was held in frigid weather, three hundred thousand people listened to the *Lacrymosa*, a meditation on death composed for the occasion by Krzysztof Penderecki. No one would have suspected that exactly a year later, in this same place, battalions of ZOMO would attack the shipyards and force their way through gates already flattened by tanks.

Now, in June 1987, the pope's voice rang out from beneath the very same monument. Though some had tried to convince the secretariat of the

Vatican that the pope should avoid visiting it, John Paul II himself made clear his desire to pay his respects to those it memorialized, knowing full well the significance the monument had assumed. It was eventually agreed that the Holy Father's visit to Solidarity Square would be "unofficial" — a term that of course meant nothing to the Poles, who followed him everywhere. The Security Service cleared the square of people, trying to minimize the impact of his visit. But that only had the negative effect of making the square look sinister.

So then the government created its own crowd, calling on Party loyalists and young people from state-run enterprises to turn out and welcome the pope. Some of them regarded this as a privilege — many agreed without realizing that the whole thing was being staged — and in some districts tickets to the monument were in such demand they were issued by lottery. Party members who knew what was really going on tried to wriggle out of the trip, but a bit of persuasion brought obedience: "Comrades! It is every member's duty! You must greet the pope with dignity!" Despite all this, there still weren't enough people to fill the square, so buses were driven to the state-owned farms and loaded up with people the government hoped would be ignorant of the complicated issues involved — and hence would most reliably represent the interests of the state. Those chosen gathered at the shipyards (which were closed for the day), and they stood around smoking and waiting for instructions. They were told to react neither too coldly nor too enthusiastically to the pope, and of course there were to be no upraised hands, no V-for-victory signs, no cheering. Each of them was handed a small flag and assigned a place to stand. Solidarity Square was at last ready to greet the guest from the Vatican.

The line of vehicles passed quickly through the silent crowd. There was no clamoring, no emotion, only small flags waving mechanically back and forth. The figure in white approached the monument, followed close behind by Cardinal Glemp and Archbishops Casaroli, Colasuonno, and Martínez. The pope knelt, prayed, and gazed thoughtfully at the three anchors. "Divine Providence could not do better," he said. "In this place, silence is a cry!"

A moment later, he returned to his car and was driven toward the jubilant crowds decked out in traditional costumes. Meanwhile "the guardians of society" stayed behind to protect the monument from the common people who had gathered five hundred yards away; those who had been designated to stand closer went off to get the hot meal the government had prepared for them.

For me the image of these puppets around the monument remains a nightmarish one. On one side of the monument, a few hundred yards away, was a joyous throng of men and women singing songs and children holding flowers, while on the other stood a morose crew sullenly waving little flags and then waiting in line between the endless rows of police dogs and the silent ZOMO agents for their ration of pea soup.

That afternoon, I was able to receive Holy Communion from the hands of John Paul II, with his ringing words echoing in my ears:

> One of the state's most important tasks is to create a space in which everyone, through his work, can grow and develop. Individual development in this created space is the precondition of the common good. If it does not exist, if life becomes too constricting and too narrow for human initiative — even if in the name of some collective good — that will work against society and against the common good. . . . Shoulder each other's burdens!

These words, spoken not far from my gray apartment complex, touched a million hearts along with my own. Seeing the hundreds of banners, and feeling the enthusiasm of a crowd no longer cowed by the police, I became sure all at once that the era of intimidation was over. General Jaruzelski's program of "entente and struggle" was coming to an end. Without a legalized Solidarity, there would be no social stability and no reform.

Alas, two more years were to pass before it all came true.

10
The Referendum

T he pope's third visit to his homeland in 1987 made my hopes for the future soar. I felt like Icarus, except that my wings were attached not with wax, but with steel. At a meeting of Solidarity's Provisional Council, convened to discuss what effect perestroika would have on Poland, I couldn't share my colleagues' general cynicism about how much, or rather how little, Gorbachev's policies would help our cause. This was no time for cynicism. The boisterous demonstrations held in late August to celebrate the seventh anniversary of Solidarity's founding were exuberant and spontaneous, I thought, and in no way designed to provoke confrontation with the security forces. And in September, when the members of the National Work Group once again began stirring up trouble in the union ranks, I was unfazed. All I could think about was how hard it was for nearsighted people to appreciate the beauty of a distant landscape.

On September 27, 1987, Vice-President George Bush paid a four-day visit to Poland. Our talk was both wide-ranging and concrete. Mr. Bush informed me that, following the Polish authorities' announcement of an amnesty in September 1986, President Reagan had decided to resume diplomatic dialogue with the Polish government. But, he added, relations between the two countries would not normalize until the government's respect for law, and for our nation's aspirations, had increased substantially. That could happen quickly. He cited Argentina as a country that had moved rapidly from totalitarianism to comparative democracy. The struggle for human rights was affecting the foreign policies of countries around the world more and more, including his own. Bush stressed that he had long wanted to visit Poland; the Poles had helped the United States win its independence, thanks to heroes such as Tadeusz Kosciuszko and

Kazimierz Pulaski, heroes enshrined in the American pantheon. Our joint visit to the grave of Jerzy Popieluszko was proof of the goodwill the U.S. government felt toward our efforts. Our leaders, on the other hand, showed far less goodwill. When Vice-President Bush met with opposition leaders Bronislaw Geremek, Janusz Onyszkiewicz, and Klemens Szaniawski, their own government accused them of consorting with the CIA.

Since 1945, Poles had rarely attached much importance to legislation passed by "their" parliament, the Sejm — a state of affairs that clearly suited the Communists, who routinely falsified the results of every election. In October 1987, however, dressed in their customary sheep's clothing, the Communists decided to call a national referendum over whether the progressive economic and social reforms currently taking place in Poland should continue or not. As if there were any real reforms! On October 23, the language of the referendum was made public:

1. Do you favor full implementation of the program for radical stabilization of the economy presented to the Sejm, a program that aims at significantly improving the quality of life, knowing that this will bring with it rapid change and a difficult period of two to three years?
2. Do you favor the Polish model of a profound democratization of political life, the goal of which is to strengthen industrial autonomy, increase the rights of the citizens, and enlarge their role in governing the country?

I made it clear that the nation should refuse to go along with this obvious propaganda ploy. In reality, the government's economic plans consisted merely of half-hearted alternatives to the status quo and one or two pieties about improving the quality of life. The whole point of the referendum was to quell any possible doubts that the Communists wanted to "stabilize the economy" they had destroyed, or "democratize profoundly" the political life they had stifled.

Solidarity's reply to the government's doubletalk was concrete. I called for a boycott. We needed to throw out the *nomenklatura*, introduce a market economy, subject any reform to the control of independent and popularly elected representatives, and reestablish union pluralism. The government lost the referendum held on November 29, because it did not get the required percentage of positive responses that it had set for itself — even by falsely exaggerating the percentage of voter turnout.*

---

* The official tally was calculated according to the number of registered voters and not actual votes.

The next day I was cornered by a horde of journalists wanting to get my views on the results and on Solidarity's prospects. They bombarded me with questions, and in response I gave them a brief photocopied statement in which I had written that Poles needed pluralism the way they needed air; only pluralism would prevent totalitarianism. And as for Solidarity, my deep conviction, I continued, was that it would stay a reform movement for some time yet, for as long as the government denied responsibility for its disasters. Solidarity would end its political activity and function purely as a trade union only when the situation in Poland had returned to normal.

A few weeks earlier, on October 25, 1987, at a joint session of the underground Solidarity Provisional Coordinating Board and the Provisional Council, we appointed a new leadership for the union and christened it the National Executive Board. But we didn't succeed in attracting representatives from the aforementioned National Work Group, who by then had become violently opposed to me and took no pains to conceal it. Not long afterward, the members of our National Executive Board were summoned to appear before the Militia. We breathed a sigh of relief when the meeting turned out merely to be a matter of "explanatory protocol."

At my urgent request, another meeting was held on November 7, in Warsaw, attended by those who had signed the declaration issued just before the pope's visit. We didn't know it, but that meeting helped create the framework for what was eventually to become the Civic Committee; all we thought we were doing at the time was groping for an answer to the question of where any fundamental reforms should be heading. My opening statement was:

> We meet at a time when something significant is taking place throughout the Eastern Bloc and particularly at its center. Events are rendering obsolete the way the economy has been managed and the government has been organized up to now. These events will change Poland, and these changes have begun. But we want actions, not words. We in the People's Republic of Poland have learned not to put our trust in high-minded phrases. Too often these have turned out to be only hollow words, broken promises, and broken agreements.
>
> That is why Solidarity has decided to boycott the November referendum. We are not the ones who take this referendum lightly. Those who first announced it, agreed upon the date and format, and then only afterward consulted with each other behind closed doors about what questions to put to the nation — they are the ones who make a mockery of it. Now that these questions have

been made public, these same people say that their meaning will become clear only after the referendum. Can we believe in a government that claims to recognize society's right to express its sovereign will when it also treat us like pawns? In the People's Republic of Poland the people have been the victims of more than one policy shift: first liberalization is announced, and then there is a tightening of the screws; first they give us something, and then they take it back. This can't go on. We shall have as much freedom and democracy as we need. We shall hold on firmly to what we have achieved and defend it.

At about the same time, I gave a long interview to two reporters from the *Washington Post*. With admirable stubbornness, these gentlemen of the press asked me various questions that boiled down essentially to one, and it involved the creation of the National Executive Board: why create it now? Our intention, I replied, was to counter the government's ploy, and the board was designed to coordinate and articulate our response to it.

There was another question dealing with some of the problems that, I thought, *should* have been addressed by the referendum. These problems could be grouped under three headings, I explained — economic, union-related, and political — and they should have been formulated in concrete terms.

Next the reporters asked me if the government was disposed to hold talks with certain representatives of the opposition. I tried to phrase my response to these nice Americans in the clearest way I could. I said we wouldn't have tried to force a general (Jaruzelski) to sit down at the same table with a corporal (meaning me) if the general had fulfilled his promises.

Finally, they asked: If the government made Solidarity legal once again, would we act differently than we had in 1980? I replied in the words of the electrician from the shipyards that I was: "The ship of state is leaking. For some time now the nation has been prepared to endure whatever it takes to fix it, but the government hasn't been. To its great shame, communism has turned a proud and valiant nation into a pauper."

I spent the New Year's holidays celebrating with my family, but also watching events with keen interest. Another Reagan-Gorbachev summit had taken place in Washington early in December, and its effects were already becoming evident. Right before New Year's Eve, as I recall, the Soviets announced their intention to pull all of their troops out of Afghanistan and end nine years of occupation. And in Poland, meanwhile, the government had taken a baby step in the right direction: as of January 1, 1988, Radio Free Europe broadcasts would no longer be jammed. Sitting comfortably with my champagne glass in my hand in front of the TV, listening to the sound of my children's laughter, I nevertheless couldn't help thinking about the difficult road that still lay ahead for me and my fellow Poles. The year had ended with me standing in front of scores of television crews, making all sorts of predictions and statements. How well would they stand the test of time?

I am not known for being afraid of journalists. During the second half of 1987, in fact, I made myself so available to them and gave them so much material that they should have been wildly grateful. My intention was always to explain that any progress we were making in Poland would have been inconceivable without genuine and widespread solidarity (in small letters) — whether in battling acid rain, restoring dignity to our lives, or thinking about our grandchildren's and great-grandchildren's future. Civilization is built on the efforts of everyone in the human family, but those efforts ought to begin at home. Even after an operation that restored democracy and independence, my poor homeland, drained nearly dry after fifty years of parasites and outside interests, would remain ill for a long time.

In my talks with journalists I frequently used analogies. Thus when they asked me just what kind of dialogue Solidarity wanted to have with the government, I compared the political scene in Poland to a chessboard on which the government wanted itself to be the queen — and have the unions be its pawns. What did I think of perestroika in the Soviet Union? they asked. One privately owned café in Moscow, I replied, did not constitute reform — particularly when it was frequented mainly by the KGB! If someone tried to extract my opinion about the chances for reform in the other Eastern Bloc countries, I provided what became known as "the Walesa fraction": a number whose common denominator was communism, but whose numerator was a variable that, depending on its size, increased or diminished the weight of the denominator it was sitting on top of. When I was asked how I saw Poland's current situation, I replied that although one could turn the contents of an aquarium into fish soup, the reverse wouldn't work.

More than once, I expressed alarm over what was happening to Polish youth, who, since there was no housing and no prospect of upward mobility, kept their eyes glued to the West. That is still true today. When I question the under-thirty generation, I find that all of them know someone who has emigrated. Beginning in nursery school, Polish children regale each other with stories about "capitalist" toys, stores, and cars. What is appalling is the meager standard of living we have attained because of what happened at Yalta. The average Pole earns between a seventh and a tenth of what a Frenchman or an American does — and that is why Polish youth are fed up and would rather use rocks than arguments. My own children jump all over me about material things, and I have to threaten them with a spanking before they stop. Ah, me! How much easier it would be to have a classic revolution in which you took from one to distribute to ten! But today two eras are colliding, and former Eastern Bloc countries should follow Spain's example: rather than indulge in an endless catalog of grievances over the past, or commit purges, these countries should show instead a willingness to work under humane conditions and with the goodwill of a competent government.

On December 16, 1987, when I placed flowers beneath the Gdansk Shipyards monument — as I had done so many times before — I emphasized with all the strength I had that in Poland we were condemned to live together. We would succeed only if we all understood each other, if everyone worked toward the same goals — while still respecting the individuality of our convictions and beliefs. Solidarity ought to struggle not for power, but for the kind of mandate that comes through democratic elections and compromise. The really vital reforms would involve the very structure of government (or other institutions, such as universities or the press), not just who gets chosen for what team. Time has shown that I was right.

"The government may not like the cold shower we're giving it, but it's a lot better than a bloodbath," I told reporters during the interviews I gave in early 1988. The irony was that while many individuals were mature enough for pluralism, society as a whole, forced into a "monism" by years of communism, wasn't. "The only just system," as communism was called, proved itself the most absurd of impediments. Poland was ready for reform in 1980, but the government did its best to prevent reform while still imposing endless price hikes. These price hikes, it is true, didn't bring about famine, but they induced a kind of material malnourishment. They lowered our expectations and limited our choices — rather than eat off plates, we would learn to accept eating off mess kits; rather than own ten pairs of shoes, we would own only one; rather than take showers, we would become used to sponge baths; we might own a television set, but we wouldn't expect to be able to use it. It is under conditions like these that idealists and utopians rise up to demand profound changes, and they are the ones who make the world turn. Not all their ideals are realizable, of course; but from several spadefuls of sand come several flecks of gold.

On a more practical level, I spent less and less time with my family, and began to wonder increasingly if I ought not resign my job at the shipyards. I finally did resign in February 1988, and my decision was largely influenced by unfolding political events and growing popular unrest. In late January and early February, I was visited by several diplomats, notably the West German minister for foreign affairs, Hans-Dietrich Genscher, and the United States assistant secretary of state, John C. Whitehead (both had earlier meetings with General Jaruzelski; Whitehead also met with Cardinal Glemp).

In the interval between these two visits, on January 17, I took part in an unforgettable ceremony in memory of the victims of Auschwitz, a ceremony to which I wish to devote a few pages.

11
Auschwitz

On January 18, 1988, seventy-five Nobel laureates gathered in Paris to ponder the threats facing humanity on the threshold of the twenty-first century. The date had been carefully chosen, for it was both the birthday of Martin Luther King, Jr., and the anniversary of the day the Nazis began tearing down the Auschwitz death camp. Toward the end of 1987, I had received an invitation from French president Mitterrand, under whose patronage the conference was to take place, as well as from Elie Wiesel, the Jewish writer and Nobel Peace Prize laureate, who was organizing it. To both I expressed my desire to participate, and my hope that the Polish authorities would allow it.

I reflected on the dire legacies the twenty-first century would inherit from ours and started formulating the speech I wished to give. Today, added to the already somber legacy of the death camp, was the legacy of all the totalitarian ideologies that, in 1987, still dominated large parts of the globe. I badly wanted a Polish voice to be heard in that conference hall in Paris, in front of the cameras. There was so much I wanted to talk about. I knew I could speak with authority. Despite daily signs that totalitarianism was weakening, Poland was still living in its grip. Like all Poles, I had endured the effects of ordinary human hatred and greed, even when they operated under the name of "class struggle." Like many Poles, I continued to risk everything in the struggle to do away with the twisted logic of Communist rule.

I was denied an exit visa.

And then out of the blue I learned that this same conference was going to open in Poland itself — more precisely, at Auschwitz, on January 17, 1988, the day before it was scheduled to open in Paris. A Boeing 707 carrying thirty-seven people landed in Cracow, and among them were five Nobel laureates: Elie Wiesel (who was born in a region of what is now Romania), president of the Holocaust Memorial Council; two other Peace Prize laureates, Mairead Corrigan McGuire from Northern Ireland and the American Betty Williams Perkins; the Italian physiologist Daniel Bovet and the American chemist Herbert Brown. With them were my dear friends Egil Aarvik, president of the Nobel Prize Committee, and Maurice Goldstein, secretary of the International Auschwitz Committee. It was a statement by the former American ambassador to Austria that had inspired this preconference trip to Poland. To better understand the threats hanging over the twenty-first century, he had said, one must first go to Auschwitz. He was taken at his word.

As soon as I heard the news, I too left for Auschwitz.* At eleven o'clock on the morning of January 17, we all met at the entrance to the largest and most horrific necropolis in the world. Arm in arm, we walked the camp's roads. Each step in this place of horror drew us into our own thoughts. Mine turned to my parents.

When I was born at half past three on the morning of September 29, 1943, my father Boleslaw was in a Nazi concentration camp. His arrest had come without any warning for his family, when I was still in my mother Felicja's womb. One dark night, policemen on horseback arrived, searched our home, found something incriminating, and took my father away with them. Later they came back to do another search and stole my mother's watches and rings. My mother was in despair: they had taken her wedding ring. She told me later that she was sure it meant that her husband would never return, that her married life was over.

The men arrested were first detained at Chalin, in a building that after the war was turned into a school I later attended. I remember seeing blood still staining the walls from the savage beatings the Nazis had inflicted. Afterward, my father was sent to the camp at Mlyniec. That winter the prisoners lay on the ground in unheated cells; their hair froze while they slept and stuck to the frost-covered walls; worn down by hunger and illness, they soon began dying. My mother tried every means possible to smuggle food in for my father, and sometimes she succeeded. She would slip out of the house in the middle of the night and take secret paths through the forest, so as not to be spotted by the Germans. As long as my

---

* The Polish village is Oswiecim, but it is as Auschwitz, its German name, that it lives in infamy. — Ed.

father was in a work camp, some contact was possible. Mama went through the forest, weeping, praying that her trip wouldn't be in vain.

My family had always been very close. My father's brother was killed during World War I. One day he went off to fight and he never came back. We don't even know where he was buried. Grandmother Walesa, born Glonek, was a very pious woman, and for the rest of her life she continued to pray for her son's return. She was never able to accept his death. He had been in the cavalry, and sometimes she ran out to the road, convinced she'd heard the sound of approaching hoofbeats.

The people of our village hated the Nazis, who had destroyed their world. Under the occupation, two Germans lived in Popowo: Krepiec and Broch. Two Polish families, the Bialoskorskis and Uminskis, were thrown out of their homes so that Krepiec and Broch could move in. Krepiec and Broch were themselves hostile to their Polish neighbors, but the daughter of one of them fell in love with a Polish farmhand who had snatched her from the jaws of death when she got herself caught between the gears of a combine. Love conquered all, and everyone in the village knew about it — and benefitted from it. The young woman always warned people when the Nazis were about to come to the village.

It was commonly understood that slaughtering a pig for food, like taking food to the partisans, was very dangerous. All meat belonged to the occupiers. Apparently, before he was arrested, my father had tried to slaughter a pig. He stunned the animal, but didn't stick it with enough force, so the pig came to, escaped, and trotted off into the woods covered in blood. The police followed its tracks to our house, and things looked black. But thanks to some miracle, possibly in the form of a bribe, the whole business was hushed up. The pig, however, was confiscated.

Wehrmacht deserters turned up regularly in the vicinity of the village, and I know that our family, among others, hid them. They sometimes took shelter in the stables, and children brought them soup in pails so small they looked like toys. The partisans used the forest not far from the village of Brudzenio as their hideout, and the children took food to them, too, sometimes covering a distance of nearly three miles.

After the war, corpses were discovered in Brudzenio (where today there is a cross over a mass grave). It was there that the Nazis executed people, especially the young men, from the surrounding villages. The grisly chore of exhuming the bodies was performed by those Germans who had failed to get away and were still living in the neighborhood. They were ordered to dig up the earth with their bare hands, pull out the corpses, wash them, and then line them up neatly. When they had finished, the Poles gathered to identify their loved ones. In agonies of grief they threw themselves on the Germans and beat them, until an officer forced them to stop and to stand aside. What they saw overwhelmed them all. Some of the disinterred bodies had their hands over their mouths, as though trying to keep out the dirt. They had probably been buried alive.

My father was lucky enough to die at home. After the war he returned to Popowo, but lived only another two months before succumbing to exhaustion and illness. He was not yet thirty-four years old. We, his family, were left behind. When I was thirty-four, I was just beginning to become active in the Free Union: I published pamphlets, and enjoyed my young family. Of course I couldn't remember the war, but the stories my family had told were a part of my childhood.

That January day at Auschwitz, those stories rang in my ears once again.

Walking along the wall of death, we stopped for a moment in front of Block 17, in which Elie Wiesel had been interned as a child. The building was unimaginably sinister. We were there to remind the world of the tragedy of the twentieth century, said Maurice Goldstein; those who had survived were never to forget the victims or forgive those responsible. "Forgiveness can come only from those who were cremated," he began, but broke into sobs. We came to the infamous slogan *"Arbeit Macht Frei"* ("Work Makes [One] Free") — the most complete mockery of work and freedom ever known. Only Satan in the flesh could have put such a motto in such a place, I said to myself.

Next to the small crematorium near the main gate, Jewish and Christian prayers were said for the victims. Rabbi Haskel Besser from New York said the Kaddish, and Father Henryk Jankowski read Psalm 129, *De profundus,* in Latin. We, Catholics and Jews, wept together. From the crematorium, we walked in silence to Birkenau, taking the long road from the gate of the ruins of the huge crematorium — that giant furnace of death, the grave of millions of people, mostly Jewish. There each of us spoke in turn. I began:

As a son of this land forever marked by the stigma of Auschwitz, and in praying with you and in paying homage to all those murdered, I bow to the tragedy of the Jewish people that was enacted here.

On this land, Poles and the Jews had lived together side by side for centuries, for good and for ill. The will of invaders brought this history to an end, and here were perpetrated crimes that human memory will never forget. Here they exterminated the Jewish people, from the newborn to the aged, in the crematoria of Auschwitz, Treblinka, and the other death camps. This tragedy for the Jews will forever serve as a warning of horror to us all.

We will preserve the memory of those who perished here and in other camps: Jews, Poles, Russians, French, Gypsies, Greeks, Yugoslavs, Belgians, people of all nationalities. We believe those who died are already in another realm, and perhaps they, better than we, will manage to judge a world in which such a monstrosity could occur.

For us, the living, memory and duty remain. Their death tells us a simple and deeply moving truth — that every sacred and human law by which we live is broken when we disguise hatred as ideology. Anti-Semitism is hatred. Let no other word ever conceal the shame of it.

After me, Elie Wiesel spoke.

Lech Walesa, my friend, thank you. Today there are among us men and women who wish to work for the good of future generations.

Lech Walesa, you are a Pole and I am a Jew. You are very dear to me. Both of us are convinced that we must remember, so as to give to our children dignity and hope. There is hope here. Look around you. Once I came here in the middle of the night, and I thought then that evil was infinite. Gathered together were humans from all over the world, speaking in their languages, moving ever closer to the mortal fire. I wondered then: Is this the end of the Jewish people? The end of humanity? The end of the world?

A world did indeed end here. A world we must reconstruct. A world in which human beings are free — free because they are human beings. Whatever our faiths, we are all children of the same God.

Lech Walesa, my friend! We have gathered here for the forty-third anniversary of the great evacuation from this camp, and to open the conference to which President Mitterrand has invited us. This day unfolds in an atmosphere of sadness and meditation. We see to what level humanity descends when it tolerates murder and oppression. Ours is a sad meditation, but in it there is also hope, hope that we ourselves must create. Here where hope had its terminus, we must say that humanity is worthy of hope.

Lech Walesa, we assure you that we shall not forget you. You are our representative here in Poland, and we shall be your representatives throughout the entire world. We shall speak, we shall ask, we shall remind. There has been enough suffering!

Elie Wiesel was far more effective than I at evoking the atmosphere of nightmare that still permeates Auschwitz. Listening to him speak, I understood with a stinging immediacy the real horror of the camp — and I realized that Elie Wiesel, Nobel Peace Prize laureate, was alive today only thanks to a miracle. Only by extraordinary luck did he not forever remain just one more missing Jewish child.

Will a younger generation fully understand what it means that on the side of the freight cars in which Wiesel and millions of others rode, was printed the word CARGO? The evil of the Holocaust was expressed in the language and protocol of bureaucracy. "Cargo" was designated to leave one place and to arrive at another at precisely calculated intervals. From all over Europe these freight cars arrived with their "cargo." It all required hard work and conscientious organization. Most horrifying of all is that the madness of Nazism was based upon a system and a logic. It was well planned and well executed. At a precise point in time, a certain number of Jews would be arrested, transported with expert technical skill, and then, according to schedule, exterminated.

How can any person of faith account for the existence of such places as Auschwitz-Birkenau, Kolyma, or the Solovietski Islands? How could God allow the extermination of entire peoples? These are questions that have haunted us all. I finally concluded that this example of pure evil, rather than destroying our notion of God, follows from it. If we believe that God gave us free will, we cannot imagine He will intervene and limit human autonomy. If He has truly granted us the right to choose, He must then be content to observe what we do. Perhaps He permits such horrors in order to show what our life here is worth. From the perspective of eternity, the Holocaust was only a fleeting moment of darkness. How hard it is to admit that we are here only a brief moment, and yet for that moment we must answer for all eternity.

Auschwitz showed evil to the world, but it also showed the capacity for goodness and dignity inherent in humanity. There were some transcendent moments of selfless heroism. Father Maximilian Kolbe, Dr. Janusz Korczak shepherding his orphaned charges, the rabbis going to their deaths praying, persons unknown offering their last crust of bread to the starving. Auschwitz tells us that we are not merely earthly, and that we are more than combinations of chemical elements. If that were all we were, where would some find the strength to maintain their dignity in the face of physical annihilation? Evil creates the opportunity for good to manifest itself. The Jewish people and all the other exterminated peoples delivered up their martyrdom to our collective memory. If today totalitarian regimes are crumbling, it is thanks to those whose suffering defined good and evil, now and until the end of human time.

After the ceremony in the synagogue, a glass of kosher vodka, and a farewell on the Cracow airfield, I proceeded to Czestochowa. I wanted to pray for peace, pray that never again would there be another Auschwitz. I wondered about the indecipherable plans of God, who singled out the unhappy land of Poland as the site for the extermination of the Jewish people — some of whom, despite everything, survived.

I was grateful to Elie Wiesel for his powerful message and his words of understanding. There has been misunderstanding. I recall how unfair I thought the truncated version of Claude Lanzmann's celebrated film *Shoah*, when it was aired on Polish television in 1985. Perhaps the film seen in its entirety creates a different impression, but that hour and a half was simply unwatchable. A drama as complex as the Holocaust cannot be condensed into a series of local interviews and public statements, particularly when they do not take into account the generational and cultural differences between the interviewers and those interviewed. Such an approach makes it hard to reach agreement and genuine conclusions. That approach, I remember feeling bitterly, divides people and stands in the way of mutual understanding.

It was in this climate of mistrust that the affair of the Carmelite nuns of Auschwitz exploded in 1986, creating a wave of hostility against Poland. The Carmelites — an order governed by strict rules of silence, contrition, and prayer — wanted to set up a convent, a small community, in the area around the Auschwitz camp. The sisters planned to replicate the small one set up at Dachau several years earlier. At Auschwitz they thought they had found a suitable building, a former theater adjoining the wall of the camp, which the SS had used as a warehouse for storing the deadly Zyklon B gas. The building, however, led directly into the camp and fell inside the perimeter designated by UNESCO as an inviolable cultural site.

In the Western press, the *Kirche in Not* [Church in Need] organization, which had long aided the Polish Church, published a rather clumsily worded appeal for financial aid to restore the building; it was followed soon afterward by an article appearing in the Belgian newspaper *Le Soir* about the proposed Auschwitz convent. The news triggered violent protests from the Jewish community, first in Belgium, and then all over Europe and America, reminding the Church that no religious sanctuary of any kind could be built on the site of the extermination of the Jews, in their necropolis. Over the ashes of millions of victims, at the major site of the Holocaust, an eternal and undisturbed silence must reign. Suddenly there were hundreds of articles furiously protesting the installation of the convent. Many were convinced that a new structure was to be erected within the camp's limits, so that visits to the site would also mean trespassing on Church property. They did not understand that the plan entailed merely upgrading a structure that had been in existence for decades.

The issue seemed to have been settled when Jewish, Catholic, and Protestant authorities met in Geneva in 1986. It was decided that a center for prayer and meditation for the Carmelites should be built a few miles from the death camp. But that center would take time to complete, and even today hasn't been finished. The land had to be acquired, the access road laid out, the building built — all of which took time and money, and everyone was impatient.

In July 1989, the affair took a dramatic turn. A group of Jewish youths on a pilgrimage to Auschwitz pelted the convent with rocks and even tried to break in, and this provoked a furious reaction from some Polish workers, for whom the nuns are like saints. The world press circulated an unfortunate photograph of a rabbi trying to force his way into the enclosure, while a Polish worker from the building was dumping a bucket of dishwater onto his head. The photograph was exploited, and from a small misfortune grew a huge conflict. In the United States — particularly among the younger generation, who hadn't been through the war or ever been to Poland grew the idea that the Poles had been behind the annihilation of the Jews. A friend told me that when she was in a taxi in New York and told the driver, who was Jewish, that she was from Poland, he stopped the car and told her to get out, shouting, "You people helped the Germans murder the Jews!" In reaction to this reaction, a wave of anti-Semitism swelled in Poland. Some people said, "They're fighting against the Carmelites because they want to distract attention away from the young Palestinians being killed by Israeli soldiers. They see the mote in the eye of their neighbor, but ignore the beam in their own." Obviously, these polemics served no purpose.

The signers of the 1986 Geneva agreement met again in 1989 and managed to quiet the passions the incident had inflamed. Construction of the meditation center at the new site is progressing, and it will open soon. But the damage was done, and the image of the Poles suffered greatly. That is why I so welcomed Elie Wiesel's visit, a visit intended to be constructive instead of divisive.

• • •

In Czestochowa I prayed before the miraculous image of the virgin for the
vitality and strength of the Jewish people, for the souls of all the victims
of the war, for the peace of my father's soul, for my children's future. The
children: what lies in store for them? More and more often they had been
asking me, "What should we do? Your nonviolent approach isn't working," they would say. "Nonviolent struggle won't work against communism. Only fighting works." That frustration and anger became more and
more apparent in 1987. Young people were beginning to lose patience.

In the most recent workers' pilgrimage to Czestochowa, seventy thousand workers had gone to the sanctuary of Jasna Gora, despite the obstacles set up by the Militia to discourage them, because they wanted to
demonstrate that Solidarity was alive. Looking at the frieze showing the
Way of the Cross on the fortified wall of that historic monastery, and then
at the crowds, my feelings were mixed. For the first time slogans of hatred
were appearing on banners, which numbered in the thousands. "Did you
come here to complain?" I asked.

"No! To accuse!" they replied.

The prior of the monastery told them, "Even if your woes multiply,
even if the murderers of your fellow workers behave as if nothing has
happened, even if people choose to forget history, you must still not give
in to hatred. Hatred and class struggle are not legacies of Christianity."

The Nobel Prize conferred on me in 1983 carried with it a grave responsibility for all of Solidarity's members. The prize was testimony of international support for Solidarity and its causes, but it also linked that support
to nonviolent methods. There at Jasna Gora, I prayed that we would not
resort to accusation. Our strength lay in our faith that good shall triumph
over evil. Those who walked through the gates that mockingly proclaimed
Arbeit Macht Frei believed in this victory; so did the prisoners freezing to
death in the Siberian camps, and the workers dying from gunshot wounds
in the street; so did Martin Luther King, Father Jerzy Popieluszko, and
millions of others who gave their lives for freedom. What they believed
in, and what they died for, would bring us victory.

12
The First Avalanche

Beginning right after the government announced price hikes in February of 1988, the steepest since 1982, the word "strike" was in the air. Solidarity's Provisional Executive Board protested these price hikes strenuously, but fell short of calling for mass demonstrations. Demonstrations broke out anyway — in Warsaw, Gdansk, and Cracow. The increases were hardest on small businesses and on programs that fell within what was called the "budgetary sphere" — the civil service, health services, education, culture. This time, heavy industry managed to get a few breaks for once.

February 26 saw a significant development in Upper Silesia, near Gliwice. Solidarity's Regional Executive Board held its first meeting and openly elected as its official representative Henryk Sienkiewicz, a Ph.D. in technological sciences from Katowice, who had long been director of the planning bureau for the coal industry. He came from the ranks of the *nomenklatura* itself, a clear sign that Solidarity's base was broadening.

In March, I was denied an exit visa to go to Australia to attend the congress of the International Confederation of Free Trade Unions. Some things hadn't changed. There were times I felt nothing would ever change. In moments of fatigue, I used to compare my political prospects to those of a fly trapped in hay. Better to be trapped in hay than trapped in amber, I would say to myself; at least I can move a little. So I went on granting interviews, making myself hoarse, and quietly plotting ways to combat communism.

What pained me most was the visible increase in poverty in Poland. Young people now were beginning to form radical organizations. In Gdansk, the most powerful such organization openly called itself the Federation of Militant Youth; it was made up mainly of high-school students. The organization with the most solid "ideological" foundations, the one essentially committed to nonviolence and ecological concerns, was the Movement for Peace and Freedom — the first of its kind in the Eastern Bloc and still around today. Certain methods and styles adopted by these groups were not to my taste (the leather jackets, crew cuts, anarchistic slogans, smoke-filled meeting places), but now I realize that I didn't fully appreciate what these organizations accomplished. Their angry demands helped rekindle the spirits of young workers in the shipyards and steel mills; their raucous shouts triggered the first avalanche.

"The higher the sun, the nearer the victory." This self-confident appeal first echoed during the spring of 1982, and it came back into fashion six years later. On April 25, a day-long strike paralyzed public transportation in Bydgoszcz. The next day, near Cracow, the metal plant at the Lenin Steelworks at Nowa Huta stopped work. I was told later that neither placards nor religious images played any part in inspiring these stoppages; the workers decided on their own. The first person courageous enough to shut off his machine was a thirty-eight-year-old worker named Szewczuwaniec, who immediately organized a meeting of the workers. That afternoon, when the next shift came on, the strike spread to other divisions: the small-parts-and-wire mill, the iron forge, and the sheet-metal plant. The first to respond to Szewczuwaniec's call were the younger workers, most of whom could barely recall Solidarity's early days; soon their fervor spread to the veterans and seasoned professionals. Among the members of the strike committee (organized within a matter of a few hours), many had been interned during the state of martial law. The experience had marked them, but it had also put them into contact with intellectuals and scientists who had widened their perspective on issues.

Because we distrusted the phone system, news about the progress of the strike at the Lenin Steelworks came to me by couriers who rode the express trains between Gdansk and Cracow, a distance of four hundred miles. On the very first day, the steelworkers presented their list of seven demands. Each one involved salaries and the rehiring of fellow workers fired for engaging in union activity. So, despite what the official propaganda machine said about these demands, they did not involve fundamental questions about government organization — which could be dismissed as being unrealistic.

On the second day of the strike, messages of solidarity began pouring into the factory, notably from the editors of *Tygodnik Powszechny*

[*Universal Weekly*], the influential Cracow paper. The Cracow regional public prosecutor read a statement on television announcing that "illegal activities" would make the workers liable to legal penalties. In fact, the steelworkers had fully respected the law: they hadn't taken over the factory's printing press or radio communications by force; they hadn't confronted the guards at the plant; they had forced no one to join in the protest; and they hadn't tried to break down the doors of the canteen, which the management had closed on the strike's fourth day.

On April 27, plainly exceeding its jurisdiction, the management demanded a written commitment from all the protesters that they would resume work. Two days later, the striking workers were given an ultimatum: either return to work by ten o'clock that night or suffer the consequences. They would not be paid for the hours they missed because of the strike. Management was doing everything it could to suppress the workers' protest before the traditional May Day celebration, but the strikers stood their ground during this first phase in the war of nerves. On the afternoon of April 30, a division of the ZOMO took positions in front of the factory; early the following morning, the ZOMO returned to their barracks without having launched an attack. On May 1, spontaneous and violent clashes erupted in a dozen Polish cities, and with them came expressions of support for the striking steelworkers. Before several thousand people who assembled for Sunday mass at Saint Brygid's, I spoke about how uneasy I was over the workers' welfare. I also reiterated my appeal to the government for genuine economic, social, and political reform in Poland. "Show your solidarity with those in Nowa Huta," I said — to which those present reacted by chanting enthusiastically, "Tomorrow we strike!" Once the mass was over, ZOMO divisions set upon the faithful, provoking a riot with clubbing and stone-throwing. In a burst of military zeal, two members of the ZOMO forced open the doors of the sanctuary, but they were surrounded and disarmed within seconds.

That evening, the strike committee of the Lenin Steelworks sent an open letter to Deputy Prime Minister Zdzislaw Sadowski:

Despite our goodwill, the plant management has broken off negotiations. . . . Furthermore, the press and television are spreading false information about us, our actions, and our demands. We are well aware that a work stoppage in such a large enterprise involves material losses. . . . We also suspect that this strike will be blamed for the low levels of productivity and shoddy organization, and therefore for all of the lamentable slowness in implementing necessary economic reforms. . . . The health of every Cracow citizen, starting with us, has suffered from pollution caused by the Nowa Huta plant. . . . Because of the importance of the problems we raise, we ask that you respond to our letter without further delay.

On May 2, the steelworkers heaved a sigh of relief: a strike had begun up in "my" shipyards, initiated by the younger workers in the K-1 division. After a brief meeting called by twenty-nine-year-old welder Jan Stanecki, the striking workers raised the Solidarity logo so that it could fly with the flags left over from the May Day celebrations. Then, some four hundred strong, off they marched to management headquarters, where they selected four delegates for a core protest committee. After finalizing a few preliminary details, this committee confronted the general manager of the shipyards in his office and presented him with these five demands:

1. Raise wages substantially.
2. Legalize Solidarity's activities in the Gdansk Shipyards.
3. Free all political prisoners.
4. Rehire all workers fired for political reasons.
5. Refrain from any show of force against workers in the shipyards.

Alarmed by the scope of the demands, the manager stubbornly attempted to get them to back down, and the disgusted workers walked out of the office, slamming the door behind them. It was decided that there was no alternative to a sit-down strike.

On that day, as bad luck would have it, I had to take a brief sick leave and couldn't make it to work that morning. My feeling was that a strike at the shipyards just then was premature, since public support for the strike was not yet firmly behind us. But as the hours passed and the protest grew, it soon became impossible for me, either as a worker at the shipyards or as the president of Solidarity, to distance myself from it — although I felt like a general without an army. I had to show that I was flexible and open to any possible approach. At the same time, since I had played so prominent a role in casting the bell of liberty, I decided also to play the role of main bellringer. Journalists told me later that they saw rekindled in me something of the old Walesa, the Walesa of August 1980, the Walesa who could instinctively sense a crowd's mood. I found this only partially flattering, since the present situation wasn't quite comparable to that "glorious August." The most significant difference was that since August 1980, we had lived our lives under martial law and now knew how the Communists reacted when their backs were to the wall. It might be that Jaruzelski and his team were on thinner ice than Gierek was eight years earlier, but that didn't mean our demands would penetrate the thick skulls of the Party policymakers. Plenty of just causes hadn't, and ended in bloodshed.

My fears proved partly justified. On the night of May 4, large divisions of the ZOMO, preceded by antiterrorist teams, forced their way through the gates of the Lenin Steelworks at Nowa Huta and embarked on a particularly brutal process of "pacification." After showering some of the buildings with small explosives and tear-gas grenades, they stormed the factory, wielding clubs, nightsticks, and hatchets. They ordered the workers to lie face down on the floor, where they were kicked and verbally abused. The women were treated no better than the men. Members of the Security Service, wearing combat uniforms and military caps, joined forces with the ZOMO. Doubtless doped up on amphetamines, they went on a rampage, destroying light equipment, clothing lockers, the altars in the factory chapel along with their liturgical icons; they even trampled on the red-and-white Polish flags. Swinging wildly in every direction, and sometimes hitting the workers, they shouted, "So you wanted to go on strike? Get back to work! Hey! You, and you, and you! Get back to work! Now!" Their salaries subsidized by workers' taxes, these parasites were paying the citizens back by teaching them "a little lesson."

I was probably the first to be told about the brutality against the representatives of the Church, who had stayed with the steelworkers throughout. Priests had also come to the Gdansk Shipyards, to keep up our morale and, if necessary, to serve as mediators. Dr. Tadeusz Goclowski, the bishop of Gdansk, must be singled out for commendation. He personally was responsible for protecting University of Gdansk students — demonstrating to show their solidarity with the steelworkers — from "pacification" measures. I know that this distinguished man had wanted very badly to come to the shipyards to say mass himself for the strikers, but Party and police authorities denied him permission. But he shrewdly found a way of showing us the Church hierarchy's support for the shipyard workers: he gave Father Zbigniew Bryk, the envoy of the curia of Gdansk who had received authorization to enter the shipyards, an ecclesiastical ornament that Pope John Paul II had used a year earlier when he said mass for the workers of the world.

Like the steelworkers, we sent an open letter to Deputy Prime Minister Sadowski:

> The strike by the personnel of the Gdansk Shipyards is in its third day. Through this action, the workers are expressing their opposition to a policy that lowers the standard of living for millions of ordinary people while simultaneously denying them their right to organize in defense of their interests. . . . Reform does not mean simply reorganization, but must be based on a change in our country's social structure. And this cannot be achieved without the support of the people and without the full participation of free unions. . . . We invite you to the Gdansk Shipyards with the hope of engaging you in serious discussion about these and other issues.

The deputy prime minister, with arrogance typical of the people then in power, made no reply whatsoever to our invitation.

The May strike would end without being resolved, even though, from the very beginning, our advisors (the brothers Jaroslaw and Lech Kaczynski, Andrzej Celinski, Aleksander Hall, Tadeusz Mazowiecki, and Andrzej Wielowieyski, the last two representing the episcopate) had been ready to begin immediate negotiations with the government. I sensed the workers' skepticism. Could anyone ever settle anything in a friendly way with the Party men? From the fire of radicalism were left the ashes of suspicion. During those long years of coercive suppression against our nonviolent struggle, our conviction grew that being in the right meant very little, since the Communists did not act ethically. The acid of this cynicism burned deep and its effects would be difficult to counteract. And yet, we would have been quite willing to forget that past, if only the government had relented and told us, "We grant you total pluralism and the right to organize freely." When talking with the strikers or meeting with the press, I stressed that while our struggle might take time, success was inevitable. I felt that way even though the manager of the shipyards, like a broken record, kept repeating that he would lose face if he even talked with us, since we were so utterly lacking in any patriotic allegiance to the factory. The only response we could give to this hollow rhetoric was to laugh bitterly.

At dawn on May 7, the manager hit below the belt: rather than negotiate, he simply ordered all work at the shipyards to come to a complete halt. His action angered me — and also goaded me into making a few abusive remarks at his expense, as I remember. But angry or not, I needed to come up with something concrete, so I suggested that the workers could, if necessary, be paid out of the Solidarity strike fund, and not lose even one zloty because of the walkout. My words of encouragement didn't lift their spirits for long. News of defeat arrived from the Lenin Steelworks. That, along with the management's constant ranting over the factory radio, softened the resolution of some strikers, particularly those who lived outside of Gdansk. Shipyard manager Tolwinski ordered that fliers be distributed announcing that anyone who returned to work would be treated to a paid holiday. And meanwhile, the Polish Press Agency was announcing to the world that the Gdansk Shipyards' entire financial situation was under review. Workers began drifting from the ranks to the shipyard gates. Most of those with the greatest powers of resistance were in their twenties; by the end of the strike, they made up nearly ninety percent of those who stood firm. They badly wanted a union that would defend them against the insults, injuries, and incompetence of their foremen.

From almost the moment I joined the strike, I had a sense that this time we wouldn't succeed. Yet I knew that I had to negotiate doggedly right up to the last minute, so that no one could accuse me later of negligence or lack of faith. When the lawyer Wladyslaw Sila-Nowicki, the only voice of opposition within General Jaruzelski's Advisory Council, arrived at the shipyards (he was invited to Gdansk through private channels, but came in an official capacity), he described to a small committee his conversation with Stanislaw Ciosek, the secretary of the Party's Central Committee. Sila-Nowicki reported that Ciosek had said, "Let them strike if they want, even for months. The government can wait until they get tired. In economic terms, the shipyards are less important than the steelworks."

Some thought that this was just a smokescreen, but I felt as though I'd been kicked in the stomach. My first thought was that my role wasn't what it used to be. My second was that Ciosek was telling the truth. At that very moment, I began thinking of ways to bring the strike to an honorable end. We would need to choose the right moment to make a dramatic exit from the shipyards — in closed ranks — but without having signed any compromising agreement. Sila-Nowicki's radically different view was that we should sign anything, because it might later serve as a starting point for new negotiations.

Thanks to the efforts of Bishop Goclowski — whom General Andrzejewski, the head of the Gdansk Militia, condescended to visit — the strike committee was finally able to begin official talks with the management of the shipyards. During the first round, only the wage demands were discussed. The management would not hear of legalizing Solidarity. Nor would they take our demands seriously. I had wanted the strike to continue until most of the country might join with us. It was not to be. The government continued to use the same clichés of psychological warfare. Late in the evening, several hundred ZOMO would appear in front of the shipyard gate looking ready to attack, and then, in perfect unison, wish the strikers sweet dreams. Once, they stood at the gates for as long as a quarter of an hour, beating their riot sticks against their plastic shields. Another night, out of the darkness flew two helicopters blasting the sounds of street-fighting, gunshots, and the rhythmic chanting of "Ge-sta-po!" from loudspeakers. (The next day, half of Gdansk was sure that people must have been killed at the shipyards, and penitents lined up in front of Father Bryk's confessional.)

On Sunday, May 8, talks resumed with the management, whose aggressive attitude was doubtless due to instructions given to them over the "red telephone." Our negotiators had the feeling they were being deceived in an effort to prod them into saying things they would later regret. Some hours later, manager Tolwinski even threatened to dismantle the shipyards, which provoked a stern declaration from the strike committee. Meanwhile, Sila-Nowicki, just off the phone from Warsaw, told me that General Kiszczak, the minister of the interior, was favorable to some of the workers' demands. He had given his word of honor that "nearly all the political prisoners" would shortly be released. "We're just starting to spar," I said to a fellow striker, "and they're getting ready for the knockout punch."

The ensuing three hours of talks — beginning at dawn on May 9 — brought nothing new. In fact, they degenerated into finger-pointing. The management was irked that "advisors, whose aim was to drag the proceedings out," spoke for the workers. The strikers were presented with a humiliating new ultimatum, and the strike committee simply got up and walked out. After phoning Warsaw, Sila-Nowicki, who appeared now to have his own agenda in mind, declared that Interior Minister Kiszczak had hardened his stance, although he still desired a "nonviolent" settlement to the conflict — no doubt to erase the unfortunate impression created by their vicious "pacification" of the Nowa Huta complex. "They want to resolve things with us by promising they won't crush us underfoot, and they think we'll all gratefully go back to work. But we don't want a handout. We want Solidarity!"

The strike at the shipyards ended on the evening of May 10, 1988. I had arrived at the decision to end it the morning of that day, but I still had a few things to do before it was over: finish writing the final statement, pay the strikers the amount that they had been promised, and pack up all the paperwork. During the course of the day, there were several altercations among some young people who — it later appeared — had been mobilized into the civil defense and then let into the shipyards to spread confusion. The idea was to provide the ZOMO with a pretext for getting involved. Fortunately, many of these young people didn't have their hearts in this kind of unsavory work; they asked us "to toss them out on their ears." The "management's men," on the other hand, were thugs — pugnacious, vulgar, sometimes drunk — and they behaved quite differently. For instance, to help pass the time, almost every day during the strike there were electric-cart races. Once, carts driven by these management men tried to ram into some of ours, and we replied in kind. This was mostly just sport. This said, the management trucks were in the minority, and had we really wanted to we could have taught them a lesson or two.

Before lunch, the head of the strike committee, Alojzy Szablewski, proposed a motion to add a new demand to the old list: that the shipyards be governed by the rights and statutes already in place before the strike. To me fell the difficult duty of reading the final communiqué aloud:

> We have failed to win the victory. But though we are not leaving the shipyards triumphant, we are leaving with our heads high, convinced of the necessity and justice of our protest against social conditions in Poland, and against all violations of our dignity. . . . Poles see no chance for life in their own country. Those who govern it continue to do so as though it were their private property, a state of affairs that threatens Poland with catastrophe. We cannot look on this with indifference. Our strike is an important step toward the realization that we will need to struggle in order to prevail. . . . The workers of Nowa Huta and we of the Gdansk Shipyards have won something priceless: the conviction that our numbers haven't dwindled, even after these years of passivity and despair. Young people in particular, now more than ever, realize they are fighting for their own rights. This strike ends without an agreement, and that's proof that Poland's political, social, and economic paralysis will continue and worsen, and that resolution still lies beyond our reach. . . . We remain faithful to the slogan of our strike: "No Freedom Without Solidarity."

And so we did leave the shipyards with our heads high, a unified phalanx of workers and students. My conscience was clear, for I felt I had done my best. I had run to the microphone dozens of times when spirits were flagging; I had tried to keep everyone going, from my comrades on the strike committee, down to the rank and file; while the strike was on,

I didn't let anyone know of my doubts, even when I felt my back was to the wall and, bombarded from every direction, I would have gladly said, "The hell with it!" and gone off fishing. I was truly convinced that this first jolt would be followed by others. Our strike had failed only because it was premature.

We left the shipyards a thousand strong. The cordons of the ZOMO opened to let us through, and we walked to nearby Saint Brygid's, where Bishop Tadeusz Goclowski came to give us greetings and blessings. Within the Gothic walls of that sanctuary, we stood among our banners, weeping and singing, "At Your altar, we raise this prayer: O Lord, let our land be free."

13
Between the Sickle and Hope

I felt better about things once I'd caught up on my sleep. Greetings and
expressions of support poured in from foreign unions, and journalists
continued to seek me out, since I was still the nominal leader of Solidarity.

Because of the May protests, I had also attracted a number of young
radicals who, for better or worse, were now my allies. I played the part of
old fogy with them, trying to make them see that while their demands were
based on worthy principles, it didn't always make sense to demonstrate
just for the sake of demonstrating. One needed to have the strongest possible hand while maintaining ideals.

Some eat butter and others lard, but nearly everyone wants to live in a
free country. Some countries gain freedom on their own, others need a
push from the outside. When President Reagan earlier had insisted that
civil liberties be instituted in Nicaragua, the government of that country
responded immediately by permitting freedom of the press. In contrast,
the help we got from our neighbors only made things worse. Poland is the
sixth-largest European nation in terms of territory, but we were reduced to
a country of paupers. For close to half a century, our Party leaders bowed
to the Kremlin, our children were compelled to study Russian and learn
all about socialist theory, and our economy was forcibly integrated into an
inefficient foreign system in which our status was little more than that of
a colony. For decades we were told, "If you challenge their authority,
they'll crush us all." This argument prevailed until as late as 1985, when
Mikhail Sergeievich Gorbachev assumed the leadership of the USSR —
and threw the dinosaurs of the old guard into a panic.

I followed Gorbachev's career with mounting hopes, but did not envy
him the job his predecessors had left him. Lenin had built a system of

self-governing socialism; Stalin destroyed that and built the gulags; Khrushchev briefly threw socialism into chaos; Brezhnev restored it and cast it in stone; Andropov and then Chernenko let the old system tumble into disrepair. Gorbachev was to try to mend all the cracks and fix all the flaws that had accumulated in this Marxist "edifice" over seventy years. He had to go back to the drawing board — clear the ground, dig for new foundations, mix the cement. Would he have the time to erect even a few stories of a pluralistic skyscraper?

I don't mind admitting that the key terms "perestroika" and "glasnost" seemed suspect to me for quite some time. Under communism, highflown phrases too often turned out to be hollow sounds, and concepts such as "democracy," "freedom," "dignity," and "patriotism," as they were actually applied, were utter shams. All the same, when the new Soviet leader showed himself to be practical, precise, patient, and diplomatic, he began to earn my trust. The Russian Empire had waited hundreds of years for a Gorbachev to take the helm, and from the very beginning of his tenure as Party secretary, things started happening. During the first half of 1988 alone, he authorized the creation of several independent organizations, began withdrawing Soviet troops from Afghanistan, and held a new summit meeting with the president of the United States. On April 29, 1988, Pimen, the orthodox patriarch of Moscow and all the Russias, was invited to the Kremlin on the occasion of the millennial anniversary of the Christianizing of Russia. That was a reversal of policy, since during the years of Soviet rule, out of the 846 churches that were active in 1917 in Moscow, 426 had been completely destroyed and 340 had been closed and desecrated.

The press announced late that spring that Gorbachev would come to Poland in early summer. There were those in the opposition who greeted the news with cynicism, but I was convinced that his visit could be another turning point for us. After all, independent analysts in Poland and abroad had long been predicting that a thaw in the East was coming. Where there was once only artificial red, they said, homegrown colors would soon fly again — they meant the white and red of Poland's flag, the red, white, and green of Hungary, the white, red, and navy blue of Czechoslovakia, and the black, red, and yellow of Germany. There would be an end to the Lie. Gorbachev's report to the Nineteenth Communist Party Conference of the Soviet Union was a document of some importance in that it confirmed the seriousness of his previous declarations. Though it was still laced with references to "socialism," "Marxism-Leninism," "revolution," and "the

Party," under this moldy rind it was possible to detect hints of fresher thinking.

But before Gorbachev was to begin his visit to Poland — on July 11, 1988 — Solidarity had an issue on the home front to address: the June 19 boycott of the nondemocratic elections of local governments (called national councils). The rhetoric of the official press tried to inflate voting in this election into a patriotic duty. Several journalistic rags, only too delighted to do the dirty work of the propaganda machine, seized the opportunity to besmirch "Lech Walesa and the political gamblers around him." Despite their combined efforts, independent tabulations revealed that less than 50 percent of the eligible voters turned out. The figure would have been even lower had some people not still believed that if you didn't vote, the Communists would deny you a passport or get you fired from your job.

Embittered by the slowness of reforms and under fire from the hard-core radicals, I wrote — on my own, and without first consulting with my advisors — a widely disseminated statement about where things now stood in Poland:

Poland is a country of unsatisfied needs. . . . There is no doubt that the reasons for this are profoundly structural in nature. . . . The current guardianship — for that is what it must be called — violates the fundamental rights of both the individuals and the groups that constitute this country. . . . That guardianship was challenged during the period when Solidarity was legal, and despite its best efforts, the government has never been able fully to reestablish the system of power. . . .

Today it is no secret to anyone that the most effective economic system is a free-market system. . . . Poland needs a new system based upon respect for workers as individuals, and a system that recognizes their right to organize and to create associations that act collectively to defend their interests. This new system will emerge only when there is a return to union pluralism and, above all, when Solidarity is legalized once again. . . .

Solidarity and the activism it has given rise to have eliminated the government's monopoly on the organization and control of every form of social and cultural life. . . . Any cultural change must consist of, and stem from, the right to free association and free circulation of ideas. . . . Those freedoms should be limited only when they include conspiring to commit felonies or misdemeanors. . . .

Political changes must exert their influence on social life. . . . particularly in the way political thought is circulated (through clubs, appropriate activities, and so forth). And they must also involve the institutions. . . . Before change can come about, we must fundamentally rethink the (Stalinist) conception of law as a tool to benefit those holding power. . . . Guaranteeing the legality of any form of government means reforming the judiciary so that it is independent of political power. . . . We must enact laws prohibiting discrimination on the basis of religious or political point of view. . . .

The success of these critical changes in Poland will depend upon dialogue between the government and the opposition — particularly between the Party and Solidarity. We are not trying to avoid this dialogue. Certain conditions must be met, however, for dialogue to be fruitful. First and most important is that all participants be accorded full recognition and meet as equals. Second, that we stop proposing specious solutions that are merely cosmetic. Third, that both parties be allowed to make their views public.

Gorbachev arrived in Poland on schedule. In his address to the Sejm, he recalled that Poles and Russians were linked by a long history, albeit not always a harmonious one. Their association had been most successful when they worked together cooperatively for the development of their own countries, as well as in the international arena. "At present, equality, autonomy, and the joint resolution of problems facing us have become the indisputable norm in our relations. These relations have become free of any taint of paternalism; they are now going forward, in the best interests of both sides, in a partnership of goodwill, and in the spirit of true brotherhood."

Officially, the major event of this official visit by the first secretary of the Central Committee of the Communist Party of the Soviet Union was the signing of a joint Polish-Soviet declaration, which provided for broad cooperation in this new era of relations between our two states. I was anxious to know if this meant that our own government, now that its hands were free, would reach out to the opposition.

The Sejm passed a law introducing civilian service as an alternative to military service, which was encouraging. On July 26, however, the government spokesman destroyed any illusions I might have had by flatly declaring that Solidarity was a thing of the past.

"Well, we'll just see about that!" I said to myself, switching off the television.

Three weeks later, miners in Silesia began a series of strikes.

14
The Second Avalanche

T he Silesian miners' strike heartened us all, especially since in earlier demonstrations the miners had usually been the last to get involved. They revealed themselves to be as politically aware as the shipyard workers, if not more so. The first to protest, beginning on August 15, was the July Manifesto Mine in Jastrzebie. One of the main sources of discontent was the previous month's wage "adjustment." But topping the miners' list was the demand for free unions. Over the next few days, the number of mines to go on strike rose to sixteen. All of them demanded one thing above all else: the legalization of Solidarity. It was the same in the port of Szczecin, where a strike broke out on August 17 and immediately spread across a wide area. On August 20, the North Port of Gdansk declared a work stoppage. Workers at the Gdansk Shipyards made it known they would join the strike on August 22 if government representatives refused to negotiate. Had the government negotiated, the whole of the Gdansk coastline would have kept to its part of the bargain. Unfortunately, the brains of the Party proved much slower than the wits of the workers.

The strikes of August 1988 demonstrated how fruitful the May movement really had been. The bitter honor of that first "failure" was now to be sweetened by a taste of real victory. Throughout the period of martial law and my internment, I had repeatedly urged those in government circles to wake up to the fact that the whole system of centralized control was breaking down. I wanted the country to make the transition to the next stage and follow the example set by Spain. But no one listened. At that time, Brezhnev — that heap of rusting iron — was still in power, and continued to oppose reforms. Several more years were to pass before the *apparatchiks* finally woke up to the danger. Between the end of April and the beginning of May 1988, Deputy Prime Minister Zdzislaw Sadowski did make vague noises about opening discussions, but I sensed that this gesture was designed only to cool passions, and that we would have to wait until things heated up again before we got a more serious offer. On August 21, Pope John Paul II said, "We are mindful of the events unfolding in our homeland. We pray for Poland, we pray for peace — a peace based on the stability of truth and justice, not on violence."

On August 22, the strike committee of the Gdansk Shipyards, newly created under the leadership of Alojzy Szablewski, issued its first declaration, and it was immediately picked up in a special strike issue of the bulletin *Rozwaga i Solidarnosc* [*Courage and Solidarity*]:

> Because the rulers of the People's Republic of Poland have not undertaken to negotiate with the various strike committees and have not begun the talks with Solidarity announced* by President Lech Walesa on August 21, the Gdansk strike committee . . . has declared that they will join the strike out of protest and solidarity.

That same day, the first declaration issued by the joint strike committees, with headquarters at the shipyards (presided over by Jacek Merkel, a naval construction engineer), listed five demands — identical to those issued during the May strike. Demand number one: "Legalize Solidarity."

That afternoon the Gdansk strike committee issued a statement:

> In exchange for making the internal radio transmitter available to the strike committee, and in recognition of the economic situation of the shipyards, the strike committee has proposed to the management to complete work on the outfitting of two ships (a ferry for Finland and a container vessel for the USSR). The management did not agree to the proposal, arguing that no decision had been reached by the regional committee of the Polish United Workers' Party of Gdansk. We have therefore not resumed work outfitting those vessels.

Lastly, here is an excerpt from the televised speech made that evening by the minister of the interior, Czeslaw Kiszczak:

> Militia forces have been ordered to secure the areas immediately surrounding a certain number of enterprises. . . . With the consent of the head of the Bureau of the Council of Ministers, I am asking the regional prefects of Katowice,

---

* Proposed, in fact. — L.W.

Szczecin, and Gdansk to establish curfews in those areas where the security of the citizens appears to be in danger.

The August strike, characterized by noise and bustling activity, differed materially from the comparatively sedate May strike. The popular singer Piotr Szczepanik lent us some sound equipment, and we set up a printer by pirating typewriter parts. By word of mouth, the workers at the Gdansk Shipyards lost no time in calling on workers at neighboring firms to join the strike: the naval repair yards and the North Shipyards, then the Radunia Shipyards, the Wisla Shipyards, and the commercial maritime port. There were stirring moments when ebullient workers from various quarters came together, waving flags and shouting at the tops of their lungs, "No freedom without Solidarity!"

On the second day of the strike, we held an ad hoc meeting at the main gate, where I spoke out at some length. I recommended throughout the strike, here at the shipyards, the cradle of Solidarity, that we had to set an example — even though we had not been the ones to start the strike. I reminded them all of the years of humiliation we had endured at the hands of the authorities in Warsaw, and here at our own workplaces. I asked them to think about our children's prospects. I made an appeal to all those who had driven our country to ruin. At the same time, I also slightly moderated my tone, to leave the way open for conciliation and negotiation.

Since I was not a member of any of the strike committees, some might wonder what my role in all this was. Without false modesty, I can say that I was the trump card, the matador, who, after the toreadors have finished enraging the bull with their jabs and pokes, enters the arena carrying his sword and *muleta*. Despite the government spokesman's derisive claims that I was merely a private citizen, destiny had at some point turned me into something of an institution, a fact taken for granted as much by the Party leaders as by the strikers themselves. My job was to goad when things got stagnant, to add water when the vine was withering, to keep up morale, to encourage, to soothe. I couldn't show signs of resignation, or even just stop to catch my breath. The strikers kept their eyes on me. They drew their strength from me. I had to be hard, strong, and unyielding, while not letting myself be lulled into inaction when the time came to make a move.

Jacek Merkel was right when he said that it wouldn't be easy. In 1980, we had been forced to strike for eighteen days before our management "comrades" understood that we wouldn't give up. It looked as though it was going to be the same this time, although more and more cracks were appearing in the monolith of power. Though we had no access to the latest updates, we did have access to prominent people who were in a good position to guide and counsel us as events developed. Jaroslaw and Lech Kaczynski were at the shipyards almost the whole time. Professor Andrzej Stelmachowski (representing the episcopate), the lawyer Wladyslaw Sila-Nowicki, and Professor Bronislaw Geremek made flying visits. We all discussed compromises of various sorts, but on one point we remained firm: Solidarity had to have its legal status restored. This wasn't from arrogance or obsessive nostalgia, but from resolution. We would never be able to exert any real influence without a powerful, independent union, and we knew it. It was precisely because we had no union organization that we had to go on strike periodically to protest the growing number of injustices.

The daily schedule and duties of the strikers needed to be organized and regularized in order to combat tedium and fatigue. Assurances of support from the outside, visits by important figures, moments when the tensions would ease — all of them were of great importance. On the third day of the strike, several visitors of note arrived at the shipyards. Luigi Cal, the director of the foreign division of the Italian Confederation of Christian Unions, affiliated with the ICFTU, managed to get inside that morning. In the afternoon came the secretaries-general of the two larger union organizations to which Solidarity belonged: Jan Kulakowski of the World Confederation of Labor, and John Vanderveken of the International Confederation of Free Trade Unions. A few days later, Raymond L. Flynn, the mayor of Boston, paid us a visit, as did Björn Cato Funnemark, secretary of the Norwegian branch of Helsinki Watch. All had come to an international conference on human rights in Cracow. Having heard about the strikes, they didn't want to miss the opportunity to come to Gdansk. Declared Kulakowski, "We believe Solidarity to be critical not just to Poland, but to the union movement the world over." John Vanderveken added, "We are here to underscore the world's solidarity with the demands of your workers."

The days passed quickly, although at first there were no tangible results. Maintenance crews had been organized with orders that covered everything, down to the smallest detail. Order prevailed throughout the shipyards. As in May, everyone felt cheerful. A lot of the credit for this goes to the young people, who, on the fourth day of the strike, issued a public statement:

We, the young workers of the North Shipyards, call on the government of the People's Republic of Poland immediately to supply us and our older comrades with four hundred tents. It is our belief that if the government of the People's Republic of Poland can aid the homeless of New York by sending them tents, it should do the same for Polish young people. After all, they are their homeland's "glory and future."

Younger workers also began building a shantytown made entirely from sheet metal bound with wire (like the one begun during the May strike). Some constructed these shelters by night, while others made them more permanent by adding doorways and thresholds. They painted inspirational messages on the walls. Strikers' surveillance patrols occasionally looked into them to check for illegal caches of alcohol.

We started the fifth day of the strike with hearts uplifted. It was the feast day of the Virgin of Czestochowa. Mass was said for the occasion near the main gate of the shipyards. And that afternoon there was a television broadcast that gave us the news for which we had been waiting: General Kiszczak proposed an immediate meeting with representatives of the various social and labor groups. "This could take the form of a round table," he said.* "I am setting no preconditions regarding even the topics for discussions or the composition of the delegation." He was making an obvious concession, for earlier proposals had included the restriction "with the exception of Lech Walesa and Bronislaw Geremek." Another Polish irony, I thought. they have chosen the minister of the interior — until now a stern and faithful retainer to the totalitarian regime — to initiate reform in Poland.

At the pre-negotiation meeting of the strikers, Jacek Merkel welcomed at long last the fact that a round table was being proposed, instead of a square cell. This was only the beginning, said he; and the hardest part still lay ahead. Alojzy Szablewski's reaction was more emotional. "I want to embrace each one of you, for while others went off to their snug little beds you stayed here, sleeping on sheet metal!" he cried. Later came the traditional parade of electric trucks, several dozen of them. On the loading platforms men stood shoulder to shoulder, chanting slogans, while the trucks, with their passengers, passed in front and made their way into the depths of the shipyards. Several times a day these trucks crisscrossed the shipyards in a show of strength, determination, and solidarity.

---

* It didn't grow into the Round Table with capital letters until a bit later. — L.W.

Late that evening, I worked out a statement in response to the question
the authorities had asked me, through Professor Stelmachowski, about my
position with regard to the proposed talks. My general position was that I
was always ready for dialogue that imposed no preconditions and that left
wide open the topics for discussion. I also suggested that the legalization
of Solidarity remained the key issue in any future political discussion; this
second wave of strikes in this year alone demonstrated that clearly. Both
sides needed to normalize relations to correct past errors, so that Poland
would not slide into a permanent state of paralysis. I proposed (trying not
to sound strident) adding the following topics to any discussion: union
pluralism (including the legalization of Solidarity), social and political
pluralism, and the signing of an anticrisis pact (or a prereform agreement).
In conclusion, I stressed that any actions that might outrage public opinion
were to be avoided — meaning any attempt to stop the strikes by force.

The next morning, in the sacristy of Saint Brygid's, I met with Bishop
Tadeusz Goclowski, who once again was actively playing the role of me-
diator. Our advisors Tadeusz Mazowiecki and Adam Michnik were also
there. On the basis of our joint decisions, and the steps Bishop Tadeusz
had already undertaken, I was to get ready to go to Warsaw. I had won the
support of the Szczecin and Silesia regions (Bogdan Lis was there to help
coordinate the movement), and now had full authority to negotiate for the
legalization of Solidarity.

Day after day, the citizens of Gdansk demonstrated their support for our
strike. Despite the cordons of ZOMO, people continually brought us —
by routes known only to them — food, blankets, and cigarettes, while
"go-fers" ran back and forth on both sides of the fence carrying leaflets
and letters (Saint Brygid's served as our mail drop). The trams that ran
along the outside of the shipyard walls rang their bells as they passed, and
from their windows outstretched hands made the victory sign. Passengers
on the train did likewise. For their benefit, the workers painted messages
on the shipyard roofs: "WE SHALL OVERCOME," "THE STRIKE GOES ON," and
of course "SOLIDARITY."

On August 29, on the eighth day of the strike, I decided the time had
come to inform the workers that negotiations would be beginning very
soon now, and that in those negotiations we would have to make some
concessions — at least in the beginning. Using the loudspeaker, I told
them that the government had finally shaken off its apathy. This didn't
mean that it was about to surrender any prerogatives without a fight. We
would have to do some bargaining. "Are you with me?" I asked.

There was a dead silence, and it so unnerved me that I couldn't speak. I hadn't expected such an extreme reaction to the idea of concessions; did they want civil war? The workers stared at me warily, unsure what to do next. Breaking the silence, I said that I would keep on preparing for the negotiations.

At the next press conference I pulled fewer punches as far as concessions went: "No negotiations without Solidarity," I said, mostly for the benefit of those Party leaders who at the plenary session the night before had mumbled something about the need to consolidate the economy in order to usher in the "second stage" of socialist reform. The seesawing that went on that day ended by giving me a raging migraine, only exacerbated by Bronislaw Geremek's news from Warsaw. "Our chances don't look good," he said.

During the strike, entertainment and distraction were provided by singers and actors, but also by the strikers themselves, who sometimes put on shows. In one of those shows, workers had rigged up three electric trucks to look like armored vehicles, and they drove them up to the second gate. Two resembled ZOMO trucks and the third a tank. They approached a group of young workers waving flags and chanting, "Sol-i-da-ri-ty," and proceeded to drench them with water shot out of a sheet-metal cannon. Then "ZOMO" in visored helmets jumped out and began hitting people with rolled-up paper nightsticks. That was exactly the cue the crowd was waiting for. They took pieces of sheet metal out of their pockets and threw them by the hundreds at the "ZOMO." This onslaught scared off the "ZOMO," who beat a hasty retreat back to their vehicles. They made a slow U-turn and headed back to the shipyards' canals, displaying signs reading "CLUB THE HOMELAND," "MIGHT MAKES RIGHT," and "WE WELCOME DIALOGUE." Meanwhile the "soldiers" attempted in vain to launch a styrofoam missile. The whole show was accompanied by laughter and hooting.

On Wednesday, October 31, the lawyer Sila-Nowicki arrived at the Gdansk Shipyards and announced, "Kiszczak wants to meet with Walesa right away, as long as it is understood that each must place confidence in the other's good intentions. The talks will focus mainly upon setting a date for the round-table talks." That he did not mention Solidarity disappointed me, but this was no time to sulk. I got to Warsaw before lunchtime. Jerzy Dabrowski, the secretary of the episcopate, and Stanislaw Ciosek, secretary of the Central Committee of the Polish United Workers' Party (who spoke from time to time), listened while I was told of the decisions reached during a three-hour meeting they had had with the minister of the interior. General Kiszczak set several inflexible conditions: Solidarity's legalization would be possible only when the round-table talks had concluded with the signing of a national accord; in the meantime, the strikes were to end within eighteen hours. Any further decisions regarding the talks would be made in the next two weeks, and during this time we were to draw up a provisional list of negotiators and advisors. I protested as much as I could, but I also knew that I couldn't act as a spoiler. Only several dozen enterprises were striking, not the several hundred of August 1980; and the general stated outright that Party hard-liners would shoot down any offer of entente with the opposition. I sensed that he was being sincere, but I wondered how the expectant workers and unshaven miners would look at me when I delivered this news. What would it matter that I had right on my side?

By the time I got back to the shipyards, the Polish Press Agency had already published a special bulletin. I still had a long uphill climb ahead of me in my discussions with the members and advisors of the joint strike committee. Alojzy Szablewski muttered that he felt demoralized and paralyzed. Bogdan Borusewicz (the legend of the underground) declared that for better or worse we had played right into the hands of the hard-liners. Only Jacek Merkel and Jaroslaw Kaczynski understood that I had gotten as much as was possible.

On Thursday, September 1, we left the shipyards in closed ranks and headed for Saint Brygid's, and Father Henryk Jankowski declared, "The strike really continues — through our dialogue." Somewhat later, Bishop Tadeusz Goclowski stressed that after Thursday comes Friday, and after the Crucifixion comes the Resurrection: "We are the sons of a millennial nation."*

---

* In 1966, Poland celebrated the millennium of its Christianization.

15
The Prime Minister's Revenge

A fter the strike ended, I had to go to Silesia, where the bitterly disappointed miners greeted me with whistling and abuse. On September
3, 1988, protest movements in the mines themselves were halted, as were
those at the last bastion of the strike — the Stalowa Wola steelworks. Now
I could begin to put into motion the next tactical phase. I use the military
term intentionally, to indicate that these tactics were components of a
broader strategy of war: not an all-out war, but a partisan war of countless
skirmishes carried out by limited forces. In the not-so-distant future I knew
I would be able to initiate a sweeping offensive. My army would be the
Polish people.

On September 10, I won the support of Solidarity's national leadership
on the matter of the preconditions for the Round Table talks, and the next
day I presided over a meeting — our fourth such meeting — of prominent
figures, who came to Gdansk at my invitation. There were lively discussions about the issues that were to be raised during negotiations with the
government, as well as who would make up the delegation.

During this period, those who had formerly been on the strike committees, as well as Solidarity's underground organizers from the various factories, came out in the open and formed commissions. This provoked a
vindictive response by the Party press, which was renewing its efforts to
discredit our union. On September 15, I met with General Kiszczak, from
whom I secured a promise that there would be no further retaliation
against the strikers. I acquainted him with the makeup of the delegation
Solidarity would send to the Round Table.

On September 16, in Magdalenka, near Warsaw, an organizational
meeting between representatives of Solidarity and the government took

place. Also participating were members of the pro-government union OPZZ, who did little to conceal their hostility to our union movement. Despite what the communiqué issued that day said, we weren't able to accomplish much other than agreeing that the Round Table discussions needed to begin by mid-October.

On September 19, I had a second meeting with the minister of the interior, representatives of the pro-government "patriotic" organization called PRON, and Church officials. The results were as fruitless as those of the meeting three days earlier, but we kept the target date for the Round Table. That very day, the Sejm disbanded the government of Prime Minister Zbigniew Messner, who was criticized by members of the Sejm for his inconsistency, and for having undermined and delayed economic reform, despite the breadth of his special powers. The Sejm committee charged with monitoring the progress of reform stated that the current social unrest indicated all too clearly how Messner's government had lost the nation's confidence. Messner — whose main concern always seemed to have been to keep the part in his hair impeccable — himself indulged in some exemplary self-criticism, and announced that the entire cabinet was resigning. This comedy had of course been stage-managed from the wings.

Finding a replacement for Messner was a problem. The new prime minister turned out to be Mieczyslaw Rakowski, a self-styled champion of democracy who was in fact openly hostile to Solidarity, as became abundantly clear less than five weeks later. But in the meantime, the hubbub over the Round Table suddenly quieted down.

On October 13, three days before the emotional ceremonies marking the tenth anniversary of John Paul II's pontificate were held, the new prime minister presented the Sejm with a plan for his new government. During his inaugural address, which was crammed with false promises about dialogue and openness (the road to hell is indeed paved with good intentions), he declared:

> We shall not hesitate to pledge, with a firm hand, the security of the state and its citizens that is necessary for reforms consistent with Poland's socialist orientation to take place. I know that for this I can count on the vigilance of the services assigned to maintain order and the rule of law, and on the unshakable loyalty of the Polish People's Army as well. . . . Our economic and political reforms have much in common with the Soviet perestroika. . . . If they were to end in failure, and if the agitation and political tension were to result in unrest, chaos, and a threat to socialism, the credibility of Soviet reconstruction

— which is so beneficial for Poland, Europe, and the whole world — would suffer serious harm. Let this be remembered by anyone who through short-sightedness would paint anticommunist slogans, or accord interviews in which they say that the signing of any agreement is a death sentence for socialism.

The last sentence was a fairly unambiguous allusion to me. I was genuinely surprised to discover that Rakowski — a consummate politician — still seemed to have absolutely no idea what was happening.

The prime minister's attitude obviously toed the official Party line. On October 21, General Wojciech Jaruzelski, the first secretary of the Central Committee of the PZPR, met with the activists of the Ursus tractor factory and revealed his hostility to any talk whatsoever about union pluralism. He could accept legalizing Solidarity, but only after a number of indignities had been imposed upon it. All this posturing was accompanied by an escalation in the propaganda campaign by the Communist press, which even accused us of trying to thwart the very idea of a round table. And the official Soviet Communist paper was called *Pravda* [*Truth*]!

On October 29, 1988, the fortieth anniversary of the first postwar launching of a ship in Gdansk (a coal-hauler, the *Soldek*, now a floating museum), Prime Minister Rakowski instructed the minister of industry to liquidate the supposedly unprofitable and outdated Gdansk Shipyards! This contemptible act of political manipulation was, among other things, Rakowski's revenge for an earlier humiliation. On August 25, 1983, Rakowski, then deputy prime minister, had come to the shipyards to put "extremists" led by me in their place. He was roundly booed. Now, as prime minister, the time for his personal revenge had come. He fixed his attention on the Gdansk Shipyards, even though it ranked only forty-fifth out of some five hundred enterprises that were in the red. In an interview with the West German magazine *Die Zeit*, Rakowski arrogantly declared, "Symbols are of no concern to me; we've had our fill of them in Poland. The fact that Solidarity was born in the shipyards means only that — it is just a historical fact." The announcement of the closing was supposed to shake up the other enterprises that were facing the specter of bankruptcy, although the prime minister knew perfectly well that the main reason the shipyards were unprofitable was the forced contracts for ships ordered by the Soviets. Quite simply, the ships built in Gdansk were fitted out with expensive equipment purchased in dollars; then they were sold in rubles in exchange for Russian-made tanks. How could the Polish economy benefit from such transactions?

The decision to liquidate was signed and sealed as the demand for ships was beginning to grow. Ten thousand technicians, nearly a third of whom had worked in the shipyards for more than a quarter of a century, were forced to look for work elsewhere. Fortunately, the news created an enormous stir throughout the country, and it was therefore announced on November 7 that, in conformity with the most recent instructions from the minister of industry, the shipyards would begin closing down operations on December 1, 1988, with the process to extend until December 31, 1990.

In connection with this announcement, the employment office where our men had intended to stage a protest meeting closed its doors. On November 23, the workers' committee presented a motion to the regional court of Gdansk to overrule Rakowski's decision. On November 30, the official union sent a similar document to the constitutional court. Solidarity, which had not yet been legalized, could not do anything official to help in these efforts.

The ensuing struggles lasted a year and a half. The government initially instructed journalists on its payroll to decry the shameful state of affairs when a nation is willing to coddle freeloaders. Articles with headlines like "A DIFFICULT BUT LOGICAL DECISION," "HOW MUCH DOES IT REALLY COST?" "THE HOUR OF CHOICE," and so on, began to appear. Could anyone seriously believe these so-called analyses, written by governmental decree? Once again, the workers were made to bear the burden of responsibility for the actions of the Communist *nomenklatura*. Once again, the *nomenklatura* shamelessly stated that the whole issue of closing the shipyards had first been discussed publicly before any action was taken — a complete lie. Actually, shipyard manager Czeslaw Tolwinski had been summoned to the Ministry of Industry and was reportedly rendered speechless by the news that they were going to shut down his enterprise. Another member of the management delegation was said to have murmured to himself, "Now? Just when we're beginning to get back on our feet?"

Despite the announcement that the closing would be stretched out over a period of more than two years, many of the workers panicked. A feeling of injustice inflamed the debate about what to do next: go on working or get out now? Some declared that the shipyards would be closed only over their dead bodies. Others began a frantic search for new jobs; but most of the openings turned out either to be low-paying or to require retraining. It's a good thing Rakowski never showed up at the shipyards. The workers would have broken his legs. Families were being robbed of their livelihoods by a single vicious signature. That there were forty-four newly signed contracts for orders on file made it all the more incomprehensible.

It cannot be said too strongly that no objective and concrete financial assessment lay behind the government's momentous decision; the government had formulated no plan for how the shipyards' assets were to be liquidated — proof once again that politics rather than economics was behind it all. Employees at the Office of Naval Shipyards had long been saying that the fiscal policies instituted by the central planners were detrimental to the shipbuilding industry. For example, no account was taken of the rate of inflation — which, given how long it takes to build a ship, swallowed most of the profits. Furthermore, some faceless bureaucrat had arbitrarily fixed 20 percent as the maximum allowable profit on the sale of ships to Polish buyers. Finally, the Gdansk Shipyards delivered most of their goods to Soviet buyers, and since they paid with rubles fixed at a rate of exchange higher than that for the dollar, the ships were inevitably an unprofitable export. There even came a point when the government declared that though it would no longer provide subsidies, the current contracts were still to be honored. So that's how you reconcile your accounts with despots.

As everyone was resigning themselves to the closing, and the *nomenklatura* had begun plundering the shipyards' assets, there was an unexpected turn of events. The Polish-American multimillionaire Barbara Piasecka-Johnson (widow of the former head of Johnson and Johnson pharmaceuticals) appeared like a fairy godmother and proposed creating a joint venture in which she would hold a 55 percent share (that is, about $100 million) in the shipyards.

We reacted like children to this extraordinary offer. But our jubilation was premature. Mrs. Piasecka-Johnson, an art historian by training, proved to be more of a romantic (in May 1989, she bought a dilapidated seventeenth-century château in Pilica, near Zawiercie, to house her fine collection of paintings) than a realist. Accustomed as she was to Western ways of doing business, she set about evaluating the situation by hiring experts from the consulting firms of Arthur Andersen and Appledore. Assistance in dealing with the Polish bureaucratic tangle was to be provided by Doradca (which means "counselor" in Polish), a cooperative from the Gdansk suburb of Sopot. Despite this excellent technical infrastructure, the American and English specialists needed enormous amounts of time to wend their way through the labyrinth of government regulations. Once all the paperwork was collected and organized, it was forwarded to a Miami law firm. Further, the question of ownership of shipyard property had never been resolved. More importantly, it was discovered that the enterprise constituted a danger to the environment (due mostly to fumes from the galvanizing process). These and many other revelations were to leave our experts stupefied.

The experts continued dissecting the enterprise until the end of 1989, and their conclusions were kept secret for a few months after that. On September 14, Mrs. Piasecka-Johnson met with Solidarity's Enterprise Committee at the shipyards, assuring them of her continuing wish to enter into the joint venture. She pleaded for the workers' patience and support, and for the management to set wage levels guaranteeing "a reasonable standard of living." When questioned, she reiterated that the moment was rapidly approaching when words would have to be replaced by deeds. By then Rakowski was no longer prime minister, three thousand workers had left the shipyards, and the enterprise had been forced to turn down twenty-nine contracts.

The delays in finalizing the contract were poisoning the atmosphere. People had assumed that Mrs. Piasecka-Johnson would simply buy the shipyards and turn them into a modern and functional business, but as it turned out, with $2 million already spent on consultants, she was still stalling before making the final decision. The bombshell hit at the beginning of December 1989, when the experts returned to Poland to make public their preliminary findings: the shipyards had been put into liquidation, so in principle their value was zero; the machines, equipment, and material were worth between $4 million and $6.5 million. The assessment stunned the Polish group, because we all knew that the real value of the assets was at least ten times that amount. Upon learning of the results of the study, the shipyards refused any further negotiation, and the experts were frostily told to leave.

But all that negotiating convinced the new Polish government to rethink its strategy, and instead of closing them, on January 3, 1990, the government announced that the Gdansk Shipyards would forthwith be turned into a stock-based business, with the exclusive participation of the state treasury. On February 5, Mrs. Piasecka-Johnson turned up in Gdansk yet again with her group of advisors, wanting to look into the possibility of buying stocks from the government. "In any case," she kept repeating, "I love Poland and intend to invest in it." These were not mere idle words, for in earlier years our kinswoman from America had spent several million dollars for medicines, provisions, and medical supplies for Poland. Furthermore, her generosity had made possible the creation of several welfare centers and orphanages, along with a private foreign bank head-quartered in Gdansk. A profoundly religious person, she had made substantial donations to the Polish Church. But as for the shipyards, she never succeeded in buying them.

The breakdown in negotiations with Mrs. Johnson created tensions at the shipyards. As president of Solidarity, I was accused of several "misdemeanors," although I had done my utmost to lend support to the joint venture and campaigned hard for it. But people had fallen into the habit of attacking me for anything that went wrong, no matter what the cause. When asked about the conditions imposed by the experts, I expressed caution, although — to be honest — they hadn't seemed so very hard: a reduction in the number of workers, a decrease in production, a temporary lowering of wages. Of course all this would later improve, and the experts were right to point out the massive amount of money it would take to modernize the shipyards. But when one has enough to eat, can one really understand those who don't?

Toward the end of April 1990, consistent with the earlier announcement, the Gdansk Shipyards were converted into a joint-stock company belonging to the Polish treasury. The capitalized stock, amounting to some 400 billion zlotys (about $42 million), was divided into shares of one million zlotys each, with the understanding that the shipyards' workers, retirees, and pensioners could buy up to 20 percent of the shares at half the nominal price. It has been predicted that the shipyards should be out of the red by 1993.

16
The Debate

L et's go back to the fall of 1988. On November 2 — that is to say, the day before the official announcement of the decision to liquidate the Gdansk Shipyards — government spokesman Jerzy Urban read Prime Minister Rakowski's appeal for an immediate start to negotiations with the opposition. This was received as the brazen sneer at the Solidarity activists that it was. The next day, acting as if nothing had happened, General Kiszczak proposed meeting with the principal players to lay the groundwork for the Round Table discussions. At first I was indignant, even ready to shoot back a barbed reply, but I soon realized that the minister of the interior (in whom I retained a tiny amount of trust) was not the prime minister. After consulting with my advisors, I agreed to a two-day meeting two weeks from then. I used the interim to hold interviews that helped me figure out our basic demands and priorities for the immediate future. These would revolve around our conviction that in the heart of Europe, here at the close of the twentieth century, the only possible method for establishing a new form of government was free elections, not violent revolution.

A welcome relief from the daily haggling with the Communists was the visit from the British prime minister, Margaret Thatcher, on November 4. I had long admired her ideas about free-enterprise society and its system of rewards, and was pleased that she found a few hours during her three-day stay in Poland to come to Gdansk to talk about them with me. Mrs. Thatcher's visit to Gdansk included several stops, the most solemn of which was a wreath-laying at the monument to the shipyard dead, and the most pleasant a ceremonial dinner in the rectory of Saint Brygid's. While delicately cutting into her pheasant, the prime minister said to me, "You have already made great strides on the road to freedom. Your accomplishments have been driven by moral conviction, and that is why you will never give in."

On November 11, ceremonies were held throughout the country to mark the seventieth anniversary of Poland's recovery of its independence. Because in most cases the ceremonies had been organized separately from those that the Communists had, for the first time, decided to sponsor, here and there the ZOMO continued their tradition of harassing nonviolent demonstrators. This harassment did not prevent the government from pompously organizing a session of parliament during which the very individuals responsible for decades of repression sang the praises of Marshal Jozef Pilsudski, the man who defeated the Bolsheviks during a bloody 1920 battle. On that same November 11, Alfred Miodowicz, president of the OPZZ group of pro-government unions (which during the state of martial law had pillaged Solidarity's property), as well as a member of the political bureau of the Central Committee of the People's Republic of Poland, sent a confidential Telex to his "federations," instructing them not to allow a vote for union pluralism in the factories. Miodowicz's strong-arm tactics angered me enough to accept an invitation to debate him on television.

Meanwhile, I met with General Kiszczak on November 18 and 19 to attempt once again to secure a promise of restoring Solidarity to legal status. Once again, the general, just like Ciosek, the secretary of the Central Committee of the People's Republic, made it clear that any suggestion of legalizing Solidarity was out of the question. The question would have to be postponed indefinitely. I was sick of being led on, and bluntly stated that if a definite timetable was not established for legalizing Solidarity, nothing would come of the Round Table talks. Sputtering with rage, Kiszczak and Ciosek repeated and confirmed their negative position. That was that.

A few days later, they literally began to dismantle the round table — no small feat, since it had been custom-made at the Henrykow furniture factory and was nearly twenty-eight feet in diameter. Since mid-October, the table had been waiting in the Jablonna Palace near Warsaw, now the seat of the Polish Academy of Sciences. It was returned in its many pieces to the manufacturer, where it was to remain in storage for ten weeks.

On November 24, Alfred Miodowicz announced with obvious glee on national television that he was pleased I had agreed to debate him.

I put in a lot of homework in preparation for that debate, knowing full well that Miodowicz was counting on "Mr. Walesa's weaker intellectual capacity" — as he later admitted in an interview. I also knew that this would be the first debate of its kind in a socialist country, and that my winning or losing could have international repercussions.

I decided to come out swinging. In front of Saint Brygid's three days later, I accused the president of the OPZZ of misrepresenting Polish reality and described the ongoing Third General Assembly of the OPZZ as "a circus with no one watching." I also declared that I did not plan to debate the role of unions, but would take the opportunity to present Solidarity's position. This provoked a speedy reaction from the spokesman for the OPZZ, who expressed his pained astonishment that in response to his offer of honest dialogue, Mr. Walesa had made it known that he would speak not with Miodowicz, but "with all of you, with Poland. All Mr. Miodowicz has to do is stand there."

Shortly before the debate, Solidarity and the OPZZ representatives agreed on various technical details. We were to be seated during the debate, which would last forty-five minutes, and the first to speak would be Miodowicz. Eight hours before I left for the studio, a group of distinguished colleagues helped me unwind and collect my thoughts, among them Jacek Kuron, Tadeusz Mazowiecki, Andrzej Wielowieyski, Adam Michnik, Bronislaw Geremek, and Janusz Onyszkiewicz. Also present was the editor Andrzej Bober (who had been fired from his television job during the state of martial law). He gave me some practical advice on how to handle the spotlights. His advice proved extremely valuable, if only because the television executives, ever submissive to the Party, refused access to people who sided with me — with the exception of my personal secretary, Krzysztof Pusz. Although Miodowicz was also to come alone, he was comfortable in the knowledge that television was controlled by his comrades at the Political Bureau.

When we entered the studio, I felt like a prizefighter before a championship bout. I turned to Miodowicz and said, "I'm going to punch your lights out!" The flustered Miodowicz gaped at me, but didn't have time to reply, since the television crew was already giving us instructions and settling us in front of the cameras.

In Poland, the last day of November is Saint Andrew's Day, one of our most popular saint's days. On Saint Andrew's Night, happy couples, dressed to the nines and carrying flowers and bottles, hurry through the streets on their way to parties — at which, following tradition, they read each other's future in the dripping wax of burning candles. On November 30, 1988, however, the streets and squares of Polish towns were all but deserted. (A poll conducted later revealed that 78 percent of all Polish adults were settled in front of their television sets.) At ten o'clock, two tense faces appeared on the screen: Alfred Miodowicz's and my own. A few hours later I received the transcript of the discussion. Here are some of the most important passages:

Alfred Miodowicz: It's been years since I last saw you at Nowa Huta, Mr. Walesa, and looking at you, sir, I must say . . . that it's a little like looking in a mirror. I too have lost some hair and gone gray; I see that your mustache, Mr. Walesa, is streaked with white. Years have passed, the setting is different, but Poland's problems have remained the same. These are the same daily problems: the lack of medical supplies, lines stretching out in front of stores, lines for buses and trams, the inability to balance the budget of the old pension portfolio, the difficulty of continuing to improve productivity because the machinery is aging, the national debt, the disaffection of our youth. The important thing is to figure out what to do so that things change. I am resolutely opposed to dividing the workers by introducing union pluralism. There has already been a dramatic split among workers at factories because of the strikes of last April and May and August — a split between the strikers and those who opposed striking. I think such divisions are so deep they will last for years. They won't lead to stability.

A second, very important, question: Can union pluralism solve all our problems? I am convinced the answer is no. Mr. Walesa, you say that we'll never get our economy off the ground without Western financial aid. And that we can't get this aid without legalizing Solidarity first. That may be so, but where will that put us? At each other's throats, repeating the lessons of Lebanon. Poland will be not just the poorest but also the most unstable country in Europe. Moreover, that aid would make us crawl on our knees, not walk on two legs. That's why we should count mainly on our own strengths. We are unionists, but above all we are Poles. It pains me to hear you say that we are the beggars of Europe.

In all those interviews you have given, you have unveiled your plans for transforming the Polish economy. You say that every sector (state, cooperative, and private) must be on an equal footing, that there must be a free market, that we must deflate the swollen bureaucracy. I think you're right. But I ask you to read the OPZZ proposals carefully.

A year ago, we ourselves suggested such an idea and called it the "economic alternative." True, it wasn't adopted. But what the new government team has announced fills us with optimism. As for free trade, it seems to me that in our vulnerable state, we would be exploited by speculators and frauds who act as intermediaries and actually produce nothing.

The OPZZ is prepared to agree to union pluralism, but on one condition. There must be only one union in each enterprise. Just which one can be decided by a free vote.

You say our government has wasted forty-four years. That's unfair. In 1981, it was Solidarity that caused the wave of panic that emptied the shelves in our stores.

Lech Walesa: Good evening, ladies and gentlemen. I am pleased to be here. And I want to thank those who didn't lose hope these last seven years. I, too, could list all the hardships and problems, and also accuse someone else of being responsible for them, but this is not the time for settling old scores. All I will say is that in 1980 and 1981, circumstances outside of Poland kept Solidarity from pushing through the reforms that it proposed. Brezhnev lived two years too long. But today the circumstances are favorable. It's just that we're not taking advantage of them. For instance, tonight's meeting should have been organized seven years ago.

Mr. Miodowicz, you're right about one thing: We must try to work together and stop fighting each other. Solidarity is ready to make some basic concessions, but on the condition that other basic assumptions be reexamined. It is no coincidence that a wave of reform is spreading across the Eastern Bloc countries. It is time to break away from political monopoly, union monopoly, economic monopoly.

You say that this is not the time for pluralism, that there are more fundamental matters to deal with first. I say we can't settle basic questions without pluralism! The world teaches us that pluralism works. What doesn't work is your hostility to it. That's what's keeping us from all sitting down at the Round Table. So let's not debate whether or not Solidarity is necessary; let's talk about how to get it working again.

AM: Our society needs stability, not slogans like "No freedom without Solidarity." There is more and more freedom in Poland. Our meeting here tonight proves it. But I agree with you that conditions are now ripe for bringing about important new changes in Poland.

LW: I'm glad you see that, because I think history will judge us harshly if we don't take advantage of them, and if we continue to govern by privilege. We need better methods, legal methods. Let's organize a meeting of specialists, each representing the two sides, and let them talk it out for five or six weeks, or until they reach some agreement. These sessions could be

Flashing the V-for-victory salute while leaving the Gdansk shipyards during the 1980 strike.
Stefan Kraszewski.

Standing with Father Henryk Jankowski and Father Jerzy Popieluszko, 1984.

Portrait of me at the time of the Round Table negotiations in 1989.
Stefan Kraszewski.

monument to workers killed in the 1970 shipyard demonstrations in Gdansk:
e anchors affixed to three crosses.
re Cottin.

Being embraced by the Holy Father at Castel Gandolfo, August 27, 1990.

One of my weekly meetings with workers, 1990.
Stefan Kraszewski.

My family in 1987.
In back, from left: Bogdan,
Danuta (holding Brygidka),
me, Slawek, Przemek.
In front, from left:
Jarek, Ania,
Maria Wictoria, Magda.
Ryszard Wesolowski.

Playing goalie in a game
between journalists and
politicians, 1990.
Stefan Kraszewski.

Welcoming President Bush to Poland in June 1989.
Stefan Kraszewski.

Following page:

Meeting with
Prime Minister Tadeusz Mazowiecki
in August 1990.
Stefan Kraszewski.

With Danka standing behind me,
I take the oath of office
as president of Poland,
December 22, 1990.

Accompanying British prime minister
Margaret Thatcher during her 1988 visit to Poland.
Stefan Kraszewski.

broadcast live on television. I repeat: We need to rethink basic principles, and as soon as possible.

AM: I also think discussions are a good idea, even though up to now I haven't been in favor of the idea of the Round Table. The table has been taken apart, but it can always be put back together. A sign of this is our sitting here tonight. I propose that this discussion be continued at the Round Table.

LW: I'm sorry, but I simply don't have the time or desire to fool people by claiming that something is happening when it isn't.

This is how things should go: first, careful analysis done by experts; second, far-reaching reforms. The Round Table will give us a chance to solve our problems. Enough pretense, enough slogans, enough indignity. We chat and our best-trained young people, meanwhile, are heading to the West! Poles are no more or less skilled than other peoples, but they have been badly governed for too long. The absence of pluralism is Stalinism. I will continue to push for Solidarity because Poland needs Solidarity. Together we can put the Round Table back together.

AM: Is union pluralism the answer to Poland's problems? No. We need to look for opportunities within the Party, opportunities that can and will bring about significant change. I agree that our greatest hopes lie with our experts, and we haven't made full use of them.

LW: When I say pluralism, I mean pluralism in three areas: in the economy, in the unions, and in political life. We must agree on this, because sooner or later pluralism will win. No one organization can have a monopoly on some universal truth and make others kneel to it. That's why we fight for pluralism.

AM: Mr. Walesa, I know we each believe in what we say.

LW: You should be encouraging freedom of assembly instead of opposing it. If you really want what's best for Poland, that is.

AM: Poles are a volatile people, and diversity must take place within unity. Otherwise we'll just tear our country apart.

LW: You can't *force* people to be happy. Give them freedom, and they'll stop running in circles. Look at the Hungarians and how far they've come.

AM: You don't think anything has changed in Poland?

LW: We're still on foot, while others are riding in cars.

AM: Soon we'll be getting into those cars, too.

LW: I'll take you at your word. I only hope that we'll take the people with us, because we're supposed to be fighting for them.

17
The Round Table

I don't know exactly how much my debate with Miodowicz affected the government's attitude toward me, but it was easy to see afterward that something had changed. A thaw was in the air. After seven years of waiting, I got my passport back, and this meant I could accept President Mitterrand's invitation to visit France. Bronislaw Geremek, Andrzej Wielowieyski, and I had been invited to take part in the ceremonies on December 9 through 12, 1988, commemorating the fortieth anniversary of the Universal Declaration of the Rights of Man.

The most memorable part of the trip was my meeting with the Paris Polonia.* Poland was coming to its senses, I told them. Finally both sides were realizing that compromise didn't necessarily mean surrender. The expatriate Poles asked about Solidarity's program for Polish independence. We needed first to *feel* free and independent, I answered. Could I comment on emigration? The place for Poles, I said firmly, was Poland.

Back in Gdansk, I was swept up in a whirlwind of events, and on December 18, for the fifth time, I urgently summoned to Warsaw 135 prominent figures from around Poland (119 actually made it). We decided to form the Civic Committee, under the aegis of Solidarity, which would act as a kind of intellectual base in the event that free elections were called. Its second function was to identify independent experts capable of conducting Round Table negotiations.

On December 20, the Tenth Plenary Session of the Central Committee of the People's Republic began. First Secretary Wojciech Jaruzelski, ascribing to himself and his brethren all the initiative and credit for bringing about change, declared:

---

* Polonia is the name used for Polish colonies abroad.

We have not been toiling in fallow fields. Since the latter half of 1980, we have followed the path of socialist renewal. . . . We can be proud that our Party — after so many difficult and frankly dramatic trials — has succeeded in working out, presenting, and instituting into social reality a viable, rational program of transformation as profound in the political as in the economic sector.

A little later, Prime Minister Mieczyslaw Rakowski referred to what was happening in Poland, and in particular to my televised debate with Alfred Miodowicz:

After listening carefully to what people are saying, it appears not only that Lech Walesa's post-debate popularity has risen, but that support for the reactivation of Solidarity has increased. . . . We can't be blind to these realities. The debate has created a new political atmosphere in Poland. Is it worse? The man who won the approval from most Poles because of that debate is not the same Walesa who in the fall of 1981 spoke at Radom of "violent confrontation." This Lech Walesa has a different political profile. He came across as the partisan of entente and compromise. . . . He has continued to give that impression in statements to the press and in interviews. He didn't disavow it during his stay in Paris, even when some in the expatriate community egged him on to take a more hard-line anticommunist stance. . . . The second part of the current plenary session will be held in mid-January. I am positive we will need to return to these topics.

The year 1989 began, and while I sipped champagne I reflected on what the old year had brought us. Mikhail Gorbachev had consolidated his position as the leader of perestroika by being elected president of the presidium of the Supreme Soviet of the USSR on October 1, 1988. (He had been the first secretary of the Central Committee of the Communist Party of the Soviet Union before that.) American voters had elected Vice-President George Bush, a personable man, president. The pope was healthy and continued doing missionary work throughout the world. Maybe the priest Andrzej Klimuszko had been right when, some years earlier, he predicted, "In the next fifty years, I see not even the hint of dark clouds over Poland."

When I looked back at the year with respect to Solidarity, I saw that, far from being a marginal organization with a skeletal crew, it had evolved into a highly organized popular movement. True, we weren't yet legal; but it seemed only a matter of time now. Some companies were already holding open elections, and the many notices on factory bulletin boards were

clear signs that Solidarity was preparing for the day when it could participate officially.

On January 16, 1989, after a break of nearly a month, the second part
of the Tenth Plenary Session of the Central Committee of the People's
Republic began as planned. In the meantime, the political bureau's proposals (which focused on some form of entente with Solidarity and other
opposition organizations) were being discussed by the Party "leaders."
Opening the session, General Jaruzelski remarked, "There is a growing
awareness that the difficulties that beset us cannot be solved by a miracle,
but only by joint efforts and mutual compromise."

He then presented evidence that there was general support within the
government for the Political Bureau's proposals. He made it sound as
though he and his comrades had just discovered the New World: "Our
studies have confirmed that the central focus of the political system . . .
has to be a powerful parliament, which would be the supreme and representative power of the nation, constituted by virtue of a democratized electoral process."

Then Jaruzelski touched the most painful nerve of all: the necessity that
Solidarity be legalized once again. This provoked, as the press agencies
reported it, "a stormy discussion" — so stormy that Jaruzelski had to demand a vote of personal confidence. The vote went heavily in his favor,
and this settled the matter: at 3 A.M. on the morning of January 18, 1989,
the Party leadership, without any fanfare, took a historic step.

Nine days later, General Kiszczak and I worked out the procedures that
would be followed by the three working teams participating in the Round
Table. We fixed February 6 as the date for the first session. The fourteen
pieces of the round table itself were shipped again from Henrykow, and
were now assembled in the Hall of Columns of the Namiestnikowski Palace (the seat of the Council of Ministers) in Warsaw.

On February 6, 1989, fifty-seven people sat down at that table. Why was
it twenty-eight feet wide? The joke going through the corridors had it that
it was because the world's record spitting distance is only twenty-five feet!
The official propaganda machine divided participants into two camps:
pro-government and pro-Solidarity — a convenient classification, though
only partly accurate; perhaps it would be better to speak of the government
and the opposition.

General Kiszczak spoke first: Solidarity, he insisted, would exist again
only if its representatives helped work out a program of economic recon-

struction and took part in Sejm elections — "without confrontation." I was the next to speak, and I stressed that we could still feel Stalin breathing down our necks. "There is only as much co-responsibility as there is co-partnership," I said.

In the course of the first day, the three principal work groups (called "small tables") were formed to negotiate the following topics:

1. Economic and social policy (Witold Trzeciakowski was the leader of our team at this small table).
2. Union pluralism (Tadeusz Mazowiecki led our team).
3. Political reforms (Bronislaw Geremek led our team).

Within these groups, subgroups and working groups (nicknamed "end tables") were formed. They soon began work on legal reform, the courts, the media, local government, associations, secondary education, university education, science and technology, youth, housing policy, agriculture and social policy in the countryside, mining, health, and ecology. The discussion involved the efforts of several hundred negotiators, advisors, and experts, and Lord knows how many assistants.

National surveys showed that most Poles wanted consensus among all the groups, and nearly all those who claimed that they would cooperate with state reforms accepted the invitation to take part. Excluded from the Round Table were members of nonallied groups — extreme Communists, extreme nationalists, sectarians, Party hard-liners allied with the Security Service, and the army.

Some in Poland, though, did not want entente. On January 21, 1989, a priest named Stefan Niedzielak was assassinated in the sacristy of the Church of Saint Charles Borromeo in Warsaw. Ten days later, another priest, thirty-one-year-old Stanislaw Suchowolec, was killed in Bialystok in an apartment that had been rigged up as a gas chamber. Both priests had been heavily engaged in political activity: Niedzielak, a former chaplain of the Home Army and of Freedom and Peace, had created the Polish Sanctuary for Those Who Died in the East (in Russia, in other words), and Father Suchowolec was associated with the Confederation for an Independent Poland (KPN). Both had been receiving death threats right up to the moment of their murder, just before the Round Table talks. It wasn't difficult to guess who was involved: not all of those responsible for Father Jerzy Popieluszko's murder had been brought to justice.

It turned out that the official group — including among others the pro-Party union members — were engaging in some dubious practices up until just a few days before the Round Table discussions began. First, the OPZZ — for reasons best known to itself — had declined to send a delegation to the preliminary talks held at Magdalenka. Then, on February 6, Miodowicz's men called a strike in the Belchatow coal mine, known for its extremely tough working conditions. Soon after, seven thousand out of the twelve thousand workers there joined the strike. Negotiations began only on February 8. The situation deteriorated. Meanwhile, members of the OPZZ attempted to touch off another strike at the nearby power station at Belchatow, but were prevented from doing so by the local branch of Solidarity's Organization Committee. Fortunately, the striking miners recognized that at some point there were more important causes to fight for than immediate wage hikes, and the strike ended. The miners of Belchatow didn't realize that they had been manipulated by the government.

The town of Magdalenka became synonymous in the public imagination with secret concessions and secret agreements. I can state categorically that no corollary agreements were ever concluded there. It was purely and simply a place where top representatives from both sides could discuss issues in private, far from cameras and spectators. Often the public discussions lasted ten hours and produced agreement on only a phrase or two. The quiet meetings at Magdalenka helped us overcome obstacles through our open and often brutally honest discussion. General Kiszczak and I would just listen to the arguments advanced by the experts on basic questions. Our presence seemed to sanction their esoteric findings. Anyone with any experience in diplomacy knows that this kind of informal discussion can take place only far from official negotiations. Some concessions, some brainstorming and bartering, can happen only in private meetings, if only because there is is possible to avoid premature disclosure of agreements in progress.

I personally did not take part in the Round Table discussions following the meetings in Magdalenka, but kept going to the palace of the Council of Ministers to get the latest word. Things seemed to be heading in the right direction, and I could begin to make plans for national elections. I traveled around the country, talking about the general aims of the negotiations. Several thousand workers joined me at the Maximilian Kolbe Church in Mistrzejowice near the steelworks at Nowa Huta. On February 9, a group of us Solidarity standard-bearers gathered at the altar in this two-story church. Father Henryk Jankowski of Gdansk and ten other priests joined together to say a mass for the smooth progress of the Round Table talks. I was made an honorary member of the Union of Steelworkers and asked to take the microphone. I felt at ease, and as a result my little talk was effective. Afterward, answering questions, I warned my listeners to resist the illusion that there was any one political group in Poland capable of leading the country. The next day, Cardinal Francieczek Macharski, archbishop of Cracow, and a group of professors from Jagiellonian University met with me to emphasize the need for grassroots efforts to reform Polish society. "These individual movements will combine to give us all a more modern country, a democratic and well-governed Poland," I said.

On a cold and rainy evening, a week later, in Stalowa Wola, I stressed, "You are your own guarantors! Don't believe in Walesa, in the government, or in anyone else! Put faith only in the structures you yourselves create!" I carefully resisted the temptations of demagoguery; I didn't want to spare my fellow citizens painful truths:

> The time is past for fighting among ourselves or indulging in recriminations. It is time to seek agreement. . . . The Round Table can only begin to help you to take command of your own fates. Without local initiative, nothing will come of it — not even of the most glorious-sounding resolutions. We need radical change in Poland, but we can't boycott the coming elections. We will overhaul our country gradually, through civilized, nonviolent methods. Even when it is legal, Solidarity should not present itself in these elections as an organized party. I want very badly for Solidarity to be strong, but it won't achieve strength through monopoly.

Later, in Lodz, Warsaw, Bielsko-Biala, and other towns, I spoke along the same lines.

As fate would have it, every time I went to the headquarters of the Council of Ministers, which buzzed like a beehive (particularly after some quarrel had broken out at Magdalenka), I ran smack into a demonstration or a picket line forming behind a fence — usually farmers demanding the organization of an agricultural Solidarity, or students striking for the recognition of the Independent Student Union (NZS). One could hear groups of Solidarity members chanting, "Down with communism!"

My hand was sore from shaking so many hands, and my mouth ached from all the smiling. I greeted many and exchanged a few words with many others. I remember hearing Jacek Kuron tell his interpretation of events:

The opposition has always gotten into power either by leading an armed revolt, or by invitation — when the government thought that an alliance with them was a good idea. There has been no third method. Now both sides have started using the same language, and finally some of them mean the same things. Until very recently, the word "democracy" meant its absence, "fraternal assistance" meant armed intervention, and "security" meant danger.

As for the Round Table participants, Bronislaw Geremek (in the subgroup on social policy) was asking, "Is there such a thing as shared responsibility for one's own country when it is completely monopolized?" Adam Michnik (social policy) pointed out the paradox: "You say we must respect the law, but you also want to hold onto the Party's leadership role in the judicial apparatus." There was also Zbigniew Bujak (social policy): "You are specialists in a police state, and we are specialists in a people's state." Janusz Reykowski (political reform): "We are to remember one point only: that the next step toward democracy not be a step toward destabilization." Marcin Krol (social policy): "If the governing Party considers elections to be a part of the social contract, we consider free access to radio and television a part of this contract." To which Jerzy Urban (political reform) responded, "Anyone in Poland can mouth off as much as they want to — just not on television." Krzysztof Kozlowski (social policy): "To recognize the role the press plays as a normal secondary channel doesn't settle the question, because since Polish culture is unitary, it needs only a primary channel." Piotr Nowina-Konopka (social policy): "Whatever official propaganda might say, we have excellent specialists and we know precisely what we want."

I soon heard that disagreements had brought the discussions to a grinding halt, and I was summoned to attend a meeting in Magdalenka. During those first days, the three main groups had brought up so many problems that they seemed insurmountable. At the "small table" handling union pluralism, the government side maintained that the issue of pluralism had been satisfactorily settled at the Party's Tenth Plenary Session, to which the social-policy subgroup responded by demanding a change in the law governing unions (enacted in 1982, during the state of martial law). As to whether several unions could operate in the same enterprise, our side proposed Tadeusz Mazowiecki's formula: competing but not confrontational unions. At the political-reform "small table," the basic impasse had already taken shape: in exchange for registering Solidarity, the opposition would agree to elections in which the government coalition would win regardless, because of the percentage of seats guaranteed to it in the parliament; after the elections there would be a transitional period during which the Party would give up its monopoly, but true democracy would still not exist. Most of the bargaining involved how to combine elections with access to the mass media. At the economic "small table," the social-policy subgroup at first rejected the government's plan for so-called economic consolidation, pointing out its inconsistencies on a number of points. It was a collision of two incompatible ways of thinking, and the OPZZ representatives played the role of spoilers (just as they did at the union-pluralism table).

Lines of demarcation shifted, sometimes hardening, sometimes blurring. Negotiators from both sides had met each other on other occasions, and they began to demonstrate greater and greater tact, political acumen, and goodwill with each other. They could also smile, and then stab each other in the back on fundamental questions. Feeling the weight of its responsibility to see that the discussions progressed, the social-policy section was fully aware how social "pluralization" might lead to polarization. They knew that the time had come for the "moderates." Which way would these moderates go? Only the elections could provide the answer.

Meanwhile, Round Table participants assumed tasks that under normal conditions would have been handled by the state. That's why they sometimes acted like the Sejm, sometimes like the executive branch, without really being either. Only the goal was clear: to construct a framework for democracy.

It was one thing to say that we wanted a new order, and something else to agree on its shape. It took more than a month for the Round Table to move from the discussion phase into the decision-making phase. But at some point everyone knew that there was no going back.

I did finally become convinced that an agreement would be reached. Yes, there were a few logjams and sandbars still blocking the path, but we all wanted to get beyond them. Despite the setbacks of 1970 and 1981, we all believed we would succeed this time, if only because now our ranks had swollen with frustrated young people prepared to pay for their ideals in blood. The opening of the Round Table talks had been a turning point; now we needed to ensure that they went down in Polish history as one of the nation's greatest triumphs. In the final days the government party began using our terms: "anticrisis pact," for example, meant a nonaggression pact. And the accords we reached now made it possible to transform Poland without any one political force stacking the deck. All this was done at the negotiating table, not in the streets — eloquent testimony that Polish society had matured.

The major objectives were achieved. There were plans for new laws on union pluralism and resource allocation. Thirty-five percent of the seats in the Sejm would be open to free election and all of the seats in the Senat; and the post of president of the Republic was created, a position with broad executive powers. There were dozens of agreements on modernizing the economy.

The Round Table completed its mission on the evening of the sixtieth day, April 5, 1989.

It was time for a formal announcement. The OPZZ militants were still trying to muddy the waters, saying that if Alfred Miodowicz wasn't accorded the right to speak directly after "Kiszczak and Walesa," the OPZZ delegation would leave the hall in dramatic fashion and refuse to sign the last-minute accord on wage-indexing. The pro-government union activists were just trying to get attention, but since we wanted to bring the talks to a successful close, we submitted to their blackmail. Their tactics surprised me a little. Here was Miodowicz, self-styled defender of the oppressed, ready to refuse to sign one of the most important documents in our history, just to further his own ambitions.

Summarizing the achievements of the Round Table, General Kiszczak declared:

> We have completed a truly collaborative piece of work. The experience was shared, and so should be the satisfaction. Speculation about who won and by how much, or who lost and by how much, is unproductive. There's been only one victor: our homeland. . . . We have not worked in a vacuum nor behind closed doors. We have sought advice from society at large, we have listened to the voices of public opinion, we have read letters and telegrams from around the country. The future will reveal the practical, concrete results that come of these discussions. One thing is certain: they have already created precious political and moral capital, and have demonstrated once again that when confronted with serious problems, when their homeland needs them, Poles are able to rise above their divisions, their differences, and their prejudices.

It was then my turn to take the floor. I cleared my throat, faced the cameras, and said:

No freedom without Solidarity — armed with that truth we came to the Round Table. We have come to this table from prisons and from under the clubs of the ZOMO, carrying with us the living memory of those who shed their blood for Solidarity. . . . That is why all the committees of the Round Table have tried to reach concrete decisions that might be carried out immediately. . . . Our demands have been accepted by the government coalition party; and so we have what we need to begin the road toward democratic reforms. . . . We realize that the Round Table negotiations have not lived up to every expectation. But for the first time, we have talked among ourselves using the force of arguments and not the arguments of force. . . . So we look to the future with courage and hope. We look to the words inscribed on the monument at Gdansk:

> *The Lord gives strength to His people,*
> *And to His people the blessings of peace.*

At a long press conference on April 6, 1989, I stated, "The framework of the talks needs to be translated into action, fast. Too often, Poles have laid down their scythes after a victory, and watched how their sacrifice achieved nothing. A beautifully bound book may hide a bad story." Responding to personal questions, I remarked, "Many people have grown to resent me or deplore me, saying that I've changed, that I used to be more spontaneous, and that my smile used to be sincere. You know, sometimes I've had to climb down from my tree and quit making faces. I had to learn to be more calculating, more flexible, and more crafty. That's why people who used to praise Lech the Brave are now wondering, 'Which is he, a worker or a politician?'"

18
Among Ourselves

On December 18, 1988, the group calling itself the Civic Committee was formed under the aegis of Solidarity. By April 1989, in the basement of the church on Zytnia Street in Warsaw, the battle for power had begun. Guided by the four points of the program adopted the day before by Solidarity's National Executive Board, we stated:

1. Solidarity would become part of public life as a legal organization during the election campaign.
2. The Civic Committee was to direct the electoral campaign under the name Civic Committee of Solidarity; the union's regional organization would form regional civic committees.
3. People from different social backgrounds and political orientations were to appear on the lists of candidates.
4. Writers and artists were to play a particularly active role in the campaign.

On April 8, the Civic Committee, now committed to this agenda, began its discussions. Here are a few excerpts:

Lech Walesa: My proposal is this: We should try to win the elections to the Senat and the Sejm not only on the basis of an individual candidate's program, but also on a platform. Our union is still not legal (though it's only a question of days), but there are already opportunities we must seize. We should approach the elections as a single group able to unite all of the opposition forces that exist at this point.
Bronislaw Geremek: There is a commonality of principles within the Civic Committee, a sense that we all share the same basic values about public life.

We know that the Round Table's achievements can be measured only in terms of their application to life, but from now on we'll begin to confront a big problem — the election campaign. These elections will not be fully democratic, and yet, for the first time in forty-five years, something really does depend upon how the citizens vote. We can exploit this piece of freedom, but we have only a sketchy organizational structure and extremely limited access to the media. We should also realize that to lose these elections is simply not an option, because the elections will be like a prism, and through them the strength of Solidarity and civil society will be measured. I share Lech Walesa's conviction that this could prove risky for the union's legendary reputation and its achievements, but right at the moment we have to place all our bets on a single card. We have only a few weeks to collect the huge number of signatures required for each candidate.

Fortunately, our activity will soon have the backing of *Gazeta Wyborcza* [*Electoral Gazette*], the first independent newspaper in Poland since before the war. Now I think we should answer sincerely the question of whether we are responding affirmatively to the call of Solidarity's central authorities. If we are, we should move on immediately and decide how to proceed.

Edmund Osmanczyk: Building a democracy is not a job for those of little faith, limited knowledge, or a lack of imagination about the real world. Our electoral strategy should be to form a tight political circle of civic opposition, with Lech Walesa as our symbol of unity. In my opinion, women will play a decisive role in the election, so mobilizing them will be crucial. We should clearly outline the main problems the new parliament will have to face. Our deputies not only should build a pluralist political wing within the Sejm, but must also have a wide knowledge of modern solutions to matters of state.

Andrzej Wajda: If we're going to win, we first need to ask ourselves this question: Under what banner? I think the banner will be Solidarity. I know that Solidarity is a union, but it is also a national movement. "Vote for Solidarity" is the only battle cry that will give us a chance to win. If we want to run a real electoral campaign, we should address young people over the radio of the Independent Student Union and in the schools of fine arts. The heart of our campaign will be *Gazeta Wyborcza,* as well as the local radio and television stations. There's no point in being ashamed that we'll need money, even foreign money.

Aleksander Hall: What is essential is what works, and will largely depend on how rapidly we concentrate our forces. But the elections should also let us show that Solidarity and the opposition mean what they say when they talk about democracy and pluralism, and that they practice what they preach. That is the first and most important lesson society will learn. I believe we have three frameworks with which to approach the campaign:

1. Solidarity directs and underwrites the opposition campaign (the weakness of this idea is the fact that though Solidarity is the most important opposition member, it isn't the only one).
2. The campaign is directed by the Civic Committee, but really by Solidarity (the drawback to this approach is that it fudges reality).
3. The Civic Committee takes on the job assigned to it by Solidarity, but only on the condition that it consult with and call upon all groups in the opposition to join with them in a coalition for democracy. I believe that members of the National Executive Board had this possibility in mind.

Andrzej Malanowski: I agree with Aleksander Hall. We have just begun a difficult game in which the Civic Committee needs to represent all the various political shadings within our opposition.

Adam Strzembosz: Given that we face a government coalition, we should counter with an opposition coalition, thus providing opportunities for those who otherwise wouldn't have any. In my opinion, a political body should be created within the Civic Committee and assigned the task of attracting various representatives of the opposition. What is at stake here are the interests of all the Poles, not just various political options.

Jan Maria Rokita: I don't see much of a future for Solidarity if the militants in its executive branch link their union mandate with their political mandate in the reformed branches of the government. This linkage would inevitably result in their either having a limited parliamentary role (in other words, having to raise their hands like marionettes), or completely neglecting their union activities. Furthermore, I do not think that decisions about the lists of candidates should be heavily weighted toward the middle-of-the-road Solidarity (under the assumption that anything radical is bad). Finally, I think the elections ought not to paper over differences within the opposition; instead, the opposition's job of putting everything into question should continue. We in the opposition cannot let ourselves be drawn into becoming another *nomenklatura*.

Jacek Bartyzel: I represent the people of Lodz, who at the beginning of March started an organization called the Entente of the Citizens of Lodz. It's a kind of forum for public debate involving twelve very different political groups, so it's not surprising that these people want to present their own candidates for parliament. This shows how sound Aleksander Hall's remarks are.

Tadeusz Mazowiecki: The electoral campaign won't replace the organization of the government; and the elections won't slow the rapid process of Solidarity's organization. All these "higher" tasks have to be taken on at the same time. For me, the most important thing to do now is to strengthen — if I can put it this way — the oppositional imagination. Where there is no democratic structure there is manipulation. The members of the Civic Committee come from various sectors of our society, but they all recognize the primacy of Solidarity's ideals.

In the future, however, we will need an internal democratic structure so that we can see just what we are. From the trunk of Solidarity will grow different branches.

The second question is whether the Civic Committee of Warsaw ought to assume a position of higher authority than those of other committees. These and similar dilemmas compel me to side with Mr. Strzembosz's proposal to create a political subcommittee, which would mark a turning point in our work. To guarantee Lech Walesa's authority, it is important that this subcommittee be formed democratically. We must not win a mandate in a way that could later turn against us.

Halina Bortnowska: I support Mr. Strzembosz's proposal, but I would take it further. Let's ask those here at this meeting right now whether, instead of being Mr. Walesa's guests, they would rather form their own committee to run the campaign. Do we all feel strongly enough about this kind of activity to sign our (often well-known) names? Every person has the right to be asked this question one more time. It can be organized so that only those who have decided to act will come to the next meeting. I also think that the core of the next political subcommittee could be formed today, for time is pressing. I propose a Solidarity League for Electing Independents, or something of that kind.

Lech Walesa: My friends, life has put us where it has put us, and that's why I don't think we'll be able to settle everything democratically just at the moment. We should use the elections to the best of our abilities — meaning to wake society up. This is already a kind of manipulation, but we have no other choice. After listening to all these opinions, I repeat my request: Let's create a single organism that will assume the heavy burden of bringing the electoral campaign to a successful conclusion consistent with our ideas. Failure is unacceptable: there are 161 seats to win in the Sejm and 100 in the Senat. Don't force me to be a dictator; let me be a democrat.

Jacek Kuron: We haven't had a parliamentary democracy in Poland for forty years, and we don't have any real politicians. So nothing can justify our drawing up a list of candidates centrally. This list must be worked out regionally; the most that the Civic Committee can do is to keep careful track of it, with help from of its campaign subcommittee. As for what to call it, I propose that it remain the Civic Committee, so as not to fuel more rumors.

The discussion went on for seven hours. What emerged was a short resolution in which the Civic Committee declared that as the Solidarity Civic Committee it was ready to sponsor the opposition electoral campaign for the Sejm and the Senat. Sixty-nine voted for Aleksander Hall's motion, and nineteen against; there were thirteen abstentions. The Solidarity Civic Committee would draw up a "central" list of opposition candidates based on regional lists, which would be monitored carefully by Solidarity union activists. The committee created five teams for the election: one to deal with matters of organization; one for radio and television; one to coordinate the lists of candidates; one to deal with matters concerning *Gazeta Wyborcza*; and the last to handle questions about the platform. The committee would also create a group to manage finances.

On April 17, 1989, after more than eight years of struggle, the Warsaw regional court once again permitted the registration of the Independent and Self-Governing Union "Solidarity" (in Polish, abbreviated NSZZ "Solidarnosc"), listed officially as a national organization with headquarters in Gdansk. It was an extraordinary moment, but it took place without ceremony and without much media attention. We Poles love victory to be accompanied by cannon volleys and drum-rolls, banners flying. Nonviolent "administrative" victories such as this one, on the other hand, we consider definitely less dramatic, even if they do attest to a greater political maturity. At the beginning of its "second life," Solidarity would clearly no longer be the party of "all the people" against the Communist *nomenklatura*, but a mature, less populist, and more permanent structure. An enormous amount of union-organizing lay before us. But for the moment the union ranks (regional and national) still had to play politics. Until after the elections, at least.

19
The Light from the Vatican

On April 19, 1989, Danka and I waited in Warsaw for the plane that was to take us to Rome to see the pope. With us were Bronislaw Geremek, Tadeusz Mazowiecki, Witold Trzeciakowski, and Tadeusz Goclowski, the bishop of Gdansk; a little farther off, a crowd bid us good-bye. We felt elated and happy, as if we'd drunk champagne: the Round Table accords had been signed two weeks earlier, and Solidarity had been officially registered just two days earlier. Our eight years of struggle had not been in vain.

Under my arm I was holding a copy of *Trybuna Ludu,* the Party paper, and this issue, for the first time in a long time, carried no slurs against me, but instead a large photo of Jaruzelski and myself, taken at our meeting the day before. After all those years when he and I had been locked into a "war of attrition," each trying grimly to convince the other of the force of his argument, events had suddenly fast-forwarded, as in a film. No longer was I only a "private" citizen of the People's Republic of Poland. The climate had changed radically; one felt it everywhere. A congenial crowd surrounded me in the tiny lounge of Okecie Airport, while smiling customs agents pretended to inspect the contents of our luggage.

We boarded the Tupolev 154 for the two-and-a-half-hour flight, accompanied only by the team of the Church-run Gdansk Video Studio, journalists in whom we had complete trust. For years they had been secretly making videos to be used later for a documentary history. Marian Terlecki, the head of the team, had been imprisoned for nearly two years because of his association with Solidarity.

Let me try to give a sense of the various chats that took place during our flight to Rome.

187

Ryszard Grabowski (of Video Studio): Aren't you afraid of flying in this plane? [A number of crashes of the Soviet Ilyushin had occurred in recent months. Fortunately, we were flying in one of the Tupolev 154s, which crashed less often.]

Lech Walesa: Speaking as an electrician, I don't see any malfunctions. I don't know much about the mechanics of it. Everything is in the hands of God.

RG: What is the purpose of your visit?

LW: The makeup of our delegation speaks for itself. First, a bishop — to give thanks to the pope (and the Church) because they did not forget us, and because he continued to speak of the ideals that inspired us to hold on and wait for the end of communism. The struggle is over, the work is beginning, and we seek his blessing for the journey that lies ahead. Also with us are the knights of the Round Table: Tadeusz Mazowiecki, leader of the group that handled union matters; Witold Trzeciakowski, who presided over the economic group; and Bronislaw Geremek, head of the political group.

RG: What were your emotions at your first meeting with General Jaruzelski in eight years?

LW: Oh, I got rid of emotions a long time ago. Our meeting marked the end of the phase of struggle and the beginning of a period of cooperative reconstruction. Sure, I had some fears, since it was General Jaruzelski who had declared martial law, interned thousands of people, and blocked political reforms for many years, but what would we gain by opening old wounds? I agreed to talk with him because in my mind it was already the future. We discussed entente.

RG: Why isn't there more enthusiasm, now that the Round Table talks have ended successfully and the opposition will be taking part in the elections?

LW: Because everything's still in the organizational and theoretical stage. For the guy in the street, freedom is mostly a matter of economics, and he hasn't seen any progress on that score yet. Unlike in 1980, people are suspicious. There was a lot of emotion then, but no political opportunities. Now it's the opposite. . . . Ah! I have forgotten to introduce yet another member of our delegation: my wife.

RG: She's played an important part in Solidarity since the Nobel Prize.

Tadeusz Mazowiecki: When I saw him in Gdansk after my internment and congratulated him on his wife's political acumen, Lech was not pleased.

LW: Yes. Because for me to do what I do, I must have peace and quiet at home. That's why I don't want my wife to get involved in politics.

Bishop Goclowski: However, there were moments when your wife played an important role, don't you agree?

LW: Yes, but people shouldn't try to do everything. We have a large family, and up to now my wife needed to be at home.

Danuta Walesa: I'm the one who keeps the family organization on its feet on behalf of Solidarity.

TM: Then I'll sign up.

The plane flew along the Adriatic coast, and through the windows we could see marvelous countryside. From above, Italy looked so tidy and organized. I envied those who lived down there. How much would we have to do for Poland to advance to that level?

TM: The point of our visit is to tell the pope personally what has been happening in Poland. The negotiations are not the stuff of legend, maybe, but that they took place at all shows what is possible today that yesterday was not. So we're going to Italy to express our very special gratitude to the Italian trade unions, which are marvelous organizations. They are separated from us by differences in worldview, but for all these years every one of them helped Solidarity — even the Communist ones.

Witold Trzeciakowski: As for me, I want to assure the Italian industrialists that political stability has already been established in the Polish market, so they should begin investing in us. I also want to convince the Club de Paris to allow us to defer debt payment, because otherwise we'll lose any real chance for economic growth.

At almost the same moment we were preparing to land in Rome, the pope, in his weekly general audience, said:

Beginning on December 13, 1981, I have prayed to the Virgin every Wednesday, asking Her to take this difficult period in our lives under her protection. Today I wish to thank You, Holy Mother, for all the good that has emerged out of these trying times. I commend to Your maternal protection Solidarity, which will again be legal on April 17, 1989. And in connection with that happy event, I commend to Your care the process that hopes to restore a national life consistent with the rights of a sovereign society.

Those Wednesday audiences had played an important role during the state of martial law in Poland. Everybody in Poland listened to the pope. People sat around their radios trying to tune in to the Polish programs on Radio Free Europe because they wanted to hear that their resistance to authority was morally justified. The voice of John Paul II reached not only Poland, but also Lithuania, the Ukraine, Latvia, Bohemia, Slovenia, and all other parts of Communist Europe. His teaching forced cracks to form in the wall of totalitarianism. I wonder what Stalin would have thought — Stalin, who asked the famous question, "How many army divisions does the pope have?" — had he watched the Soviet empire crumble and his invincible armies surrender one after the other to the "pope's armies."

I spoke of this at the University of Sacro Cuore, part of which is the famous Gemelli Clinic. I was invited there to meet with professors and students from the medical school, a meeting at which I received a medal stamped especially in my honor. "We came here to thank you for saving Solidarity," I said.

They gave me a puzzled look.

"Yes!" I continued. "It was you who saved the Holy Father after the assassination attempt in May 1981. And it's hard to imagine that Solidarity would have survived without him."

The Italian press circulated this comment widely, and not all the response to it was favorable. In the eyes of many journalists, we were all basically just clerical types. Rather than go into Polish history I took a kind of intellectual shortcut: Where would Solidarity have been if the Church hadn't let us use all those thousands of catechism rooms and church basements for our meetings and discussions during martial law? Where would we be if we hadn't repeated the Church's messages that violence breeds violence, and that people cannot build happiness on the unhappiness of their neighbors? Or that we could remain strong only so long as we avoided terrorism? In 1989, communism was in retreat worldwide, and in the city squares, people at long last could yell out what they thought and wanted. Five years ago, I continued, Poles could express themselves only in churches or during street demonstrations, but street demonstrations always threatened violence. There were plenty of young people whose specialty was provoking confrontations with the police, and they could do so with great skill. It is but a small step from there to terrorism. If we managed to avoid that route, it's also thanks to the Church.

I expanded on the theme I had raised at the Gemelli Clinic during my meetings with the Vatican's secretary of state, Agostino Casaroli. Monsignor Casaroli asked how events in Poland were unfolding and what role the new Solidarity would play. I replied that the time for struggle was over, and that in order to become part of Europe we needed to build a democracy. If what I said may have sounded like a simplistic slogan, it told a complex truth. Because of all that has happened in Poland over the last forty-five years, building a democratic system there was like learning the Chinese alphabet. I also reiterated to the cardinal what the pope had meant to us during the past few years. He had been as necessary as the sun. Without the Church, we all knew, communism would have led us further and further into darkness.

On April 20, 1989, the pope granted me an audience. It took place in his library, immediately following his reception of the president of the Irish Republic. Thanks to him I got to tread on red carpets, and my approach was heralded by ceremonial clashes of halberds wielded by the Vatican's Swiss Guards. Of course, I knew that I wasn't a head of state, but this was the Holy Father's benevolent gesture.

We spoke for forty minutes. I brought him up to date on the latest events, and briefed him about the intentions of the parties at the Round Table, Solidarity, General Jaruzelski. I talked about our nation's endurance. We reminisced about the past. I assured the pope that we were not seeking vengeance; we would demonstrate that, to us, Christian principles were more than mere lofty phrases. We were fully aware of having entered our most difficult phase. No longer benefitting from the excuses and special status granted a society oppressed by communism, now we had to prove that we could do more than struggle and conspire. We were facing a new reality. My conversation with John Paul II was warm and straightforward. Our exchange — reassuring in its simplicity — raised my morale, and I came away with sound advice.

As I was leaving, the Holy Father asked after the children and noted that Danuta looked less well than previously. She had in fact lost weight. The last few months had taken their toll. I was hardly ever at home, and we still had no one to help with our eight children. The pope gave me a copy of the mosaic of the Virgin of Ravenna as a parting gift; I offered him an album of photographs taken during the strikes that had opened the doors to change in Poland. Then, as the other members of the delegation came in, the pope jovially encouraged the photographers to take a number of pictures. Speaking to the Gdansk Video Studio team, he said, "Ah! You're from Gdansk? I remember. The light from Gdansk." Those words were to become the motto of their future broadcasts.

During the rest of our Italian visit, I met with the secretaries of the three union groups — the CGIL, the CISL, and the UIL — and warmly thanked them all for their steadfast help and support, especially when we were

under martial law. During General Jaruzelski's January 1987 visit to
Rome, Italian unionists had actually convinced him to open a dialogue
with Solidarity. What interested us now was how the unions — part of
whose job is to foster Italy's economic development — also managed to
look out for the workers' interests and keep an eye on legislation designed
to uphold social justice.

I had also come to Rome as a semiofficial ambassador in pursuit of
economic aid. On the evening of April 21, I paid a visit to the CNEL,
the Italian Committee for Labor and the Economy, founded to encourage
entente between union leaders and industrialists, where I tried to present
reasons to invest in Poland. In a country where goods were scarce, I said,
the expanding Italian industry could do great business. As a result of that
discussion, the idea of organizing an economic forum in Poland to study
possible cooperation with Italy was born. Some of those present had previously confronted the jungle of Polish tax policies, and the experience
had cooled their enthusiasm.

We also met with the Italian president, Francesco Cossiga; the president
of the Italian Senate, Giovanni Spadolini (who had visited in Gdansk in
November 1988); the prime minister, Ciriaco de Mita; and the minister for
foreign affairs, Giulio Andreotti. Thanking them all for understanding our
people's hopes for democracy, we laid out the main principles behind the
Round Table's philosophy for them. We were then ushered off to meet the
heads of the largest political parties: Arnaldo Forlani of the Christian
Democrats, Bettino Craxi of the Socialist Party, and Achille Occhetto of
the Communist Party. I reminded everyone of Bettino Craxi's many efforts on behalf of the imprisoned Polish opposition militants, and invited
them all to visit Poland.

The Communist leader, Achille Occhetto, expressed the keenest desire
to do so, and my private meeting with him was a spectacular success. Occhetto confided that Poland's servitude in 1981 had had a profound influence on the Italian Communist Party. For Comrade Enrico Berlinguer it
had afforded the chance to offer bitter criticism of the so-called "real socialism," and to argue for the need for profound reform in the whole of
Eastern Europe. His position triggered the process that has now passed
into history under the term "the collapse of the Communist world."
Solidarity's struggle, Occhetto continued, was an inspiration to all the
forces in Europe that believed in democratic socialism. The Italian Communist leader kept calling me "comrade" and "friend." Inviting him to
Poland, I stated that I would greet him personally at the airport in Warsaw

as a demonstration of Solidarity's gratitude to the then-secretary of the Communist Party, Alessandro Natta, who had publicly jolted Jaruzelski by asking him about the legal status of the opposition.

The mayor of Rome presented me with a magnificent replica of the she-wolf of the Capitol — the symbol of the Eternal City. Europe was a single entity, I said to the press, and Poles had as much right as anyone to belong to it. The journalists asked me about Solidarity's new agenda. I replied:

Solidarity is a reform movement whose main purpose is to break up monopolies. We want to exist only as a union, but under the conditions of post-Stalinist monopoly, that's not immediately possible. First, as a movement, we have to break the stranglehold of the existing political system, while also taking care that we don't ourselves turn into a monopoly. In time, other organizations will emerge and they will help create pluralism. We're not the same organization we were in 1981, because now we must unite the people who founded Solidarity with those who were only twelve or thirteen years old at the time. What price will Solidarity pay for working with the government? Most people understand how necessary it will be to work with government, in some sense to "collaborate." What I wonder is: Will those once imprisoned for their beliefs be satisfied just because they can now become deputies?

20
Turning West

When we returned from Rome, events accelerated. We had to address pressing national questions needing immediate attention. Our view on Poland's place in Europe and in the world in the light of the Round Table accords had to be formulated. We listed the five principal goals of the Polish nation:

1. Achieve national sovereignty.
2. Maintain and consolidate peace.
3. Break down divisions between Poland and Europe.
4. Develop international relations.
5. Strengthen and expand human rights.

We could actually summarize our declaration in a single sentence: Our goal is a free and secure Poland, living at peace in the world.

On May 5, the leading members of Solidarity and I were received by Cardinal Glemp. The cardinal, to whom we explained the selection process for our candidates, pressed upon us the ethical imperatives of public service. As expected, he also raised the issue of abortion.

On May 7, I attended an electoral meeting in Plock. After participating in the procession of the relics of Saint Zygmunt, the patron saint of Plock, I gave a speech that concluded, "If we don't win the elections, don't blame Walesa. Blame yourselves!" I repeated that message as often as I could during the next four weeks in dozens of other towns.

On May 8, 1989, the first issue of *Gazeta Wyborcza* came out, with Adam Michnik, the well-known Polish opposition militant, as editor-in-chief. Our slogan became its motto: "No freedom without Solidarity." A number of journalists were hired from what had formerly been the underground press, and the eight-page format was expanded after a few months to include additional columns. From the start, *Gazeta Wyborcza*, Poland's first independent daily paper since before World War II, became an instant success, because it filled in a serious information gap. It also acted as a welcome counterweight to the propagandistic Party press and forced it into some measure of honesty. In a declaration that appeared in that first issue of *Gazeta*, I ended by writing, "I see our opportunities increasing with every passing day, and we are taking more and more advantage of them. With *Gazeta* they will increase even faster." In the second issue, Adam Michnik, paraphrasing Marx, wrote, "A specter is haunting Europe and other continents — the specter of the end of Gulag communism."*

Despite the full schedules of the election campaign, I carved out time for two important trips — to Strasbourg and to Brussels. In Strasbourg on May 9, the Council of Ministers of the Council of Europe honored me with the European Prize for Human Rights. This distinction has been awarded every three years, beginning in 1980. The previous laureates were Raúl Alfonsín, the president of Argentina, and the medical division of Amnesty International; I shared the 1989 prize with the Helsinki International Federation.

"Though I am the one to receive this medal," I said in my acceptance speech, "I know it represents your recognition of Solidarity's efforts as a whole to broaden respect for human rights in my country, and to embrace principles of nonviolence. I therefore accept it on behalf of a great many men and women from different movements, associations, and organizations, who have come to the defense of human rights in my part of Europe."

I also stressed that reform in Poland required that the West offer support and understanding, for the hopes of the weary Polish people would falter without international cooperation. In Europe, respect for human rights and personal dignity was the living heritage of Christian humanism, I concluded.

"There is one Europe," I told representatives from the business world:

But it is divided. So we must unite. No single country can solve all the problems it faces. The system that we Poles are trying to tear down shut itself off

---

* Michnik is parodying the opening sentence of *The Communist Manifesto*: "A specter is haunting Europe — the specter of communism." — Ed.

from democratic countries behind an iron curtain. We are asking you — you who have been raised in a different environment — to teach us how to build democracy and achieve economic health. We would be only too happy to have your problems of overproduction, for our stores are empty. Our absurd pricing system means that, for example, an average-quality color television costs half a year's pay. In this age of computers and satellite dishes we can only look at how others live and gaze enviously at everything we lack. Gray buildings, streets pitted with potholes, endless lines for the smallest items — those are our reality. That is why my part of Europe looks with such hope to yours, not in the hope of a handout, but for help in improving our economic condition.

The Italian president, Francesco Cossiga, and Giulio Andreotti, his foreign minister, arrived on an official visit to Poland just as I returned. Bronislaw Geremek, Tadeusz Mazowiecki, Witold Trzeciakowski, and I met with them. We discussed many aspects of the current situation in Poland. The Italians agreed that it was imperative, if the Polish political miracle were to succeed, that it be backed up by considerable material aid, the exact amount of which could be specified later. Cossiga, in the course of his state visit, strongly urged all Poland to join in the victory and vote.

Not everyone intended to join the vote. The group known as Militant Solidarity, formed under the leadership of Kornel Morawiecki of Wroclaw during the state of martial law, differed from us, mainstream Solidarity, in that it rejected any suggestion of entente. Militant Solidarity called for a boycott of the elections, which it claimed "broke with the principle of national sovereignty." I found myself flying from one meeting to another in an effort to counteract their position.

We considered it a great victory when, on May 17, the Polish parliament passed a law legalizing the Catholic Church, and restoring to it a number of privileges that had been revoked following World War II. This law represented years of negotiation between the representatives of the Church and the government, and was the first act to normalize relations between the state and the clergy. Poland, therefore, become the first country in the Soviet sphere to restore diplomatic relations with the Vatican. Once again the Church was given the right to buy and sell land, establish and run schools and hospitals, even to operate radio and television stations without government interference. The government also gave back control over construction of religious buildings, and agreed to restore, or grant financial compensation for, hospitals and other properties taken from the Church in the 1950s. A second, no less important, law provided freedom of religion for all denominations while also reestablishing state allowances and salaries for Poland's 62,000 priests and nuns. All this represented the government's acknowledgment of the Church's role in creating the Round Table.

The two-day trip to Brussels wore me out. I had been invited to speak at and attend numerous meetings between government representatives and compatriots. On January 1, 1993, Brussels will become the capital of a united Europe of twelve nations and 280 million inhabitants. There, decisions concerning some 40 percent of the world's business will be handled. That is why my visit wasn't limited to discussions about unions. Apart from gaining some prestige (a not insignificant commodity), I wanted to gain the confidence of financial backers.

While in Brussels I attended a formal session of the ICFTU, at which John Vanderveken, the secretary-general, declared, "We have stuck by Solidarity through thick and thin — during those difficult days under martial law, and during happier times. You, Mr. Walesa, and your movement now have many friends, some in unexpected places, but I am delighted to see that with all your heavy obligations you have found time to meet with the most steadfast of them."

My brief, improvised reply, in which I thanked them warmly, was applauded by a hundred representatives from the largest group of unions in the world. Also present were representatives from the Basque organization (also named Solidarity), as well as members of my delegation. Our old friend Lane Kirkland of the AFL-CIO declared that the name "Solidarity" represented the very ideals of the union movement, and that it was no coincidence that the anthem of the American unionists was called "Solidarity Forever."

During the course of political visits and meetings that followed, the Belgian prime minister, Wilfried Martens, at the end of our two-hour conversation, was generous enough to declare, "It is not Mr. Gorbachev, but Mr. Walesa, who initiated the changes in Eastern Europe." The president of the European Economic Community, Jacques Delors, strongly affirmed the possibility of cooperation between the EEC and Poland, through a rescheduling of our debt repayments and a lowering of interest rates. That, of course was extremely important for us.

The second day of my visit began with a religious service at the Polish Catholic mission and a meeting with the Polonia of Brussels (nearly a hundred thousand Poles live in Belgium). I was taken to the king of the Belgians, Baudouin I, with whom I talked freely for about fifty minutes. This was, I was told, the first time that a union leader had met with the monarch, who by constitutional law is allowed to receive only heads of state. This exception didn't seem to make His Majesty uncomfortable; he appeared very much at his ease.

The General Federation of Belgian Workers had extended considerable help to Solidarity during the darkest of times, and I was pleased to be able to express our gratitude to them. During that visit to Belgium, I also received a gold medal for encouraging solidarity among the workers of Eastern and Western Europe. "Mr. Walesa, this is your home, this is the house of Solidarity," said Jan Kulakowski, the secretary-general of the WCL. "We have supported you from the first. We supported you when you were operating underground, and we will also support you while you build a new Poland."

During the dinner given in Solidarity's honor, a declaration of cooperation between Poland and Belgium was read aloud and signed by Philippe Moureaux, the deputy prime minister and minister of governmental reforms:

> The success or failure of your experiment will have incalculable consequences for the future of Europe; that is why we will not neglect our duty to show you our support and our solidarity. You realize more clearly than anyone that economic development depends on more than just governmental action. That, among other things, is what distinguishes our two economic systems.

At Solidarity's Brussels office, three hours before taking off for Poland, we again met with the leadership of the International Labor Organization, which, after martial law was declared, had most strongly opposed the government's decision to forbid free unions in Poland. Their opposition had nearly forced Poland's withdrawal from this organization. Now that the source of the conflict had vanished, we could discuss Solidarity's participation at the next session of the ILO.

During the flight home, I wondered whether these two days had brought us closer to Europe. Only time would tell.

In Prague, Vaclav Havel, who had been arrested that January during a demonstration, had been freed from prison. I was also told that there had been demonstrations in front of the Soviet consulate in Cracow, which at first I was inclined to regard as a Soviet provocation. I calmed down, however, when I was assured that young radicals were solely responsible. On May 17, I was named honorary president of the Polish Peace Committee.

Meanwhile, the mass media were preoccupied with the news that the Supreme Soviet of the Soviet Socialist Republic of Lithuania had adopted a declaration of national sovereignty. The republic was actually seceding from the Soviet empire! I told some friends that if things continued like this, the Berlin Wall would come down.

On May 23, the Independent Student Union (NZS) was denied official status, and this immediately provoked a wave of strikes within institutions of higher learning. On May 24, I met with representatives of the Hungarian League of Independent Unions.

On May 28, I was able to visit Piekary Slaskie and the icon of the much-venerated Piekarska Virgin during the annual pilgrimage there. That year the pilgrimage had attracted a quarter of a million of people. It was the first and only time that I spoke before a crowd so large, and my knees shook. Nevertheless, I couldn't pass up such an opportunity. I talked about the elections. Then I appealed to them to vote for the candidates from Solidarity's Civic Committee list.

The response I got was enthusiastic — almost as enthusiastic as the welcome they gave to the man who followed me onstage, the French singer and actor Yves Montand.

21

The Thirty-Five-Percent Democracy

The election campaign officially began on May 10, 1989. It lasted twenty-five days, and generated more emotion and excitement than all of the other postwar campaigns combined. At the time of the Round Table, we seemed assured of winning up to 35 percent of the seats in the Sejm (all the rest were to be occupied by a coalition of the Party and its look-alikes), and, depending on the outcome, possibly all one hundred free seats in the newly created Senat. The government still controlled the basic components of the propaganda machine — radio and television. We, on the other hand, had the Church and *Gazeta Wyborcza,* whose third issue carried the twenty-five-point election platform of the Solidarity Civic Committee. This platform touched on the most painful areas of Polish reality — from an inadequate constitution to the harshness of daily life. We would make a nonviolent transition from a totalitarian system to parliamentary democracy, transform a command economy into a market economy, and exchange a society mired in apathy for the flexible dynamism of a new order.

Fortunately for our candidates, the government coalition didn't get into the campaign until two weeks before the election, and even then in awkward fashion. The hardest task it faced was overcoming the entrenched habits of the old system; it almost certainly learned from Solidarity how to conduct a real campaign. All of this played in our favor, since we were treating June 4 as a plebiscite in which Solidarity would demonstrate beyond doubt the total absence of national support for the government in power.

The government was hoping to snatch what it could of the "free" seats in the Sejm by nominating "non-Party" candidates who enjoyed its confidence. They quickly circulated a "National List" on which appeared the thirty-five names of the leading government Round Table participants. Voters could accept or reject this list as a bloc, but they were also free to show which candidates they preferred over others. Knowing that some of the people on that list were better than others, Solidarity's Civic Committee urged voters to choose those names that "have your confidence." Our appeal proved effective in only two cases; the other Party members were rejected wholesale.

The time had come for me to draw on my popularity and on the credit that the nation had ascribed to me for change in Poland. According to data gathered from the Center for the Study of Public Opinion on May 1989, my approval rating was 74 percent, and my disapproval rating only 7.5 percent (13 percent were indifferent, 5 percent refused to express their feelings publicly, and 0.5 percent didn't know who I was). To bolster Solidarity's 161 candidates for the Sejm, and the 100 candidates for seats in the Senat, I had myself photographed with each of them, either in groups or individually. These photographs then appeared on billboards, "road signs" for the silent majority: "Get the message? Vote for the guy standing next to Walesa."

I gave nearly forty interviews to the foreign press and participated in dozens of rallies. Everywhere I went, I urged Poles to vote for the candidates from Solidarity's Civic Committee list, and occasionally cited the Church's view on these elections, as expressed in bulletin 234 of the Episcopal Conference of May 2, 1989 — namely, that by ending the monopolization of power, elections represented an important step on the road to self-government. To give that message more punch, I told people that at Przemysl, Bishop Ignacy Tokarczuk — famous for his feistiness — had said to his parishioners, "You know very well how the Good Lord Himself would vote in these elections!"

Despite these little games, I tried to play fair. No one was going to accuse me of manipulation. On the other hand, Prime Minister Rakowski committed a serious infraction of the electoral rules. At his May 10 meeting with the mayors of the cities and towns, he declared that the most important task now facing state administrators was to convince voters that the government candidates deserved their confidence. He added that the government expected from its regional representatives "their utmost commitment in the struggle to obtain the largest possible number of votes for the coalition candidates." I knew that in every civilized country, the organs of state were bound to remain strictly neutral in elections, and to treat all the office-seekers equally. Abuses of this principle generally end in scandal and defeat for the party in power. And that was what the Polish prime minister, a man supposedly versed in the ways of the world, was courting.

The Western press was expressing doubts that Poland was politically mature enough to hold elections. We were proving that despite having leapt into the deep end, we could keep our heads above water. The Round Table accords were only the beginning — the "small table" on social reform had settled scarcely half the problems on its agenda — but they were a strong beginning. We were on the road to parliamentary democracy. What we had going for us was the name of Solidarity and, such as it is, the myth of Lech Walesa. In a remarkably short time we had built a workable platform, both pragmatic and progressive. But we knew full well that how much weight it could hold depended on the outcome of the elections.

Since the end of World War II, Poland had awakened out of its stupor only twice to take any active part in elections — in 1947 and again in 1957. Both times the results were falsified, and these betrayals had made a deep impression in the memories of people over thirty. Now we had to get those people to believe again. We had to do everything possible to squeeze through the crack that had opened for us, or else we would never break down the monolithic Communist rock and move beyond it.

The elections were our chance to set up a transitional system that in itself represented a kind of victory. The Senat, even taking into account its restricted sphere of activity, controlled some matters now settled in arbitrary fashion by the PZPR — and election to it was unrestricted. As Bronislaw Geremek pointed out, winning a majority in the Senat would be a symbol of moral strength and popular will.

Sometimes that popular will needed guiding. In the early days of the campaign, I made this statement about minorities within Poland:

Poland is home to Ukrainians and Belorussians, and, in lesser numbers, to Lithuanians, Jews, Slovaks, Germans, Czechs, Armenians, Tatars. . . . They comprise an unusually important heritage in this old multinational republic. At a time when national hopes are again stirring, we should underscore our tradition of tolerance and respect for these groups not only in the name of our common past, but also in the name of the future. They are Poles . . . and bear the same burdens we do. They have the same fears and hopes. In addition, they have their own specific concerns: to preserve, within Poland, their own religious and cultural identities, their schools, and their places of worship. They want to preserve their dignity without masquerade. . . .

Let us remember, especially in this election campaign, that these people are our neighbors and fellow citizens. . . . Let us find a place for them in this campaign and respect it. Let this be a campaign in which they can play a dignified role. It is a human and moral duty, as the Holy Father so eloquently reminded the whole world in his recent message. It is also our political duty: millions of Poles live outside our current borders and are protected by laws that respect their identity, Poles for whom we hope — do we not? — that they live under conditions permitting them to take part in public life. . . .

Here is how we should test the qualifications of our senators and deputies: in this period of entente, this third millennium of Christ's teachings, this time of promise for those who live on the banks of the Vistula, are they seeking wisdom, truth, and humanity for Polish citizens of all backgrounds, cultures, and beliefs?

I made two other appeals, the first to Polish farmers and the second to all the citizens of the republic. In the first, I asked the farmers to remember to vote as responsible land managers — courageously and with a sense of justice, so that the land their fathers had protected stayed in the hands of their sons and daughters; so that their land would be fertile, cultivated for the benefit of the country; and so that they would reap the rewards of their efforts. In the second, broader, appeal, I wrote that no good comes of passivity, of a wait-and-see attitude, or of anger. The alternatives Solidarity offered proved that it could impose what was just and right, whatever the conditions. And it deserved their vote.

The time had come for Poland to become a country in which every citizen could feel at home. It was also necessary for our country to return to the fold of Europe. The coming elections were to mark a turning point. Poles could no longer wait until it was too late to show involvement and concern; it had to be demonstrated right now, before the elections.

Hoping to prod anyone sitting on the fence into action, I made it abundantly clear everywhere I went that I knew perfectly well these elections wouldn't solve Poland's problems, not right away. But this didn't mean we should give up on change, on progressive thinking, and on parliamentary methods. We also knew that the independent minority in the Sejm wouldn't be able to form the kind of government the country really needed, nor bring to power a president who shared our ideas. But it could still mobilize public opinion and give voice to the popular will.

In keeping with the principles agreed upon at the Round Table, and confirmed by a law passed by the Sejm, the Senat would be in a position to reject any legislation that it judged harmful to the nation. There was leverage here.

For such legislation to be enacted, it would first have to receive a two-thirds majority vote in the Sejm, or 66 percent. But it could not get that percentage if the 35 percent representing Solidarity voted against it.

We had to win that 35 percent.

The Solidarity Civic Committee's list of candidates featured only ten workers, but I didn't consider that percentage necessarily bad. The workers'-and-peasants' state formed in Poland in 1944 had, after all, dragged the country's economy into a swamp and reduced the country to slavery. At the time, a joke made the rounds of the salons of the intelligentsia: "Who invented socialism: the workers or the scientists?" The answer? "The workers. The scientists would have experimented first with rats!" So what if the joke was a terrible simplification and a serious injustice to the old revolutionary ideals? Those ideals are a little hard to explain to people who have been governed by the carrot-and-stick approach for forty-five years. The common wisdom about the old workers'-and-peasants' state was, briefly put, "It's like trying to get the whip and the horse to get along with each other."

On the list of candidates were representatives from many currents within the Polish opposition: from veterans of the struggle for power in the 1940s to members of the Polish Youth Movement; from the Polish Socialist Party (PPS) to the Independent Student Union (NZS); from the Committee for the Workers' Defense (KOR) to the Freedom and Peace group (Wolnosc i Pokoj). Despite what the Party propagandists said, this diversity proved that Solidarity had never assumed it was the sole base for democratic change, much less a political party. If in crucial moments it had acted as if it were, this was simply by default.

The feeling in Poland just before the elections could best be described as depressed. The monthly income of most households barely covered basic needs. And an appreciable part of the society was convinced that both personal income and the price of goods depended entirely on the government. Forty-five years of the diktat system had accustomed people to believing that all economic questions were decided by politicians. This pattern of thinking would be reflected in the elections, but in itself this was not a good thing, it seemed to me, because a vote for Solidarity would then be little more than a vote against the government. All of the unfulfilled hopes rallied around Solidarity, adding further weight to the responsibilities of our future deputies and senators. Some people felt that all that would really happen after the elections was that one empire would simply replace another — Solidarity would pick up where the government left off.

We went to the polls on June 4, 1989. Our signs were everywhere — on walls, in store windows, hanging from trees, draped on cars. Near all of the polling places stood Solidarity representatives, ready to explain to anyone who needed help how to pick a candidate from the Civic Committee's list. Some of the older people were casting a vote for the first time since before World War II; relatively few younger people had ever voted. Yet we knew that what was happening before our very eyes was an experiment that would hold good for several generations, and that, beginning the next morning, Poland would be a different country. By taking part in the election, and by voting for our candidates, we were showing the world that we stood for change without bloodshed.

The scenario could have been different: that same day, in Tiananmen Square, the very center of Beijing, the army massacred many of the thousands of students demonstrating for democracy.

Altogether, about two thousand candidates from various movements presented themselves in the first round of the elections, or about three candidates for each deputy's seat in the Sejm and almost six candidates for each seat in the Senat. The voter turnout proved lower than expected; it reached only 62 percent. Millions of Poles did not bother to vote. Why not? Adam Michnik has written with good reason that this reflected a lack of confidence not only in the Round Table accords, but in the future itself. The low turnout was a sign of persistent apathy.

We in the opposition could still openly celebrate the election results the day after the first round. After all, we had won 91 out of 100 seats in the Senat and 160 out of the 161 contested seats in the Sejm; our candidates intended to present themselves for the second round. Of the seats in Sejm, only one escaped us. It was won by Henryk Stoklosa, a millionaire from Pila who owned a salvaging firm with 210 employees, more than 100 trucks, a gas station, and a plane. He had spent a fortune on his campaign, and for his money he got 2.8 percent more votes than the candidate from the Solidarity Civic Committee.

On Thursday, June 8, a session of the Entente Commission presided over by General Czeslaw Kiszczak and myself was held at the Sejm. The social-reform "small table" confirmed its decision to stick by the Round

Table accords while still respecting the law already in effect. The government coalition said it would ask the State Council to create the legal grounds for filling the thirty-three vacant seats in the Sejm — those that had been "assigned" to the candidates on the "National List" who had been crossed out on the first round.

During the second round of elections, we won the remaining eight seats in the balloting for the Senat and one in the Sejm. Now it became a matter of finding a group from within the government camp interested in bringing about nonviolent change. We had to begin to get along with them right from the start. Otherwise the accumulated problems of forty-five years of totalitarianism might provoke an explosion of social discontent on an enormous scale. We needed time and money to rebuild our economy; the country had neither. Western aid, in search of which I had expended so much energy in France and Belgium, would be forthcoming only when other countries gained confidence in the new Polish government and in its program for ending the crisis.

22
The Presidents

O nly two days before the election, the first issue of *Tygodnik Soli-darnosc* [*Solidarity Weekly*], with Tadeusz Mazowiecki as editor, was published. We were very proud of our effort, a full-size newspaper of sixteen pages. On the first page, beneath a photo of the Round Table talks, was the headline for an interview I'd had with Malgorzata Niezabitowska (later to become the government spokesperson). In response to a question dealing with some of the unhealthier emotions the elections had stirred up, I agreed that it would have been better had there been genuine political pluralism. Since this wasn't the case, we had no choice but to act under the only banner that could unite us all — Solidarity.

The momentous events taking place in the other Communist countries around the world, with the exception of China and Cuba, encouraged us enormously. On June 13, Mikhail Gorbachev and Helmut Kohl signed a joint declaration, a real turning point in relations between the USSR and the German Federal Republic. Among other things, that declaration stated, "All people and all nations may freely determine their own destinies." That sentence contained the hope of a permanent break with the past, and the notion that future relations could be based on confidence and trust. Few predicted the wave of nationalist movements that were to sweep across the Soviet empire, spreading to nearly every republic. We could barely understand what was behind an ominous series of prison riots that were beginning in our own country.

On June 14, between the first and second rounds of the elections, French president François Mitterrand came to Poland for a two-day visit, accompanied by six of his ministers and a group of eminent figures from French

207

business and industry. Mitterrand, a true statesman, had long asserted the importance of a Europe free of the cold-war legacies of Yalta. He had also repeatedly and publicly emphasized that Poland was one of Europe's oldest and most deserving nations. Economic cooperation between our European nations was very much on his agenda. He acted on his convictions. On the first day of his visit, Mitterrand concluded an agreement with the Polish government to defer for four years the payments on a third of Poland's debts to France (including interest) — a total of more than $1 billion.

The next morning, President Mitterrand breakfasted with Prime Minister Rakowski and then visited Warsaw's old city. Before noon, he took the plane for Gdansk, accompanied by General Jaruzelski, who had also been with him during his trip to the Monument to the Defenders of Westerplatte, his meeting with war veterans, and his visit to the City Hall museum. At 2:45 in the afternoon, Mitterrand and his wife arrived at the Hevelius Hotel to meet with me and a group of my closest colleagues. I told him my views on the situation in Poland and on the dangers that threatened reform, meanwhile trying to convince him that providing economic aid to Poland was good business. We were a country of nearly forty million inhabitants, and once we got back on our feet we could become a significant economic partner. Mitterrand for his part spoke in favor of Poland's right to a place in a Europe moving toward unity, and said that he had recently proposed that France play the role of arbitrator between Poland and its creditors, given that Poland's enormous debts (some $40 billion) needed to be restructured to provide more realistic repayment schedules. We parted friends. Shaking my hand, the president noted that France, conscious of the traditions it held in common with Poland, felt that it had a duty to help fulfill the expectations of the Poles, and those of younger Poles in particular.

François Mitterrand's visit to the indomitable city of Gdansk was further proof that Warsaw was relaxing its grip. Not long before, the government had showed decided ill-will toward any idea of flying visiting political figures to the coast to meet with "Mr. . . . [grinding of teeth] . . . Walesa." Until Mrs. Thatcher's arrival, it was suggested that any meetings with "Mr. . . . [ahem!] . . . Walesa" should take place at the appropriate foreign embassy. Now Warsaw no longer made a fuss.

Some things hadn't quite changed, though. During the French president's visit, I recall clearly, the Polish-French security service performed their duty with diligence, knocking out two overzealous photographers. And after our luncheon, during which we were served French wines and cheeses, we went to the base of the Monument to the Shipyard Dead, where our guest placed a wreath. A crowd of over three thousand Gdansk residents chanting "Vive la France!" witnessed the event. The presence of the crowd took the government by surprise, for neither the press nor the television — both government-controlled — had had the courtesy to inform Gdansk that the president of France was coming to town.

At the next session of the Civic Committee on June 22, debate raged over a resolution by Solidarity's national authorities to dissolve the local civic committees. Members of these committees objected to the resolution. During the campaign, close to a hundred thousand citizens throughout the country had committed themselves to Solidarity, they argued. Why slap them in the face now? The Round Table accords required active civic organizations responsible for coordinating action for the good of local communities.

Having voted for the resolution, I refrained from speaking out for quite some time, and finally admitted that the National Executive Board's decision had been in error. The next day I took part in the decision to create a joint parliamentary Civic Club, which would include members from the local committees. I proposed that Professor Bronislaw Geremek be made president, and he was elected. Andrzej Wielowieyski was elected vice-president. The debate cooled down.

Despite the torrid heat of summer, my workload was such that I couldn't find a spare minute to go fishing. I was driven by one obsession: no one, but no one, was going to pass us in the race toward democratization. On July 1, Mikhail Gorbachev, in a televised speech about the nationalist revolts in his country, declared, "Today we are reaping the harvest of injustices to which we have consented in the past few decades: the deportation of people hounded out of their homelands, the denial of nationalist sentiment." That same day, East German authorities decided to prohibit border guards from using weapons, while in Hungary censorship was lifted.

Buried up to my neck by the avalanche of events, I had no choice but to stay put at home. Otherwise I would have accepted an invitation to visit the United States, where, as I mentioned earlier, I was asked to take part in the city of Philadelphia's Fourth of July celebrations and to accept the Medal of Freedom. In my stead went Danka (and my youngest son, Jarek), equipped with a speech I'd written for the occasion. Its theme was my conviction that nations deprived of freedom suffer more than other nations. Nonetheless, suffering can inspire. The American Declaration of Independence of 1776 and the Polish Constitution of May 3, 1791, could not have been written if their authors had submitted to servitude. The desire for freedom is stronger than the power of fear, and trying to reduce humans to slavery is like trying to stop a river's course. Poland has lost its freedom time and again; Poles have never resigned themselves to that loss. And in their country's glorious though brief periods of independence, they have always remembered this simple truth: he who stands by while his neighbor is reduced to slavery is never free.

On July 5, I attended the opening session of the newly elected Sejm, as did General Jaruzelski. The deputies were sworn in using a new oath whose wording had been hammered out between representatives from Solidarity and the State Council. That same day, the Senat convened for its first debate. I didn't stay for the debate, but slipped out for a meeting with the delegation from the World Confederation of Labor, headed by the Filipino John Tann. This was its first official visit to Poland, and so along with Tann came the confederation's secretary-general, Jan Kulakowski. Major figures from Solidarity's leadership joined me at the meeting — Zbigniew Bujak, Zbigniew Janas, Tadeusz Mazowiecki, and Bogdan Lis.

I was overjoyed when, on July 8, I read the final communiqué of the Warsaw Pact meeting that had been held in Bucharest. There was no universal model of socialism, it read in part, and each member nation of the pact had the right to follow its own political destiny without any outside interference. The Brezhnev Doctrine really was dead, then. What was alive was the chance for autonomous domestic and foreign policy among Moscow's former satellites. Henceforth, the Communist bigwigs in Poland could no longer use their favorite old argument: "Stop acting up, or they'll invade!" Their arguments that we should cling to the old system could now be seen for what they really were — a desperate attempt to hold onto their jobs.

On the evening of July 9, President George Bush landed in Poland for a forty-hour visit. Apparently there had been some anxiety in Washington just before the trip as to which Polish authorities would greet the president, since the National Assembly hadn't yet had time to elect a president of Poland. Mr. Bush, however, said he would go to Poland regardless of who might be there to meet him. Fortunately, it turned out to be someone he knew — the first secretary of the Central Committee of the PZPR, General Wojciech Jaruzelski. Without any false modesty whatsoever, he had agreed to act as head of state. On July 10, the meeting between President Bush and General Jaruzelski, originally planned to last for forty-five minutes, lasted two and a half hours. That gave rise to speculation that the American president thought his interlocutor had presidential power. There was nothing surprising in this, as I for one hadn't presented my candidacy for the job, knowing that I could be more effective for the time being doing other things.

In his speech before the Polish parliament, President Bush announced a six-point program for American aid to Poland:

1. A proposal at the forthcoming economic summit in Paris of the seven most highly industrialized countries to intensify and coordinate their efforts to promote democratic reform in Poland.
2. A request to the U.S. Congress to provide a $100 million to capitalize and invigorate the private sector in Poland (while also encouraging similar contributions from the other industrialized countries).
3. Pressure on the World Bank to grant $325 million in new loans toward helping Polish agriculture and industry reach the production levels of which they are clearly capable.
4. A request to the industrialized members of the Club of Paris to reschedule part of Poland's debts.
5. A request to Congress for $15 million to help fight air and water pollution in Cracow's old city, a Renaissance gem.
6. The creation of an American cultural and information center in Warsaw.

President Bush remarked further that economic hardship had burdened the Poles for decades, but that the nation's newfound determination made it possible to predict that there would be an end to the crisis. This would require patience and unremitting effort, but the Polish people were no strangers to hard work. "Follow your dreams," he said, "and you will see a flourishing Poland." America's attractiveness is due not just to the beauty of its land, but also to its work ethic. Poland is a beautiful country, too; it is also a country with immense agricultural potential and many talented people, and together they can lead their country to success in all areas. Poland is where World War II began, and now it is the place where the Cold War ended; Poland's example can help bring Europe back together:

> While I've been to Poland before, I did not expect to return so soon nor to such altered circumstances in your country, and so, too, perhaps many of you didn't

expect to be here serving in this or any Polish parliament. . . . When Coperni-
cus discovered the natural disposition of the planets and had the courage to
cast doubt on previously accepted ideas, the world changed forever. Today, the
range of political and economic changes in Poland is on a Copernican scale.

Before noon on Tuesday, July 11, President Bush, his wife, and members of the official American delegation landed at Rebiechowo Airport on
the outskirts of Gdansk. The visitors went first (the president in his bulletproof car) to the residence of Bishop Tadeusz Goclowski. After visiting
the cathedral of Oliwa outside Gdansk and attending a short organ concert,
the Bushes came to lunch at my new address, the century-old house at 54
Polanki Street. Meanwhile, a luncheon was held at the Hevelius Hotel for
the American secretary of state, James A. Baker, to which were invited
several Solidarity militants from Gdansk: Bogdan Borusewicz, Bogdan
Lis, Lech Kaczynski, Jacek Merkel, and Edward Szwajkiewicz. From the
Warsaw chapter came Andrzej Stelmachowski, Bronislaw Geremek, and
Adam Michnik.

The menu for our luncheon for President and Mrs. Bush had been
planned well ahead of time, down to the smallest detail. For hors-
d'oeuvres we were offering smoked eel and salmon, hard-boiled eggs,
crayfish, salami, pork chops with prunes, several cheeses, and a variety of
our regional sausages. We then served two kinds of soup — cream of
mushroom and a cold Lithuanian borscht. Roast turkey and veal, loin of
pork with mushrooms, and loin of beef followed, all garnished with pota-
toes, vegetables, and morels. And to conclude the feast, our deserts were
chocolate cake and raspberry tart, along with fresh strawberries. All in all,
a royal spread!

The president and I seemed to have a great deal to say to each other
during the luncheon, and I felt sorry for our poor interpreter, who never
had a chance to swallow even one bite of his lunch. I kept guiding the
conversation back to one main idea: that the world must correlate political
reforms with the economics that too often lag behind them. Sensing the
importance of this moment when I was seated next to the head of a world
power, I stressed the urgency of our hope for foreign investment of about
. . . $10 billion. Not a loan, much less a gift, but rather capital that would
be deposited in the subsidiaries of large banks for use by Poles showing
some enterprise and initiative. President Bush listened attentively and
seemed receptive to the idea. Though he had met me two years earlier (on
September 27, 1987), he seemed somewhat surprised by my powers of

persuasion. Concrete proposals, he said, would have to be examined. That was encouraging.

After lunch and a short walk around my garden, we went to the center of Gdansk, and to the Monument to the Shipyard Dead, where a speakers' platform, protected on two sides by bulletproof glass, had been set up. President Bush had apparently been rather disappointed by his reception in Warsaw. Instead of cheering crowds of thousands, he had been greeted by small clumps of perhaps ten. Gdansk — center and symbol of change in Poland — gave him a somewhat different reception. Some forty thousand people came to the monument, all waving little flags that the American Secret Service had distributed especially for this occasion. There were crowds everywhere. Father Jankowski had sent an honor guard of five hundred oblates from the parish of Saint Brygid, and forty persons had been chosen to accompany Bush right up to the monument, wearing T-shirts emblazoned with "PRESIDENT BUSH'S VISIT TO POLAND," which they had been given by the American Embassy. NBC, ABC, and CBS had flown in several tons of equipment for satellite transmission of live coverage of the president's stay in Gdansk. I was later told that all of the major American networks cut into regularly scheduled programs for periodic updates from their reporters on location in Gdansk. The largest amount of air-time was devoted to the ceremony at the monument and to our two speeches.

I spoke first. Political reform in Poland was unavoidable, I said. A slave never makes a good worker, and a developing civilization will never endure monopolies that impede its progress. The very nature of democracy and pluralism demands that political and economic changes go hand in hand. The example of China has taught us that where that isn't the case, events can lead to Tiananmen Square. If we want Solidarity Square, where we now stand, to represent forever a place of hope in the minds of future generations, we must work together to see that economic changes follow right behind political changes. As an economic world power, the United States was in a position to affect the course of reform in Poland. I tried to convince the president that our country deserved his country's assistance.

President Bush's reply was this:

> I salute Solidarity, I salute Poland, and I salute everything you have succeeded in accomplishing since my last visit. Poland has a special place in the American heart and in my heart, and when you hurt we feel pain, and when you dream we feel hope, and when you succeed we feel joy. . . . Coming to Poland

is like coming home. . . . This special kinship is the kinship of an ancient dream, a recurring dream, the dream of freedom. . . . Just before I left Washington a few day ago, I was asked by one of your journalists, 'If you were a young Pole, would you leave Poland and go to America?' And I answered that in this time of bright promise, of historic transition, of unique opportunity, I would want to stay in Poland and be a part of it — help make the dream come true for all the Polish people. . . . And just as the son of Poland has shown the world the heights of spiritual leadership in the Vatican, so the people of Poland can show the world what a free people with commitment and energy can accomplish.

We parted like two brothers — though maybe half-brothers is more like it, since he is a good deal taller than me. From the shipyards, the president returned to Westerplatte, accompanied by General Jaruzelski, where he laid a wreath at the monument there. After that he flew off to Hungary, the second island in the growing archipelago of freedom.

That afternoon I went home pretty pleased with myself (and with Gdansk too). From the very moment martial law had been declared, on December 13, 1981, the United States had taken a radical and very tough attitude toward the Communist regime in Poland. They had condemned from the very beginning the military takeover, the violation of human rights, and the lack of compromise. They backed up all this by introducing stringent economic restrictions and by suspending all financial assistance. The Round Table accords had cut through this impasse. The president's visit to a Poland only now ridding itself of its demons, a Poland that had given birth to Solidarity, augured well for the future. Unlike his other Western allies, George Bush felt that political changes by themselves provided enough of an argument for offering his country's assistance.

On July 19, 1989, the National Assembly elected the president of Poland. General Wojciech Jaruzelski received just one more vote than the minimum necessary to get the job. A sizable portion of the government coalition in the National Assembly (consisting of both the Senat and Sejm) — virtually appointed by the government, we should remember, under the old system — actually voted against him.

More than likely my July 14 declaration had had an impact on this positive outcome. I had said that at this time only a member of the government coalition should be elected president. I also declared that I was prepared to cooperate with whoever was elected president for the coming term. The good of Poland demanded it. I sent General Jaruzelski my congratulations (I was one of the first to do it), though I couldn't refrain from getting in one good dig: "For your sake, sir, and for Poland's sake, I hope that the next president elected by the legislature owes his job to the voices of all Poles." In my second statement on July 19, I wrote that history's final judgment of General Jaruzelski would depend essentially on what he did during the next few years.

I met with the president-elect at the Belvedere* on July 25 to discuss the ten-point declaration Jacek Kuron had made five days earlier at the meeting of the parliamentary Civic Club. I also wanted him to know my own thoughts on the new government. Because of ever-worsening economic conditions and ever-growing tensions, the only reasonable course of action would be to assign the task of forming a government to those who enjoyed the support of the country's majority. Since the government coalition was in all likelihood unprepared to accept this idea, it was up to them to take full responsibility for the composition of the cabinet. I meanwhile intended to form a "shadow cabinet," which would prepare solutions to the problems that would inevitably arise, sooner or later.

General Jaruzelski proposed that the opposition representatives should enjoy limited participation in the new government, with one to be named deputy prime minister. I counterproposed that the cabinet should consist entirely of representatives from the opposition, or of a coalition with the opposition — but with the concession that none would come from Solidarity's leadership. On this point we never reached any final, binding agreement.

On July 31, 1989, President Jaruzelski resigned as first secretary of the Central Committee of the Polish United Workers' Party. Outgoing Prime Minister Mieczyslaw Rakowski was quickly elected to replace him in a job that wouldn't be around for long–nor even be worth so much as an honorary doctorate!

---

* A palace that is now the official residence of the president of Poland.

23

The Government of Solidarity

In "Your President, Our Prime Minister," his celebrated article in the July 4, 1989, issue of *Gazeta Wyborcza,* Adam Michnik wrote that Solidarity's overwhelming victory in the elections proved that the Poles wanted radical changes in their government. How could the democratic movement defeat the Stalinist *nomenklatura* with neither revolution nor violence? asked Michnik. Only by a partnership between the democratic opposition and the reform wing of the faction in power. Poland was offered an opportunity that up to then no country had managed to seize. And so we had to try to do what no country had ever done before: create a system of power that was both strong and representative. Simply changing the façade, substituting one candidate for president or prime minister with another, wouldn't be enough. We needed to create a new form of government, one supported by all the country's major political forces; a brand-new government, but one that guaranteed continuity. Michnik's conclusion was clear: such a government could be put in place only if the office of president were filled by a candidate from the PZPR, and if the office of prime minister, with the task of forming the government, fell to a candidate from Solidarity.

Though initially Michnik was widely attacked for his opinions, they proved prophetic. It just took a little time for the prophecy to come true. On August 2, President Jaruzelski named his minister of the interior, General Czeslaw Kiszczak, to be prime minister, and the Sejm confirmed this appointment. That arrangement lasted only three weeks.

A tumultuous three weeks. On August 7, I issued a statement saying that the government's appointment of the new prime minister proved beyond doubt that those in power meant to cling to their monopoly. My statement accelerated a crisis of confidence in the government by validating the general perception that the elections had changed nothing, and that there never really had been any hope of change. With that perception in mind, I expressed my categorical opposition to General Kiszczak's forming a new government. Rather than revert to the concession I had proposed to Jaruzelski about Solidarity's participation, I argued that now the only legitimate political solution would be for a new cabinet to be formed with ministers drawn from Solidarity, the United Farmers' Party, and the Democratic Party.

In fact, Kiszczak hadn't wanted to be appointed prime minister, and accepted the nomination only because he was "moved by a sense of duty." He knew he would be doomed to a lonely position. When, as the head of Solidarity, I was asked why I had thrown a wrench into the works by opposing him, I replied that just because we were granted some (twenty or so) unimportant ministerial posts didn't mean that Solidarity should take the fall for whatever disaster now happened — especially since Jaruzelski had rejected my efforts at a compromise. No: now it was all or nothing. After it won the election, the opposition must be in a position to seize the reins of power. If we didn't form a coalition to be ready for that moment, we would remain only a shadow cabinet.

When Prime Minister Kiszczak tried to drum up support for his government by knocking on everyone's door (even on Cardinal Glemp's) — an exercise in futility — I knew that it was time for Solidarity to make its move. I felt confident. After all, we were a force recognized by the West, and the efforts I had made personally, and in record speed, by calling at the golden gates of the wealthier countries had produced better results than all of the efforts of all the preceding governments combined. For example, on August 8, Poland signed an agreement on the sale of Polish products with the EEC amounting to some $120 million. The money earned from the sale of these goods was to be transferred to Polish banks.

On August 10, Lech Kaczynski, one of my closest advisors, met with the leaders of the Democratic Party (SD) and the United Farmers' Party (ZSL) to discuss my new position regarding the makeup of the cabinet. When sounded out about his views on which candidate ought to be proposed for prime minister, he hinted that it should be Lech Walesa. He knew full well I had no intention of seeking the position.

On August 15, the embattled General Kiszczak announced publicly that my final proposals for a coalition with the SD and the ZSL had wrecked his plans (he claimed to have already formed a skeleton government). He offered President Jaruzelski his resignation as prime minister — possibly in favor of the president of the ZSL, Roman Malinowski.

I was not fond of Malinowski, who I felt was much too much under the thumb of the PZPR, but I decided not to make a scene about his candidacy. I didn't want to fight a war on two fronts. So my reaction to General Kiszczak's declaration was in the form of a short statement reiterating the views I'd expressed on August 7: "A government representative of the whole nation, and formed — in conformity with the prerogatives of the president of the People's Republic of Poland — by a coalition of Solidarity, the ZSL, and the SD, now remains the only chance we have to alter the dangerous turn of events in our country." Finally, on August 16, I got what I had been waiting for. The chairmen of the Central Committees of the SD and the ZSL declared support for my views on forming a truly representative national government. I received a similar show of support from the parliamentary Civic Club.

On August 17, Jaroslaw Kaczynski and I marched to the Myslewicki Palace in Warsaw for intensive talks with Jerzy Jozwiak, the head of the SD, and ZSL head Malinowski. These discussions proved heavy going, for we were testing each other and looking for weak spots. We all agreed on the need to form a national government as fast as we could. Later, the same group sat through a two-hour meeting with President Jaruzelski. After offering many reservations — but getting not one assurance in return — he accepted the formation of a government possessing the broadest possible popular support. But, he added, this could happen only "with the participation of all the national political forces."

That's as far as the bargaining went. I was trying to sell yet another idea: that the government should be made up of Solidarity members and open to other political groups. Jaruzelski wouldn't buy it. He did, however, give me the assurance that the prime minister would be chosen by Solidarity. It was still too early to finalize details about the distribution of ministerial portfolios, but interior and national defense would fall to the PZPR candidates.

A good day's work. That evening, on the way home, I stopped by to see Cardinal Glemp and thank the Church for its wise counsel and foresight.

Now all I had to do was silence the blowhards from the PZPR who were on the warpath, accusing *me* of upsetting Poland's precarious political balance! Rakowski, the new first secretary of the PZPR, declared that, though the situation was serious, this was no time to capitulate. On August 19, the Central Committee of the PZPR adopted an obfuscating platform for fundamental reform. At midnight of the same day, the leadership of the Romanian Communist Party proposed to the leadership of the PZPR and the other Communist leaders within the so-called Eastern Bloc that they act jointly for the "defense of socialism and the Polish people." You almost had to admire Nicolae Ceausescu.

Finally, on August 21, my hopes were realized. President Wojciech Jaruzelski designated the candidate I had suggested, Tadeusz Mazowiecki, as prime minister. By becoming prime minister, Mazowiecki — former editor of several Catholic publications, veteran politician of the opposition, and recently named editor of *Tygodnik Solidarnosc* — solved the dilemma that had confronted Catholics since the end of World War II: whether to share power or to oppose it. Moreover, along with Bronislaw Geremek, Tadeusz Mazowiecki had been there from the beginning — the first intellectual not from Gdansk who actively supported the August 1980 strike. They both came to the shipyards from Warsaw to offer their services as advisors. It was thanks to them that we were able to get the government to concede to a number of our demands. Both of them had stayed on Solidarity's side through thick and thin, all the way up to the Round Table.

I was overjoyed by Mazowiecki's appointment. Once again, my intervention had proven effective and timely. Mazowiecki was ready to take on the responsibility. He announced that his first actions as prime minister would involve preparing a report to present to the International Monetary Fund. That fall, the IMF was to decide whether to allocate emergency credit to Poland.

Three of my statements in which I discuss the situation since the elections were published. In the first, I stressed that Poland's political parties would acquire credibility only if they worked out concrete reforms. The threats and blackmail that the Central Committee of the PZPR in particular engaged in neither inspired confidence nor promoted the national good. I also expressed satisfaction that, by nearly 90 percent of the votes, the Sejm had confirmed Tadeusz Mazowiecki as prime minister:

> His concerns are rooted in the pains and the protests of those workers for whom, pushed to extremes, the only option was to fight back — even when their struggle meant financial sacrifice. We survived that phase, and now we have to leave it behind. That doesn't mean that the problems have been solved. Working conditions are still miserable and unfair — and wages are still unbelievably low. These injustices can and must be done away with. . . .

We must save Poland — not just one part at the expense of another, but all of Poland. For forty years, we have waited for this chance. Let's not waste it.

A group of fifteen deputies from the PZPR proposed to eliminate the passage in the Constitution stipulating that the leading political force for building socialism be the Polish United Workers' Party. A party's program, platform, and vision should determine its role in politics, not the Constitution, wrote the deputies. This was like closing the barn door after the horse has fled, and for two reasons. First, the nation had rejected socialism, so the idea of "building" it was senseless. Second, the most important task before the newly elected members of the Sejm was rewriting the Polish Constitution from scratch, not rephrasing one passage.

In his speech to the Sejm, Prime Minister Mazowiecki made a statement that was to become famous. There were to be no witch hunts, he said: "What has happened in the past must be dropped. What we must deal with now is the state of collapse in Poland *today*." Despite Mazowiecki's honorable and patriotic efforts, the corridors of the Sejm buzzed with news about how the PZPR's *nomenklatura* was still planning to play the spoiler for some time to come. We would have to act concretely and decisively to make good on all the promises.

On August 26, I met with Elizabeth Dole, then American secretary of transportation, and her husband, Robert Dole, leader of the Republican minority in the U.S. Senate. Secretary Dole gave me a letter from President Bush inviting me to visit the United States. The American ambassador to Poland, John R. Davis, was also present at our meeting and, like the Doles, congratulated me on my efforts in getting Tadeusz Mazowiecki appointed. He also assured me that the American government would offer its support to any government that Solidarity formed in the future.

But not everyone was as supportive. The next day, ATA, the Albanian press agency, calmly asserted that the selection of Tadeusz Mazowiecki as prime minister had been "an act of bourgeois counterrevolution." The agency took Gorbachev to task for "giving the green light to antisocialist forces throughout the world."

At the beginning of September, Tadeusz Mazowiecki met with Mieczyslaw Rakowski, the first secretary of the Central Committee of the PZPR, and Marian Orzechowski, head of the Deputies' Club of the PZPR. Following the meeting, Rakowski declared that after becoming more familiar with the new government, he had changed his unfavorable opinion of the prime minister. When I was asked at a press conference about this change of heart, I replied that I was displeased by its patronizing tone. Our "comrades" seemed to think that they were undisputed masters of any situation, and I thought someone should set them straight.

Since there was every indication that it would take until mid-September to form a government, I thought it safe enough to accept an invitation for a three-day visit to the Federal Republic of Germany made by the union group DGB (Deutscher Gewerkschaftsbund) and its president, Ernst Breit (curiously, this invitation had been extended every year since 1981). Despite the warmth with which I was welcomed, it turned out to be an exhausting trip. At meeting after meeting I repeated what I had already said in Italy, France, and Belgium: Poland was looking not for a handout, but for mutually profitable investments. The need was urgent. If the West held back now, all the political changes we had made didn't stand a chance. "Right now you industrialists are acting like wallflowers at a dance, " I chided them. During my visits to various cities in Germany, I was distracted by all the attractions (like the marvelous cathedral of Essen), but the real purpose of my visit haunted me: to convince major capital to invest in Poland so that it could become a real European partner. I repeated *ad nauseam* that a united Europe did not mean a uniform Europe. I also stressed this in my talks with the all the major figures in West German politics — President Richard von Weizsäcker, Chancellor Helmut Kohl, SPD president Hans Vogel, and former chancellor Willy Brandt (another recipient of the Nobel Peace Prize), as well as in my meetings with the president of the East German Economic Commission, Otto von Amerongen, and during a meeting with the workers at the Krupp factory in Bochum.

Five days after my return to Poland, Prime Minister Tadeusz Mazowiecki announced the composition of his government. Each of the forces of the coalition — the Parliamentary Civic Club (OKP), the ZSL, the SD, and the PZPR — was given a vice-presidency. Furthermore, the OKP was given eleven cabinet posts, the PZPR four, the ZSL four, and the SD three. A professor from Poznan, Krzysztof Skubiszewski, a "non-Party" person (although sympathetic to Solidarity and close to the episcopate), was named to the post of foreign minister. Up to then, Skubiszewski had been little known, but he was to prove very helpful because of his connections.

The new government signaled the end of one-party rule. The crowning symbol of the coalition's goodwill was the nomination of Jacek Kuron, one of the historic leaders of the democratic opposition, to the post of labor minister.

On September 16, I went to the basilica of Jasna Gora in Czestochowa, where three hundred thousand pilgrims from all over Poland were gathered. It was the largest assembly of the faithful Czestochowa had ever seen, and there was good reason for it: not since the war had there been such an occasion for thanksgiving.

"We must reestablish the work ethic, patriotism, and our belief in the state," declared Tadeusz Goclowski, the bishop of Gdansk. "The government and the parliament can do a great deal, but to heal this nation, and to strengthen its moral fiber, we have to dig deeper. That is the task facing both the Church and Solidarity."

24
The Domino Theory

The next two months are something of a blur — an uninterrupted string of meetings, smiles, handshakes, and well-wishing. I am obviously speaking from the perspective of my own little backyard, for the government and its business were taking place on a different plane. As president of Solidarity, I supported every action that might help the government move along during the early stages. After a point, however, my services were less and less necessary, and so I could devote myself more and more to union work and to "receiving." Suddenly, new invitations, greetings, and requests for meetings, were pouring in from around the world. I instructed my secretary to buy something I had never owned before: an appointment book marked off in hours. And by mid-September 1989, I was installed in a new office at Solidarity's new headquarters at 24 Waly-Piastowski Street in Gdansk. I was surrounded by Solidarity's seasoned veterans — the veterans of prisons, strikes, and negotiations. The office was renovated following the departure of I know not which director of I know not what, so that I could now perform my official duties and ceremonies outside of my home and Father Jankowski's sacristy.

On September 19, the presidium of the Solidarity's National Executive Board met. Normally what happens at these meetings is not worth reporting in detail, but this one was of special significance. It was the first time we'd met while "our" government was in power. I was the first to speak, and recommended that as a union our job was to continue to stimulate the kind of political thinking that ends up putting bread on people's tables. What I meant was that 80 percent of the national wealth should be taken away from the state (and privatized) as quickly as possible. The next issue

I raised was whether the local civic committees should be disbanded. I was in favor of their continuing, but not under the banner of Solidarity. Another question was whether Solidarity should create a stock-based company to coordinate all of its economic activities. We closed, as we always did, by voting on a declaration urging the government to go full speed in its drive for reform.

On September 26, the French newspaper *Le Figaro* printed an interview that one of its journalists had done with me a week earlier. He had asked whether I thought the Communists would return to power if the present government failed. There was no chance of that, I replied, at least not soon. Why not? Because they alone were responsible for all the current difficulties. Did I have confidence in President Jaruzelski? No, I said, I didn't. But, I added, I had to admit that for the first time in many years the general had finally done something right: nominating a member of Solidarity to be prime minister.

On September 20, Robert Mosbacher, the American secretary of commerce, came to visit me. He had come to Poland for informal talks with the administration about such matters as protection of investments, guaranteed transfers of profits, and open access to advertising. On September 21, Robert De Niro, the American actor, came to my home with two expatriate Poles, the film director Roman Polanski and the former tennis champion (and now businessman) Wojciech Fibak. I enjoyed the visit very much. September 23 was a Saturday, and though I had wanted to go mushroom-picking, I had a slight cold and resigned myself to staying home and catching up with my mail. On September 24, I watched the television coverage of the Polish delegation's visit to Washington. Led by the deputy prime minister and minister of finance, Leszek Balcerowicz, the delegation was being interviewed by officials from the International Monetary Fund and the World Bank. I was particularly pleased to talk with Czeslaw Milosz, recipient of the Nobel Prize for literature and a countryman who now lives in California, when he paid me a visit in Gdansk.

Around this time I decided to make some changes in the leadership of *Tygodnik Solidarnosc*. Now that Tadeusz Mazowiecki, its editor, had become prime minister, it risked becoming a government paper, and I wanted to avoid that. On September 28, for the first time since the dismissal of the widely disliked Jerzy Urban, a new government press spokesperson appeared on television: Malgorzata Niezabitowska, formerly a reporter for *Tygodnik Solidarnosc*. That same day, it was announced that ZOMO — probably even more hated than Urban — had been disbanded, and I was asked by all the television and studio stations to discuss the fallout.

The days and weeks that followed were no less hectic, and among others I recall with particular pleasure my audience (me, the shipyard electrician from Gdansk) with the Spanish royal couple, King Juan Carlos I and Queen Sofia. On October 5, the Wolnosc i Pokoj (Freedom and Peace) movement and Polish-German Solidarity organized a demonstration on the market square in Cracow. Their slogans? "Destroy the Berlin Wall!" and "Freedom for East Germany!" Using bricks and fast-drying cement, demonstrators erected a wall over three feet high in front of the East German Cultural Center in Cracow.

On that same October 5, I wrote an open letter to the president of Chile, General Augusto Pinochet:

> As you must certainly be aware, I intend to visit Chile at the end of October of this year. I hope that the goal of my trip, which is to establish cooperation with the Chilean unions, can be achieved without hindrance. I wish to meet personally with Manuel Bustos and Arturo Martínez, to express — like so many other union leaders — my admiration, respect, and support for their spirited struggle to defend the interests of Chilean workers. I am counting on meeting them as free men, able to exercise fully their civic and union rights.
>
> The fact that your government has ignored so many petitions from both within your own country and abroad demanding the freedom of union leaders is a cause of deep concern. My Solidarity colleagues have endured the severe penalty of total isolation merely because they had the audacity to proclaim ideas that are accepted and respected throughout the civilized world. . . .
>
> I expect you to free Manual Bustos and Arturo Martínez. I also call upon you to restore to them their full rights, so that they can fulfill their duties as union leaders and work for the welfare of workers in Chile.

I got no response to the letter and didn't expect one, but Bustos and Martínez were freed on October 23. So I pushed back the date of my grand entrance.

Let me go back to the beginning of October. I began warning "my" government against any further price hikes at a time when the new economic program was already causing the Poles further hardships. Spiraling inflation threatened to cause an explosion of discontent whose magnitude could have tragic consequences, including civil war. In Washington, Deputy Prime Minister Balcerowicz fought valiantly to secure $2.7 billion in emergency credits, but for the average Pole the only thing that mattered right now was his empty wallet. There can be no water in the reservoirs when there's a drought in the mountains. The government, as expected, compounded the problem by being unable to convince citizens of the necessity of its actions. So people were wandering around aimlessly like lost sheep, grumbling about the almost weekly increases in the cost of living. Sensing the general mood, I forcefully declared that the time for professionals had come and that I was a mere amateur. But the workers didn't make that distinction, and I got earfuls of what the government should have heard. It was no coincidence that the crime rate rose by 15 percent.

The government's backward and outdated economic policies made things worse — the financial *nomenklatura* was none too eager to adopt a new management approach, and it continued to transfer the costs of the crisis on to consumers of nonindustrial goods. Now and again this even led to tacit agreements between the OPZZ (the pro-government unions) and Solidarity, enabling both groups to join forces to combat the Party mafia. Unfortunately, this had little effect, for the higher-ups were well aware that for the time being, at least, severe cuts in government spending — cuts that would mean closing down the dinosaur enterprises and forcing massive unemployment with consequent retraining costs — were out of the question. One ray of light, however, beamed on us during this dark time: on October 19, the U.S. Congress decided to allocate $837 million in loans to Poland and Hungary ($714 million of which were for Poland).

There were always new rounds of meetings with representatives from various groups who wanted to be photographed with me, or who asked for my support in one struggle or another. Sometimes I had to play the supplicant myself. Such was the case when the deputy secretary-general of the World Confederation of Labor, Flor Bleux (with whom I exhaustively discussed the problem of international cooperation), came for a visit, or when I met the Swedish prime minister, Ingvar Carlsson. "We are close neighbors," I told him, "but our economic interaction is negligible." The visit of Fred Zeder, president of the American Corporation for Foreign Investments, and that of Robert Bernadzik of the Department of Labor, involved hardheaded discussions about stock-based companies partly financed by non-American capital.

My talks with Bernadzik took place on October 16. That same day more than twenty thousand refugees from Romanian Moldavia crossed into Hungary, and in Leipzig a large demonstration took place demanding free elections, a free press, and reform of the political system. The domino theory had become a reality: the Poles and the Hungarians were toppling their systems, and they would be followed by the East Germans, Czechoslovaks, Bulgarians, and Romanians.

On October 22, I received a delegation from the Congress of the American Polonia, founded in 1944, headed by its president, Edward Moskal. Our good countrymen from America had collected a million dollars for the Children's Hospital in Cracow. The next day, I met Pierre Méhaignerie, president of the French Democratic Socialist Party (CDS), whose visit was intended to establish contact and exchange between regions and towns in Poland and France. Of course, I couldn't pass up the opportunity to urge them to invest in us — if only indirectly, by setting up bank subsidiaries.

On October 23 came the announcement that Hungary had once again taken the lead in the race toward democracy by proclaiming, on the thirty-third anniversary of the Soviets' bloody repression of the 1956 uprising, that it had become an "independent republic." The great red star on the roof of the parliament building, a beacon of communism, was turned off; those affixed to military caps were taken off. In the meantime we in Poland had to go on living in a state called the People's Republic of Poland — though fortunately not for very long.

October ended with the announcement that the Peruvian terrorist organization, the Shining Path, had sentenced Gorbachev and Deng Xiaoping to death "for betraying communism and the ideals of Mao Zedong."

I was getting ready for a transatlantic trip in early November, but I didn't let it slow me down. Of the endless sequence of meetings during this time, the one with the Cuban poet Armando Valladares, whom Fidel Castro's regime had condemned in January 1960 to thirty years in prison for having criticized the new dictator — not publicly, but among some of his own friends — stands out particularly. Valladares was twenty-four years old when he was jailed. He passed through one prison after another, spent seven years in solitary confinement, and endured unspeakable torture. And all because he didn't want to ask for a pardon. He felt that would be lowering himself, a form of moral and spiritual suicide that ran contrary to his Catholic faith. In 1969, Armando Valladares married Martha López. They had met in prison when she was visiting her father, also a political prisoner. She left Cuba in 1972, smuggling out poems that her husband had written in prison. By 1976 she had succeeded in getting them published, making them available to the whole world.

Martha's determination saved Armando, who would not otherwise have survived. (Following a forty-six-day hunger strike in 1974, he lost the use of his legs for five years.) On October 22, 1981, at the personal request of François Mitterrand, Fidel Castro allowed the "counterrevolutionary" Valladares to go free, and he emigrated to the United States with his mother and sister (his father, judged politically dangerous, was not allowed to leave). There he has devoted himself to the struggle for human rights. When he came to Gdansk on November 9, 1989, he said that he had first heard of me in 1980. I was deeply flattered. We talked warmly for nearly an hour, and afterward this indomitable poet presented me with a copy of his book, *Against All Hope*, a memoir of his years in prison. I was very moved, for I remembered what it felt like when the first part of my autobiography, *The Way of Hope*, was published.

On Thursday, November 9, the Polish seeds helped bring in a new European harvest: the Communist Party of East Germany decided to grant freedom of travel to its citizens (visas were required, but granted without problems). This decision touched off a wave of joy among the normally stoic and depressed citizens of Berlin, which for twenty-eight years had been a city divided. Several hundred thousand East Germans poured into West Berlin, weeping, drinking champagne, and kissing passersby. At the same time, bands of young West Berliners crossed into East Berlin, shouting, "It's the end of the Wall!" "The Wall is crumbling!" And the next day, it fell. Half of East Berlin went picnicking between the famous checkpoints. People brought hammers and saws to demolish chunks of that hated concrete barrier. Destiny does not take a straight course. Barely a month earlier, Erich Honecker, the corrupt dictator of East Germany, had boasted that the wall would stand for another hundred years. History, I think, deals in farce.

That same momentous November 9, Helmut Kohl, the chancellor of West Germany, arrived in Warsaw for what was to have been a six-day official visit, during which he asked to talk with me and Prime Minister Mazowiecki. Once again, our talks focused on financial support. But they also concerned the likelihood of the unification of Germany and the need, in that case, for guarantees of Poland's western border; Germany had never renounced its claims to Polish territory in the Upper Oder area. Unfortunately, our talks remained unfinished — because of what was happening in East Germany, Kohl decided, after a day or two, to take a quick trip to Berlin. The Polish government accepted his decision with mixed sentiments. And the doubts it felt about German-Polish relations weren't laid to rest when the chancellor returned to Poland to take part in a joint German-Polish mass held in Krzyzowa (Kreisau in German), near the Oder River, on November 12.

25

A Shower of Dollars

America is beautiful, America is huge, America is rich. The first thing that struck me about America was the people walking backward. Everywhere I went, it seemed, right in front of me appeared a small group of people walking backward, holding their cameras or recording equipment. Most of the time, however, I wasn't on foot but in an official limo with windows thicker than my index finger. I know that no one will credit me with being an oratorical Columbus when I say these platitudes, but America *is* beautiful, huge, and rich. After my dizzying, nonstop visit to Canada, the United States, and Venezuela, my inner images and thoughts were like film footage with the sequences all mixed up. I admit to loving those days — crazy, hectic, filled with smiling faces and rounds of applause (applause is highly welcome) — but I can't put them into chronological order. I do remember the most outstanding things, just as I do the faces of the most important people I was continually meeting, but they are like almonds buried in cake dough. Sometimes it's easier to remember a pretty girl in a miniskirt than some tedious civil servant or local politician shaking my hand for the sake of his reelection.

In the course of my twelve-day transatlantic trip (November 11 to 22), I met three great leaders: Brian Mulroney, prime minister of Canada; George Bush, president of the United States; and Carlos Pérez, president of Venezuela. All of them received me like royalty, and President Bush, on whose "turf" I stayed the longest, honored me at the White House with the highest American civil decoration, the presidential Medal of Freedom. I sat in an armchair bearing the inscription "SOLIDARITY" while I listened to the short ceremonial speech. When I stood and bowed my head to receive the medal, only my mustache stopped my tears from falling freely.

230

I watched the daily street activity with great interest — though mostly, alas, through car windows. A few observations: In Canada, it isn't cats that scurry around in the garbage, but black squirrels. In New York, the motorcycle police have boots so highly polished I could see my reflection in them; but right in midtown I saw homeless derelicts the likes of which I had not seen in Poland for twenty years. In Venezuela, everything smells of fish and gasoline, and the women have long legs. I also observed that the Canadians play the Polish national anthem ceremoniously, like a stately polonaise, though it's actually a lively mazurka. Americans are exuberant and are always on the lookout for puns and plays on words, which they pass along with complete openness.

My moments of greatest emotion occurred in the United States. Nevertheless, I will never in my life forget Polish National Day in Toronto, where they compared me to the first Lech, the legendary founder of the Polish state. In my speech, I traced Poland's journey toward the third millennium. I was later presented with a magnificent cake decorated with the Solidarity logo — it must have weighed twice as much as I do. In the United States, I spoke with so many cabinet members, congressmen, and agency directors that I would have to add an appendix to this book in order to list all of their names.

Of all my meetings during that trip, four stand out in memory: the one with the Chilean union leader Manuel Bustos, about whom I had written that letter to General Pinochet; another with Cardinal Jan Krol, who celebrated a magnificent Polish mass in the sanctuary of Doylestown, Pennsylvania; one with AFL-CIO president Lane Kirkland, whose congress I visited on November 14 and 15; and finally the one with members of the Jewish community in New York (about which I shall talk in more detail in the next chapter). For good measure, let me add that I spoke several times with Zbigniew Brzezinski, Edward Piszek, Edward Derwinski, Dan Rostenkowski, Barbara Mikulski, Paul Simon, and Edward Moskal, all great supporters of the Polish cause in America. During all my business meetings, I was always assisted by members of the Solidarity delegation: Bronislaw Geremek, Bogdan Lis, Janusz Onyszkiewicz, Wladyslaw Frasyniuk, and Jerzy Milewski. My personal secretary, Krzysztof Pusz, watched over my physical and mental well-being and helped me combat stage fright. The presence of the same Gdansk television team that had traveled with me to Rome, led by Marian Terlecki, also boosted my morale.

The main purpose of my American expedition was to address a joint session of Congress on November 15, 1989. The press made much of the

fact that I was the second foreigner in American history without high political office on whom such an honor had been bestowed (the first, in 1824,
was the marquis de Lafayette), and when I entered the chamber, I was
greeted by an ovation lasting several minutes and done in full Western
style, with foot-stamping, whoops, and whistles. Though it was meant to
cheer me on, the welcome made my knees go weak and my mouth go dry.
Fortunately, Jacek Kalabinski, my interpreter and a man who deserves his
full share of the credit, was next to me. He always knew how to modulate
his voice to get the right effect at the right moments.

Americans love people who start with nothing and go someplace, so
the sight of a short (I'm just under five-foot-six), stocky electrician from
Gdansk, father of eight, pleased them as much as the part I had played in
overturning communism in Europe. You can't help feeling strange when
some of the most powerful people from the richest country in the world
scrutinize you as an oddity, even if their hearts are open to you. I was
terribly nervous. I've never been able to assume that cold, mechanical way
in which — toward the end of his life — Brezhnev, for example, used to
address the Supreme Soviet.

I talked for only about an hour, but to listen to the Western press you'd
think it was a major historical event. All I did was speak my mind about
what I thought were the most important questions facing Poland and all of
Europe. To summarize:

> We, the people . . . These are the words with which I wish to begin my address,
> and I don't need to remind anyone where they are from. Nor do I need to explain
> why an electrician from Gdansk such as myself might also have the right to use
> them. . . . I stand before you, citizens of a country and continent watched over
> by the Statue of Liberty, to speak to you in the name of my nation. . . . I know
> Americans to be a people both realistic and pragmatic, a people who believe in
> good sense and in decency, for those qualities lead to the triumph of what is
> right. You are a people who prefer actions to words. I understand these feelings
> well. I am not wild about words myself. I prefer facts. I prefer what works.
>
> Ladies and gentlemen, the thing I want most of all to impress upon you is
> this: that social movement born in Poland, so magnificently called Solidarity,
> is working! After many long years, our struggle has produced results, and
> today anyone can see those results with their own eyes. Through that struggle,
> we have learned what to do and where to go. It has touched the lives of millions
> of people around the world, undermined the power of monopolies and even
> broken some of them up, and opened up new horizons.

And yet, above all else, it was a nonviolent struggle. We have been thrown into prison, fired from our jobs, beaten, and some of us even killed; but we have never struck anyone, destroyed anything, or broken so much as a single window. Instead we have been guilty of stubbornness, sacrifice, and abnegation. We knew what we wanted, and that made us strong.

The Solidarity movement was successful because at every point it fought for whatever solution was the most humane, the most worthy, and for whatever was an alternative to brutality and hatred. When it needed to be, it was also a movement that was persistent, obstinate, unyielding. And that is why, after many long years — and moments of real tragedy — we have succeeded. That is why we are showing the way for millions of people in Poland and in other countries. . . .

Ten years ago, in August of 1980, a famous strike began in the Gdansk Shipyards, and it led to the founding of the first independent union in a Communist country. . . . I was ten years younger then, and known only by my co-workers in the shipyards. I was also a little thinner then. The fact that I was thinner turned out to be important. Though I had been laid off for trying to organize the workers and getting them to fight for their rights, I climbed back over the fence, returned to the shipyards, and led the strike. That's how it began. We have come a long way since, but I still remember climbing over that fence. Today, around Eastern Europe, others are climbing over fences and tearing down walls. And they are doing so because freedom is a human right.

A second thing comes to mind when I think about how far we have traveled. At first, voices from around the world warned us, lectured us, even condemned us. "What do those Poles want?" they asked. "They're madmen. They're threatening world peace and the stability of Europe. They should stop rocking the boat." Other nations might have the right to live in prosperity, the right to freedom and to democracy. But Poles, they implied, should renounce these rights so that it wouldn't disturb the peace.

In the days before World War II, there were some in the West who wondered why they should risk their lives for Gdansk. "Why not just stay home?" they asked. But war found them anyway, and they had to risk their lives for Paris, for London, for Hawaii. Some of those isolationist voices complained about what was going on now in Poland: "There's that Gdansk, disturbing the peace again." What they did not understand was that what was happening this time was not the start of a new war, but the end of an old one. What was beginning was a new, democratic, and more secure era in the history of our world. It was no longer a question of dying for Gdansk, but of living for it. . . .

Whatever it is that threatens European stability today, it isn't Poland. The path of profound change has been nonviolent, gradual, and negotiated, and that is why it has been possible to avoid the violence. Solidarity's way has become a model for other countries. We of all peoples know that changes do not always occur nonviolently. . . . How can anyone who understands the world around him now say that it would have been better had the Poles kept quiet? Shouldn't we say, rather, that the Poles did more to preserve and consolidate peace than many of their intimidated advisors? Shouldn't we say that stability and peace are in greater danger in those countries that have not yet managed to pass long-range and comprehensive reforms — those that cling to old and discredited forms of government, despite the will of their peoples?

Things are different in Poland now. And I have to say that what we have done has been viewed with understanding by our neighbors to the east and by their leader, Mikhail Gorbachev. This understanding has permitted us to lay a new foundation for improved relations between Poland and the USSR. And these new relations will also promote stability and peace in Europe, allaying those fears that are our worst enemies. Stretching behind them, Poles have a long and hard history. No country favors peaceful coexistence with all peoples and all nations more than Poland — peaceful coexistence with the Soviet Union in particular. We believe that now is the right time for friendship. . . .

Poland was the first victim of World War II. Her losses in human life and property were among the heaviest. . . . In 1945 we were theoretically on the winning side. But theory had little to do with practice. While her allies looked on in tacit agreement, an alien system of government was imposed on Poland, a government with no roots in Polish tradition and no popular support to back it up. Add to those a foreign economy, a foreign legal system, a foreign social philosophy. . . . The lawful Polish government-in-exile, recognized worldwide for having led the country's war effort, was vilified. Those who remained faithful to it were rewarded with brutality. Many were murdered. Thousands disappeared in the East; they shared that fate with those who had joined the underground army in Poland to fight the Nazis. We are still finding their bones in unmarked graves scattered throughout our forests.

The atrocities of the war were followed by the persecution of all those who dared think and act independently. All those solemn pledges made in Yalta about free elections in Poland were broken. . . . After 1939, this was the second national catastrophe. While other nations celebrated their victory, Poland went into mourning, a bitter mourning, for the Poles felt that the Allies had abandoned them. Many still feel that way. In spite of it all, the Poles began rebuilding their ruined country, and in the early postwar years they were quite successful. Soon, however, a new economic system was imposed that killed individual initiative. The economy was run by individuals without any mandate from the people.

Stalin prevented Poland from using aid provided by the Marshall Plan — the aid that was used by every other country in Western Europe, including those that had lost the war. It is worth invoking the name of this great American plan that helped Western Europe protect its freedom and a peaceful order, for now Eastern Europe awaits an investment of this kind — an investment in freedom, democracy, and peace.

The first government in fifty years to be elected by the people and to serve the people has inherited a crushing burden of debts from its predecessors. . . . Today, every country of the Eastern Bloc is bankrupt. The Communist economic system has failed in every part of the world, and the result is a massive exodus of citizens from these countries: by sea and by land, on ships and in planes, swimming and on foot. . . . But Poland has irreversibly committed itself to a new path. Our struggle will end when we have created hope and opportunity at home, so that no Pole need seek them abroad.

I want everyone to know and to remember that the same ideals that forged the magnificent American republic endure in distant Poland. Forces may have tried to cut us off from those ideals, but Poland never accepted that isolation, and today it aspires to the freedom those ideals produce. Joining Poland on its path to democracy are the other nations of Eastern Europe. The Wall has come down. May it never rise again.

I was flushed with emotion when I finished reading. The members of Congress interrupted me twenty-five times with applause and standing ovations, but what meant even more to me were the comments I heard afterward: Poland, some of them said, had returned to the international arena and could now speak in its own name. That very evening, when I talked with Secretary of State James Baker, the main topic was investment in Poland — as much as possible and as soon as possible. During the formal dinner that the House of Representatives gave in the Capitol in honor of Solidarity, many of the guests wore red-and-white buttons that said "MAKE THE CHECK OUT TO LECH." They agreed that it was better business to invest in democracy than in arms. I feel that my modest contribution had tangible results. It was said that my speech had been the best-paid speech in the world, for Congress granted Poland nearly $250 million in credits more than it had intended a few days earlier.

• • •

I had been told that Americans are raised on slogans and "sound bites," so I made an effort to try and come up with something witty and concrete. At the AFL-CIO convention I said, "Poland has opened its doors wide to you; it has even taken them off their hinges. What we want is cooperation on the order of a few billion dollars." Later I said, half-jokingly, "You have ninety-nine cents and I have a penny. But my penny still makes a dollar." I told leaders in Washington, "Throw Poland a life preserver."

"After that storm of words," I told the reporters who had come to see me off, "I expect a shower of dollars."

26
Healing Old Wounds

On November 17, 1989, I met with representatives of the American Jewish community in New York. Holding a small clay pot in his hands, the organizer of the meeting said to me:

This pot was made fifteen hundred years before our era, in the land of Israel. To the Jewish community in America, it symbolizes the link between ourselves and our ancestors. We offer it to you as an expression of our friendship and appreciation. In America, we often hear people complain that when you really need an electrician you can never find one. From now on things will be different. A Polish electrician has taken charge. He came here when we needed him most. And it is in large part thanks to his efforts that the world is lit again. Ladies and gentlemen, Lech Walesa!

The room could barely hold the seventy-five people assembled in it, but I still had a bad case of stage fright. Seated in front of me were important people, most of them elderly, and many of them with prejudices about Poland and about me as the representative of the Polish people:

Ladies and gentlemen, I'm not sure exactly what to do. I have written what I think is an important speech, into which I have put a lot of thought, but I have many questions to ask you, just as you no doubt have many to ask me. My meeting with you separately is no accident, because the history of your people is the most tragic of all. You have been persecuted throughout history, while we Poles have experienced only periodic persecution. Of course we could dwell on the grievances that have arisen from our shared history, but such is life. Yet I believe there are fewer things that divide us than there are that unite us. What divides us most of all is misunderstanding and the games played by people who would try to use the Jewish tragedy for their own ends. I am here today to help do away with any divisions, to show that they are not real, but products of vile and perfidious manipulation.

I went on speaking, my voice still trembling:

> You represent the major Jewish organizations in the United States, and I Solidarity, which for ten years now has been working for change in Poland. Our meeting is thus an occasion for a new level of dialogue between Jews and Poles, a special dialogue. It is a dialogue that can no longer take place in Poland, because Polish Jews no longer enrich our lives by sharing theirs with us. They perished in Auschwitz, Treblinka, Sobibor, Majdanek. Only a handful survived. We want to have nothing to do with anything that has poisoned the relations between Poles and Jews, poisoned them despite the efforts of so many in Polish society. We want to have nothing to do with that legacy of evil, a legacy sometimes exploited by self-serving individuals. The events of 1968 were testimony to that legacy. But today we need to work harder to further understanding — in the name of our common past, and in the name of everything that unites us. I would like this meeting to accomplish something concrete, something that will move us toward that understanding. I do not have a single drop of Jewish blood in my veins, but I respect history and I cannot permit lying by anyone — even if it were being done by the head of our Church. Let the truth be victorious.

My words were received warmly. But as I waited for questions, from the corner of my eye I could see that there were still angry and bitter faces. Finally someone rose to speak:

> My name is Menachem Rosensaft. My parents were sent to Auschwitz and Bergen-Belsen. They came from Poland, from Bedzin and Sosnowiec. Mr. Walesa, I would like to ask you, as a representative of the postwar generation, the generation to which we both belong, to take a position on the fact that during the war Cardinal Glemp's predecessor kept silent about the crimes being carried out against European Jews. It was forty years before the Church officially recognized the Jewish tragedy at Auschwitz. I also would like you to comment on the fact that after the Holocaust, after the Nazis had left, pogroms against the Jewish population still occurred — such as at Kielce.

(What I *might* have said in response is the following: "Sir, many of your own countrymen, maybe even some seated here, also didn't hear their agony. In 1944, as the excellent Polish reporter Hanna Krall wrote in her book *Hypnoza* [*Hypnosis*] — which I recommend to you — a little Jewish girl was taught to recite the Lord's Prayer so she could behave like a Christian child. She and her playmates were taken to the zoo, where a giraffe laughed once he saw how the sadness on the faces of the Jewish children betrayed them. The hero of Hanna Krall's book says that the Jews of the Warsaw Ghetto resented the Poles because the underground Polish Home Army had given them only fifty revolvers. But Zion? Did it send even fifty revolvers to the ghetto? Ten? It would not have been easy, but they might at least have sent someone to see what was going on. The Jews in Palestine didn't send a single revolver, a single emissary, a single letter to the Jews in the Warsaw Ghetto. They traveled back and forth between New York and London, because the only thing that was important to them was the future Jewish state and arms they would need to fight the wars to found it.")

I answered Mr. Rosensaft's questions as calmly as I could:

I could find many Jews, even some here in this room, who didn't hear your cries. And if you had wanted to, you too could find them. Only you don't want to. Instead you want to blame the Cardinal and reopen old wounds. I am not going to defend him. If he didn't do as he should have, I won't defend him. As to the Kioloo pogrom, that was an infamous crime done by people who, after all the tragedies of the occupation, shamefully dared to raise their hand against those few Jews who survived. It was without doubt a heinous crime, and I would be the first to spit in the face of these criminals.

Now it is up to us to break the vicious circle and begin again. What happened was appalling. After the war your people deserved least of all to be treated like that. But all Poles don't deserve to have accusations flung in our faces. Let's not dwell on the past. If Jews still lived in Poland today, if the Nazis had never come, our country would be prosperous and I wouldn't have to come to the United States and beg. My people have been suffocated, and you have been uprooted. We have much in common, and that is why we say painful things to each other. My wife and I have arguments. But she loves me, and I love her. . . .

I felt and understood the bitterness of the man questioning me. He had lost all his loved ones at Auschwitz, that anteroom to Hell. I could even understand his animosity toward the Church. Over the centuries Christians have blamed Jews for the crucifixion, and the result has been pogroms and persecution. But what did Cardinal Glemp have to do with them? For years, particularly since Vatican II, the Church has recognized anti-Semitism as a sin and actively condemned it. Cardinal Glemp may be guilty of awkward phrasing, but he's no racist.

There, in New York, I wanted very badly to improve Polish-Jewish relations, and to confront the charges of Polish anti-Semitism. Few Jews still live in Poland (barely a few tens of thousands survived the German occupation), and yet the foreign press continues to allege that there is Polish anti-Semitism. Can there be anti-Semitism when there are so few Jews? It would seem so.

Rabbi Israel Miller, former president of the Council of Jewish Organizations, declared that the Israeli people needed support, and not only from the Jews. He asked me what Tadeusz Mazowiecki's government was doing to help Israel. I wasn't sure what the current state of diplomatic relations with Israel was, so I couldn't answer the question. Shortly afterward, however, I learned that the Polish government had offered to help fly Soviet Jews to Israel — the Hungarian airline, which up to that point had been helping Jewish émigrés, had halted these flights because of terrorist threats from Arab groups. One day when I was at the Warsaw airport I saw the effects of the Polish offer. The terminal was crawling with police patrols checking every passenger and every car.

In the end, I didn't manage to persuade the American Jewish community that relations with the Poles would be better if we stopped dwelling on the past. A few months later an opportunity to make relations somewhat better did come along. Late in February 1990, a delegation from the World Jewish Congress came to see me in Gdansk, a delegation led by the multimillionaire Edgar Bronfman — a striking man in his sixties with a penetrating gaze. The World Jewish Congress was founded in 1936 in Geneva (its current headquarters are in New York), and is estimated to have a million and a half members, yet it is neither the largest nor the wealthiest of the Jewish organizations. The goals of the Congress are to promote Jewish unity, to further the interests of the state of Israel, and to protect Jewish minorities around the world, so that they can preserve their cultural and religious traditions.

After some polite small talk, Mr. Bronfman came to the point: "We are again observing signs of anti-Semitism in your great country, even though barely ten thousand Jews still live in Poland. It would help immeasurably if you, Lech Walesa, were to take a public stand on the matter."

I replied that my position had always been clear: I had never promoted or condoned anti-Semitism. Then I tried widening the conversation by talking about the history of Polish-Jewish relations:

> Mr. Bronfman, my prayer is that we don't have to talk to each other like dip-lomats, but can address each other in simple, straightforward language. There never was any genuine racially based anti-Semitism in Poland, and there still isn't. Theorists might find lots of signs of hostility toward Jews, especially in our past, but I am a pragmatist who lives in the here-and-now and I just can't live by theory. There may at one time have been discrimination and differ-ences in interests between these two powerful peoples who lived side by side in Poland — Poles and Jews. Nowhere in the world was there a larger Jewish population, and this necessarily gave rise to conflict, in the same way as there is conflict in any multicultural society. Some Poles might have said to the Jews, "These are our streets"; and Jews might have said back to the Poles, "But these are our houses." What I'm merely suggesting is that the conflict wasn't racial, but economic. Poles never enacted any law or devised any theory promoting racial superiority or inferiority. There is talk once again about how Poles aren't providing the Jewish minority with better living conditions — and I under-stand that. But I have always had people of your faith around me, though I personally have no family ties to the Jews.

It is Poland's loss that so few Jews now live there. What the Nazis did to the Jewish people was the most inhuman and the most heinous crime ever devised by man. I was ready to do anything to attract Jewish interest in Poland once again, though I knew success was unlikely: "Jews needed Poland when they needed a home. Now they have one and they live well. I'm putting it bluntly because I am blunt, and even perhaps impudently frank."

Nothing was impossible, Mr. Bronfman replied, now that the outlines of a new Poland were appearing; perhaps some Jews might wish to return. As for the Germans, they cannot be allowed to have the atomic bomb, and the constitution of a unified Germany must guarantee the security of all national minorities.

Edgar Bronfman's mission must have been widely publicized, because four weeks later — on the forty-fifth anniversary of the Arab League — I was visited by a delegation headed by Abdallah Hijazi, a representative of the Palestine Liberation Organization. In the delegation were ambassadors to Poland from nine Arab countries: Algeria, Egypt, Iraq, Yemen, Libya, Morocco, Jordan, Syria, and Tunisia. Mr. Hijazi began talking in language much too formal and affected to get anywhere. So, as is my habit, I decided to help him by suggesting he express himself sincerely and drop the diplomatic embellishments.

He burst out laughing and said, "That makes me feel young again." Then he put away his notes and talked briefly about the Arab stand on what was going on in Poland. When he'd finished he invited the others to speak. All of them stressed, as I remember, that Arab businesspeople did not meddle in the domestic politics of the countries in which they wanted to invest. They set no political preconditions, though they expected clear support for "the just cause in the struggle for peace."

I knew right away that this was an allusion to Poland's having recently reestablished diplomatic ties to Israel. I argued that different fruits could ripen in the same orchard — something I believe very strongly. Jews had lived with us for centuries, and they helped create Polish culture. They are gifted at business, and now they have their own government and resources. We want them on our side. We also want the Arabs on our side. There is only one Israeli ambassador in Poland, after all, and there are no fewer than nine Arab ambassadors!

Their general response was:

We are not prejudiced against the Jews, especially now that more than 56 percent of the Israelis favor dialogue with the Arabs. But the Israeli army and Israeli settlers must withdraw from the occupied territories. Is it not a pity that Israeli settlements today are built around town squares named for Arab kings? Our vision of reconciliation between Arabs and Jews is humanitarian. But there is no such thing as a "pretty" occupation. Your national anthem includes the line "Poland is not dead so long as we live." That is how Arabs feel about Palestine.

But we seek peace not at the expense of Israel, but next to Israel. We preach for peace on the same Palestinian land where Christ preached for humanity. But peace cannot mean slavery. On this historic land there should be a state for each nation.

I stressed that as president of Solidarity and recipient of the Nobel Peace Prize, I want with all my heart to see true reconciliation between

Palestinians and Jews. I wish peace, happiness, and stability for both parties in the conflict. I also wish for Poland to do more and more business with both.

I was intrigued by their reply: "You Poles are betting too much on Western Europe and too little on the Arab world. We know that from an economic standpoint, you cannot compete with the West. You ought to be designing your export market around the Middle East."

We continued our discussion and addressed again an earlier question regarding the now-free Polish media. It had to do with an article in *Gazeta Wyborcza* about a fire that had ravaged a Libyan factory (probably manufacturing chemical weapons) with the headline "FIRE IN THE LUNATIC ASYLUM." As a matter of principle I could only advocate total freedom of the press, I told the ambassadors, and went on to tell them that I too had received my fair share of abuse from it.

After posing together for an official group photograph, they left. Their parting gift to me was an example of Bethlehem craftsmanship: a bust of Christ sculpted in olivewood.

Auschwitz and what happened to the Jewish people will forever stand as warning to us all, for at any moment in history a criminal ideology of racial superiority can emerge. The largest number of European Jews lived in Poland. In their flight from persecution in Western Europe, it was in Poland that they had found a home. The largest group in the Diaspora, therefore, had stayed on the banks of the Vistula. And that is why they were annihilated there in such numbers. With World War II, that madness that gripped first Europe and later the whole world, the Germans built Auschwitz in the heart of Poland. Military transport trains jammed the other railway lines, but at Auschwitz, not far from Cracow, there was a fast track direct to the gas chambers.

For those in the West who have never been to Poland, the perception is: "The graveyard of the Jewish people is in Poland, and that must mean that the hands of the Poles are stained with guilt." It is a horrible simplification. My father wasn't Jewish, and he didn't die at Auschwitz. He was an ordinary farmer from Mazowie. I never even knew him, for he died from exhaustion after surviving another of Hitler's concentration camps. He departed life only two months after being set free; I wasn't yet two years old. There were hundreds of those camps in Poland.

27
Stirring Things Up

In one of the short stories from his collection called *Kolyma Stories,* Varlam Shalamov, a Russian writer who spent half of his life in Stalin's gulags, describes how paths were made in the snow-covered wasteland of Siberia: rows of prisoners wearing chains and rags, five or six across, would head out into that expanse of endless whiteness, until the collective tramping of their feet had created one. As president of Solidarity, I sometimes felt like one of those trampers. No one had gone before me to clear a path between totalitarianism and democracy. No one knew exactly which direction to take. We had to rely on instinct alone, and it was like trying to follow the movement of the sun through a fog. As one of my colleagues put it, it was like being the first through a minefield: the easier job was waiting to follow behind.

A great wave of demonstrations had begun in East Germany, Czechoslovakia, and Bulgaria. The dominos were falling at full tilt. Colleagues would say to me, "See what you've started, Lech? Now they're all going to be lining up, looking for subsidies from Europe!" "'Lining up' is exactly the way to put it," I replied. "We'll all have to go through the gates of Europe one by one, because we can't go all at once." In their struggle for democracy, all of these countries were confronting the same basic problems — collapsing economies, chronic budget deficits, huge debts. In Poland, we needed to start depoliticizing the economy and shifting property to the private sector. The next battle would be to control inflation — rocketing to a rate of nearly 300 percent a year — and to do that we would need at least $1 billion in foreign aid. By December, the Sejm had approved twenty-one new laws allowing for setting up private enterprises in Poland.

On November 29, in London for a four-day trip, I said to those greeting me, "I have come to you wearing three different hats — those of a union leader, a politician, and a businessman." As a union leader, I had been invited to take part in the fortieth anniversary of the founding of the International Confederation of Free Trade Unions, where I met the members of two British unions: Norman Willis's leftist TUC and the rightist Electricians' Union, headed by Eric Hammond. As a politician I had the honor of visiting with Prime Minister Margaret Thatcher at her residence at Chequers, after earlier meeting the foreign minister, Douglas Hurd. As a businessman, I was invited to speak by the powerful and influential lobby at the headquarters of the British Industrial Confederation, with whom I spoke bluntly: "You do business with people who need things. Poles need everything — from buttons to satellites. Do business with us."

I wore a fourth and less official hat when dealing with the English Polonia, and in particular with the Polish government-in-exile set up in London after Hitler's invasion. There were the Polish Social and Cultural Center in Hammersmith and the Sikorski Institute to visit. Czeslaw Zychowicz, president of the Association of Polish Combatants, and Artur Rynkiewicz, president of the Polish Union (which consists of some seventy Polonia organizations), came to meet with me. The former president of the émigré government, ninety-six-year-old Edward Raczynski, its current president Ryszard Kaczorowski, and the generals Stanislaw Maczkowski (ninety-seven years old!) and Klemens Rudnicki were all looking forward to a visit with me.

No matter what hat I was wearing I made it an unwavering point to raise the issue of credit for Poland. I was constantly explaining the two major difficulties that Polish reform would now face: first, the economic disaster, and second, what might be called human factors — the absence of truly democratic habits and the widespread ignorance about what pluralism really means. There was no real middle class in Poland, for our "protectors" had effectively liquidated it. We needed a new one.

The anticommunist opposition had finally taken over some control of government, and we had begun to demand that it share responsibility for the country's fate; but the political climate left a great deal to be desired. Public apathy about politics ran very deep.

What did I get for my labors? Very little. The first day of my visit the British government doubled the funds earmarked for technological development — though that still amounted to only $75 million. Another $23 million was granted for additional emergency food aid to Poland, along with $100 million — representing Britain's contribution to the "stabilization funds" (as they are called) that are managed by the International Monetary Fund.

I was given to understand that alleviating Poland's indebtedness was a sensitive political issue, for were it done, Latin American countries would demand the same treatment. But something needed to be done. Eugenio Lari, head of the Eastern Europe department of the World Bank, had estimated that in 1992 Poland would need new loans and credits of nearly $20 billion.

Mikhail Gorbachev had visited the Vatican, and this, in part, is what the Holy Father said to him:

> As we approach the end of the second millennium of the Christian era, the Church calls on all those who care deeply about the fate of humanity to unite in a common commitment to its material and spiritual health. Such concern will not only help to ease tensions between nations and to bring an end to geopolitical confrontation, but will foster universal solidarity, especially with regard to the developing countries.

Gorbachev replied:

> The Soviet Union and the Holy See are involved in the same pan-European process of change. Each in its own way has seen to it that this process is balanced — helping to resolve European problems by creating the conditions under which each nation makes its own choices freely. Respect for a people's national, political, and cultural identity is critical, so that in a period of massive change — such as the one we now are in — change can occur peacefully.

Life was soon to confirm the sincerity of Gorbachev's words: the Soviet Union didn't lift a finger when the Romanians overthrew the hated tyrant Nicolae Ceausescu and, on Christmas Day, executed him.

On December 12, I poked a stick into the anthill by issuing a declaration calling for greater powers for the new government — powers making it capable of reorganizing the economy; amending the laws on property; de-monopolizing the state and cooperative sector; reforming the tax structure, the accounting system, and bank operations; and restructuring regional and local governments. For these powers to be effective, I continued, the judicial acts by which they were accorded would have to go into operation immediately. It was understood, of course, that these special powers would be granted only for a clearly defined period of time, during which the Senat and the Sejm could work on other important legislation, while also reserving to themselves the right to modify all changes instituted by the government.

My declaration stirred things up far more than I'd expected. What I was trying to address was the widespread frustration that things were going too slowly. But the perception was that I wanted to become a dictator.

My colleagues' position was that as long as the apparatus of the previous government (now called the "fifth column") was still intact, it would be foolish to accord anyone greater power without parliamentary checks and balances. There were even those who said outright that my proposal lacked common sense: what was the point of using shock therapy to get things going? It would only play into the hands of the Communists, everyone said, since they alone could manage the kind of "firm-handed" government I had in mind. Every group in the government categorically rejected my ideas.

Be that as it may, my troublemaking had some good side effects: people began talking about the need for fast legislation, and they argued openly that the parliament should take more responsibility for the country's fate.

28
Death of a Dissident

O n December 13, 1989, for the first time, Poles showed in public how
they felt about having lived under the state of martial law decreed
eight years earlier (which "officially" lasted nineteen months, but in fact
continued for five years). Demonstrations broke out in a few places, and
though they were not large or numerous, some — despite all the appeals
from the media — were violent. In Warsaw, demonstrators went to
General Jaruzelski's residence, chanting, "We want a president and not a
secret agent!" In Katowice, crowds smashed the windows of the building
housing the Regional Committee of the PZPR and burned a gasoline-
drenched effigy of Jaruzelski. In Cracow, the crowd tried to burn down
the headquarters of the PZPR Committee. In Szczecin, the PZPR and Militia headquarters were attacked. In Gdansk, Wroclaw, Lodz, and Poznan,
the demonstrations were much milder.

Jaruzelski himself did not appear in public. As Prime Minister
Mazowiecki later revealed, Jaruzelski intended to take "the secret of December 13, 1981" to his grave.

It was a dirty secret. The Communist apparatus had systematically
looted the country under martial law. Casting patriotism aside and thinking only of themselves, Party members had committed thievery on a grand
scale, abandoning any attempt to control or regulate those parts of the
economy that still worked. No one investigated the apparatchiks of Edward Gierek's time (December 1970 to August 1980). Gierek, in exchange
for huge bribes placed in foreign banks, had been "persuaded" to use
Poland's funds to buy patents and technology that were outdated and often
incomplete. No one tried to estimate how many credits granted by the
West had been transferred — more or less directly — to Brezhnev's

Soviet Union. No one revealed how much was looted by Party function-aries, the Security Service, the prison authorities, the Militia, and certain army officers. Contempt and the arrogance peculiar to a government with no checks on its power so completely clouded any sense of duty that many Polish representatives — there is no other way of putting it — stopped being Polish. They became thieves. Bankrupt factories, empty stores, a grim and dour populace: this is what the most corrupt regime of all, Gierek's, had left behind.

Under these sorry conditions, it had become imperative for the government of Solidarity to do anything it could to pull Poland out of the swamp. But all it had at its disposal were a totally ineffective banking system, inadequate business laws and money-changing mechanisms, and a pathetic telephone system.

Polish agriculture posed yet another problem. After forty-five years of a command economy, it was now up to the government to deal with problems such as the price of milk and diesel fuel. The incredible short-sightedness of farmers in the Congress of Rural Solidarity (poor planners, though they were expert at making demands) meant that painful changes lay ahead — including basic changes in the thinking of Polish farmers. When I went to "listen to the people's mood" I was attacked for the high price of meat, the stagnant dairy industry, and the stupid leadership; and when I replied, "You need to set these problems right by yourselves, and not just blame Walesa," people shouted back to me, "You're closer to the ministers!"

There were many times I felt like giving up. In moments of panic I was convinced that nothing would ever really change in my lifetime. But then something would happen to raise my spirits. Often it was something small — small but significant, because it heralded something new. In the first issue of the underground newspaper *Policjant* [*The Policeman*], I read this encouraging passage:

> The world is changing. Poland is changing. The changes are even affecting those areas where habit and immutability seemed like the only guarantees of existence. The challenges we face fill us with anxiety, but they should also imbue us with a sense of certainty: what has been can be no longer. Over many long years we were told there were certain boundaries that could not to be crossed. Today the impossible is possible. This does not exempt us from making painful choices. We do not want readers to think that our views present "the only just way," for life has shown us, often painfully, that there is no such

thing. But we must remember that our fears can't destroy the hope that, some-day, everything will be normal.

On December 17, one of the most eminent spokesmen of the Russian people died: Andrei Sakharov, a man of great integrity and courage. One of the inventors of the Soviet hydrogen bomb, Sakharov later became the best-known of Russian dissidents and for his efforts was awarded the Nobel Peace Prize in 1975.

I decided to attend his funeral in Moscow, set for December 18, after sending his widow, Yelena Bonner, my telegram of condolence: "A man who was the symbol of wisdom and courage has left us. Today, the wave of reforms for which he fought is overtaking Eastern Europe. With it are arising new and difficult problems and sadly his voice will not be there to help us resolve them."

With me aboard the plane to Moscow were Adam Michnik and Senator Edward Wende. After two hours of flying, the pilot was told that the airport in Moscow was closed: due to a sudden drop in temperature, the runways had frozen. So we landed instead in Leningrad, where, together with the Polish consul, we visited the dilapidated older part of the city. Two hours later, we were able to leave for Moscow. We finally arrived — five hours after the funeral. The same thing had happened, we learned, to several other foreign delegations.

We went straight from the air field to Vostriakovski Cemetery. Soldiers had replaced the men who earlier had guided the funeral procession of some sixty thousand people. The cemetery walls and the area around the front gate were covered with flowers, as was the grave, where we placed a wreath in the name of Solidarity (the letter V framed by flowers). That evening, at the Hotel Rossija, we took part in the official funeral banquet. More than four hundred people were there.

At the Berlin Wall Museum, next to Checkpoint Charlie, there is a permanent exhibition entitled "From Gandhi to Walesa." Outside, on the museum's wall, there is a plaque bearing these words: "Solidarity. Struggle without force. Only when we are free can we fight for peace. Gandhi, Martin Luther King, Sakharov, and Walesa are building your future, too." How honored and how humble I felt when I learned that my name appeared next to those of such monumental figures! Lech Walesa, an electrician from Gdansk — I didn't feel worthy of being compared to these men who had done so much for freedom and human dignity. I have always been much more a pragmatist than an idealist. Of the figures whose names appear on that plaque, I remarked to myself that I remained the only one still living.

The year 1989, called by some "the people's autumn," was coming to an end. In Poland, the official sign of the year's close could be found in the changing of the country's name back to what it was before World War II: the Republic of Poland. Changed also was the country's emblem: the white eagle was back, with its golden crown. Rather than being done all at once, the reprinting of official stationery and currency would be spread out over a five-year period. The symbols of sovereignty and independence had been returned to the people of Poland. Soon even the misleading name "Civic Militia" was replaced with the simpler term "Police." Personally, I thought that the army should have reissued those square kepis worn by army officers since the middle of the eighteenth century as a symbol of honor. But perhaps not everything ought to be brought out of the museum of the past.

29
The Final Days of the PZPR

During almost every interview I gave in early 1990 I was asked whether the Round Table accords were still in force. Answering affirmatively, I added that they would need to be interpreted according to the new circumstances. Even the Holy Scriptures are interpreted differently today (though the dictates of the Ten Commandments are timeless). I explained that when we first sat down to negotiate at the Round Table, the climate in Poland was tense, and there wasn't much room for maneuvering. Now, nine months later, the political landscape had changed and a new government was in power. That's why it was still just as important as it ever was to hold to the ground rules established by the Round Table talks — so that all the emerging political forces could get along.

Further, I was opposed to any kind of settling of old scores: revenge begins a vicious circle, and terrorism is repaid with terrorism. Of course, those who had been in power during the years of corruption and mismanagement should be held accountable for their actions — but by the historian, and not by the judge. When asked about the future of the political left, I suggested that it was necessary for new leaders to emerge, leaders whose credibility was not tainted by association with Stalinism. Poland needs a powerful left, because locating all power in the political right creates a dangerous imbalance. I concluded that the glorious era of the PZPR, the Polish United Workers' Party, was over.

From January 3 to 5, representatives from the democratic opposition in East Germany visited Poland at the invitation of the Senat. Among them were Professor Jens Reich, the painter Barbel Bohley of the New Forum movement, and the philosopher Wolfgang Templin of the organization Peace and Human Rights. On January 4, they came to Gdansk to see me.

From meeting with them I became aware of how different the East Germans' preoccupations and concerns were from those of their West German counterparts. Since German reunification meant that the Western Big Brother would have to take on East Germany's economic problems, East Germans were worried that this meant they would be relegated to second-class citizenship. What, for instance, would happen to the unions in East Germany? As the differences in economic power leveled out, relations between the two German halves would become more harmonious. But all agreed about the Berlin Wall: rather than being moved to some other border, such as the German-Polish border, it should be dismantled right down to its very foundations.

On Sunday, January 14, I had an hour-long conversation in Warsaw with the Japanese prime minister, Toshiki Kaifu, who had been received a few hours earlier by Prime Minister Mazowiecki. We mainly discussed the prospects of increased Japanese investment in Poland. He formally invited me to visit Japan. That same day, Mazowiecki told me that he was considering a proposal before the Sejm to push up the date for local elections. Since I had myself suggested the same thing earlier, I thought that the moment was right to issue a statement on the subject:

> The reforms passed by the Sejm and the government are in my view being implemented too slowly by mid-level government branches. Changes are occurring at a pace that makes it impossible to ensure these reforms will be adopted quickly and effectively. The only solution is to call on the Sejm and the government of the Republic of Poland to schedule elections of local authorities ahead of the planned date.

Mr. Mazowiecki was offended by my initiative. He claimed I had stolen the idea of earlier elections from him, even though he knew perfectly well otherwise.

On Thursday, January 18, Soviet Ambassador Vladimir Brovikov came to visit me in Gdansk. I remember telling him that the Communist system, maintained by military might, was slowly but surely receding into the past. To establish a basis for new relations between our governments, we should first fill in the blank pages of Polish-Soviet history: those involving the USSR's attack on Poland on September 17, 1939; the massacres at Katyn Forest and elsewhere of fifteen thousand Poles, mostly officers and intellectuals; and the deportation of hundreds of thousand of Poles to Siberia for forced labor. I also told Ambassador Brovikov that Poles must be al-

lowed to travel freely anywhere in Poland, or in what was once Polish
territory, where the bones of our ancestors still lie and the monuments of
Polish culture still stand. The Soviet Communist Party had always been
on the best of terms with the Polish Communist Party; what we really
needed to see was true friendship between our peoples. I said, "We do not
wish to impose our values on you, but by the same token you should not
impose yours on us; your domestic woes were in part caused by that kind
of forced intervention."

My Soviet guest graciously replied:

> I share your concerns. I too no longer feel the need to protest when I hear bitter
> recriminations about the tragedies in our shared history. If Polish-Soviet his-
> tory could be rewound like a videocassette and recorded again, I would be
> among the first to record it in a different way — in a way that would make us
> co-authors of our fates. But history is unchangeable. Mr. Walesa, you have said
> that we are condemned to remain neighbors. That is true. Therefore, we need
> to ask ourselves how we can face each other, how best to avoid turning our
> backs. A path to understanding has been cleared, and the ideology that divided
> us has been removed. Let both our nations aspire to greater things.

I took a deep breath and returned the conversation to specifics:

> Mr. Ambassador, to say that the Molotov-Ribbentrop Pact is no longer in force
> answers only half of the question; the second part of the question is, What have
> the effects of that pact been? Obviously, we have no intention of attacking the
> Soviet Union to get back our lost territory. However, we must be allowed to
> visit them if the old wounds are to heal. We do not want to drive your soldiers
> out of Poland. We know they will go by themselves when the time is right. And
> I know that Mr. Gorbachev has inherited a legacy of problems from the times
> of Stalin, Khrushchev, and Brezhnev. But we cannot wait to see what the future
> will bring. If everything really is changing, we need to speak openly and not
> out of constraint.

The ambassador coughed lightly and began a stiff recitation of the Party
line: the border that now lies between our two countries is an irreversible
historical fact. He added that in the Ukraine and Belorussia, nationalist
voices were clamoring to take Bialystok, Przemysl, Chelm, and other
towns back from Polish territory; this kind of demand, he stressed, was
unreasonable and unproductive. As for the presence of the Soviet armies

in Poland and other countries, it was true that their presence was gradually becoming unproductive — so long as no need for them arose, of course. "Naturally, Russians take a different view of these matters than Poles," he said, "but that doesn't mean that if the Polish government requested Soviet army units to withdraw from its territory, the Soviet government wouldn't conduct an intensive examination of the matter."

We went on debating economic problems, disagreeing on subjects such as technology, finance, and reform. Finding a common language was a struggle. The USSR was like a tractor-trailer truck, I said — big and powerful, but unwieldy; Poland was smaller and cornered better. We also broached the serious problems of the youth in both of our countries — to them, rhetoric about "patriotism" and "the interests of the Eastern Bloc" meant nothing. We (I more than he, actually) brought up a variety of new concerns: the lies printed in history textbooks; the legitimacy of the current Polish government; our plans to catch up as quickly as possible with, and join, the European Community. Discussion about all these topics was open and frank. But when I mentioned the Polish impatience for political change, the ambassador visibly stiffened. He replied, "Today, all the wisdom of politicians — whether Polish or Soviet — needs to be directed toward preventing any kind of explosion in society, for that will bring bloodshed."

On January 25, I began holding each of my press conferences in a different setting. Naturally I had to start at the Gdansk Shipyards. There I said to both the press and the workers:

> Lately I have been hearing charges that we're ignoring the masses, that we talk only with the elite, that we drink cognac, and that the concerns of the workers are no longer our concerns. To prove how false these charges are, I've decided that my weekly meetings with journalists will take place among workers and farmers, so that we can all keep in touch. Think of me above all as a union man, and only a little as an amateur politician. If I have made nondemocratic decisions in the past, it was so that others, in the future, could live under democracy.

On Sunday, January 28, I sat in front of my television watching the final congress of the Polish United Workers' Party (known all these years simply as "the Party"). Along with the rest of Poland, I was waiting for the event we'd been expecting for some weeks now: the collapse of the PZPR.

It finally happened at 1:36 A.M. on Monday, when a majority of the delegates voted to dissolve the PZPR and to transfer its privileges and powers to a new political party called the Social Democratic Party of the Republic of Poland, led by a young and gifted apparatchik named Aleksander Kwasniewski. Those in the minority formed a separate party called the Social Democratic Union of the Republic of Poland, and elected a Gdansk native as its president, Tadeusz Fiszbach. And so the "unity" of the left in Poland — a unity based on Communist hegemony and propaganda — collapsed.

The reign of the PZPR had been long and unchallenged. From the beginning of its existence, it was the only real power in the country, and that fact very quickly and profoundly dehumanized its leaders, who were primitive and vindictive people to begin with. You couldn't have a career in industry, science, the civil service, or any field, if you weren't a member of the Party. All of the highest civil-service positions (from the national government down to the town councils) were filled only by Party members. Party officials stole routinely from state coffers and drew "supplements" to their salaries. Criticism was not permitted. Demonstrations were broken up; people were thrown into prison or fired (and often prohibited from finding other work within a radius of a hundred miles of their former jobs); "oppositional riffraff" were regularly denied admission to universities or training centers. How unsurprising, then, that after forty-five years of this the PZPR became a symbol of despotism and a focus for hatred. No one would cry at its funeral.

Out of the ruins of the PZPR rose two new parties, both calling themselves social democrats. One result of the split was the resignation of Mieczyslaw Rakowski, leader of the Party conservatives. Tadeusz Fiszbach took a more realistic stand:

> If we use the same people to create a new party, that party will lack credibility — and credibility is more important than unity. And that is why there is no truth in the assertion I have brought about a schism in the Party. An activist doesn't become a social democrat overnight. What I have done is to gather together activists who share a new view of the Polish left.

The basic difference between the two new parties lay in their assessment of the PZPR's past. Tadeusz Fiszbach — who had been the first secretary of the PZPR's Regional Committee in Gdansk until he was forced from office when martial law was declared on December 13, 1981 —

thought that declaring martial law topped the list of the Party's errors. His counterpart in the new Social Democratic Party, Aleksander Kwasniewski, declined to comment on the past and spoke only of the need for future reform — though he had consolidated his power with the help of some former hard-liners.

So here we were again at the forefront of change in Eastern Europe. Now that the Soviet army no longer threatened Poland, now that we had gained domestic independence and international recognition, it was time to address as best we could the hardships of daily life, hardships that the crisis had intensified. It was true that because of Deputy Prime Minister Leszek Balcerowicz's plan (and because "stabilization funds" from the West had finally come through), the government had managed to slow inflation. But the average Pole continued to earn between only eighty and a hundred dollars a month, and meanwhile the cost of living was approaching that of Western Europe. That's why when journalists asked me why Solidarity didn't limit its activities to union matters, my reply was that first we had to create a working economy. Then and only then could we concentrate on workers' demands. (Meanwhile, of course, union leaders under the OPZZ banner were claiming in a self-serving manner that *they* were the ones concentrating on the workers' interests.)

Again and again I was asked to comment on unemployment projections, which varied between half a million and three million Poles. What could we do? First, we needed to keep encouraging Western banks to open subsidiaries in Poland, and do so by creating conditions in which investment would be attractive. Second, we needed to start modernizing Polish industry, and plan and implement a complex network of public works throughout the country. Eighty percent of our cities needed massive rebuilding, and half of the country's roads needed leveling and paving. Our problem was that there were several workers for every shovel. We had to either increase the number of shovels or find other jobs for these workers.

In the Polish town of Poronin, on January 30, 1990, young radicals toppled the statue of Lenin (donated forty years earlier by the workers of Leningrad). That same day, in Strasbourg, Prime Minister Mazowiecki formally requested that Poland be admitted to the Council of Europe. "As a people we have always been a part of Europe," he declared. "Now we want to be a part of it as a nation." The council stated outright that the basic condition for considering Poland's candidacy was fully free elections. On the other hand, the conditions set by the International Monetary

Fund were economic rather than political, and it therefore granted Poland a loan of some $725 million. We continued to face financial hardship and price hikes, but now we could at least hope that in six months inflation would level off at 1 or 2 percent. Once we had put the economy back on track, we could begin discussing changing the system — privatizing industry, passing an antimonopoly law, filing bankruptcy papers for the more unprofitable enterprises, and reforming the banking system. We were trying to revitalize in a few years what the Communists had allowed to deteriorate for nearly half a century. We knew that Moscow would be watching us closely.

30
The Gloves Come Off

O pposition to the Communist Party had united nearly everyone in Poland. Once the Party was dissolved, differences of opinion began to
emerge within Solidarity's leadership — at first over unimportant problems, then gradually over more fundamental issues. They centered chiefly
around three major questions:

1. How long would people support Mazowiecki's government, which seemed
   to promise only sweat and tears for the near future?
2. Had the Round Table accords arrived at by Solidarity and the Communists
   lost their validity now that the PZPR no longer existed? For example,
   should the general elections, which had been scheduled for 1993, be moved
   up as far as possible, so that Poles could have a fully democratic parliament?
3. Should Poland maintain a special relationship with the USSR (as Prime
   Minister Mazowiecki wanted), or should it turn more clearly toward Western Europe (as Bronislaw Geremek, president of the Parliamentary Civic
   Club, seemed to suggest)?

Later, some regrouping within Solidarity occurred because of what was
called "autocratic tendencies in the leadership of Solidarity." Beneath this
concern was the question of whether we should move straight ahead
quickly under my leadership, or build a democracy slowly, step by step.

I realized that I was putting Mazowiecki's government in an awkward
position by speaking out, and I was criticized for my lack of courtesy. I
didn't care whether or not I was rude, I replied; all I wanted was to be
effective. I would support the government up to the Second Congress of

259

Solidarity, and after that I would reevaluate my position. The fact was, I was fed up with being raked over the coals for someone else's mistakes (the workers I met with every week didn't mince words).

I tried to explain to people that dismantling the *nomenklatura* — those who had clung to the Communist Party ladder and had permanent positions in the civil service, the army, and the police — was going to be a headache. But it had to be done. Social tension was growing largely because of the impunity and arrogance of that tight-knit and entrenched group. Every letter I received said the same thing: "Nothing has changed. The *nomenklatura* is still abusing power and openly sabotaging the decisions of the government and parliament." The only way to remedy things was to hold local elections as quickly as possible.

As head of Solidarity, I had never presented myself as a candidate for political office, nor had I tried to intervene in government activities. However, since the present government needed to hear grievances, I took on the sometimes thankless job of being the spokesman for those grievances.

I performed my duties vigorously. In the fall of 1989, there were three forums for public opinion. All had originated in the same opposition movement, but each one had gradually became autonomous: Solidarity was the first forum; the Parliamentary Civic Club (OKP), headed by Bronislaw Geremek, was the second; and the third was the government of Tadeusz Mazowiecki. The OKP was often critical of the government, which for its part was trying conscientiously to strengthen its executive power. Solidarity continued to be the support and guarantor to the government, providing structure and suggestions about platform.

As the final arbiter, I rarely said my piece, but when I did, I did it in style, I am told. I am self-educated, and maybe that's why I watch those around me carefully. I make my own observations, draw my own conclusions, ruminate over them, analyze them over and over, and learn from them — so that I don't make the same mistake twice. I'm not comfortable playing the diplomat, but if pressed, I can do it. If I have managed to get somewhere in life, it may be that I play to win and avoid making abrupt moves.

From February 8 to 11, the Second General Regional Assembly of Solidarity was held in the Gdansk Shipyards, and I was elected to be a delegate to the Second National Congress. My goal was clear: to make another bid to be president of Solidarity. Beginning early enabled me to work out new plans, such as in the international arena. As a union leader, I was tired of also having to be a teacher of political ways and means, but it looked as if I would have to continue being both for a while longer.

By mid-February, because final preparations for German reunification were underway, the problem of guaranteeing Poland's borders began to assume some importance. To protect Europe from any future German territorial expansion, the four great powers — the United States, the USSR, Great Britain, and France — established conditions for reunification. They invited representatives from both Germanies to take part in their talks. The Polish government sought actively to be allowed to join in.

Wanting to add my own two cents, I wrote an open letter to Ernst Breit, president of the West German DGB group of unions, on March 1, 1990, in which I said:

> Dear colleague, I ask you, as a friend of Solidarity and a friend of Poland, to use your authority, and the authority of the union organization you represent, to support Poland's request to take part in the conference of the four powers and the two German states, and, furthermore, to support a treaty that will assure the inviolability of the Oder-Neisse border. Elaborating on the arguments for this is pointless, since you know them perfectly well. Europe is on the verge of a transformation that will also change the character of the German nation.
>
> The desire for reunification is natural, and I follow its progress with great interest. Knowing how much you value stability and nonviolence, I count on your understanding and hope that you will support our position.

For all I know, this letter had some effect on the final negotiations, but I got no words of thanks from Mazowiecki's government. The only message I was getting from them was that individual initiative was no longer welcome.

But how could I keep quiet when each and every day I saw signs that the dramatic rise in the cost of living and the freeze on salaries were eroding popular support for Solidarity? There were even some fools who declared that they missed the old Communist system, moaning, "There was more food in the stores and it was cheaper, thanks to subsidies." This kind of "full-belly-today" thinking has always exasperated me. So my advisors and I continued to preach that the important thing was to keep tight control over state spending. Controlling spending would, we were convinced, create a stable rate of exchange and slow inflation. Of course, this meant hardship, and people reacted by calling even more loudly for pay hikes. But giving in would have destroyed state subsidies and emptied government coffers.

I waited anxiously to see if Poles would swallow this bitter pill and not go on strike — and if they would understand that the success of *any* reform was at stake.

On March 17, I met with the newly elected president of Czechoslovakia, Vaclav Havel, at the Karkonoski Pass in the Carpathian Mountains. The meeting had been arranged by Polish-Czech Solidarity activists Adam Michnik, Zbigniew Janas, and Jan Litynski, who accompanied me in the helicopter ride to the Czech mountain refuge of Spindlerova Bouda. They hadn't picked the location at random, for it was at this border post, toward the end of the 1970s, that Polish and Czech dissidents (Havel among them) held regular meetings to discuss the political situation and to work out joint communiqués.

The Czech president arrived forty minutes later than I (I took advantage of the time to visit the "dissident photo exhibition" recently set up in what had been an official Polish border post). When Havel arrived, it took us a good ten minutes to work our way toward each other through the crowds of enthusiastic tourists, mainly Czech, who pressed around us, despite the efforts of our Security Services. It was like two colliding cyclones, with each of us in the eye of a storm, until finally we managed to find each other. We went into the Spindlerova Bouda to have lunch, and we spoke warmly about a great many things, rejoicing at finally meeting one another. That's how we described our meeting an hour later at Odrodzenie, the Polish mountain resort a few hundred yards away, during a press conference at which we gave journalists copies of the declaration we had just signed.

Someone quipped that Walesa, by profession an electrician, and Havel, a chemist, should be able to arrive easily enough at the electrochemical process needed to charge storage batteries.

On Tuesday, March 20, I was awarded my first Polish honorary doctorate, by the senate of the University of Gdansk (fourteen foreign universities had already given me honorary degrees in absentia). After the ceremony, the journalist Zbigniew Gach, who since the beginning of 1990 had published satirical articles about me in Solidarity's weekly newspaper, *Tygodnik Gdanski*, wrote:

> For the first time, wearing the cap and gown with the University's colors, the president of "S" accepted an honorary doctorate in person. Marching in the

ceremonial procession, he could hardly keep from laughing when someone from the Associated Press bowed to him, or when the canon's aide knelt before him. But as soon as University rector Czeslaw Jackowiak said, "Mr. Lech Walesa, I confer on you the title, dignity, and privileges of a *doctor honoris causa* of the University of Gdansk," our president's eyes filled with tears. Then the university choir intoned a fourteenth-century hymn, *"Gaude, mater Polonia, prole fecunda nobili"* ["Rejoice, Mother Poland, fertile in noble descendants"].

Despite all the pomp and circumstance, I didn't forget about what I thought was the most important issue of the moment, and toward the end of March I was back on the warpath: "For the past six months the government has been riding on the backs of the unions. What it should have been doing the whole time was making sure it had something to fall back on, or even creating a political party. If pushed to it, I'll take over and demonstrate how to govern."

I knew very well what I was saying. In March, our union began meeting with government representatives. Their chief concern seemed to be to remind us that we had to write a joint communiqué in which we were to show agreement over such basic issues as privatization, wage indexes, budget allocations, and minimum wage. Our so-called joint communiqués symbolized divisiveness more than unity, and were in that respect reminiscent of the Round Table negotiations. At the third meeting, held on April 4, union leaders were so irritated by the wishy-washiness of the bureaucrats that they threatened to walk out. They had discussed the "ideology" of the struggle against unemployment; the role of Solidarity in the hiring and firing of workers; and the interests of retirees, the sick, the young, and those in the liberal professions. Scandalously, not one concrete decision on any of these topics had been reached.

I got so angry I started swearing. For months I had been telling the government that we needed to speed up reform, so that we all wouldn't wake up some fine morning with "one hand in the chamber pot," as the expression has it. Since no one in the government seemed to be listening, or even to care, I decided to throw a little more weight around. Solidarity is supposed to be a true union, I said to myself, and the basic duty of a trade union is to battle unemployment. If the economy gets hit with high unemployment, the union must do everything it can to help workers and minimize the effects. It was time for Solidarity to take off the gloves.

31

The Second Solidarity Congress

I n early April 1990, I had interesting meetings with two visiting deputy prime ministers, Don Mazankowski of Canada and Jan Carnogurski of Czechoslovakia. During Mazankowski's visit, I said, "In Poland, there is a saying that when things go well, it's almost like living in Canada. I can't hide the fact that I would like Poland's standard of living to equal that of Canada. But the truth is that we can't do it without your help, or without your investments." Mr. Mazankowski replied that twenty-nine business representatives had come with him for just that purpose. He assured us that in addition to a general aid package, Canada would sign a declaration of intent to assist in the modernization of Polish agriculture.

Jan Carnogurski's visit was more of a courtesy call. He is a Slovak and is fluent in Polish. I raised the issue of the Polish-Czech border. The Czech Communists had closed their border with Poland in 1981, on the pretext of protecting their country from a smallpox outbreak in the border area (doubtless Solidarity was the infecting agent). This made family contacts impossible. The "smallpox" continued until 1990, although now that half of the Czech opposition had been released from prison and occupied important government positions, we expected a change in border policy.

In Moscow, on Friday, April 13, the Tass agency published an official declaration regarding one of the topics I had raised during my talk with Soviet Ambassador Brovikov in January:

> At meetings between the Polish and Soviet leadership, as well as in society at large, there have long been questions about the circumstances surrounding the deaths of the Polish officers taken prisoner in September 1939. Historians

from both countries have done extensive research into the tragedy of Katyn Forest in an effort to bring to light new evidence.

Recently, Soviet archivists and historians have come across documents pertaining to Polish soldiers held in NKVD camps in Kozielsk, Starobielsk, and Ostashkov in the USSR. It would seem that in April and May 1940, some 15,000 Polish officers were detained in these three camps; 394 were transferred to the camp in Griazowiec; the others were handed over to units of the NKVD in the areas of Smolensk, Voroshilovgrad, and Kalinsk. NKVD reports after that time do not mention them. . . .

The Soviet people would like to express their profound regret for the Katyn tragedy, which stands as one of Stalinism's worst crimes.

The long-awaited Second National Solidarity Congress met from April 19 through 24 in Gdansk. Though I tried to smile for the cameras and appear upbeat, the period right before the congress had been a test of nerves. My ulcers had recurred (my secretaries know how many cups of mint tea I drank every day), I had frequent headaches, and my blood-sugar level rose alarmingly. I prayed to the Virgin Mary for strength and health for the coming weeks. Still, I felt tired and weak. Every year of fighting the Communist regime aged you two.

Furthermore, journalists and diplomats seemed to be ganging up on me, barraging me with questions about whether I wanted to become president in the event that there were new parliamentary elections. The questions irritated me. I had given no signals about starting a campaign for the presidency. A week before the congress opened, I appeared on the popular television program *Interpelacje* [*Interviews*], a program on which politicians are put on the spot. There too I was accused of having my eye on the Belvedere, the presidential residence. It was time to fight back.

How could I aspire to be president, I asked, when Polish intellectuals always wanted someone fluent in foreign languages, someone who knew how to entertain, who bowed elegantly, and who practiced all the social graces?

But could we afford that luxury? I asked. Did the president of Poland really have to be fluent in French to help the workers? No? Then perhaps what the country needed instead was a firm and decisive hand, I said. You can't catch thieves by committee.

I prepared quickly for the congress, but with great care, not wanting to be caught off-guard by the first loudmouth to come along. If I had any fears, it was at the prospect of the congress degenerating into a senseless griping session over the grievances accumulated in the last eight years. Not that I personally felt vulnerable to any charges, but because of Solidarity's radical streak, reasonable dialogue could fast turn into senseless bickering.

Fortunately, the radical wing did not keep us from getting at the basic order of the day: electing a president and members of Solidarity's National Board, voting on statutes and their amendments, and finally, adopting level-headed resolutions on various aspects of the Solidarity platform.

At the first congress, in 1981, I had spent most of the time running to the microphone to berate delegates or tell anecdotes. I had said then that as long as I was at the head of this movement, I would not surrender power to the Party, to the Committee for Workers' Defense (KOR), or even to the Church. I kept my word.

In 1990, however, I couldn't do as much running — if only because I'd gained weight in the last ten years. I didn't take part in the debates and I took the platform only three times during the six days the congress lasted. My first and longest speech took place when I introduced my candidacy and platform just before the presidential election, an election in which I was pitted against two other candidates. I argued that the reduced size of our union membership (now barely two million) was a legacy of martial law, which had frightened many honest people away from joining us. Should I be reelected, I warned, I would reorganize things and seek investment from around the world. I said straight out that what I would do would earn me a few medals for my chest and a few kicks in the ass.

I still have a copy of the tape of the press conference I held immediately following my reelection on April 21, 1990 — a conference at which I barely escaped being crushed by the reporters and photographers:

Question: How will this Second National Congress change Solidarity?

Lech Walesa: As a union, we want to be there when people are suffering, when they are fired from their jobs. But we also have a role to play in Poland's reform process.

Q: What are the first tasks that need doing?

LW: We need to see local elections are held, so that we know the reforms ordered from above make it all the way down to the bottom, and local elections are the way that happens.

Q: Should Solidarity create a political party?

LW: I don't know. We are a democracy and so that's not something I would decide on my own. But my feeling is that it isn't a good idea.

Q: Are you going to run for president of the Republic?

LW: I must ask you once again not to get what I say mixed up. I have said many times that I had no intention of seeking the job, and I honestly don't know whether I'm right for it. I am who I am because of Solidarity, because of you reporters — who shout out questions when you take photos — and because of the Polish people. If things had been different in Poland, I might have stayed an electrician and be rewiring lights right now. Extraordinary circumstances elevated me into a lofty position.

Q: What do you make of the criticism that's been leveled at you?

LW: I can be criticized for the fact that talented people like Andrzej Gwiazda and Marian Jurczyk were pushed out of the picture. Certainly, from one point of view, that's even a sin. I'm committing another sin when I say to young people that I think they need a good spanking. That's a father's sin. Another is the way I criticize intellectuals — who I think have been hitting below the belt. I try to understand everyone and sometimes I don't succeed. But only people who don't do anything avoid making mistakes.

Q: What's the future of Solidarity's Civic Committee?

LW: That was my baby, and it's still a platform for helping Poland work toward democracy. It may even become independent, provided that it wants to serve the country.

Q: Aren't you ever afraid things won't work out for you?

LW: Ladies and gentlemen, I am afraid only of God. No one and nothing else.

Q: What are your thoughts on privatizing the Polish economy?

LW: I have already said a thousand times that there are two Polands. One is a Poland burdened with the huge monopolies it inherited from communism. The other is a private Poland that we are just beginning to build. To catch up with a Europe that continues to forge ahead, two-thirds of Polish industry needs overhauling.

I was elected president on the third day of the congress, and by day six I must have given some twenty interviews. When the moment came for me, together with the other national leaders, to take the oath of office, I was very moved. We swore to remain faithful to the spirit of solidarity born in August 1980, to defend human rights, and to respect our statutes. At the end, when I reflexively added, "So help me God," the other members of the National Board added, "So help us God!"

There were many guests at the Second National Congress from all over the world — labor leaders and other dignitaries. And letters of support

came from John Paul II, President George Bush, Jacques Delors, president
of the European Community, and many more.

The delegates and guests were much interested in the display table set
up by Amnesty International, which was distributing information about
violations of human rights. On the fourth day of the congress, nearly two
thousand people signed a petition calling for the freedom of imprisoned
union workers in Yugoslavia, Sudan, and China.

Gathering that many people together is no small feat. A well-organized
medical team watched over the health of the delegates and staff during the
congress. Doctors and nurses from the regional section of Solidarity's
Health Service in Gdansk volunteered to maintain a clinic and stood like
guardian angels in the discussion hall. An ambulance stood by in case of
emergency. Over the six days of debate, more than three hundred persons
ended up needing medical care — mainly bandaging wounds, treating
viral infections, and curing conjunctivitis, though there were also a few
serious cases, such as a stomach ulcer and a cardiac arrest.

Discussion about Solidarity's identity revolved essentially around its
political positions. The delegates clearly expressed their wish that Solidarity remain a union movement, even though about 60 percent of the participants were also members of the regional civic committees. The idea of
workers' ownership of companies was rejected roundly — and without
much discussion.

The noisiest controversy was the one surrounding the structure of Solidarity. Two positions clashed: some favored territorial organization, and
others organization by "branch." In the end the "branch" advocates were
forced to yield to the "territorials," but I predict that at the next congress
the issue will come up again — territorial structure strengthens Solidarity
as an organization, but it doesn't do much to facilitate cooperation with
foreign organizations.

The Second National Congress of Solidarity was like Poland: lots of
discussion, plenty of questions, few solutions. Although my own agenda
was very short and simple, I accomplished what I wanted. I was reelected
president, and I declared that Solidarity would maintain its independence
from the government and all political parties.

32
Speeding Things Up

I f anyone thought that my political machine couldn't pick up steam, they were making a big mistake. Assured of my place in the driver's seat after the Second National Congress of Solidarity, I instinctively wanted to step on the gas, so I checked the gauges, put in the clutch, and prepared for a fast start in second gear. Meanwhile, I met with two prominent figures from the European political scene.

On May 2, 1990, Douglas Hurd, the British foreign minister, visited me in Gdansk. I told him that Poland was once more in the vanguard of reform, and to say that was not to exaggerate reality but to report it. Unfortunately, although we had controlled inflation, unemployment was still a problem. The operation had been a success, but the patient remained in serious condition. At Yalta, the four great powers, including his own country, had allowed Poland to be stripped of everything it had. Wouldn't freezing part of the Polish debt now be the right thing to do?

On May 4, President Richard von Weizsäcker of West Germany arrived in Gdansk as part of his four-day visit to Poland. He met first with city officials, to whom he said that Gdansk was one of the most beautiful cities in the world. Then he went to Westerplatte, the University of Gdansk, Oliwa Cathedral, and finally Solidarity headquarters. Given that unification of the two Germanies was already underway, I thought that his visit was very important. Our forty-minute talk dealt essentially with the prospects of Greater Europe and the crystallization of Polish-German relations, somewhat damaged by Chancellor Kohl's second thoughts about our borders. I expressed the opinion that political changes in Central Europe were headed in the right direction, but that the dismal economic situation could undermine everything and result in new waves of emigration, which, in turn, would destabilize Western Europe. "What would you do," I asked rhetorically, "if millions of people suddenly massed at your borders with signs proclaiming 'Freedom,' 'Down with the Borders,' 'Equality,' 'Human Rights,' 'No Visas, No Passports'? Would you send out the army?"

I was a little flustered by trying to get von Weizsäcker to speak, for I soon discovered that what impressed American or Soviet officials left this inscrutable, coldly intelligent German untouched. President von Weizsäcker is a highly respected figure, and not just in Germany. How could an ordinary electrician with just three years of education and all the cunning of a farmer from Mazowie challenge an intellectual with an intimidatingly aristocratic "von" in his name? I tried to say exactly what I meant and welcomed him in Polish. Was this tactless? I don't think so. But on the other hand, I can say that his visit would have gotten more attention from the government had they known that von Weizsäcker, unlike Chancellor Kohl, did not intend to raise fresh doubts about our common border.

Soon after, I was interviewed by the *New York Times*, and this gave me a chance to respond to some really substantive questions about what was going on in Poland. I declared — knowing full well what I was saying — that we were beginning to wallow in the mud. There was too much talk and too little action. What we needed was a small bombshell that would start a "political war" (within legal bounds, of course). My thinking was that those in power — the "higher-ups" — should yell at each other in order to break old stereotypes of power, reject old thinking, and force everybody to earn his own place. That's the only way ordinary people — the "lower-downs" — will have access to fresh thinking, whether or not such scrapping fits into accepted wisdom. A political shake-up would give us the chance to win back Polish young people.

Almost immediately, all the old guns, the venerable elders, trained their sights on me. "What are you saying?" they cried. "What do you mean by a 'political war'? A war between whom? Hasn't there been enough war? We need to get to work, and begin at the beginning!" Not one to split hairs, I fired back: "If the president is a tortoise and the prime minister a snail, the *nomenklatura* and opportunists will pillage this country before we can institute reforms. The office of the president needs to wield an axe to clear the way and cut down theft and crime. Otherwise the parasites will bleed us white." Once again my words were garbled in transmission to the public. It was reported that I had said the president ought to run around with an axe chopping off people's hands. Ouch! And to think that I myself had wanted a free press.

My theatrical appeal to throw Poland into higher gear was calculated to counteract a growing national mood. The press was circulating rumors that the former opposition militants, now that they were in power, were doing nothing more than feathering their own nests and creating a new *nomenklatura*. Even if that were true, why was everyone blaming *me*? Choosing competent and honest leaders was their job, not mine, as I tried to explain at each of my meetings. Tadeusz Mazowiecki's government was a coalition government consisting of a number of parties. Why blame everything on Solidarity? If the government had been made up exclusively of Solidarity representatives, then, fine, they could accuse us of monopoly and graft and greed. "Even if the rumor were true," I said, "Poles must still do all they can to elect responsible people. Let the elections be a true test of civic duty."

Around the middle of May, the nucleus of a new political group was formed and baptized Porozumienie Centrum (Alliance of the Center), and Jaroslaw Kaczynski, then editor of *Tygodnik Solidarnosc*, was elected to lead it. So my challenge to revitalize political life in Poland was beginning to have an effect. Centrum's main goal was to work out a program that would accelerate political, economic, and cultural change.

1. In the political realm, the first thing Centrum had to stand for was the dismissal of any official who in the public's eyes represented antidemocratic, anti-Polish, or antimoral attitudes. Letting people like that keep jobs of public trust would slow everything down and breed even more cynicism.
2. Economic acceleration meant acting as a catalyst for Deputy Prime Minister Balcerowicz's reform program (to calm the *nomenklatura*, the program was designed to conform with the principle of negative selection).
3. Cultural acceleration meant encouraging the movements and artistic currents that had been blocked by the government.

By its very existence, Centrum was a dam-breaker — already bigger and more effective than all of the marginal and extremist movements, which by 1990 numbered nearly a hundred. A few weeks later, some intellectuals from Cracow formed the Alliance for Democracy to compete with Centrum, and later still — another branch to grow from the trunk of Solidarity — the Civic Movement for Democratic Action (ROAD) was born, led by Zbigniew Bujak, Wladyslaw Frasyniuk, Adam Michnik, and Henryk Wujec.

On Monday, May 27, free local elections took place for the first time since before the war. Although I had urged Poles to take local matters into their own hands, barely 42 percent of the electorate voted. The low turnout surprised everyone; it meant a continuing deep social apathy. As if there weren't problems enough, so-called militants from the OPZZ stirred up trouble, and railway workers went on a preelection strike that paralyzed a quarter of the country. I went to Slupsk twice, since that was where the main strike committee had been formed. My argument that the strike could deal a deathblow to an already ill state fell on deaf ears. Some of the protesters continued a hunger strike; they demanded unrealistic wage hikes, not caring that the state's coffers were empty and that the West would not grant Poland new credit if it went further into debt. Fortunately, the workers of Slupsk reconsidered and ended the blackmail.

Ten days after the election, Poland took another small step toward democracy: censorship was abolished.

33
Three Cities

S cores of ministers, ambassadors, presidents, "patrons," and directors visited me from the moment Solidarity was legalized. There are simply too many of them to talk about. Some said they wanted to learn from me; others came to offer advice. I received everyone politely (a Polish proverb has it that a guest in the house is God in the house), although I confess I didn't want to spend as much time with them as I did. I also came across plenty of self-servers and fanatics during my trips around the country. Most of those trips are not worth mentioning, so in these pages I will recount only one or two.

On the other hand, I'll go into more detail about the trips I made abroad between December 1988 and June 1990, since each of them had a definite impact upon me and my homeland.

On Sunday, May 20, 1990, I went to the Nineteenth Congress of the DGB group of unions being held in Hamburg. I had been invited as a guest of honor, along with such notable figures as von Weizsäcker, former chancellor Willy Brandt, and the German minister of labor, Norbert Blöm. Most of the welcoming address given by Ernst Breit, departing after serving two terms as president, was devoted to the role Solidarity had played in the European "people's springtime" that helped bring about the reunification of Germany. My own words echoed his theme:

I am convinced that the cooperation between Solidarity and the DGB will be crucial to reconciling our two countries, and to helping us through a particularly complex moment in European history. . . . European unification challenges Poland above all in an economic sense, for only if we can create an efficient market economy can we become a partner in a unified Europe. . . .

Given the challenges of reunification, the 1990s mark a new era in the history of Germany as well. However, I ask you, my esteemed colleagues, not to be surprised if reunification doesn't leave us indifferent. . . . I would like to point out that to some extent a united Germany was possible only because of Solidarity's struggle to free itself of totalitarianism — a struggle that involved millions of Poles, a struggle that cleared the way for other countries in Central and Eastern Europe, including East Germany. Solidarity represents human rights, the rights of workers and citizens, and the desire to restore truth, liberty, and human dignity. It is a contribution to the heritage of Europe by Poland, the country where the first shots of World War II were fired, and the country that awoke to find itself transformed when the last shot was fired.

On trips abroad I always played a number of roles besides that of union leader, and this was true also in Hamburg, where I had meetings with businessmen and highly placed civil servants. I knew that the real purpose of my visit was to bring Poland — forcefully embodied by "old mustachioed Lech" from Gdansk — to the attention of the Germans. I reminded myself again and again that I had to do everything necessary to keep the door to the new Europe from slamming in our face. So I stuck my foot in it. My role wasn't to make specific proposals or offer concrete solutions, or anything of the kind. I limited myself to pointing out the political dimensions in which economic realities take place, hoping that potential investors wouldn't be put off by all the red tape that we had only begun to cut through.

On June 14 and 15, I went to the Seventy-Seventh meeting of the International Labor Organization being held in Geneva. An official Solidarity delegation had arrived four days before, headed by my deputy Lech Kaczynski, to clear the ground for my three main activities: a working lunch with the director of the ILO, an address during the general session, and a press conference. What I said at that session was this:

Solidarity's struggle for the right to exist lasted eight long years. But when our union was made illegal and thousands of its members were put into prison, the ILO did not forget us. . . . By putting the interests and rights of the workers first, Solidarity participated in the profound transformation of a political system produced by decades of Communist experiment. Solidarity has supported the reforms put forward by the government, but we are still worried about the slowness with which they are being implemented. Particularly in the political field, the pace needs to be picked up. . . .

Moreover, just because Solidarity acknowledges the need for economic reforms doesn't mean we don't oppose their effects, some of which are disadvantageous to workers. Yes, we need a market economy, but there can be no question of any return to the barbaric capitalism of the nineteenth century. . . .

It is with great satisfaction that we welcome this new stage in our cooperation with the ILO. . . . We want to be worthy of our name, and worthy of the tradition of fighting for human rights, liberty, and truth.

According to the Swiss press, what most surprised people was my having remained in such good form. During my press conferences, I played lengthy verbal ping-pong with the journalists, not stopping until I managed to mollify and then win them over. I felt very keenly that these bloodthirsty creatures were just waiting for me to trip and make a mistake. Surely, I thought, Western readers have had their fill of Lech Walesa, the patron saint of unions.

What I needed to do was spice up leftovers that had been reheated I don't know how many times. Some of their questions suggested they had been disillusioned by Solidarity's Second Congress, which was even criticized for showing a right-wing orientation (unions in the Western industrialized countries come from left-wing orientations). I tried until I was hoarse to explain that the West wasn't making enough of an effort to understand Poland; that was why it resorted to oversimplification. How could I convince them that before unions could make demands from the system, there had to *be* a system? How much did I have to stress that we couldn't conduct collective bargaining as a union when the whole economic structure itself was in such bad shape? All this they immediately labeled centralization, manipulation, and any number of other words ending in "-ation."

At the conference, Czechoslovakia was pointed out to us as a positive example. It was a country where the trade unions still struggled valiantly for workers' rights. We were told that in Poland, on the other hand, union positions were filled by small-time politicians who forgot about the needs of the workers right after the election, when they cozied up to the government. Andrzej Slowik, the regional Solidarity leader from Lodz, was the man some union leaders looked to with admiration. Yet while his ideas won approval abroad, in no way did they match the realities of our devastated country.

On the whole, I thought my trip to Geneva was a success, if only because Lech Kaczynski was elected a deputy member of the ILO Administrative Council. Some African countries, where a fairly strong Communist influence lingers, raised objections, but by and large the voting went smoothly. I did notice, however, that some union leaders from developing countries — particularly in Asia, Africa, and South America — perceived all the attention given to changes in Eastern Europe as a threat to their own interests.

Toward the end of June, I went to Vienna to take part in the inaugural ceremonies and first-day deliberations of what has been called the Small Congress of Vienna. This year the congress was to consider Central Europe and the paths to democracy. It was organized by the Viennese Institute of Human Sciences — itself created in 1984, thanks to the support of Pope John Paul II (who every two years invites members of the Institute's Scientific Council to his summer residence at Castel Gandolfo for several days of discussion). Father Jozef Tischner from Cracow and Professor Krzysztof Michalski, who has one foot in Vienna and the other in the United States, are codirectors. In addition to the congress participants (nearly one hundred eminent figures from the political, intellectual, and financial circles of Europe and America), about fifteen hundred Viennese (of which a good percentage spoke Polish) came to my talk.

The congress began on June 28, 1990, at seven in the evening. Following a brief introduction by Professor Michalski, a few words of welcome by the Austrian chancellor, Franz Vranitzky, and a short talk by the minister of science, Erhard Busk, I was invited to take the podium. I spoke for a good twenty minutes about Solidarity's history of nonviolent struggle, about the new Europe taking shape, and about the new forms of political action. In conclusion I said:

> The nationalistic ideologies that carry in them the germ of intolerance form a great temptation for societies undergoing rapid democratization. It would be a real tragedy for this new Europe if its central portion were torn apart by ethnic and nationalistic enmity. With the exception of Poland, which is ethnically almost homogeneous, all the countries formerly under Soviet influence contain the seeds of ethnic conflicts. The Latvians, Estonians, and Lithuanians fight against the Russians; there is conflict between Czechs and Slovaks, between Hungarians and Romanians, between Bulgarians and Turks, and between Albanians and Serbs. The list goes on and on. After years of Moscow's "internationalistic" politics — really anti-national politics — those long-repressed aspirations may take an extreme and sometimes violent form. We must not be surprised at this; we should be prepared.

On Friday, June 29, I attended a mass at the Church of the Resurrection in Kahlenberg, where the Polish king Jan III Sobieski prayed before his victorious battle of September 12, 1683, with the Turks, who held Vienna under siege. The mass was said jointly by Father Jozef Tischner and Father Jerzy Smolinski, who later showed me around the small museum devoted to the siege of Vienna. At ten that morning, I went to the building that used to house the stock exchange, to take part in the first day of the Congress. Thanks to the generosity of the American multimillionaire Saul P. Stein (the financial sponsor of the whole Small Congress of Vienna), I later flew back on his private jet, so I was able to have lunch at home with my wife and kids.

I returned ready to pick up where I had left off and keep stirring things up. Over and over I declared that the government's procrastination was becoming dangerous. The growing number of strikes by farmers and the growing complaints from the miners provided ample testimony.

34
Electing a President

I remained loyal to Prime Minister Mazowiecki's government longer than I should have, particularly to that group of activists who because of my support occupied many of the key positions. Finally the day came when I said, "Enough is enough! You've been lounging around and hiding out in the bastions of power too long." I was surprised that these otherwise-intelligent men could lack the imagination to grasp that. Those moving in would very soon sweep them out of the glittering corridors of the Council of Ministers' palace. Public disillusionment would lead to a sudden outburst. No one should be fooled by our compatriots' seeming apathy.

Sipping their cappuccinos, my detractors replied that I was making a mountain out of a molehill. Nothing irritated me more than their glib rhetoric. My mailman had gotten a hernia from carrying all the sacks of anonymous complaint letters. Because I was still "only" the leader of a union — with a couple of million members — these gentlemen from Warsaw were increasingly dismissive of me. When I mentioned the need for a strong president to handle the growing chaos, I was told that the Polish people didn't want a despot. When I warned of a new *nomenklatura* taking shape right before our eyes, this time from within Solidarity ranks, I was scolded and told not to soil my own nest. When I lambasted the government for not speeding up privatization, I was simply told to go to hell.

Problems were worsening daily, and there was mounting evidence that the government was not responding to them. I ended up making a formal commitment to join the political struggle. It was because of this commitment that some of the members of the elite circle around Prime Minister Mazowiecki began attacking me more and more, claiming that I was irre-

278

sponsible. I fully realized I was paying the price for my recent decision to revoke the right of the newspaper *Gazeta Wyborcza* to use the Solidarity logo, which I had done to distance the union from current government practices. But I wasn't going to back down. I continued to be blamed for the stupidity of certain ministers, and I continued to take my quarrelsome positions at meetings. The social and political climate in Poland was becoming more and more tense as the cost of shifting to normal economic life rose. The sluggish government, meanwhile, was trying to save its own hide.

During a private two-hour conversation on July 26 with President Jaruzelski, I also told him that as the Sejm and the Senat elections of the year before had been won overwhelmingly by the antigovernment opposition, and as the worsening economy did not augur well for the coalition in power, Poland needed bold new solutions to the problem of who should rule. Our only choice, I argued, was to pass government power to those who had the support of the majority — quite simply, that meant new elections. I concluded by declaring that I would prepare for the inevitable by forming a shadow cabinet.

On August 9, I issued a statement in which I declared, without pulling any punches, that the current political establishment no longer enjoyed popular support and that therefore it would be necessary to elect a new parliament and also a new president before the end of their terms of office:

> I think, and I have always thought, that Poland needs a strong president with a popular mandate, a president who, with the parliament, will get things moving, who can make decisions under political pressure, and who has the courage to wield power. . . . It's a matter not of finding people, but of finding programs that can bring Poland closer to democracy. Our struggle should be about programs, not name-calling.

I called for tolerance, political maturity, and an end to personal attacks during the election campaign that inevitably lay ahead, a campaign that would have to include electing a president to represent the whole nation — rather than allowing one to be chosen by a parliament that was only partially representative.

I should note that six days earlier I had asked the well-known Catholic journalist Andrzej Micewski to head my group of advisors, which was composed of professionals trained at assessing key issues. Micewski accepted the responsibility partly because of his own belief in pluralism. He also warned me that it would take at least five years to achieve full democracy in Poland. Five years, I thought, would represent a productive first term for a new president.

Before making a final decision about my own candidacy (though I had been launching trial balloons for some time now), I went to Italy for a two-day visit at the invitation of the organizers of the annual Assembly of Christian Young People. Naturally I took sought an audience with John Paul II. One of his envoys had led me to understand that he wanted to know more about the goals of my political campaign. Getting away from Gdansk just at that moment wasn't easy — toward the end of August, a series of demonstrations were being held to celebrate the tenth anniversary of Solidarity's founding. The prospect of visiting the pope, however, overshadowed all other obligations. The Italian newspapers gave my visit wide coverage, calling me the most important Christian figure in the world after the Holy Father and Mother Teresa. More than three hundred journalists crowded the press conference I held in Rimini, and the number of bodyguards I was assigned would have done justice to any head of state.

The pope received me at Castel Gandolfo on August 27. After greeting me warmly and saying a brief mass in the chapel of the Roman bishops, he led me to a little anteroom. There I knelt before him, along with the bishop of Gdansk, Tadeusz Goclowski, who had come with me, and four other members of my delegation (including the security agent assigned to protect me). Then the pope took me to his private apartments for a confidential talk about the situation in Poland. My batteries were recharged. My doubts and anxieties vanished. Together, the pope told me, we had accomplished a great thing: we had halted the march of communism. Now we had to commit ourselves to lead Poland into the twenty-first century, while also remembering that our country was Catholic and that our society would follow the teachings of the Church. I flew home that same day. On August 29, during his Wednesday general audience, the Holy Father honored me by quoting a long passage from that speech I had given to the United States Congress.

My countrymen were kept guessing during the next few weeks as to whether or not I would announce my candidacy to be president. This was deliberate on my part. In interview after interview I stressed that I wanted to see more candidates throw in their hats: only then could I win over their supporters by speaking out at meetings and in publications. I wanted to force the political factions to show their hands. The elections, I said, would either free me of my public duties to Poland or force me to play a bigger role. It seemed less and less important that we had defeated a totalitarian system. What counted now was what we would build for future generations.

My strategy seemed to have an effect on the ROAD party. At the beginning of September, they increased the pressure on Prime Minister Mazowiecki to announce his candidacy. Both the ROAD people and my supporters from Centrum strongly contended that the presidential election should take place before the parliamentary elections.

I had no objection to this. I read the following statement on television on the morning of September 17: "Today I have made my decision. I submit for approval my candidacy in a general election to become president of the Republic of Poland. For me, this would represent an opportunity to see through to successful completion the pledge I made in August 1980."

To the hordes of journalists I then made it clear that it wasn't that I wanted to run for president, but that I had to. If I should happen to lose, I could still look each Pole in the eye, because I would continue the fight whatever happened.

I had chosen the date of my declaration carefully. On September 18, along with twenty-seven of the most eminent figures in Polish politics, I took part in a discussion in Warsaw organized by Cardinal Jozef Glemp. First there was an informal luncheon that included Cardinal Glemp; President Jaruzelski; Prime Minister Mazowiecki; the marshal of the Sejm, Mikolaj Kozakiewicz; the marshal of the Senat, Andrzej Stelmachowski; and myself as president of Solidarity. Two hours later, the remaining guests joined us for coffee, which turned into a meeting that lasted until dinner. Nearly all the participants agreed the presidential election should be held as soon as possible, in order to ease the tension that had destabilized the country over the past few months. President Jaruzelski got the message. On October 1, he signed a decree cutting short his term of office.

During meetings with journalists and with people from all sectors of the workforce, I laid out my platform point by point. I made it clear I had thought through these main points, but that I wouldn't be explicit, because it was a matter more of general concepts than of specific "prescriptions." My presidency would assume the character of an open forum, I said. I wanted to exercise power while listening carefully to what people thought. My government would attend to the needs of a nation impoverished and in many ways backward, but without resorting to the methods of our Communist predecessors. Asked if I wasn't overplaying the populist note, I replied in all sincerity that as a public figure I was born out of a widespread anger, and that I would grow to transform it.

The downfall of most revolutionaries is that once they gain power, they merely replace the deposed tyrant. True democracy, as Professor Leszek Kolakowski has pointed out, is based on three basic conditions: a system of checks and balances, an independent judiciary, and equality under the law. In discussions with Western politicians, I have always made an effort, in my own rough way, to assure them that I understood these conditions. I did this on September 10, when two members of the Israeli Knesset, Professor Shevek Weiss and Dr. Uzi Landau, came for a visit. I made it clear again in mid-September, when former president Ronald Reagan and Manfred Wörner, the secretary-general of NATO, were visiting Gdansk. Mr. Wörner flattered me by calling me the spark that had ignited a new democracy.

Those who had difficulty seeing me as president pointed out that everything I had accomplished up to now had been easy. What they meant was that though I had enormous political influence and could say whatever I wanted, I had never had to implement policy.

I thought that accusation highly unfair and told them so. Perhaps I had been unpredictable, but only to my adversaries, never to others. At critical moments, I had never let myself be guided by my emotions. I had never tried to lead men with no weapons into battle. Look at Bulgaria, I said. Look at the Soviet Union, and especially at Romania. How many human lives had the fire of revolution consumed in those countries before people began to understand that the vicious circle of revenge leaves a wider trail of blood with each turn? I may not have experience in some areas, even a great many areas; but in political matters I know what I'm doing.

From the beginning, my presidential campaign created shifts in allegiance in the Western press, which up to then had been favorable to me. There was an underlying sense of patronization by those who were "more civilized" (and who therefore "knew better" and hence displayed a tendency to preach.) Some of my former colleagues and advisors got onto their soapboxes and accused me of being an anti-Semite, a cleric, and a populist. In newspaper columns, I was once again transformed into an ordinary electrician, a laborer of limited intellect with the crazy ambition of governing a nation of thirty-seven million people located at the heart of Europe.

On October 3, 1990, Solidarity's National Board voted by secret ballot to support my candidacy for the president. Sixty-seven members voted in favor and ten against; there was one abstention. So from early on my campaign enjoyed powerful backing. I named Jacek Merkel — a deputy in the Sejm and a naval engineer at the Gdansk Shipyards — to head up my campaign staff. Polish communism, one commentator noted, hadn't simply been an external reality; the experience of it had deeply infected the way Poles thought about the world and about themselves. I believe that to be true. We did not submit to it, however, and a handful of us pulled ourselves out of the Communist swamp. Once we had set foot on dry land, we began looking for someone to help drain the swamp and transform it into fertile soil. Solidarity thought that I was the right person for the job.

On October 23, Jacek Merkel took charge of safely transporting to Warsaw petitions containing half a million signatures supporting my candidacy. Only a hundred thousand were actually required. On October 24, my candidacy was officially registered by the National Electoral Commission.

In fact, I had begun campaigning some three weeks earlier. Over the course of fifty-three days, I covered nearly ten thousand miles, spent close to 160 hours riding around in a government car, visited forty-six towns and cities, and attracted several hundred thousand people to my meetings. In all, I was away from home for more than three weeks.

The announcement of my candidacy quickly prompted the appearance of other candidates, and eventually we were fourteen in all. In the end, only five (besides me) managed to collect the number of signatures required to register with the National Electoral Commission in time. They were: Tadeusz Mazowiecki, the current prime minister; Roman Bartoszcze, president of the Polish Farmers Party (PSL); Leszek Moczulski, head of the Confederation for an Independent Poland (KPN); Wlodzimierz Cimoszewicz, socialist deputy in the Sejm; and finally the little-known Stanislaw Tyminski, who had long been living in Canada, where he ran the rather marginal Libertarian Party. Most students of politics predicted that the first round of the election on November 25, 1990, would be sufficient to elect a president, since there were really only two serious candidacies, Prime Minister Mazowiecki's and mine. No one predicted that Stanislaw Tyminski would enter the line-up as a dark horse.

Mazowiecki's camp relied heavily on negative campaigning, much of which focused on me. Many who had up to then looked to me as a living symbol and a national hero wore Mazowiecki buttons. They slung mud at me, attacking me for my efforts to accelerate democracy, efforts that they called crazy and unrealistic. They portrayed me as an unskilled proletarian whose time was past. Sometimes I was called a madman who wanted to take an axe and chop Poland off from the rest of Europe.

My campaign staff didn't resort to such methods. Centrum, which supported me, worded its electoral appeal this way:

WHAT LECH WALESA WOULD DO AS PRESIDENT OF POLAND:
- •Accelerate democratic changes in Poland.
- •Unlike Prime Minister Mazowiecki, look into the crimes committed by the *nomenklatura*.
- •Provide justice to those who have been deprived of it.
- •Create a future that everyone can share in.
- •Keep Poland faithful to herself and to Europe.

Nearly 280 organizations, from radicals to industrialists, supported me. So did foreign politicians, such as Carlos Saúl Menem, the president of Argentina, who happened to be visiting Gdansk just then.

We went to the polls on November 25. Despite appeals from all the candidates, and despite the fact that these were the first free elections held in Poland since the end of World War II, voter turnout barely reached 61 percent. The results, posted that evening, stunned everyone: Prime Minister Mazowiecki got only 18 percent of the vote and was now out of the running. He submitted his resignation the next day, as did his cabinet. The remaining candidates were myself, with 40 percent, and none other than Stanislaw Tyminski, with 23 percent.

The chaos that erupted following this unexpected turn of events exceeded that of a natural disaster. Tyminski, whose campaign staff contained many former Communist Party and Security Service members, was most frightening of all to the honest and patriotic voters who had supported Mazowiecki. Tyminski seemed to have come out of nowhere — a man without a country, a *hochstapler* [adventurer], a screwball — and managed to bamboozle nearly five million people by playing on their cynicism, their ignorance, and their weariness with poverty. What I had warned might happen did: Poles voted for an "independent" candidate to protest the government's procrastination and incompetence.

I was now left with a nightmare: How could I defeat an opponent who had sunk to blackmail, claiming that he had damaging documents about me in his possession? How was I to conduct a campaign against someone who was utterly devoid of integrity (he had made hundreds of campaign promises he could never keep) and who thus posed a mortal threat to the country he had fled twenty-one years before?

35
Between Rounds

I was only partly gratified by the first round of elections. My own success pleased me, of course, but that so many voters could be led astray
so easily was worrisome.

When I compared what Tadeusz Mazowiecki had done for his country
with what Tyminski had done (or not done), I had trouble believing that
Poles would think Tyminski the worthier choice. It was Mazowiecki's humane intelligence and integrity against the cynicism and opportunism of
a dream merchant. Those who had voted for the demagogue had fallen
into the old trap of false promises.

Only work creates wealth. Consistent effort and work of good quality,
when combined with competition, produce the best results. Individual
success becomes the success of society as a whole. But before we can
compete economically, we need to establish rules that we can all abide by.
Thus wealth is inextricably linked with social justice, and that is why
economic reform is so closely tied to political reform.

The election results surprised only those who had underestimated the
effect of those years of frustration, or forgotten the contempt with which
the totalitarian powers had treated society. As for me, I knew I was the
right man for the job of being the first elected president of Poland's Third
Republic. I couldn't hide my feelings. I knew that I would stand by my
principles and maintain — as well as be inspired by — the loyalty and
energy of my supporters, particularly the younger ones.

Above all, I knew that I would have to reconcile social forces and
implement true reform — and do it quickly.

As the second round of elections approached, I grew confident and
calm. I wanted to reach a position of power democratically, through

elections. Once I became president, I would not perform miracles, but I would create the reforms our country needed so badly.

One struggle was ending; another was just beginning.

Part III
Keeping Faith

36
The Virgin on My Lapel

E ach morning, when I get dressed, I pin a special little badge bearing the image of the Virgin to my jacket lapel — and only after having done so do I feel ready to face the world. This, as one might easily guess, has been the subject of both sarcasm and sympathy. Many have wondered why a political man, someone who speaks and mingles with presidents and prime ministers, who travels all over the world making speeches and granting interviews, should make such a display of piety. But this pin is now accepted as part of me.

The badge was a gift, blessed by Cardinal Wyszynski and pinned on me publicly in Jasna Gora. For centuries, the Poles have made pilgrimages to the Jasna Gora monastery in Czestochowa, convinced that the Virgin's presence there — represented in the miraculous icon called the Black Virgin would help them in their afflictions. The hundreds of canes and prosthetic devices affixed to the wall of the chapel testify to their faith and her miracles, as do the countless number of commemorative plaques. She has also helped Poland as a whole: in the monastery are hundreds of pictures of monarchs offering their thanks. Over the centuries, religion in Poland has always served to unify the nation, from Saint Wojciech, patron saint of Bohemia and Poland in the tenth century, to Florian, and from Bishop Stanislaw Szczepanowski, whom King Boleslaw Smialy the Bold had drawn and quartered for disobedience, down to the revered image of the Virgin Mary at Czestochowa.

The white-habited Paulist Fathers of Jasna Gora tell every visitor the legend behind the Black Virgin painting, with its dark, Byzantine look. Legend relates that the first icon of the Virgin Mary was done by Saint Luke himself on a cypress plank taken from the stable in Bethlehem.

Later, Saint Helena transported the icon from Jerusalem to Constantinople and presented it to her son, Constantine the Great. It passed from him to Charlemagne, and eventually into the hands of the Ruthenian prince Lew. The next owner was Prince Wladyslaw, who gave it to the Paulists on August 30, 1384. Around 1430, the original icon was replaced by a painted version, the version we know now, and went to Jasna Gora, which by then had become Poland's most important sanctuary. Because of the number of miracles that had taken place there, the icon's fame grew and spread far beyond the country's borders.

During the years 1655 to 1657, the years of a war between Poland and Sweden, the monastery was the only fortress not to fall into Swedish hands, and this strengthened the people's faith in the picture's miraculous and sovereign nature. To thank the Virgin for protecting Poland, King Jan Kazimierz made a vow in 1656 to name the Mother of God queen of the *Res Publica*.* Henryk Sienkiewicz, the Polish writer who won the Nobel Prize for literature at the beginning of the twentieth century, recounts the episode in *Potop* [*The Deluge*], a novel that is part of the patriotic literature every Pole is supposed to read. We had this book at home when I was growing up, and sometimes our mother read to us from it. Sienkiewicz had written *Potop* in the 1880s to strengthen the nation's will: wounds from the crushing defeat of a second insurrection against czarist Russia in 1863, and the repression that followed it, still had not healed when he wrote it.

The reversal of Poland's fortunes had begun much earlier — during the time of Stanislaw August Poniatowski, the last king of Poland, who was elected in 1764. Weakened by internal strife, Poland had been unable to oppose Catherine the Great's invasions, though a confederation of the *szlachta*† (called the Confederation of the Bar) was formed in 1768 to rid the country of the Russian invaders. This patriotic movement was crushed by the Russian armies. Nevertheless, the Confederates, under the leadership of Kazimierz Pulaski — later a hero in the American Revolution — made the monastery at Jasna Gora their headquarters and defended it successfully for nearly two years, firing the enthusiasm of the Poles. This was the period when "The Anthem of the Confederates" was composed. Part of it goes like this:

---

* After the Jagiello dynasty died out, Poland became an elective kingdom called the *Res Publica*, also known as the Nobiliary Republic.

† "*Szlachta*" refers to the lesser nobility — land ownership was the only criterion — to distinguish them from the "magnates," the great lords who possessed estates the size of the smaller American states.

> *Never shall we be allied with kings,*
> *Never to force shall we bow our heads,*
> *For we are the soldiers of Christ,*
> *We, the servants of Mary.*

Jasna Gora eventually surrendered, and the end of the Confederation of the Bar marked the beginning of our national misfortunes. On August 5, 1772, Russia, Austria, and Poland signed a treaty of partition, beginning a state of crisis for Poland that continued until the third partition, in 1795.* That third partition was to last more than a hundred and twenty years, until 1918. From their place in heaven, the Confederates must have been surprised when in 1980 they heard their anthem intoned by Lech Walesa and echoed by a crowd of workers at the gateway to the Gdansk Shipyards.

During the Nazi occupation, the German governor, Hans Frank — head of the "General Gouvernement" of occupied Poland, whose capital was in Cracow — noted in his diary on February 2, 1940, "To the Polish imagination, the Church is the central point of reference, constantly shining in silence and thereby playing in some way the role of the eternal beacon. When all the lights went out in Poland, the Church and the Madonna of Czestochowa remained. This must never be forgotten."

Though German soldiers bivouacked at Jasna Gora, the monastery remained intact. After the war, the Communist authorities tried every means to limit Jasna Gora's role: they permitted only a few cheap restaurants and one or two hotels to be built on the road to Czestochowa, which was used each year by millions of pilgrims. Public transportation functioned miserably along that route. At the train stations, pilgrims, pious though they might be, had to fight to get onto the trains. Meanwhile the Party press rubbed its hands in glee: "Look, citizens, at the chaos these 'invasions' bring about." But all the propaganda and all the obstacles were for naught. During the 1960s, a copy of the painting was widely exhibited in Poland. The oath of fidelity to King Jan Kazimierz was put back into use in the dioceses and the parishes, with the approval of the Church hierarchy.

Finally Wladyslaw Gomulka, the first secretary of the Central Committee of the PZPR, could no longer bear seeing the copy of the painting attract the kinds of crowds that he could only dream of attracting himself. He had the picture "arrested" when it was on one of its trips around the country — in order, supposedly, to "bring it back safely" to Jasna Gora. For several months, the Militia made sure that the monks didn't take the

---

* In which the Polish state, as such, ceased to exist.

picture to other dioceses, but the assemblies continued nonetheless — in front of empty picture frames.

The long struggle against the Virgin Mary proved futile. One of the first things the workers did at the beginning of the strike at the Gdansk Shipyards in August 1980 was to hang a copy of the Black Virgin on the gate.

My pin with the image of the Black Virgin makes me feel connected to my family. My grandfather venerated the Virgin Mary, as did my mother, whose fondest wish was to make a pilgrimage to Jasna Gora. She was never able to fulfill it. Life at home was too hard: she had hungry mouths to feed and little money. But her prayers helped me to go in her place. I now visit the monastery nearly every time I travel to southern Poland. The Paulists have made me an honorary member of their order, and I am very proud of this, even though I am aware of the misunderstandings that it causes. Union leaders and Western politicians remind me that I'm not a religious activist. And I always remind them that Solidarity wouldn't have survived without the Church.

As long as I am part of Solidarity, I will wear the pin on my lapel; when I no longer am, I will discreetly wear a medallion of the virgin under my shirt.

During my internment, my jailers insisted that I take the pin off. "Mr. Walesa," they would say, "one of these days we're going to negotiate, and things will definitely change. But first take off that pin." My reply was consistently negative. Those Party members saw it not as a symbol of faith, but as a symbol of will — I knew this — and the point was to make me yield. If I had yielded, they would have exploited it by immediately telling the priests that it was proof I wasn't a true believer after all. They could have verified my faith before August 1980, when I met the world, but they hoped, with their policemen's mentality, that it had started to "go soft." They would interrogate those closest to me about my faith, hoping to glean my weaknesses. What they were hoping to uncover was that I merely pretended to be an ardent Catholic. But they kept running up against my deep connections with the Church, such as the fact that my children were singing in the choir well before 1980.

I first went to Czestochowa in October 21, 1980. My mother's prayers that I make the pilgrimage to Jasna Gora came true thirteen years after I had left home. I had always told myself that if and when I went to Jasna Gora, it would be when I was at peace with myself and with the world. While

October 1980 wasn't really a time when I felt this peace, I nevertheless went.

I traveled to Nowa Huta, Cracow, Nowa Sacz, and Silesia. As an ordinary worker I experienced a triumphal trip through southern Poland, a land echoing with the patriotism of previous struggles for independence. In the course of my travels, on practically every square foot, I saw a statue, a monument commemorating the fall of some past national hero. I unwittingly was following in their footsteps. After years of a Communist "class struggle" in which the individual had no place, the national thirst for a hero was so powerful that sometimes — even before the doors of my car could open all the way — I was swept up into the embrace of some enthusiastic procession. Over and over I told the crowds that I wasn't a hero: "Look! I'm one of you! My hands are calloused by tools and blackened with machine oil. Pay no attention to my fancy speeches!" They wouldn't listen to my protests.

In 1956, when Wladyslaw Gomulka got out of prison and came to power, he was greeted as a savior. Nearly a million people gathered in Warsaw to cheer his pledge that the torture of innocent citizens would stop. The same thing happened in 1970, when Gomulka was overthrown and Edward Gierek, a technocrat educated in Poland, was greeted as the leader who would change Poland's destiny. There was applause and still more applause; but in 1980 he too was gone — overnight, dishonored.

As I went through the doors of the fortified monastery, my thoughts once again were of my mother, and of how she had never had the chance to come here.

Inside, an exposition had been set up illustrating the continuity of Polish history. It has been no ordinary feat, maintaining this continuity in a country continually ravaged by foreign armies. Looking at the rows of pictures, and admiring the hundreds of standards presented to the monastery after skirmishes and victorious battles, I was reminded once again that Poles had long lived with a heavy cross tied to their backs; they couldn't have carried it without help from God. All those times when we were entangled in desperate political and military situations, our faith saw us through. That is why Jasna Gora became the nation's guiding light.

My acts of faith contained no fatalism about the future. Our ancestors may have had to lay down their lives in the struggle against oppression, but all I had to do was make good use of the opportunities that came my way. I felt humbled by the thought that there were worthier men than I, who, in the name of all Poland, had brought the nation's gratitude to the sacred image of the Virgin here at Jasna Gora. I had never intended to become that kind of hero. I had not tried to become a leader.

But when circumstances turned me into one, as a Christian I had to accept my part in the larger design. "Guide me, Holy Virgin," I said. "Let me be your instrument for the good of my country, my Church, and my neighbor. Protect them all, so they'll be fit for their struggle to regain their just rights." When I had finished my prayer, I felt like a man who has put the important things in his life in order. The symbol of this order was the badge pinned to my lapel.

I returned to Jasna Gora on the morning of December 12, 1983, after having spent many long hours in the car traveling from Gdansk to Warsaw to welcome Danka back from Oslo, where she had accepted the Nobel Prize for me. She was still imbued with the warm welcome she had received from the Norwegians, their king, the Nobel Committee, and journalists; back in Warsaw, though, she was greeted by a squad of Militia men carrying nightsticks.

We left for Czestochowa late that afternoon. I had decided to donate the commemorative certificate and the medal to the monastery. The SB followed closely behind us. Sometimes the agents sped up next to us, peering inside the car. Maybe they were curious to see what the medal looked like. In my mind I kept hearing the words of Egil Aarvik, the head of the Nobel Prize Committee:

> We who watch from the outside are especially impressed by how Solidarity has shown its desire for peace and understanding through its devotion to the Church. We have seen crowds of tens of thousands gathering in and around their churches to pray for their country and their cause. We have seen them weeping for the victims of the struggle before crosses adorned with flowers. We have understood that their nonviolent struggle endures not only for their sake, but also for the sake of all who aspire to peace.

There are only two living Polish Nobel Prize winners, and I am proud to be one. That honor conferred on me a prestige that was of enormous help to the cause.

The other living Polish Nobel laureate is Czeslaw Milosz, a poet and professor at the "capitalist" University of California at Berkeley. His winning the prize surprised many people, for he was almost unknown in Poland (where the censors had a file on him). Those who had had the chance to read the slim volumes of poetry delighted in his work. I unfortunately had scarcely had any associations at all with his name, which figured so often on the covers of books published by underground presses. I envy writers like Milosz, who can find the right words and strike the right chords. One writer with a gift for language can raise in people's hearts a greater desire for truth and good than thousands who don't possess that gift. Sometimes a pope will have it and sometimes a beggar, sometimes a wise man and sometimes an idiot. Both child and elder might receive the blessing of knowing divine intentions. And surely poets are the most blessed of all.

I very much wanted Czeslaw Milosz to attend the unveiling of the shipyard monument in December 1980, but he couldn't be there. We met for the first time on June 12, 1981, at the Catholic University of Lublin, where he was being given an honorary doctorate. The intellectual elite had gather.d for the occasion — and along with all those eggheads was me, the electrician from Gdansk. Milosz spoke about the meaning of words, and used me as an example of someone who knew something about them. Totalitarianism had found ways of distorting fundamental concepts, sometimes by reversing their true meaning. Holding a monopoly over the meaning of words is a twentieth-century phenomenon. What is happening in Poland, he said, is that human meanings are being restored to words — yet another interpretation of the Polish revolution, and one that I fully agreed with.

Later, Milosz did pay a visit to the shipyards, where he was greeted with a standing ovation by the workers in their coveralls. The spectacle moved him. He was amazed that his poems and the work he had done in faraway Berkeley had not fallen into a void. Unlike previous years, when he was accustomed to address a small circle of university colleagues, here in Gdansk he was speaking to a crowd of thousands of workers — gathered at the base of the most famous monument in Poland, a monument on which some lines from one of his poems were engraved.

Every morning, on their way to work, the workers read these phrases:

> *The Lord gives strength to His people,*
> *And to His people the blessings of peace.*

These words were the foundation of much of what we had done during the period of martial law. They also served as the motto for a number of Solidarity's small underground newspapers. History had made these words, so that they could make history.

As I write about Czeslaw Milosz, my thoughts go back to that December ceremony when, to the notes of Penderecki's *Lacrimosa*, I lit a torch before a crowd of 150,000 people. My hands were shaking, and it was so cold that I could hardly raise the torch. The music, composed for that ceremony, harmonized beautifully with the scenes depicted on the monument — a woman with a child, outlines of figures breaking bread together, widows grieving for their husbands. Those figures weren't only on the monument; they were also standing right next to me, there, at the ceremony. And Milosz's words were meant for them:

> *You who have injured the ordinary man,*
> *Laughing aloud at his distress . . .*
> . . . .
> *Think not you are safe. The poet remembers.*
> *Kill that poet — and another will be born,*
> *Words and deeds will find inscription. . . .*

The great poet was right. Ideologues who persecute innocent people should never feel safe. There, at the base of the monument, feeling the eyes of Poland and the eyes of all of Europe watching me, I knew that those who laughed were no longer safe.

In 1983, labeled a "private citizen" by the government, I placed my Nobel Prize medal in the glass case next to the pen of Henryk Sienkiewicz. I have returned to Jasna Gora a number of times, and each time, from its parapets, I have observed with emotion the number of people carrying Solidarity banners, a confirmation of how our movement was reviving, how Poland was advancing toward freedom. There I understand the meaning of a nation. There, no one is surprised that I wear the badge of the Virgin on my lapel.

37
Beginnings

F aith was as natural to me as my mother's milk. Faith in my family was passed from generation to generation because it accomplished two goals — it preserved our national identity and it eased our suffering. My maternal grandmother, born Dobrzeniecka, came from a family with twelve children, who despite their poverty never forgot daily prayers — morning, afternoon, and evening. Women gave birth with a prayer on their lips, and the dying passed away whispering a prayer. In nearly every generation one child became a priest or a nun, and parents dreamed of a religious vocation for their little ones. World War I, the defeat of the German and Austro-Hungarian empires, the Russian Revolution, and the Polish-Bolshevik War: they were all unfathomable signs of divine will. Priests made the sign of the cross over the men who headed off to war and welcomed them with the sign of the cross when they returned; one prayed for their souls, at church or at home, if they didn't.

Toward the end of the 1940s, as I was becoming aware of the world, nothing had changed very much. It was still true that no Walesa ever skipped morning prayer, and before noon he always prayed, together with the entire family, to the angel of the Annunciation. Sitting in a semicircle in the largest room, eyes fixed on the image of the Virgin, we recited our prayer in unison. Often, we prayed after having run a long way, or while we were working in the fields, or in the stables — they were moments of rest. And every May, the Walesas went to the festivals honoring the Virgin Mary to offer our prayers of adoration to the Mother of God. That was part of our life. Every Sunday we walked four miles to church, and along the way we prayed before all those statues of the Virgin spread out along the road from Popowo to Chalin. Mass in the chapel or church wasn't enough.

Additional religious services were held in the house, and everyone at home took part in them, chiefly the women, since the men were out working. The Walesas sang and prayed a great deal, especially during Lent and Advent.

The high point of the vigil before Christ's birth was the *posnik,* or fast-day, evening, when we could eat only lean dishes, the recipes for which were family traditions. Our stepfather presided over the ceremony at our house. He would freshen up after coming home from work and put on his Sunday best; then, as we all knelt with him, he would lead us out loud in prayer—as the head of the family, he performed the functions of a priest. To commemorate the star of Bethlehem, we never sat down to eat until the first star had risen in the evening sky. We would tear out of the house into the twilight at least a hundred times to see if any stars had yet appeared; sometimes the sky was clouded over and we couldn't see any. Finally our stepfather would give the signal to sit down. After the prayer, we exchanged wishes and broke the customary wheaten *oplatek* — a thin wafer of unleavened bread. That was the best moment of the most beautiful evening of the year.

But as life went on we didn't have much time for expressing any feelings, especially since the head of the house was not our father, but our stepfather. Though he did his best for all four of us, the children of his wife's first marriage, we never grew close to him. My sister Izabela could not accept the idea that our mother had married her first husband's brother only because she didn't want to live alone.

Our stepfather wasn't a bad man. He always urged us to finish school so that we could move away from the countryside, where life was poor and hard. He had married a widow with four children, and by so doing fulfilled the last wish of his brother, who on his deathbed had asked him to take care of his wife and children. He had made great sacrifices for us.

But this didn't keep us from remaining inconsolable over our father's death. None of us at the time understood that our mother had been twenty-seven when she was widowed and that she couldn't raise a family alone. She was afraid of taking her four young children to a strange city, for she had no income and only a small plot of farmland. But we still couldn't understand.

When I was four or five, I learned that our father was buried in the graveyard. Izabela had taken me to see his grave. My older brothers Edward and Stanislaw had already asked our mother about him: Why was it that a widow married for the second time had the same last name as her deceased husband? She relived her tragedy each time she told us the story.

But when we shared the *oplatek* and sang *koleda* — Christmas carols — together around the table each year on Christmas Eve, we did so as one big family. We always left an empty place at the table, according to age-old tradition, so that if some lost soul knocked on our door, he could join us immediately as a member of the household. No one ever did come, but the chair and the dishes were always ready.

In my mind the image of the empty chair is associated with the war. My mother and stepfather often said that after the war many had been sent to Siberia, and that some had managed to make their way back home many years later. To me, that was the reason for the place waiting.

My mother would scatter some straw under the white tablecloth. The Christ-child had been born in the straw, and it was a reminder of His poverty, she always said. The bread was blessed — mainly because sometimes there wasn't any bread at all. One of our own village traditions was that before putting a loaf in the oven, the mistress of the house made the sign of the cross over it; if it fell onto the floor, she retrieved it reverently and then kissed it to ask for forgiveness, so that God the Provider wouldn't be offended.

The Walesa Christmas vigil was ceremonious but modest. Before the vigil was the koleda, when the priest came to bless the cottage, read a prayer, and ask after everyone's health and happiness, especially the children's. In preparation, a major housecleaning would have taken place, with every nook and cranny carefully swept. The dining table with its white tablecloth was set with two candles and a cross. Then everyone waited in an atmosphere of excited anticipation. The children had to be told to stay quiet so they wouldn't disrupt the seriousness of the moment.

The old Slavic word *wieczerza* ("vigil") refers to the religious significance of gathering around the table, not to the food eaten there. Noodles with poppy seeds, beans, cabbage, wild mushrooms, sometimes fish — everything was prepared according to the Lenten rules, which stayed in effect until midnight. The presents under the tree were mostly symbolic: a cake, a bit of candy, a trinket. Spending the evening together as a happy family — that was the real gift.

Later in the evening, we all went to the *pasterka*, the midnight mass. What a celebration that was! Everybody who could walk went to the church. Sometimes the snow was waist-deep, and when we got there we were stiff with cold — but also happy, because you were *supposed* to be stiff with cold when you went to the *pasterka*. The one preceded the other, like going to confession before taking communion.

For Epiphany, the letters K + M + B were written on the floor in chalk bought from street peddlers in front of the church — the letters were the initials of Kaspar, Melchior, and Balthazar, the three biblical Magi. This was done not only to commemorate their trip, but also to protect the household from misfortune, just as Jews marked the lintels of their doors with lamb's blood during Passover. You could also buy incense from the peddlers, but we never did because it cost too much.

Lent and Easter were also important holidays. We began eating lean on Ash Wednesday, when the older people went to church to have their foreheads smudged with ashes. The younger kids had their foreheads smudged at home, and even though the ashes of course symbolize mortality, the dust to which we all return, children are pretty untroubled by such thoughts. Most people had to work on Good Friday, but for those who went to church, it was a day of silence and meditation. The church was usually packed and the atmosphere stifling hot but dignified. The old people said they liked it when it was stifling, because drafts made them ill.

From early in the morning on Good Friday until three or four in the afternoon, everyone bustled around trying to outdo each other, hurrying to get the house ready for Easter and still have time to go to the Passion service, devoted to the memory of Christ's sufferings. A stylized replica of Christ's tomb, beautifully decorated with flowers, was placed at the altar. Fasting was not the only mortification of the flesh that day: drinking any liquid was forbidden, to remind us that when Christ was nailed to the cross he suffered from thirst. In some houses, the mirrors were covered as a sign of mourning.

On Easter morning, adults and young people joined in a procession to the Resurrection service. And only after it was finished could we have the holiday feast at which we all shared the blessed food. The rest of Easter Sunday was spent eating and relaxing.

Easter Monday, on the other hand, was the most fun for the children and young people, who passed the morning splashing each other with icy well-water. The practice, called *smigus-dyngus* in Polish, dates back to the Middle Ages. The boys run after the girls, who scream and throw pails of water at them — partly to observe tradition, partly to tease. I don't know the origin of the game, but it would seem that the Poles borrowed it long ago from the German bourgeoisie in Poland. My mother always felt that it had religious significance — something to do with baptism.

Fifty days after Easter comes Pentecost, which in Poland we call "Little Green Festival" or "Festival of the Gift of the Holy Ghost." The church and the front gates of farms are decorated with birch or ash branches. The greenery symbolizes joy and renewal, which the Apostles felt when they saw the tongues of fire and knew of the presence of the Holy Ghost. It used to be that on this day shepherds and peasants walked through their fields carrying the image of the Virgin and church flags, singing to the glory of Mary, and then sitting down to a picnic in a meadow. Postwar hardships might have limited the number of ceremonies and religious observances, but they still accompanied practically every step of life.

When someone in the village was dying, the priest was called, and his unction of holy oil could relieve the suffering and even — if the Good Lord willed it — restore health. Everybody made confession and took communion, not just the sick person but his whole family. If a neighbor died, we went to his house, as a family or part of a delegation, to spend that "empty night" — the night without the one now dead. From six in the evening until dawn, the dead person was watched over, the vigil being punctuated by prayers and songs of mourning. My mother knew them all. Candles were lit in the darkness in the hope that there would be a miracle and the dead person would revive. Everything took place to the accompaniment of sobs and moans. The point of all this was that the mourning family should not have to be alone; everyone in the village joined them in their grief.

As children we were sometimes frightened by these vigils: Mother had told us that the dead like to visit a house in mourning to tell its occupants what the next life is like. In our family, though, we talked about death pretty often and in a familiar way. We were, after all, part of the generation that had lost many of their own in the war, and war makes plain the vanity of earthly life. My mother continually reminded us that if we weren't good Christians we wouldn't meet up again at the Last Judgment. She was unhappy that she couldn't go to church every week; raising us, she always said, took too much time. So she made up for it by praying at home, and by constantly worrying about whether she was following all of the Commandments. That's why she wanted more than anything for one of us to become a priest or a nun. I was the one she expected to enter the priesthood. But I knew that it wasn't the life for me, particularly after I discovered girls.

The one in our family who came the closest to priesthood was Grandfather Kaminski, who was a sort of secular cleric. This meant that he had to be above reproach and go to mass every single day. One morning in 1944, he went to mass, sat down, yawned — and died.

The greatest experience of my boyhood was my first communion. The evening before, the whole family had gone to confession, and all the kids, me especially, asked the adults to forgive us for misbehaving; we also had to kiss our stepfather's hand, and settle old quarrels with each other. The day of the ceremony, without having eaten, because, of course, one must take communion on an empty stomach, we headed to church in our finest clothes. Inside the church, I remember, it was stiflingly hot. Some children fainted — that always happened at times like this, after all the buildup and preparation. During the whole year before first communion, a nun and the priest had taught us the catechism and the articles of faith; at the end of the year we were grilled on what we'd learned. In those days the church ceremony wasn't followed by a noisy celebration, as it is today, nor did people try to outdo each other with presents. We were very poor, and our festivities consisted of a formal dinner; it was a spiritual and communal occasion.

The four-mile trek to church wasn't always as easy as it was the day of my first communion, when I felt as if I were walking on air. Four miles is a long way for a child. My shoes gave me blisters, and sometimes I was nearly in tears by the time we got there. We usually arrived for ten o'clock mass, even when it got really hot, and along the way there was no cold Pepsi-Cola, but only the dust of a country road. Nevertheless, my sister Iza liked going to church so much that she sometimes found a pretext to return the same day — especially when there was housework that needed doing.

Every August 15, we made the twelve-mile pilgrimage from Popowo to Skepe for the greatest of all the Marian celebrations, the one called the Virgin of the Harvest. Through woods and fields we went, singing hymns. To us it seemed like an expedition to a faraway place. At the ceremony itself the harvest was blessed, for it was not only the product of hard work, but also a gift from God. Women brought sheaves with blades of wheat and grasses of every color braided together, to decorate the altar. The priest blessed these sheaves so that when they dried, their seeds could be used for the first sowing next spring.

Electricity didn't reach Popowo until the 1960s, so our lives followed nature's cycles. At night, we were too scared to leave the cottage, because of the ghosts outside. Along the edge of the field, marked by a horizon of distant hills, the will-o'-the-wisp moved like a speeding ball of fire, and the worst thing that could possibly happen was that it would get into the house. We stayed away from the fallow fields between Ruszkow and Sobow after dark — that was where the will-o'-the-wisp had chosen to live. Our little village was widely spread out; several hundred yards separated one farmhouse from another. People tended to stay close to home and tried to be completely self-reliant.

Lightning sometimes started fires, despite our praying throughout every storm and placing a saint's picture or a votive candle in the window. Not far from us, there was a stone that was often struck by lightning. That stone must have had some symbolic power, but what could it mean? It was just one of the mysteries of my childhood.

I spent my childhood on a farm, and country life formed my character. But I never grew to like it. I knew how much labor it took for a peasant to work his plot of land in his own way. His helplessness before the powers of nature frustrated me, as did the fact that I couldn't ride a bicycle to church or school, and that the snow buried me in winter and the dust choked me in summer. I wanted to stay in school, but I felt guilty because it meant that my mother had to support me.

"Don't worry about that," she would tell me. "You should develop your God-given talents."

"Who cares about my talents when they make life so hard for you?" I would reply.

I left home to go to vocational school. The idea of work didn't faze me in the slightest. Every country boy knows how to use a scythe, an axe, and a blacksmith's tools. During the summer, I had worked at a brickyard to bring in a little extra money. The clay was heavy and the work was done by hand. I carted raw bricks to the oven, and when they had been fired I stacked them one by one. My hands were covered with gashes and calluses. You couldn't slack off or complain that you were too tired to work. When I tried, my stepfather, more than once, used his specially braided whip on me.

I grew up respecting hard work, but also rebelling against it. All that work didn't seem to improve anyone's quality of life. I still feel no love for country life, even though it made me who and what I am, and created the strands that make up the fabric of my life: my sense of morality, my belief in tradition and stability, my respect for my elders, for priests, and for religion. Everyone has his own fabric and measures life by its dimensions. Some strands are formed early, some we are born with, and everyone's weave is different. Growing up on a farm, poverty, the absence of a father, the postwar years, work, church — all these are strands in my fabric, and they are woven tight.

The home I grew up in valued religion deeply, but not fanatically. I was convinced of God's existence in a natural way, and without dogma. So too, in a natural way, grew my conviction that without faith, action means nothing. Christianity provided me with a fabric, with standards that I could use to judge the world and my own conduct in it. It has helped me determine what really are the most important things; it has helped me to define my goals, and then inspired me to reach them. Things that are of no importance pass through my fabric like sand through a sieve: the sand makes it through, the more valuable gravel cannot. If you have the right sieve, you know instantly what is of value and what is worthless. My sieve has sometimes helped me to make quick decisions — without endless consultation and paralyzing hesitation.

The country life that I've depicted here no longer exists. Currents of change accompanied communism and its propaganda. There was some industrialization, and "tribal" bonds became looser. Young people began to emigrate to the city, and in 1967 I was among them. New strands were woven into the fabric of my life. But the older ones still have sturdy roots in the soil on which I was raised.

Epilogue

At precisely noon on December 22, 1990, I stood before the Parliament of Poland, the first president to be elected directly by the nation as a whole, and having won by more than 73 percent of the vote. Many Poles had stayed home on election day, though — we were only beginning our apprenticeship in democracy. But nothing could take away from the fact that the Third Republic had been born before our eyes.

I began my address with these words:

> A period in our history has come to an end, a period during which government authorities were appointed according to the will of foreigners, or by enforced concessions. Today we are taking another crucial step along the long and bloody route that leads to independence. Providence has granted us the privilege of following in the footsteps of past generations, but not with violence.

While I spoke these words, Danuta's eyes filled with tears. She was sitting not far from me. Poles have always had to die defending their freedom. My family, the whole Polish family, has lived through enough tragedy. Let us hope those tragedies are at an end.

The deputies and senators assembled there in the Sejm, and Poles everywhere in front of their television sets, listened to what a worker from Gdansk had to say after being elected to the highest post in the land:

> Independent Poland wants to be within the peaceful order of Europe as well as to be a good neighbor. For centuries a common history has linked us to the Ukraine, Belorussia, and Lithuania. We also share history with Germany, which now we hope is a friendly and open gateway to Europe. Our culture

305

> connects us with the West, but we will continue to nurture a spirit of fellowship
> in our relations with Russia.

I thought of the Soviet Union, and of how it was being torn apart by internal dissension.

I spoke slowly and forcefully. There was no room for mistakes: my critics were all too ready to seize on even my smallest slip. They had found it impossible to admit that a mere worker had become president. The nation should have chosen a businessman, a professor, an intellectual, somebody who embodied learning and deft manners. Instead, the nation had chosen me.

Above all, I wanted to be an effective politician, but a politician who listens to public opinion.

> I come from a family of farmers, and for many years I was a worker. I shall
> never forget the place I left to begin the path that has led me to this office. I
> would hope that from my example every Polish worker, and every farmer,
> feels directly involved in the governance of their homeland.

Uppermost in my mind were all the promises I had made to the Polish people. I had promised that their lives would change. It was in their name that I had fought for the presidency — to be able to bring about the reforms begun ten years earlier by means of a strike.

On December 10, 1990, the day after the election, I had gone to the Gdansk Shipyards. I emerged from the bulletproof Volvo that was now my official car and went directly to my former workshop. I got choked up when I looked at the small metal locker where I used to store my tools. Workers in overalls, looking embarrassed, congratulated me. I was no longer one of them. But I wanted them to understand that I knew how they felt. Shyly, they said, "We hope you will be able to change our lives, Mr. President."

The workshop where I had spent half my life looked like a technological museum. When I began working there in 1967, it had been one of the most modern in Poland.

The day after my inauguration, I flew to Czestochowa. I wanted to thank the Black Virgin of Jasna Gora, whose image I had carried for ten years, and I wanted once again to carry out the wishes of my mother, who hadn't lived long enough to get there herself. Now she could be proud of her son, who, as president of Poland, had made an oath of fidelity to the republic and to the sacred image.

I was beginning a journey into unknown territory. But to guide me I had the inscription on the Monument to the Shipyard Dead:

> *The Lord gives strength to His people,*
> *And to His people the blessings of peace.*

As a person and as a leader, I had the duty to do whatever I could to make those verses come true.

A Note on Polish Pronunciation

Polish, like all other Slavic languages, contains some sounds that the Latin-based Roman alphabet never contemplated. Russian and other eastern Slavic languages use the Cyrillic alphabet, based on the Byzantine Greek, with additions. Polish, on the other hand, under western influence, modified the Latin alphabet with a few accents and other diacriticals (which are not used in this book). Here is a partial guide to pronouncing Polish names:

Pronunciation of the vowels is uncomplicated: relatively short and open, without the sliding diphthongs used in English. For the most part you can use the simple vowels contained in

　　pa pen pin plop plume puppy

for sound-alikes. But **a** and **e** have nasalized forms, represented by

　　ą, as in French **bon**, and

　　ę, as in French **bain**.

Many of the consonants are close enough to English so that the English sound will serve:

　　b d f g(hard) **h k l**(sometimes) **m n p s**(sometimes) **t**

Some are similar to their sounds in some other European languages:

　　j is always pronounced as **y**

　　w is always pronounced as **v**

　　r is trilled (usually)

These consonants are more problematic:

　　z alone is pronounced much as in English; in combination, it's the key
　　　　to a lot of puzzles:

　　　　z after **c** or **s** acts exactly like **h** in those positions in English; see below

　　　　z after **r** produces as **zh** sound; see below

　　c is usually **ts**, so the common name ending **-icki** is pronounced **-itski**

　　　　ch is pronounced as a hard, breathy **h**, as in German **ach** or Scots **loch**

　　　　cz is pronounced like English **ch**; **ć** is similar, but a bit softer

　　sz is pronounced like English **sh**; **ś** is similar, but a bit softer

　　rz is pronounced as the **zh** sound represented by the **s** in **measure**

308

l has two forms:

    l plain is pronounced at the front of the mouth, with the tongue touching the gums just behind the upper teeth, as in English **late**

    ł with a slash is another sound, pronounced so deeply that it can resemble an English **w**

In this book, we have refrained from using the special letters and accents, so the reader won't have all the clues he needs for proper pronunciation, but the incomplete list above should help. So: **Walesa** is actually spelled **Wałęsa**, and if you know that **w** = **v**, **ł** = **w**, and **ę** is a nasal **e**, you know that it's pronounced something like **Va*wen*sa**. Similarly, **Częstochowa** is the proper spelling, which is pronounced, roughly, **Chensto*hh*ova**. **Wyszyński** is pronounced **Vi*shin*ski**, and **Mazowiecki** is pronounced **Mazov*yet*ski**.

Names and Acronyms

AK (Armia Krajowa — Army of the Country or Army of the Interior or, most commonly, Home Army). During World War II, the leading organ of the Polish resistance, directed by the government-in-exile in London.

Army of the Country or Army of the Interior — *See* AK.

Centrum (Porozumienie Centrum — Alliance of the Center). Parliamentary group formed by supporters of Lech Walesa.

Civic Movement for Democratic Action — *See* ROAD.

Committee for the Workers' Defense — *See* KOR.

Communist Party — *See* PZPR.

Confederation for an Independent Poland — *See* KPN.

Democratic Party — *See* SD.

Freedom and Peace — *See* Wolnosc i Pokoj.

Home Army — *See* AK.

Independent Student Union — *See* NZS.

KOR (Komitet Obrony Robotnikow — Committee for the Workers' Defense). Founded by a group of intellectuals after the workers' riots in Radom in June 1976.

KPN (Konfederacja Polski Niepodleglej — Confederation for an Independent Poland). Right-wing nationalist movement founded and led by Leszek Moczulski.

Militia — *See* MO.

MO (Milicja Obywatelskiej — Civil Militia). The urban police; *see also* ZOMO.

Motorized Units of the Civil Militia — *See* ZOMO.

National Alliance of Trade Unions — *See* OPZZ.

NZS (Niezalezy Zwiazek Studentow — Independent Student Union). Activist student organization formed in 1980, in the wake of Solidarity, and dissolved during the state of martial law. It has resumed activities.

OKP (Obywatelski Klub Parlamentarny — Parliamentary Civic Club). Parliamentary group of 161 deputies and 100 senators elected by Solidarity supporters, the president of which is Bronislaw Geremek.

OPZZ (Ogolnopolskie Porozumienie Zwiakow Zawodowych — National Alliance of Trade Unions). Union organization created by the government in November 1984 to supplant Solidarity and led by Alfred Miodowicz.

Parliamentary Civic Club — *See* OKP.

Patriotic Movement for National Renaissance — *See* PRON.

PC — *See* Centrum.

Polish United Workers' Party — *See* PZPR.

Prokuratura. The state prosecutor's office.

PRON (Patriotyczny Ruch Ocalenia Narodowego — Patriotic Movement for National Salvation). Organization formed by the government in 1982 with the hope of attracting Poles disaffected with the PZPR.

Provisional Coordinating Board — *See* TKK.

PZPR (Polska Zjednoczona Partia Robotnicza — Polish United Workers' Party). Official name of the Communist Party; dissolved in January 1990, to create two "social-democratic" groups.

ROAD (Ruch Obywatelski-Akcja Demokratyczna — Civic Movement for Democratic Action). Movement started by the "Mazowiecki camp" at the initiative of Zbigniew Bujak and Wladyslaw Frasyniuk, in response to the formation of the Porozumienie Centrum (Center Alliance Party), formed by supporters of Lech Walesa.

SB (Sluzba Bezpiezenwa — Security Service). Name adopted by the political police in 1956; formerly the UB (Urzad Bezpieczentwa — Security Bureau).

SD (Stronnictwo Demokratyczne — Democratic Party). Satellite of the PZPR that broke free after the elections of June 1989.

Security Service — *See* SB.

TKK (Tymczasowa Komisja Koordynacyjna — Provisional Coordinating Board). Underground leadership of Solidarity.

UB — *See* SB.

United Farmers' Party — *See* ZSL.

Wolnosc i Pokoj — Freedom and Peace. Nonviolent, ecologically oriented movement.

ZOMO (Zmotoryzowane Oddizialy Milicji Obywatelskiej — Motorized Units of the Civil Militia). Anti-riot units of the urban police.

ZSL (Zjednoczone Stronnictwo Ludowe — United Farmers' Party). Satellite of the PZPR, of which it became independent, like the SD, to join with Solidarity in giving a parliamentary majority to the government of Tadeusz Mazowiecki.

Chronology

1918

November 11: Wiped from the map of Europe after the 1795 tripartite agreement between Russia, Prussia, and Austria, Poland regains its independence under the leadership of Marshal Jozef Pilsudski. The new democratic government takes the name Second Republic to link itself with the eighteenth-century Nobiliary Republic (also called the Polono-Lithuanian Union or the Republic of Two Nations). That republic, formed after the Jagiello dynasty died out, had been governed by an elected king. Along with the French and American constitutions, the Polish constitution, approved May 3, 1791, was one of the first to espouse democratic principles.

1918 to 1939

The interwar years fall into three periods: In the first (1918–1921), dominated by Marshal Pilsudski, Poland defeats the Red Army in Warsaw in 1920 and establishes its borders. On March 17, 1921, it adopts a parliamentary constitution inspired by that of the French Third Republic. The second period, from 1921 to 1926, is marked by Pilsudski's "withdrawal," and by the difficulties his successors have handling the country's growing problems. The third period begins with a coup d'état on May 12–14, 1926, which brings Pilsudski back to power. A new and less democratic constitution is adopted on April 23, 1935, shortly before the marshal's death on May 12.

1939

August 23: A nonaggression pact is signed in Moscow between Germany and the Soviet Union (the Molotov-Ribbentrop Pact). A secret agreement provides for the division of Poland between the Soviets and the Nazis.

September 1: The German army invades Poland, whose forces fall back to Warsaw — which surrenders on September 27 — and then retreat to the eastern territories.

September 17: The Soviet army invades Poland, attacking its defenses from the rear.

September 28: A German-Soviet treaty ratifies Poland's fourth partition, setting the new border between the two aggressors at the Bug River.

September 30: The Polish government flees Poland and seeks refuge in Romania, where it is interned. President Ignacy Moscicki thereupon appoints Wladyslaw Raczkiewicz, who is living in Paris, to succeed him and then resigns. The new president chooses General Wladyslaw Sikorski as prime minister, and the Allied Forces immediately recognize the government-in-exile, installed in the Polish embassy in Paris. After the fall of France in 1940, Sikorski's government moves to London. During the war it coordinates the activities of the underground resistance, known as the Armia Krajowa (AK, or Home Army).

1940

January: The Nazis begin constructing the camp at Auschwitz. The Jewish population has been confined to ghettos in Warsaw, Lodz, Bialystock, and other cities since October 1939.

1941

June 22: Germany attacks the Soviet Union, which reestablishes contact with the Polish government-in-exile. The occupied Polish territories are renamed the General Government, with the capital at Cracow and administered by Hans Frank. The Germans announce that Poland has ceased to exist.

December 5: The Sikorski-Stalin accords are signed, providing for the formation of a Polish army within the USSR. But some 15,000 Polish officers arrested by the Soviets in 1939 are still missing.

1942

January 20. The Nazis begin to carry out "the final solution of the Jewish problem": the Holocaust begins.

1943

April: In the Katyn Forest, near Smolensk, the German occupying troops discover a mass grave containing the bodies of 4,321 Polish army officers shot in the back of the neck. Despite the conclusions of an investigation by the International Red Cross, Josef Stalin accuses the Germans of the crime. When the Polish government-in-exile accuses the Soviet Union of responsibility, Stalin breaks off relations. The Polish army that has been training in the USSR, led by General Wladislaw Anders, links up with the Allies via Iran and distinguishes itself in the Middle East and in Italy at the battle of Monte Cassino.

April 19 to May 16: Revolt and annihilation of the Warsaw Ghetto. Some of the 40,000 survivors are killed on the spot; the rest are sent to death camps.

July 4: Sikorski dies in a plane crash; Wladyslaw Mikolajczyk, head of the Peasants' Party, becomes prime minister.

1944

July 22: The Polish National Liberation Committee, formed in the Soviet Union, settles in Lublin, the first Polish city to be "liberated" by the Red Army.

August 1 to October 2: An insurrection is started in Warsaw by the Home Army; the Red Army, at the city's gates, allows the Germans to wipe out the Resistance and systematically destroy the Polish capital.

1945

February 4 to 11: At the Yalta Conference, Churchill and Roosevelt agree to permit the "enlargement" of the Lublin Committee, allowing the Soviets to tighten their grip on Poland.

June 28: The Soviet-backed government takes control: the Socialist Osubka Morawski becomes president. Two vice-presidents are named: Wladyslaw Gomulka, a Communist, and Prime Minister Mikolajczyk, who agrees to take the position even though, without the approval of the government-in-exile, it is a charade. The Warsaw government gains international recognition.

Civil war breaks out in Poland's southeastern provinces; many former members of the AK are arrested.

The government-in-exile continues to exist in order to ensure the continuity of the Second Republic. (Wladyslaw Raczkiewicz dies on June 6, 1947, and is succeeded by August Zaleski (1947–1972), Stanislaw Ostrowski (1972–1979), Edward Raczynski (1979–1986), Kazimierz Sabbat (1986–1989), and finally Ryszard Kaczorowski, who will transmit the insignia of the presidency to Lech Walesa in 1990.)

1946 to 1948

The referendum of June 30, 1946, and the legislative elections of January 19, 1947, eliminate the moderate elements in the government. Mikolajczyk flees to London. In 1948, the Polish Workers' Party (PPR) absorbs the Socialist Party (PPS) to form the Polish United Workers' Party (PZPR).

1948 to 1956

The Stalinist period, marked by the arrest of former first secretary Gomulka, accused of "nationalist deviation," and later by the arrest of Cardinal Stefan Wyszynski, the primate of Poland.

1956

Following Khrushchev's speech in February 1956 on Stalin's crimes, the Communist Party's Twentieth Congress, and the Poznan riots of June 1956, a popular movement succeeds in liberating Wladyslaw Gomulka, who is elected first secretary. The episode is called "the October springtime."

Cardinal Wyszynski and many former Home Army members are freed. Soviet marshal Konstantin Rokossovsky, whom Stalin had appointed minister of defense in 1949, returns to the USSR.

The period of liberalization ends, followed by the period of "stabilization."

1968

Student riots result from the prohibition of *Dziady* [*The Forefathers*], a play by the famous nineteenth-century Polish writer Adam Mickiewicz; anti-Russian speeches provoke demonstrations. General Mieczyslaw Moczar uses the pretext to begin operations against Gomulka and begin a "cultural pogrom" against intellectuals, Jews, and dissidents.

Diplomatic relations with Israel are broken off.

1970

December 14 to 19: Workers' demonstrations against a sudden price hike are brutally suppressed and turn into riots in the Baltic ports of Gdansk, Gdynia, and Szczecin. Fifty people are killed.

December 20: Gomulka, who has been first secretary of the PZPR since October 1956, resigns and is replaced by Edward Gierek. Following new strikes, Gierek cancels price hikes in February 1971.

1971 to 1974

Thanks to massive loans from the West, Gierek's government attempts economic modernization and briefly stimulates talk of a "Polish miracle." But membership in the Eastern Bloc's Council for Mutual Economic Assistance (Comecon) and rigid bureaucratic planning soon doom the effort to failure.

1976

June: The announcement of new price increases higher than those in 1970 causes violent demonstrations by workers in the Warsaw suburbs of Radom and Ursus. They are put down brutally.

September: A group of dissident intellectuals (notably Jacek Kuron, Adam Michnik, Edward Lipinski, and Jerzy Andrzejewski) found the KOR (Committee for the Workers' Defense) to help victims of the crackdown.

1978

October: Cardinal Karol Wojtyla, archbishop of Cracow, is elected pope and takes the name John Paul II.

1979

June: The "Slavic pope" — the first in the Church's history — visits his homeland, attracting huge gatherings and bolstering resistance to the regime.

1980

July: Sporadic strikes, sparked by price increases, break out.

August 14: Workers strike at the Lenin Shipyards in Gdansk. At the prompting of Lech Walesa, a strike committee is formed to negotiate with the government.

August 30 through September 3: The Accords of Gdansk, Szczecin, and Jastrzebie are signed. For the first time in the Eastern Bloc, an independent union,
Solidarity, is given permission to organize.

September 6: Stanislaw Kania replaces Gierek as first secretary of the PZPR.

September 17: Solidarity—the NSZZ (Niezalezny Samorzady Zwiazek Zawo-
dowy: Independent and Self-Governing Union) "Solidarnosc" — seeks to register as a legal body. Because of delaying tactics by the government, however,
registration is not made official until November 10.

1981

January 15: Pope John Paul II grants an audience to Walesa in Rome.

February 10: General Wojciech Jaruzelski is named prime minister.

May 12: Rural Solidarity is registered by the Supreme Court following tense negotiations interrupted by strikes.

May 28: Cardinal Wyszynski dies.

July 7: Monsignor Jozef Glemp is made archbishop and appointed to succeed
Wyszynski as primate of Poland.

October 8: During the First National Congress of Solidarity, the union elects Walesa its president.

October 18: General Jaruzelski — still prime minister — replaces Stanislaw
Kania as first secretary of the PZPR.

December 13: Jaruzelski proclaims a state of martial law: a military Council for
National Security is formed, constitutional guarantees are suspended, and curfews are instituted. Thousands of militants from Solidarity, including Walesa,
are arrested and interned.

December 14 to 23: The U.S. imposes economic sanctions on Poland. The Western powers suspend all economic aid to Poland.

1982

April 22: Leadership of Underground Solidarity is formed.

May 1: Solidarity holds large demonstrations to protest the state of martial law.

May 8: Parliament officially dissolves all unions, until now merely "suspended."

November 12: Walesa is freed from internment.

December 13: Martial law is suspended.

1983

June 16 to 23: Pope John Paul II makes second trip to Poland. There are numerous
peaceful demonstrations for Solidarity.

July 22: Martial law is officially ended.

October 5: Walesa is awarded the Nobel Peace Prize.

1984

July 22: Amnesty is declared for many leaders of the KOR and some members
of Solidarity.

October 19: Father Jerzy Popieluszko is kidnapped and murdered by Security Service agents.

October 27: General Czeslaw Kiszczak, minster of the interior, announces that the guilty parties have been arrested.

October 30: Popieluszko's body is discovered.

November 3: The funeral services for Popieluszko are conducted by Archbishop Glemp and thirteen bishops at Saint Stanislaw's Church in Warsaw. Walesa delivers graveside eulogy.

December 27: In Torun, trial begins for Popieluszko's four accused murderers: Grzegorz Piotrowski, Leszek Pekala, Waldemar Chmielewski, and Adam Pietruszka.

1985

February 7: Defendantsare found guilty; sentences are twenty-five years for Piotrowski and Pietruszka, fifteen for Pekala, and fourteen for Chmielewski.

October 13: Legislative elections are held. Turnout percentage announced by the government — 78.9%; Solidarity's estimate — 66%.

November 6: Jaruzelski is named president of the State Council, or head of state; Zbigniew Messner replaces him as prime minister.

1986

September 11: Government decides to free all political prisoners.

1987

January 13: Jaruzelski, on official visit to Rome, is received by Pope John Paul II.

February 19: The last American economic sanctions against Poland are lifted.

June 8 to 14: Pope John Paul II makes third visit to Poland.

September 26 to 29: Vice-President George Bush visits Poland, signaling a clear improvement in Polish-American relations.

November 29: The government holds a referendum to approve further stern economic measures (notably price increases) and "democraticization" in public life. Refusing to give the government carte blanche, Solidarity calls for a boycott, and it is successful; only 67% of those eligible vote.

1988

April and May: Strikes break out across the country and are brought under control (with some difficulty) by Solidarity, which demands that the government begin negotiations.

August 31: First meeting between government representatives and members of the opposition. A "Round Table" is proposed. Solidarity sets one condition — that it be made legal again.

September 19: Prime Minister Messner is replaced by Mieczyslaw Rakowski.

December 18: Solidarity's Civic Committee is formed.

1989

January 18: At a plenary session, the Central Committee of the PZPR agrees to legalize Solidarity, effective April 17.

February 6 to April 5: Round Table discussions end with an agreement calling for unrestricted elections to 35% of the seats of the Sejm (the rest will still be reserved for the PZPR and its satellite parties) and all seats in the Senat.

June: Landslide victory for Solidarity: it wins 99 of the 100 Senat seats and all of the "free seats" in the Sejm.

July 19: Jaruzelski is elected president of the Republic (a newly created post) by a margin of one vote, thanks to Solidarity support.

July 29: Rakowski replaces Jaruzelski as first secretary of the PZPR.

August 21: Following an unsuccessful bid by General Kiszczak, Tadeusz Mazowiecki is named prime minister.

September 15: The new government wins a vote of confidence in the Sejm.

November 15: Walesa, on a visit to Canada, Venezuela, and the United States, addresses a joint session of Congress.

1990

January 27 to 29: Final Congress of the PZPR, which votes to dissolves itself. It is replaced by the Social Democrats of the Polish Republic and the Union of Social Democrats.

April 11: Parliament repeals censorship laws.

April 13: The USSR acknowledges responsibility for the Katyn Forest massacre.

April 19 to 24: Second National Congress of Solidarity reelects Lech Walesa as president.

May: Creation of ROAD, which supports the Mazowiecki government.

May 27: Local elections give victory to candidates nominated by Solidarity's Civic Committees.

September 18: Cardinal Glemp meets with Polish leaders but fails to achieve attempted reconciliation.

October 25: Jaruzelski, at Walesa's urging, presents resignation to Parliament, which sets presidential elections of two rounds, on November 25 and December 9. The National Electoral Commission registers six presidential candidates who have obtained the requisite 100,000 signatures: Lech Walesa, Prime Minister Mazowiecki, Wlodzimierz Cimoszewicz (formerly of the Communist Party), Roman Bartoszcze (Peasant Party), Leszek Moczulski (Confederation for an Independent Poland), and an émigré Polish businessman, Stanislaw Tyminski.

November 25: Voter turnout on first round reaches only 60.6%. Walesa leads the list with 39.96% of the vote; Tyminski gains 23.1%, ahead of Mazowiecki (18.08%), Cimoszewicz (9.21%), Bartoszcze (7.15%), and Moczulski (2.5%).

December 9: On second round, Walesa is elected president with 73% of the votes.

December 22: Walesa is sworn in as president, receiving insignia from Ryszard Kaczorowski, successor to the last president of Second Polish Republic.

Index

A Way of Hope (Walesa), 22
Aarvik, Egil, 129, 294
ABC News, 3, 106
AFL-CIO, 110, 197, 231, 236
Against All Hope (Valladares), 228
Agca, Ali, 51
Agence France Presse, 104
agriculture, reform in, 249
Albania on developments in Poland, 220
Alfonsín, Raúl, 195
Amerongen, Otto von, 221
Amnesty International, 195
Anders, Gen. Wladyslaw, 314
Andreotti, Giulio, 192, 196
Andrzejewski, Gen., of Militia, 143
Andrzejewski, Jerzy, 316
ANSA (Italian News Agency), 91, 105
"Anthem of the Confederates," 290-291
"Anthem of the First Pilsudski Brigade," 66
Anti-Semitism, 132, 237-238, 314, 316
    in Poland, 130, 135, 240-241
Antonowicz, Marcin, 98
Arab countries
    business with, 242-243
    representation in Poland, 242
Arlamowo (Poland), LW interned in, 36, 117
assassination
    attempt on pope, 190
    of priests, 175
Associated Press (AP), 90, 93, 95, 104, 263
Auschwitz, 46, 77, 129, 131, 133-134, 238-
    239, 243, 314
    Carmelite convent at, 134-135

ceremony at, 128-129, 131-134
    LW's speech at, 131-132

Badkowski, Lech, 57-58
Baker, James A. III, 212, 235
Balcerowicz, Leszek, 226, 257, 271
Bartoszcze, Roman, 283, 320
Bartyzel, Jacek, 184
Baudouin I, king of Belgium, 198
Bejger, Stanislaw, 112-113
Belchatow mine, 176
Belgium, LW's trip to, 197-198
Belvedere Palace, 215, 265
Bergen-Belsen, 238
Berlin Wall Museum, 250
Berlinguer, Enrico, 192
Bernadzik, Robert, 226-227
Besser, Haskel, 131
Bialystok (Poland), 175, 254
    ghetto, 314
Bielsko-Biala (Poland), 177
Birkenau, 133
Black Virgin, Shrine of
    See Jasna Gora
Blanchard, François, 111
Blaszkowski, Rajmund, 106
Bleux, Flor, 226
Blöm, Norbert, 273
Bober, Andrzej, 168
Bohley, Barbel, 252
Bortnowska, Halina, 185
Borusewicz, Bogdan, 15, 108, 158, 212
Bovet, Daniel, 129

Brandt, Willy, 221, 273
Breit, Ernst, 221, 261, 273
Brezhnev, Leonid, 7, 148, 151
Brezhnev Doctrine, 3, 210
British Industrial Confederation, 245
Bronfman, Edgar, 240-241
Brovikov, Vladimir, 253-255, 264
Brown, Herbert, 129
Brudzenio (Poland), mass graves at, 130
Brygid, Saint, Church of (Gdansk), 4, 21,
    46, 62-64, 68, 73, 139, 158, 213
  dinner for Thatcher, 166
  LW speaks on Popieluszko at, 83
  meetings at, 113
  Popieluszko at, 74, 77
  press conferences at, 168
  service after strike, 146
  support center for strike, 156
Bryk, Father Zbigniew, 141, 144
Brzezinski, Zbigniew, 24-25, 231
Bujak, Zbigniew, 108, 178, 210, 272, 312
Bulgaria, 244
Bush, George, 173, 210, 220, 230, 268, 318
  luncheon for, 212
  speech of, 213-214
  visit to Gdansk, 56-57, 211, 213
  visit to Poland (1987), 121-122
Bustos, Manuel, 225, 231
Bydgoszcz (Poland), 78, 138

Cal, Luigi, 154
Canada, LW's trip to, 230, 231
Carlsson, Ingvar, 226
Carnogurski, Jan, 264
Carter, Jimmy, 24
Casaroli, Archbishop Agostino, 119, 190
Ceausescu, Nicolae, 48, 219, 246
Celinski, Andrzej, 142
censorship abolished, 272
Center for the Study of Public Opinion, 201
Centrum (Alliance of the Center), 271, 281,
    284, 311
Chalin (Poland), 129, 297
Chelm (Poland), 254
Chmielewski, Lt. Waldemar, 78, 81, 318
Christmas traditions in LW's youth, 298-300
Chrostowski, Waldemar, 78-82, 84
Churchill, Winston S., 315
Chylice (Poland), 35
Cimoszewicz, Wlodzimierz, 283, 320

Ciosek, Stanislaw, 143, 157, 167
Civic Club, Parliamentary, 221, 259-260,
    311-312
Civic Committee, Solidarity, 61, 123, 185-
    186, 199, 201, 205, 267, 319
  candidate list, 204
  debate on functioning, 182-186, 209
  formation, 172
  platform of, 200
Colasuonno, Archbishop, 119
Cold War, end of, 7, 11
Committee for the Workers' Defense
    (KOR), 204
Communist Party, East German, 228
Communist Party, Italian, 192-193
Communist Party, Polish, see PZPR
Communist Party, Romanian, 219
Communist Party, Soviet, 173, 254
  Gorbachev's report to, 148
  Khrushchev's anti-Stalin speech to, 315
computers, 42, 43, 110
concentration camps, 4, 46, 238, 243
  See also Auschwitz; Bergen-Belsen;
    Majdanek; Mlyniec; NKVD camps;
    Ravensbrück; Sobibor; Treblinka
Confederation for an Independent Poland
    (KPN), 19, 175, 283, 311
Congress, U.S., 211
  loans to Poland, 226
  LW addresses, 231-235
Cossiga, Francesco, 196
Council of Europe, 195
Cracow (Poland), 129, 134, 154, 198, 225,
    227, 243, 271, 276, 293, 314
  as capital of occupied Poland, 291
  demonstrations in, 137, 248
  pollution in, 140, 211
Craxi, Bettino, 192
Cuba, 227-228
Cybul, Father, 62
Czechoslovakia, 148, 244
Czestochowa (Poland), 53, 134, 136, 222
  papal visit (1983), 116
  See also Jasna Gora, Virgin of

Dabrowski, Archbishop Jerzy, 84, 157
Davis, John R., 220
De Niro, Robert, 224
death camps, see concentration camps
Delors, Jacques, 197, 268

Derwinski, Edward, 231
Deutscher Gewerkschaftsbund (DGB), 221, 261, 273
Dole, Elizabeth, 220
Dole, Robert, 220
Dziady [*The Forefathers*] (Mickiewicz), 316
Dziennik Balticki [*Baltic Daily*], 58

Easter traditions in LW's youth, 300
Elblag (Poland),
    voter turnout in, 88, 91, 104
elections, 88, 204
    boycott of, 104
    "National List," 201
    for Sejm and Senat, 200-206
Electricians' Union (British), 245
emigration, 53-54
Entente of the Citizens of Lodz, 184
Europe, 7, 54
    development in, 195-196, 261
    entering, 244
    stability of, 233-234
    See individual countries and cities
Europe, Eastern, 148, 233
European Economic Community (EEC), 42, 114, 197, 217

family life, LW on, 15-17
Federation of Militant Youth, 137
Fibak, Wojciech, 224
Fiszbach, Tadeusz, 256
Fonda, Jane, 113
Forlani, Arnoldo, 192
France, and Poland, 22, 208
Frasyniuk, Wladyslaw, 96-97, 108, 110, 231, 272, 312
Free Union, 33, 41, 131
Funnemark, Björn Cato, 154

Gach, Zbigniew, 262
Gandhi, Mohandas K., 4, 118, 250
Gazeta Wyborcza [*Electoral Gazette*], 183, 186, 194-195, 200, 216, 243, 279
Gdansk (Poland), 23, 77, 143, 214
    accords of, 75-76, 317
    appearance of, 19
    arrests in, 95
    citizens support strike (1988), 156
    curfews in, 153
    demonstrations in, 137, 248, 316

elections in, 60
    headquarters of legalized Solidarity, 186
    John Paul II's trip to, 112
    LW as citizen of, 18-19
    militants in, 111
    North Port, strike (1988), 151
    not informed of Mitterrand's visit, 209
    papal visit (1987), 114-118
    Piasecka-Johnson sets up bank in, 165
    symbol of liberty, 233
    voter turnout in, 88, 91, 97, 104-105
    writers support strike (1980), 58
Gdansk Shipyards, 64
    conversion to stock company, 164-165
    demonstrations (1970), 118
    finances of, 143, 161, 163
    LW returns to after election, 306
    LW working at, 19-20, 95
    press conference at, 255
    strike (1980), 10-11, 233, 292, 317
    strike (August 1988), 151-158
    strike (May 1988), 140, 142-145
    strikers' letter to Sadowski, 142
    threatened liquidation of, 161-162
    work halted at, 142
    See also Monument to the Shipyard Dead
Gdansk Video Studio, 187-188, 191
Gdansk, University of, 42, 141, 262-263
Gdynia (Poland)
    riots in (1970), 316
    voter turnout in, 88, 91
Gemelli Clinic (Rome), 190
General Federation of Belgian Workers, 198
Genscher, Hans-Dietrich, 127
Geremek, Bronislaw, 61, 82, 122, 157, 172, 196, 202, 209, 212, 219, 231, 260, 311
    at August 1988 strike, 154-155
    head of Parliamentary Civic Club, 259
    on Civic Committee, 182-183
    on trip to Rome, 187-188
    on political reforms, 175
    in social-policy work group, 178
    as Solidarity advisor, 53, 76, 109, 168
Germany, 148, 244
    LW visits, 221
    reunification, 253
ghettos, 314
Gierek, Edward, 24, 141, 248-249, 293, 316-317

Glemp, Cardinal Jozef, 116, 119, 127, 191,
    194, 218, 238, 240, 281, 315, 317-319
    disapproval of LW's activities, 113, 114
Gniezno (Poland), 108
Goclowski, Tadeusz, bishop of Gdansk,
    106, 112, 141, 143, 146, 156, 158,
    212, 222, 280
    trip to Rome, 187-188
Goldstein, Maurice, 129, 131
Gomowski, Stefan, 63
Gomulka, Wladyslaw, 291, 293, 315-316
Gorbachev, Mikhail, 109, 124, 147-149,
    173, 197, 207, 209, 220, 234, 254
    and change in USSR, 24-25, 148
    meets pope, 246
    and perestroika, 7, 21, 113
    policies of, 121
    visits Poland (1988), 150
Gorsk (Poland), 78
Grabowski, Ryszard, 188
graffiti, 19, 77
"gray masses," 18
Gray Wolves, Organization of, 51
Grzelak, Grzegorz, 27
Grzywaczewski, Bozena, 50
Grzywaczewski, Maciek, 50-52
gulags, 4, 46, 148, 195, 244
Gust, Zosia, 26
Gwiazda, Andrzej, 267

Hall, Aleksander, 27, 142, 183, 186
Hammond, Eric, 245
Havel, Vaclav, 198, 262
Helsinki Watch, 154, 195
Henrykow factory, 167, 174
Hijazi, Abdallah, 242
Hodysz, Adam, 86-87
Holocaust, 237-238, 240-241, 314
Home Army, 113, 239, 311, 314-316
Honecker, Erich, 48, 228
human rights, and U.S. policy toward
    Poland, 121
Human Rights, European Prize for, 195
Hungarian League of Independent Unions, 199
Hungary, 148, 227
Hurd, Douglas, 245, 269

Independent Student Union (NZS), 177,
    199, 204
International Confederation of Free Trade

Unions (ICFTU), 109-110, 137, 154,
    197, 245
International Labor Organization (ILO),
    111, 198, 274-275
International Monetary Fund (IMF), 78,
    108, 219, 224, 246, 257-258
Interpelacje, 265
Israel, 316
    Polish aid to, 240
    representation in Poland, 242
Italian Committee for Labor and the Econ-
    omy (CNEL), 192
Italian Confederation of Christian Unions, 154
Italy, LW's trips to, 38, 187-92, 280

Jablonna Palace, 167
Jablonski, Henryk, 116
Jackowiak, Czeslaw, 263
Jagiellonian University (Cracow), 177
Jamrozik, Wojtek, 26
Jan III Sobieski, king of Poland, 277
Janas, Zbigniew, 210, 262
Jankowski, Father Henryk, 4-5, 20-21, 23,
    106, 131, 158, 177, 213
    aids Solidarity, 63
    as candidate for assassination, 85
    cooking of, 65
    locates house for LW, 29
    as LW's advisor, 64, 83
    and Solidarity anniversary ceremonies, 73
Jaruzelski, Gen. Wojciech, 3, 54, 73, 116,
    124, 127, 141, 143, 161, 187-188, 191-
    193, 208, 215, 224, 248, 279, 317-319
    as head of state, 210-211
    as president, 214-219
    burned in effigy, 248
    government of, 18
    on legalizing Solidarity, 174
    on Round Table, 172-173
    policy of "entente and struggle," 75, 83,
        120
    resigns as first secretary of the PZPR, 215
    resigns as president, 281
    visits pope, 110
Jasna Gora, 113, 136, 222, 289-294, 296, 306
    See also Czestochowa
Jasna Gora, Virgin of, 117
Jastrzebie (Poland)
    accords of, 317
    miners' strike (1988), 151

Jedynak, Tadeusz, 108, 110
John Paul II, pope (Karol Wojtyla), 9-10,
    53, 114-115, 120, 152, 191, 246, 268,
    276, 280, 316-318
  assassination attempt on, 48, 51, 190
  canonizes Maximilian Kolbe, 77
  Danka Walesa on, 38
  first visit to Poland (1979), 9-10
  and Jaruzelski, 10, 110-111
  receives Walesas in Rome (1989), 38, 191
  tenth anniversary of pontificate cele-
    brated, 160
  third visit to Poland (1987), 10, 111, 112-
    120
  visit to Czestochowa (1983), 116-117
  visit to Gdansk (1987), 114, 118-119
John, Elton, 66-67
Jozwiak, Jerzy, 218
Juan Carlos, king of Spain, 225
Jurczyk, Marian, 267

Kaczorowski, Ryszard, 245, 315, 320
Kaczynski, Jaroslaw, 142, 154, 158, 218, 271
Kaczynski, Lech, 27, 142, 154, 212, 217,
    274-275
Kahlenberg (Austria), 277
Kaifu, Toshiki, 253
Kalabinski, Jacek, 232
Kalinsk (USSR), 265
Kaminski, Grandfather, 302
Karkonoski Pass (Poland-Czechoslovakia),
    262
Kashpirovsky, Anatoly, 63
Kaszuby (Poland), 27, 68
Katowice (Poland)
  curfews in, 152
  demonstrations in (1989), 248
Katyn Forest (Poland), massacre in, 46,
    253, 314, 319
  monument to victims of, 113
  Soviet Union acknowledges respon-
    sibility for, 265
Kazimierz, Jan, 290-291
Khrushchev, Nikita S., 25, 315
Kielce (Poland), pogrom at, 238-239
King, Martin Luther, Jr., 128, 136, 250
Kirkland, Lane, 197, 231
Kiszczak, Gen. Czeslaw, 31, 82-83, 157,
    159, 166-167, 174, 176, 205, 217, 318-
    319

and strikers' demands, 144
  as prime minister, 216-218
  conditions for negotiation, 158
  on August 1988 strike, 152
  on Round Table accords, 180
  proposes meetings, 155
  speech at Round Table, 174
Klimuszko, Andrzej, 173
Koch, Edward, 113
Kohl, Helmut, 207, 221, 228-229, 270
Kolakowski, Leszek, 282
Kolbe, Saint Maximilian, 77, 133
  church of (Mistrzejowice), 176
koleda (Christmas carols), 299
Kolodziej, Marian, 115
Kolyma (USSR) (prison camp), 133
Kolyma Stories (Shalamov, 244
Korczak, Janusz, 133
Kosciuszko, Tadcusz, 121
Kowalczykowa, Anna, 60
Kozakiewicz, Mikolaj, 281
Kozielsk (USSR), 265
Kozlowski, Krzysztof, 178
Krall, Hanna, 239
Krol, Cardinal Jan, 178, 231
Kruszynski, Jerzy, 106
Krzyzowa (Poland), 229
Kulakowski, Jan, 154, 198, 210
Kuron, Jacek, 168, 215, 222, 316
  official view of, 15
  on choosing candidates, 183
  on Round Table negotiations, 177-178
  as Solidarity theorist, 53
Kus, Mariola, 106
Kwasniewski, Aleksander, 256-257

Lacrymosa (Penderecki), 118, 296
Landau, Uzi, 282
Lanzmann, Claude, 134
Lari, Eugenio, 246
Leczycy Prison, 94
Lenarcik, Janusz, 106
Lenin, N., 148, 257
Leningrad (USSR), 250
Lewinski, Father, 44
Lipinski, Edward, 316
Lis, Bogdan, 59, 108, 156, 210, 212, 231
  trial of, 96-97
Lithuania, declares independence, 199
Litynski, Jan, 262

Lodz (Poland), 177, 275
  demonstrations in (1989), 248
  ghetto, 314
  militants in, 111
  political debates in, 184
López, Martha, 227-228
Lublin (Poland), 315

Macharski, Cardinal Francieczek, 177
Maczkowski, Gen. Stanislaw, 245
Magdalenka (Poland), 159, 176-178
Majdanek (Poland), 238
Malanowski, Andrzej, 184
Malinowski, Roman, 218
Malkowski, Father, 85
Martens, Wilfried, 197
martial law, 10, 141, 317
Martínez, Archbishop, 119
Martínez, Arturo, 225
massacres
  of Poles by Soviet Union, 253
  at Tiananmen Square, 205
  See also Holocaust; Katyn Forest; Stalin
Mazankowski, Don, 264
Mazowie (Poland), 243
Mazowiecki, Tadeusz, 82, 196, 210
  as candidate for president, 281, 283-284,
    320
  early support from, 219
  as editor of Tygodnik Solidarnosc, 207
  on elections and opposition, 185
  government of, 240, 259-261, 271, 278,
    312, 319
  on trip to Rome, 187-189
  as prime minister, 219-221, 224, 228,
    248, 253, 257, 319
  as Round Table negotiator, 175, 178
  service to Poland, 285
  as Solidarity advisor, 53, 76, 109, 142,
    156, 168
  supporters of, 283, 312
Medal of Freedom, given to LW, 230
Méhaignerie, Pierre, 227
Merkel, Jacek, 27, 152-153, 155, 158, 212,
  282-283
Messner, Zbigniew, 160, 318-319
Micewski, Andrzej, 279
Michalski, Krzysztof, 276
Michnik, Adam, 15, 59, 61, 168, 205, 212,
  216, 250, 262, 272

contacts with Soviet dissidents, 113
  as editor of Gazeta Wyborcza, 194
  on the end of communism, 195
  and KOR, 316
  on need for president from PZPR, 216
  released from prison, 75
  social-policy work group, 178
  as Solidarity advisor, 53, 156
  trial of, 96-97
Mickiewicz, Adam, 316
Mikolajczyk, Wladyslaw, 315
Mikulski, Barbara, 231
Milewski, Jerzy, 109, 231
Militia, 76
  and unauthorized assemblies, 9
  bugging of Walesa home, 17, 27-28
  kills shipyard demonstrators (1970), 118
  renamed "police," 251
  seeks to arrest LW, 98
  surveillance by, 20, 28
  wiretapping by, 89-94, 97-103
Miller, Israel, 240
Milosz, Czeslaw, 224, 294-296
Miodowicz, Alfred, 167-168, 170, 172-173,
  180, 312
  debates LW, 168-171
  OPZZ men call strikes, 176
Mistrzejowice (Poland), 176
Mita, Criaco de, 192
Mitterrand, François, 128, 132, 172, 228
  visit to Gdansk, 207-208
Mlyniec (Poland), 129
Moczar, Mieczyslaw, 316
Moczulski, Leszek, 19, 283, 311, 320
Montand, Yves, 199
Monument to the Shipyard Dead, 75-76,
  113, 115, 126, 181
  Bush's visit to, 213
  dedication (1980), 118, 296
  Mitterrand's visit to, 209
  papal visit to, 112, 119
monuments, "war" of, 112-113
Morawiecki, Kornel, 196
Morawski, Osubka, 315
Mosbacher, Robert, 224
Moscicki, Ignacy, 314
Moskal, Edward, 227, 231
Mostowki Palace, 76
Moureaux, Philippe, 198
Mrowczynska, Lilka, 45

Mulroney, Brian, 230
Muszkowska-Penson, Joanna, 62

Namiestnikowski Palace, 174
National Alliance of Trade Unions, *see*
 OPZZ
National Work Group, 111, 123
nationalism, and intolerance, 276
Natta, Alessandro, 193
New York Times, interviews LW, 270
New York, LW in, 237-240
Nicholas, Saint, Dominican basilica of, 75
Niedzielak, Father Stefan, assassination of,
 175
Niezabitowska, Malgorzata, 207, 224
NKVD, and massacre of Polish officers, 265
Nobel laureates
 at Auschwitz, 129
 conference of, in Paris (1988), 128
 See also Bovet, Daniel; Brandt, Willy;
  Brown, Herbert; McGuire, Mairead
  Corrigan; Milosz, Czeslaw; Perkins,
  Betty Williams; Sakharov, Andrei;
  Sienkiewicz, Henryk; Walesa, Lech;
  Wiesel, Elie
Nobel Peace Prize, 4, 58, 103, 136, 188,
 250, 294, 318
 Danka Walesa accepts for LW, 32, 37
 LW gives medal to Jasna Gora, 296
 LW receives, 18, 19
nomenklatura, 10, 29, 61, 137, 162, 216,
 220, 226, 260, 270-271, 278
Nowa Huta steelworks, 66, 169, 176, 293
 pollution from, 140
 strike (1988), 138-139, 141, 145
Nowicki, Jan, 106
Nowina-Konopka, Piotr, 27, 178

Occhetto, Achille, 192
Odrodzenie (Poland), 262
Oliwa (Poland), 60, 212
 Walesa house in 29-31, 29
Olszewski, Bogdan, 26
Olszewski, Jan, 103
Olsztyn (Poland), voter turnout in, 88, 91,
 104
Onyszkiewicz, Janusz, 75, 122, 168, 231
OPZZ (National Alliance of Trade Unions),
 75, 167-170, 180, 226, 257, 311-312
 and disruptive strikes, 176, 272

as spoilers, 179
and Magdalenka discussions, 160
Orzechowski, Marian, 220
Oslo (Norway), Danka and Bogdan Walesa
 in, 37
Osmanczyk, Edmund, 183
Ostashkov (USSR), 265
Ostrowski, Stanislaw, 315
Oswiecim (Poland)
 See Auschwitz
Otwock (Poland), 36

Paczek, Janusz, 30
Palestine Liberation Organization, 242
Palestinians, 135
Palubinski, Janusz, 108
pasterka (midnight mass), 299-300
Patriotic Movement for National Salvation
 (PRON), 3, 160, 312
patriotism, changing nature of, 54
Pawlicki, Szymon, 60
Pekala, Lt. Leszek, 78, 80-81, 85, 318
Penderecki, Krzysztof, 118, 296
perestroika, 9, 125
Pérez, Carlos, 230
Perkins, Betty Williams, 129
Piasecka-Johnson, Barbara, 163-164
Piekary Slaskie (Poland), 199
Pietrasinski, Leszek, 94
Pietruszka, Col., 84, 100
Pilica (Poland), 163
Pilsudski, Marshal Jozef, 167
Pimen, patriarch of Moscow, 148
Pinior, Josef, 108
Pinochet, Gen. Augusto, 225
Piotrowski, Capt. Grzegorz, 78-81, 84-87,
 318
Piszek, Edward, 68, 231
Pivot, Bernard, 22
Placiczewski, Father, 55
Platek, General, 84
Plock (Poland), 194
pluralism, 123, 126, 171
 economic, 171
 Jaruzelski's hostility to, 161
 political, 171, 207
 union, 169-171, 180
Poggi, Archibishop Luigi, 10
pogroms, 238-239, 240
 cultural, 316

Poland, 3, 5
  anti-Semitism in, 135, 240-241
  and coming independence of USSR, 148
  change in, 3, 6, 21, 238, 249
  changing relations with USSR, 234
  debts and debt rescheduling, 12, 197,
      208, 235
  democratic reform in, 211
  dismemberment of, 5
  and elections, 202
  and "Findlandization," 7
  flag of, 251
  government-in-exile, 234
  heroism and martyrdom of, 5-6, 8
  and Holocaust, 135
  and IMF, 78
  independence, 167, 172
  need for ethnic tolerance, 202-203
  nonviolent change in, 234
  resistance to change, 253
  return to the fold of Europe, 203, 208
  stability in, 170
  in World War II, 5
Polanski, Roman, 224
Policjant (The Policeman), 249
Polish economy
  Solidarity's views on, 111
Polish Peace Committee, 199
Polish Press Agency, 143
Polish Socialist Party, 204
Polish Union, 245
  See also Polonias
Polish United Workers' Party
  See PZPR
Polish Youth Movement, 204
Polonias (expatriate organizatons)
  American, 227
  Brussels, 197
  England, 245
Poniatowski, Stanislaw August, king of
    Poland, 290
Popieluszko, Father Jerzy, 73, 82, 85, 136
  first attempt to kill, 77-79
  funeral of, 73
  in Gdansk, 77
  investigation of murder of, 48
  kidnapping of, 78, 80, 82-83, 318
  LW and Bush visit grave of (1987), 122
  murder of, 81, 84, 87, 318
  sermons of, 76

  service to strikers, 74
  at Solidarity anniversary ceremonies, 73
  "subversive" activities of, 84
Popowo (Poland), 50, 55, 95, 131, 302-303
  under Nazi occupation, 130
Poronin (Poland), 257
Potop [The Deluge] (Sienkiewicz), 290
Poznan (Poland)
  demonstrations in (1989), 248
press conferences, 8, 280
  August 1988 srike, 157
  in Walesa home, 17
Prokuratura, 21, 76-77, 89, 103, 312
  LW's appearance at, 98
  LW's appearance before, 96-97
  seeks to arrest LW, 100-101
Przemysl (Poland), 36, 201, 254
Pulaski, Kazimicrz, 122, 290
Pusz, Krzysztof, 68, 168, 231
PZPR, 55, 221
  anticlericalism of, 55
  continuing influence of, 218
  demise of, 252-253, 255, 257
  Deputies' Club, 220
  dissolution of, 252, 256
  and elections, 122
  formed (1948), 312, 315
  incapable of change, 3
  looting and privileges of, 42, 248, 260
  loses threat of Soviet intervention, 210
  opposition to, 248, 259
  post-election machinations of, 219-220
  and "reforms," 122
  role in transition to democracy, 216
  and Soviet Communist Party, 254
  subservient to Soviet Union, 147

Raczkiewicz, Wladyslaw, 314-315
Raczynski, Edward, 245, 315
Radio Free Europe, 124, 189
Rakowski, Mieczyslaw, 23, 76, 161-162,
    164, 166, 208, 215, 218, 220, 256, 319
  belittles LW, 75
  coerces officeholders in election, 201-202
  on Walesa-Miodowicz debate, 173
  replaces Messner as prime minister, 160
  rigid inaugural statement, 160-161,
Ravensbrück, 62
Reagan, Ronald, 109, 121, 124
Red Brigades, 47-48

Reich, Jens, 252
Reuters press agency, 91, 95, 104
Reykjavik (Iceland), summit meeting, 109
Reykowski, Janusz, 178
Ribbentrop-Molotov Pact, 254, 313
Rogowski, Capt. Marek, 99-100
Rokita, Jan Maria, 184
Rokossovsky, Konstantin, 316
Romaszewski, Zbigniew, 94, 110
Roosevelt, Franklin Delano, 315
Rosensaft, Menachem, 238-239
Rostenkowski, Dan, 231
round table, physical, 167, 174
Round Table accords
   durability of, 252
   skepticism concerning, 205
Round Table talks, 172-181
   attempts to scuttle, 176
   completed, 180
   constructing democratic framework, 179
   delayed pending Solidarity legalization,
     167, 171
   first session, 174
   "knights of," on trip to Rome, 188
   "small tables" and "end tables," 175
   work groups, 175
Rozwaga i Solidarnosc [*Courage and Soli
   darity*], 152
Rudnicki, Klemens, 245
Rulewski, Jan, 78
Rybicki, Arain, 26-27, 38
Rynkiewicz, Artur, 245
Rzeczycki, Andrzej, 50, 67

Sabbat, Kazimierz, 315
Sacro Cuore (Rome), 190
Sadowski, Zdzislaw, 152
   strikers' letters to, 139, 141-142
Sakharov, Andrei, funeral of, 250
Samorzadnosc [*Self-Governance*] (Gdansk
   union weekly), 58
Secret Service (U.S.) prepares Walesa home
   for Bush visit, 56-57
Security Service
   arrests LW, 33
   exemplary diligence of, 208
   interference by, 29
   plants housekeeper in Walesa home, 39
   suppresses Nowa Huta strike, 141
   surveillance of LW, 17-18

Sejm
   elections for, 175, 200-206
   Gorbachev's address to, 150
   introduces nonmilitary service, 150
   ousts Messner as prime minister, 160
   passes laws for private enterprise, 244
   thirty-five-percent open, 180
   vacant seats, 206
Senat, 180, 204
Shalamov, Varlam, 244
Shoah (Lanzmann), 134
Sienkiewicz, Henryk (writer), 290, 296
Sienkiewicz, Henryk (Solidarity representa-
   tive), 137
Sikorski, Gen. Wladyslaw, 314
Sikorski Institute, 245
Sikorski-Stalin accords, 314
Sila-Nowicki, Wladyslaw, 143-144, 154,
   157
Silesia
   LW travels to, 159
   miners' strike (1988), 151
Simon, Paul, U.S. senator, 231
Skepe (Poland), 302
Skowronska, Anna, 103, 106
Skubiszewski, Krzysztof, 221
slogans, 236
Slupsk (Poland)
   pre-election strike, 272
   voter turnout in, 88, 91, 104
smigus-dyngus (game), 300
Smolensk (USSR), 265
Smolinski, Father Jerzy, 277
Sobibor (Poland), 238
Social Democratic Party, 257
Sofia, queen of Spain, 225
Solidarity, 8, 154, 232
   calls for boycott of elections, 123, 149
   changing identity, 268
   and the Church, 8-9
   conditions for Round Table talks, 159
   Coordinating Bureau (Brussels), 109-110
   emigration of activists, 53
   equipment for, 110
   financial support, 110
   First National Congress of, 48, 266
   Legal Defense Committee, 110
   legalization of, 34, 124, 143, 152, 156,
     161, 167
   National Executive Board, 123, 223

Solidarity *(continued)*
    new headquarters, 223
    and nonviolence, 4, 6, 11, 233
    officially relegalized, 186
    office in Walesa home, 17, 26, 31, 42
    organizes election activities, 60, 205
    Provisional Council, 121, 123
    PZPR votes to relegalize, 174
    as reform movement, 21
    schism in, 111
    Second National Congress, 259, 264-268
    seeks calm after Popieluszko's disappear-
        ance, 83
    seventh anniversary of (1987), 121
    strategy of evasion, 6
    underground survival of, 3, 25, 75
    and younger radicals, 4
    See also Civic Committee
Solidarity National Executive Board, coordi-
    nates response to referendum, 124
Solidarity Provisional Coordinating Board,
    108-110, 123
Solovietski Islands (prison camp), 133
Sopot (Poland), 163
    voter turnout in, 91
Sosnowiec (Poland), 238
Soviet Union
    demise of, 7
    and Katyn Forest massacre, 314
    threat of, 3
    withdraws from Afghanistan, 124, 148
    See also Brezhnev; Gorbachev; Stalin
Spadolini, Giovanni, 192
Spain, as example of reform, 126, 151
Spindlerova Bouda (Czechoslovakia), 262
Sprawni Inaczej (Alternative Living), 39
Stalin, Josef, 148, 314, 316
    massacres under, 265
Stalowa Wola steelworks, 159, 177
Stanecki, Jan, 140
Stanislaw, Saint, Church of (Warsaw), 77,
    318
    service for Popieluszko at, 82
Starobielsk (USSR), 265
Stein, Saul P., 277
Stelmachowski, Andrzej, 154, 156, 212, 281
Stoklosa, Henryk, 205
strikes
    of 1980, 10-11, 292
    of 1988, 140, 142-145, 319

of August 1988, 151-158
    See also Gdansk Shipyards; Nowa Huta;
        and other locations
Strzembosz, Adam, 184
Suchowolec, Father Stanislaw, assassina-
    tion of, 175
Swinoujscie (Poland), ferry at, 110
Szablewski, Alojzy, 145, 152, 155, 158
Szaniawski, Klemens, 122
Szczecin (Poland), 156
    accords of, 317
    curfews in, 153
    demonstrations in (1989), 248
    militants in, 111
    riots in (1970), 316
    strike (1988), 151
    voter turnout in, 88, 91, 104
Szczepanik, Piotr, 60, 153
Szczepanski, Free Union militant, 33
Szewczuwaniec, instigator of Nowa Huta
    strike (1988), 138
Szwajkiewicz, Edward, 212

Tann, John, 210
Taylor, Jacek, 98, 103, 106
Tczew (Poland), voter turnout in, 88
television
    and LW, 21
    LW debates Miodowicz on, 168-171
Templin, Wolfgang, 252
Terlecki, Marian, 187, 231
Thatcher, Margaret, 166, 208, 245
The Way of Hope (Walesa), 115
Tiananmen Square, 205
Tischner, Father Jozef, 276-277
Tokarczuk, Bishop Ignacy, 201
Tolwinski, Czeslaw, 143-144, 162
Trades Union Congress (TUC), 109, 245
Trafalski, Col., suspicious death of, 48
Treblinka, 132, 238
Trybuna Ludu [People's Tribune] Party
    daily, 87, 187
Trzcinski, Jurek, 26, 68
Trzeciakowski, Witold, 175, 187-189, 196
Tygodnik Gdanski [Gdansk Weekly] 262
Tygodnik Powszechny [Universal Weekly]
    (Cracow) 138-139, 138
Tygodnik Solidarnosc [Solidarity Weekly],
    207, 219, 224, 271
Tyminski, Stanislaw, 283-285, 320

union monopoly and pluralism, 169-170, 180

Union of Steelworkers 177

unions
American, 110, 197
Australian, 110
Basque, 109, 197
Belgian, 198
British, 245
Canadian, 110
European, 110
German, 221
Hungarian, 199
international, 154, 197-198
Italian, 154, 191-192
Japanese, 110
Polish student, 177, 199
See also AFL-CIO; Deutscher Gewerkschaftsbund; International Confederation of Free Trade Unions (ICFTU); OPZZ; Solidarity; World Confederation of Labor

United Press International (UPI), 95, 97, 103-104

United States, LW's trip to, 230-231

Universal Declaration of the Rights of Man, anniversary, 172

Urban, Jerzy, 3, 8, 42, 49, 76, 92, 100, 105, 109, 166, 178, 224-225

Valladares, Armando, 227-228

Vanderveken, John, 154, 197

Vatican, 119, 187, 189, 191, 193, 196, 214, 240, 246
LW's visit to, 10, 190-191

Venezuela, LW's trip to, 230

Vienna, Small Congress of (1990), 276-277

Vogel, Hans, 221

Voroshilovgrad (USSR), 265

voter turnout
in Sejm elections, 205
LW on, 92

Vranitzky, Franz, 276

Wachowski, Mietek, 67

Wajda, Andrzej, 183

Walentynowicz, Anna, 59

Walesa, Ania (daughter), 33, 36, 42, 45

Walesa, Bogdan (son), 17, 37, 41-43, 45-47, 49-50, 52

Walesa, Boleslaw (father), 95-96, 129-131, 243, 289

Walesa, Brygidka (daughter), 17-18, 42, 45-46, 49, 117

Walesa, Felicja Kaminski (mother), 55, 96

Walesa, Grandmother, née Glomek, 130

Walesa, Jarek (son), 41, 44, 46, 52-53, 209

Walesa, Lech, 22, 88, 91, 94, 96, 113, 155, 170, 217, 241, 291, 311-312, 315, 317, 319
on anti-Semitism in Poland, 237-238
appeals for participation in reform, 177
on change in Solidarity, 266
correspondence of, 26, 42
the "cowboy from Gdansk," 8
daily life of, 18, 56-69
dangers of life of, 47-48
as defendant, 106-107
on election campaign, 185
as "the electrician from Gdansk," 5, 23, 49, 232, 250
eulogy to Popieluszko, 73
expectations for, 6-7
faith and religion in upbringing, 297-304
family beginnings in Gdansk, 16
farm childhood and work ethic, 303
as "farmer from Mazowie," 270
first communion, 302
interview with Brzezinski, 24
medical problems of, 94, 99, 101-102
"new political profile," 173
as Nobel laureate, 4-5
objectives as president, 305-307
on reorganizing economy, 246
on Round Table accords, 181
patron saint of unions, 275
as "plotter," 103, 109
presidential campaign of, 282
as "private citizen," 21
proposal on elections, 182
receives doctorate from University of Gdansk, 263
reelected president of Solidarity, 267
on smoking, 26
statement on "state of Poland," 149-150
statements of, 89, 95, 105
The Way of Hope, 115
trial of, 97, 105, 107
trip to Rome, 187-193
visitors to, 57

Walesa, Lech (continued)
    voice analyzed by Security Service, 89-
        90, 92
    on voter turnout, 91, 97
    wiretapped conversations of, 103
    as worker, 95
    worldwide fame of, 23
Walesa, Magdalena (daughter), 17, 33, 36,
        53
Walesa, Maria Wiktoria (daughter), 36, 42,
        45, 117
Walesa, Miroslawa (Danka) (wife), 18, 21,
        32-40, 58, 61, 63, 67-69, 99, 187, 209,
        294, 305
    as mother, 41
    as center of family, 32, 40
    character of, 33-34, 38
    cooking of, 65
    faith of, 33
    as gardener, 39
    as housekeeper, 30, 34, 39, 43
    interviews with, 38-39
    and new house, 30
    on trip to Rome, 189
    separations from LW, 33, 35
    siblings of, 61
    as surrogate for LW, 36-37, 53
    trip to Philadelphia, 38
    trip to Rome, 38, 191
    wiretapped conversation of, 93
Walesa, Przemek (son), 41-44, 48, 50-52
Walesa, Slawek (son), 35, 41-43, 45-46, 48,
        50-52
Walesa, Staszek (brother), 61
Walesa family, 41-55
    and school, 44
    outings, 27
    religious education of, 46-47
    and school, 35
    search for house, 29-30
Warsaw (Poland)
    demonstrations in, 137
    ghetto, 314
    militants in, 111
    riots in (1976), 316
Warsaw Pact, demise of, 210

Warsaw Steelworks, 73
Weiss, Shevek, 282
Weizsäcker, Richard von, 221, 269-270, 273
Wende, Edward, 250
Wesiora (Poland), 68-69
Westerplatte naval base, monument to the
        defenders of, 112-113, 208, 269
Whitehead, John C., 127
Wielowieyski, Andrzej, 142, 168, 172, 209
Wiesel, Elie, 128-129, 131, 133-135
    speech at Auschwitz, 132
Willis, Norman, 109, 245
Wojtyla, Karol, see John Paul II
Wolnosc i Pokoj (Freedom and Peace), 138,
        204, 225, 312
World Bank, 108, 211, 224, 246
World Confederation of Labor (WCL), 109,
        198, 210, 226
Wörner, Manfred, 282
Wozna, Malgorzata, 106
Wroclaw (Poland), 75
    demonstrations in (1989), 248
    voter turnout in, 104
Wujec, Henryk, 61, 272
Wyszynski, Cardinal Stefan, 9, 289, 315-317
    prison notes of, 74
    sends Popieluszko to strikers, 74

Yalta Conference, 5, 11-12, 234, 315

Zabza, Teresa, 26, 98, 101
Zaleski, August, 315
Zaspa, 28, 36, 58-59, 66, 68, 112
    apartment in, 17
Zdunowice (Poland), 68
Zeder, Fred, 226
ZOMO (riot police), 4, 66, 83, 118, 120,
        145-146, 167, 181, 225, 311-312
    alert for Solidarity anniversary, 73
    at Nowa Huta strike, 139
    attacks and harassment by, 139, 141, 144
    isolate shipyard during strike (August
        1988), 156
    isolate shipyard monument, 75
    lampooned during strike, 157
Zychowicz, Czeslaw, 245